Professional Results with Canon® Vixia® Camcorders: A Field Guide to Canon G10 and XA10

Warren Bass

Course Technology PTR
A part of Cengage Learning

COURSE TECHNOLOGY
CENGAGE Learning®

Australia, Brazil, Japan, Korea, Mexico, Singapore, Spain, United Kingdom, United States

COURSE TECHNOLOGY
CENGAGE Learning®

Professional Results with Canon® Vixia® Camcorders: A Field Guide to Canon G10 and XA10
Warren Bass

Publisher and General Manager, Course Technology PTR:
Stacy L. Hiquet

Associate Director of Marketing:
Sarah Panella

Manager of Editorial Services:
Heather Talbot

Senior Marketing Manager:
Mark Hughes

Acquisitions Editor:
Dan Gasparino

Project Editor:
Kate Shoup

Technical Reviewer:
Eugene Martin

Copy Editor:
Kate Shoup

Interior Layout:
Shawn Morningstar

Cover Designer:
Mike Tanamachi

Indexer:
Sharon Shock

Proofreader:
Sam Garvey

Printed in the United States of America
1 2 3 4 5 6 7 14 13 12

For product information and technology assistance, contact us at
Cengage Learning Customer & Sales Support, 1-800-354-9706

For permission to use material from this text or product, submit all requests online at **cengage.com/permissions**
Further permissions questions can be emailed to
permissionrequest@cengage.com

Library of Congress Control Number: 2012930796

ISBN-13: 978-1-133-70259-7

ISBN-10: 1-133-70259-7

Course Technology, a part of Cengage Learning
20 Channel Center Street
Boston, MA 02210
USA

Cengage Learning is a leading provider of customized learning solutions with office locations around the globe, including Singapore, the United Kingdom, Australia, Mexico, Brazil, and Japan. Locate your local office at: **international.cengage.com/region**

Cengage Learning products are represented in Canada by Nelson Education, Ltd.

For your lifelong learning solutions, visit **courseptr.com.**

Visit our corporate Web site at **cengage.com.**

This book is dedicated to the memory of Ricky Leacock.

1921–2011

Acknowledgments

The author wishes to acknowledge support for creating this text from Temple University, its Department of Film & Media Arts, and staff members John Sedlack, Ethan Schwartz, and Bruce Forrest Byker James. In addition, this text would not have been possible without the personal assistance of Zana Bass with photographs, graphics preparation, and general support on every level.

About the Author

Warren Bass is an independent film and videomaker. He is a full professor (and former chair) of Film & Media Arts at Temple University, where he teaches directing, cinematography, videography, and advanced documentary and fiction workshops. He was trained at the Yale School of Drama in directing and at Columbia University in film as the School of the Arts Scholar. He has taught at Yale, NYU, the State University of California, and the American Film Institute; has chaired university departments in Film, Television, and Theater in New England; served as Vice President of the University Film & Video Association; and served for extended periods of time as Director of Temple University's graduate program in Film & Television. He has directed theater at Lincoln Center, off-Broadway, and in regional professional theaters including the world premiere of the musical drama *Copernicus* at the Annenberg Center in Philadelphia. His film and video productions have been aired on PBS, syndicated television, and cable in the U.S. and on European, Asian, and Australian television. His work has received more than 100 regional, national, and international awards.

Contents

Introduction

This book is a comprehensive field guide to the concepts, strategies, equipment, and procedures for achieving the best results possible with Canon's top-of-the line palm-sized camcorders. The guide focuses on the specific features of the Canon Vixia HF G10 and XA10, but users of other camcorders in the Vixia series, the Legria series (shooting PAL), and other camcorders will find a wealth of relevant information.

The small size and ergonomics of the palm-sized camcorder are its biggest assets. Since the middle of the last century, visionary media makers have sought to make motion-picture cameras and eventually video camcorders more compact and mobile. The miniaturization of equipment has had an increasing impact on the aesthetics, economics, content, and even politics of media making.

In 1948, critic and filmmaker Alexandre Astruc theorized that only when the motion-picture camera becomes as portable and accessible as a pen is to an author, can film-making become as personal and profound as other art forms. Astruc's concept of the "camera-stylo" (camera/pen) foreshadowed the emergence of the French New Wave, Direct Cinema, Cinéma Vérité, Dogme 95, and numerous independent film and video artists, activists, and media collectives throughout the world. Yet perhaps only now, with the introduction of the first generation of professional palm-sized high-definition camcorders, have we truly entered the age of the "camera-stylo." Home video makers, aspiring filmmakers, journalists, schools, and professional media makers are acquiring high-quality palm-sized camcorders in unprecedented numbers. Temple University, for example, has 900 Film & Media Arts majors, 700 Broadcasting majors, and thousands of other students from Communications, Journalism, Theater, Advertising, Speech, Graphic Arts, Design, Psychology, and Anthropology who use palm-sized camcorders during their training. Tiny professional-quality camcorders are in the forefront of today's media-making revolution.

The increasing portability of professional, semi-professional, and non-professional motion-picture media has had a significant effect on documentary and news in particular, and even fiction film production. In 1948, documentary filmmaker Richard Leacock ("Ricky" to those who knew him) was hired at age 27 as the cinematographer for Robert Flaherty's *Louisiana Story*. The feature film was shot in 35mm and although it was a fictional story using local residents as actors, it followed Robert Flaherty's observational approach of shooting large amounts of footage at real locations, evolving the story as they went along, and piecing it together in the editing room. Their 35mm camera was lighter than studio models but still quite cumbersome. The production took 14 months to film.

In 1960, Leacock along with filmmakers David and Albert Maysles, filmmaker D.A. Pennebaker, and producer Robert Drew pioneered a new, mobile, hand-held movement in documentary called "Direct Cinema" that placed the spectator intimately in the middle of ongoing events. Leacock, who had studied physics at Harvard, and Pennebaker, who had a degree in engineering from Yale, actually developed modifications to existing 16mm film cameras for sound synchronization and portable battery operation. Commercially made portable sync sound cameras soon followed. Some of the landmark Direct Cinema films include *Primary*, a behind-the-scenes view of John F. Kennedy's presidential campaign; *Crisis: Behind a Presidential Commitment*, on a major moment in the civil-rights struggle; Leacock's *Happy Mother's Day*, on the birth of quintuplets (which ABC refused to air because it was too honest); Pennebaker's feature film on Bob Dylan *Don't Look Back*; and the Maysles brothers' features *Salesman*, *Gimmie Shelter*, and *Grey Gardens.* Simultaneous with the Direct Cinema movement in the United States was the Cinéma Vérité movement pioneered in France by Jean Rouch and in Canada with cinematographer Michel Brault. Portability was essential for the making of all these films.

Leacock eventually headed the graduate Film program at MIT from 1968 to 1989 that in turn produced a new generation of hand-held documentary makers including Ross McElwee, Jeff Kreines, Joel DeMott, Ann Schaetzel, and David Parry. Over the years, I had many long conversations with Leacock, as we served together as trustees of the University Film Study Center housed at MIT and Harvard and ran a summer film institute at Hampshire College. Leacock, more than anyone else, promoted the development of small, mobile, hand-held cameras that could shoot in available light with sync sound and provide greater immediacy with "the feeling of actually being there." He experimented with adapting Super-8 film and portable video for professional purposes long before small-format video was used commercially. Even after retiring from MIT, Leacock pushed the limits of small-format video by making *Les Oeufs a la Coque* (*The Eggs of the Cock*, a phrase for poached eggs and a pun on his name), a feature-length production shot with a tiny 8mm Handycam and broadcast in prime time on French television in 1991.

In 1990, during the Gulf War, broadcast field reports relied on consumer camcorders. Models such as Canon's Hi8 A1 proved to be mobile and effective in heat, sand, and precarious combat conditions where newscasters feared to take more expensive and cumbersome equipment. The Canon Hi8 A1 Mk II had a double seal to protect its tape mechanism from sand. Today's solid-state camcorders have considerably more ability to document reality and gather news under difficult circumstances.

In 1995, Danish filmmakers, including Lars Von Trier and Thomas Vinterberg, founded the Dogme 95 movement. They signed a 10-point "vow of chastity" declaring that they would make feature fiction films "by any means available" under almost documentary limitations: hand held, available light, unaltered locations, no filters, and no special effects. Vinterberg's low-budget feature *The Celebration* (*Festen*) was shot under these conditions by cinematographer Anthony Dod Mantle using a consumer mini-DV camcorder. *The Celebration* was blown up to 35mm for theatrical release; when it won the Jury Prize at the 1998 Cannes Film Festival, the floodgates opened worldwide to small-format feature filmmaking. In 2000, Spike Lee shot *Bamboozled* in mini-DV with a Sony VX 1000. In 2002, Dod Mantle shot *28 Days Later* under director Danny Boyle using a Canon XL-1 mini-DV camcorder, and won the Academy Award for Cinematography in 2009 for *Slumdog Millionaire*, which was shot 60% digitally with a Silicon Imaging SI-2K camera (2,048×1,142 pixels). The film itself won the Oscar for Best Picture.

Camcorders such as the Vixia HF G10 and XA10 will never produce the look of the uncompressed images of the SI-2K, the Red One, or a 35mm Panaflex with $40,000 interchangeable lenses. But not every production needs that look or can afford that technology. In their price range, the G10 and XA10 are sharper, cleaner, more compact, more portable, and more laden with professional features than any prior palm-sized camcorder. They blur the line between "pro-sumer" and professional, and in the right hands they can be powerful media-making tools for a wide range of applications.

We are in the middle of a digital media revolution. The working poor in developing nations find it essential to own cell phones, and many of these devices also record video. Camcorders from amateur to professional quality are ubiquitous throughout the world. An enterprising person can set up a video business with about the same investment it would take to acquire an auto-rickshaw to become a taxi driver in Asia or Africa. Entire countries that had never been able to produce their own movies have burgeoning motion-picture industries based on HD video. Collectives working for social change record video and exhibit via the Internet, where it can be viewed by dozens, thousands, or millions. There is an enormous democratizing potential when media ownership and access can no longer be fully controlled or stifled by governments or by institutions or owned only by the wealthy. If you have access to a high-definition palm-sized camcorder, your potential is limited only by your imagination and your resourcefulness.

Companion Website Downloads

There are several appendixes and a glossary for this book, which are available online. These cover camcorder and file precautions, Canon XA10 and G10 diagrams, a menu map, comparison charts for various camcorders, basic keyboard commands for major editing software programs, and troubleshooting. You may download these companion files from www.courseptr.com/downloads. Please note that you will be redirected to the Cengage Learning site.

1

Camcorder Basics: Getting Started

The Vixia HF G10 is Canon's top-of-the-line consumer high-definition camcorder. Canon also manufactures and markets an almost identical model, the XA10, as part of its professional line. These two camcorders are packed with more features than any other camcorder their size or in their price range. Canon describes the Vixia HF G10 as providing "professional capabilities" at a consumer price, and the XA10 as a "fully featured, ultra-compact pro video camera that shares nearly all the functionality" of Canon's professional XF100 camcorder, "but in a smaller, run-and-gun form factor." Are the G10 and XA10 truly professional? What are their advantages and limitations? This text is a field guide to producing professional and semi-professional results with these camcorders and a thorough guide to their features, operation, and accessories. It's also an introduction to their use in documentary, fiction, corporate, event, alternative, and personal media making, from amateur to professional.

Features

The Vixia HF G10 and XA10 weigh only 0.78 kilograms (1.71 pounds), not including battery, memory card, lens hood, and accessories. Considering their diminutive size, they are filled with an impressive array of professional features, including the following:

- Manual control overrides for every focus and exposure parameter
- Manual audio controls
- Audio level monitor

- 2× magnify focus assist
- Edge sharpness monitor
- Waveform monitor
- Two zebra pattern settings
- Multiple frame rates, including 24p
- Custom settings
- Cine modes
- Color bars
- Audio tone
- A 10× high-definition zoom lens with an eight-blade iris instead of the usual six blades in this price range
- 32 gigabytes (GB) or 64GB of internal memory plus two slots for removable memory, capable of simultaneously making a backup recording for file protection or sequentially recording for a total of 15 to 72 hours without reloading
- The ability to record in 1080p true HD video

Canon's third-generation high-definition image processor provides improved dynamic range and further reduces visual noise in low-light situations. The HF G10 and XA10 record AVCHD high-definition video up to a data rate of 24 megabits per second (Mbps)—the limit for AVCHD format—in what is called 4:2:0 color space (discussed later).

Canon designed a daring ⅓-inch CMOS Pro photo sensor for the G10/ XA10 with 1,920×1,080 native pixels—offering exactly the number of pixels of the high-definition television image instead of making a much higher number of megapixels the selling point to enhance still photo capabilities, like most manufacturers. This ensures that there are no video artifacts from downscaling a much larger number of much smaller pixels. With this design, the area of each pixel can be maximized, which dramatically improves low-light responsiveness. The CMOS Pro photo sensor also features a high-speed readout to minimize skew of fast-moving images, which can appear to bend like jelly (an artifact of many CMOS sensors, including video footage from DSLR still cameras).

What the HF G10 and XA10 lack professionally includes the following:

- Interchangeable lenses
- 4:2:2 or 4:4:4 color space

- Three-chip photo sensors
- 50Mbps, 100Mbps, or higher data rates
- The ability to record uncompressed images, such as in RAW format, Apple ProRes, or Avid DNX of high-end professional camcorders

This is an unfair comparison, however, to a much higher price range where just the lenses can cost many times more than an entire G10 or XA10 camcorder. People have made feature films with much less than what these two camcorders have to offer.

Differences Between the HF G10 and XA10

The XA10 costs about $500 more than the HF G10. The XA10 has 64GB of built-in memory, which can record nearly six hours of high-definition video at the highest quality setting, whereas the G10 has 32GB of built-in memory. The biggest difference is that the XA10 has a removable handle unit that slides onto the camcorder's front and rear accessory sockets and is secured into place with two screws in the rear and a tightening ring in the front. Aside from providing more options for ergonomically carrying and holding the camcorder, the attachable handle contains the following (see Figure 1.1):

- XLR microphone or line inputs for professional audio recording
- 48 volts of phantom power for professional microphones
- A full complement of manual audio controls
- An audio attenuator
- A microphone shock mount
- A standard mounting shoe for accessories
- An additional record button with a lock lever
- Additional zoom control
- A tally light
- An infrared light

This combination of features is rarely found in a package this small. Infrared recording is not present on the HF G10, nor does the G10 have a second accessory shoe or screw holes to accommodate the auxiliary handle and its professional sound inputs. Right now, the Canon XA10 is the best full featured palm-sized camcorder in its price class.

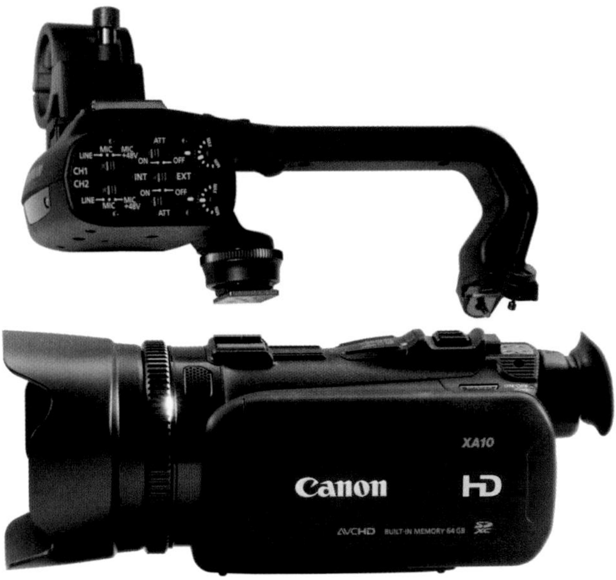

Figure 1.1 The accessory handle for the Canon XA10.

The XA10 is a good transition camcorder for individuals moving up to professional-quality and control from previous experience with consumer models. The XA10 is an ideal camcorder for college or university media programs because it is capable of operating in full AUTO mode like a consumer model, but offers students the opportunity to learn professional techniques with its XLR-balanced line sound inputs, phantom power, waveform monitor, multiple frame rates, and manual focus, exposure, and color-balance controls. The XA10 may seem expensive to some, but considering all its features, it is a great field camcorder in its price class.

The G10 would be the camcorder of choice for those on a much tighter budget. It will do almost everything the XA10 will do except shoot infrared and record on balanced line audio inputs from professional microphones. It also lacks the ergonomic convenience of the handle and its built-in shock mount. There are some workarounds with respect to sound, including semi-pro microphones with mini-plugs, XLR to mini-plug adapter cables or converter boxes, and double system sound (using a separate audio recorder). These are discussed in Chapter 7, "Improving Sound."

Single Chip Versus Three Chips

The HF G10 and XA10 are based on Canon's newly designed single ⅓-inch CMOS Pro light-sensitive chip, which uses 1,920×1,080 photo sensors. Single-chip camcorders are generally less expensive and much more compact than three-chip models.

Three-chip camcorders divide the light path with a prism onto three full-screen light-sensitive mega-pixel chips that are filtered to receive only red, green, or blue light. Combined information from the three sensors provides an accurate measure of the red, green, and blue (RGB) levels for every pixel making up the picture image. A single-chip camcorder, in contrast, employs a pattern of filtered and unfiltered pixels across its single surface, where two pixels out of every four receive white light, one of four is filtered to receive only red light, and the remaining one receives only blue. Through a complex algorithm that compares adjacent pixels, RGB values are calculated for every pixel making up the picture image. For example, the brightness value for an unfiltered pixel minus the adjacent values for blue and red will approximate its green content.

Obviously, a calculated approximation for every pixel cannot be as accurate as direct RGB readings derived from three perfectly aligned chips, but single-chip designs and their algorithms have improved so much in recent years that they have definitely entered the professional world. For example, the Red One camera, which costs about $17,500 for the body and comparable or larger amounts for accessories and lenses, uses a single 4.5K chip (which has the resolution of 35mm film) for shooting dramatic motion pictures that are shown in movie theaters. Features like *District 9, Pirates of the Caribbean: On Stranger Tides,* and *The Social Network* were shot on the single-chip Red One. DSLRs (digital still cameras with the ability to shoot professional-quality video) like the Canon 5D MKII (and Mark III), 7D, and T3i all have single chips. DSLRs have been used to shoot independent feature films including Grand Prize winners at the Sundance Film Festival (*Crazy Love* and *To Hell and Back,* for example) and professional television like the season six closing episode of *House,* which was shot on the Canon 5D MKII. A single chip is definitely capable of professional results. There will be further discussion of the HF G10 and XA10 camcorders in comparison to DSLRs and the new generation of camcorders with 35mm sized photo sensors in Chapter 16, "Integrating with Larger Camcorders."

4:2:0 Color Space

The HF G10 and XA10 have the same single ⅓-inch CMOS Pro chip, the same high-definition lens, and much of the functionality of Canon's professional XF100HD and XF105HD camcorders selling for $3,000 and $4,000—but in a much smaller package and at less than half the price. The HF G10 and XA10 are much more compact because the numerous physical switch controls found on the XF100 and XF105 have been moved to the touchscreen. Another difference is that the XF100 and XF105 can record 4:2:2 color space, whereas the G10 and XA10 record 4:2:0. On a practical level, most viewers will not be able to see the difference between 4:2:0 and 4:2:2 except in circumstances like special-effects chroma keying, which could show fringing and edge artifacts in 4:2:0.

4:2:0 and 4:2:2 have identical black-and-white resolution, and fortunately, most of the picture information that the human eye can see is in the black-and-white signal. The human retina contains 120 million rod-shaped photoreceptors that are sensitive to black-and-white values, and only six to seven million cone-shaped cells that read red, green, or blue and need up to 1,000 times more light. Consequently, video files are typically designed with much more black-and-white information to mimic the reception of the human eye and ultimately save signal space by discarding color information that can barely be perceived. The black-and-white information is often encoded separately from the color signal, which might occupy a second track alternating between red and blue (4:2:0) or relegated to two additional tracks, as in 4:2:2 and 4:1:1 encoding. (There does not have to be an additional track for green because it can be extrapolated by subtracting red and blue from the black-and-white signal.)

These sets of triple numbers describe what is called "color space." They represent the relative sampling ratio of black-and-white (the first number) to the color tracks (the second and third numbers). This concept is explained further in the glossary. 4:2:2 color sampling has double the color resolution of 4:2:0, providing finer color transitions and microscopically cleaner edges. This can be important in processes like chroma keying and advanced compositing effects, and in printing video onto 35mm film. Otherwise, unless closely compared side by side, 4:2:0 images can be hard to distinguish from 4:2:2 images.

AVCHD

The 4:2:0 signal on the G10/XA10 is encoded in a format called "Advanced Video Coding High Definition," or "AVCHD." Instead of recording onto videotape, AVCHD is a tapeless, file-based format that allows a great deal of digital information to be stored in a very small space. It does this by highly compressing the data and making the playback hardware and software work harder in decoding the image. Because it is entirely solid state, electro-mechanical errors and other limitations of tape are no longer part of the recording process. Solid-state camcorders can be more compact, are better sealed from dirt and moisture, have longer battery life, run more quietly with no motor noise or head wear, and record cleaner, more stable images. They are also less vulnerable to air pressure, humidity, vibration, shock, and mechanical damage. Not having to record at a specific physical speed like videotape, AVCHD allows for multiple frame rates, multiple choices of image quality (through a range of compression and data rates), and a choice of progressive or interlaced scanning. It catalogs its data into folders and files on a memory chip the size of a postage stamp. The format automatically numbers your shots into a series of compressed MTS files; creates directories, file levels, and thumbnail images; and records date and time information as each shot is recorded. Working with these files is discussed in Chapter 18, "Managing and Storing Video Files."

The downside of AVCHD is that you have many more decisions to make before shooting regarding frame rate, interlace or progressive scanning, and compression quality (measured in megabits per second), even when recording in full AUTO mode. AVCHD also has post-production options and issues to resolve as you expand these highly compressed files for playback, editing, and media storage. Larger hard drives, fast video cards, updated software, and faster and more recent computers are needed to work with AVCHD at the higher quality levels—up to four times the processing power compared to tape.

Prepping the Camcorder

Before you start using the camcorder, there are a few steps you'll need to take. The battery needs to be charged or the power adapter needs to be attached. You also need to enter the current date and time into camcorder. To record, you need to select a recording mode (AUTO, M, or CINEMA), a quality level (compression), and a memory location, which may also need initializing. M (for manual) and CINEMA modes will involve pre-selecting additional parameters.

When you turn the power on, the ON/OFF light shines a continuous green and the ACCESS light (to the right of the viewfinder, as shown in Figure 1.2, along with several other key components of the camcorder) momentarily blinks red as the camcorder communicates with the memory chip. The access light will also blink as you record and will continue to blink for a second or two after you stop recording. While the access indicator is blinking, do not turn off power, open the memory slot cover, or change the camcorder's operating mode. When you turn the power off, the green ON/OFF light lingers briefly and the red access light blinks while the camcorder updates data. Prematurely plugging or unplugging memory or power before these indicator lights turn dark can corrupt files, just like shutting down a computer or hard drive.

To charge the battery while it is inside the camcorder, connect the external power supply to the DC IN at the lower-right rear of the camcorder. The camcorder's power and the ON/OFF light should be dark when connecting or disconnecting the power supply. Within a few seconds, the ON/OFF light will blink red, indicating charging, and will go out entirely when the battery has a full charge.

Caution

The camcorder must be turned off and the ON/OFF light must be entirely dark when a memory chip is inserted or removed, a battery is inserted or removed, or the power adapter is connected or disconnected.

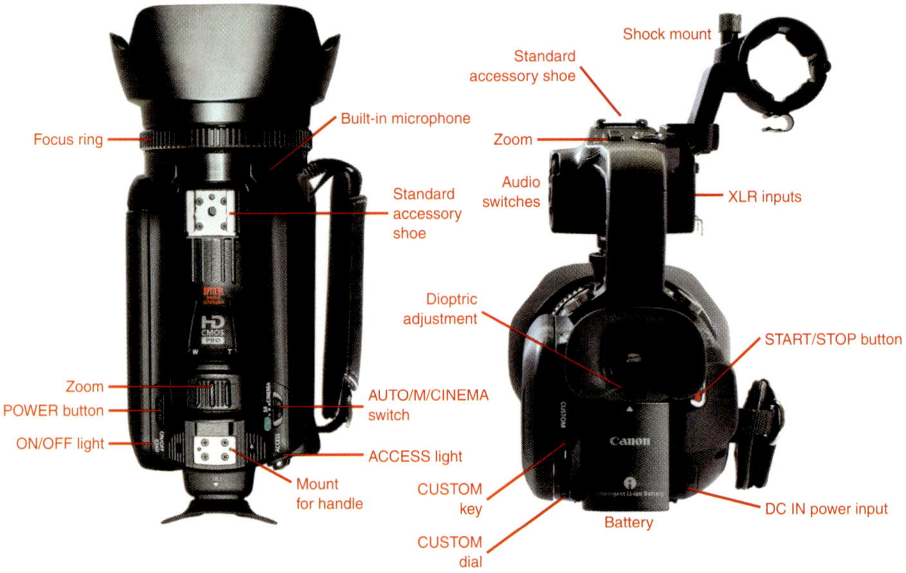

Figure 1.2 Top and rear view of the Canon XA10. The Vixia G10 is identical except for the accessory shoe and the handle.

The G10/XA10 has five layers of menus. (See Figure 1.3.) If the readouts do not appear on the LCD screen, press the DISP. (display) button on the left side of the camcorder (look ahead to Figure 1.4). The top layer is the Function display (FUNC), which indicates the status of current functions. Pressing FUNC opens the next layer; the word "MENU" appears in the upper-left corner, where the word FUNC used to be. This layer offers a number of program controls and settings when in record mode and a selection of image icons representing your recorded files when in Playback mode. Pressing MENU opens overlapping tabs for the remaining three displays, giving you a choice of a Camera/Play icon, which reveals record/play options; a Film Clip icon, where you select items like recording chip, quality mode, and frame rate; and a Tool icon, which offers additional controls and adjustments, including initializing the recording chip. See Appendix C, "Menu Map," available at www.courseptr.com/downloads, for an outline of the menu displays.

The default language of the menu and its layers is English, but there is a choice of 26 other languages. To change the language, choose FUNC > MENU > Tool icon, scroll down to Language, and select your language of choice. When you're finished, press X to exit the menu.

Setting the date and time is necessary because the camcorder's system logs each recorded segment of video using date/time information. If the camera's clock has not been set (or has lost its setting), the Date/Time menu will automatically appear

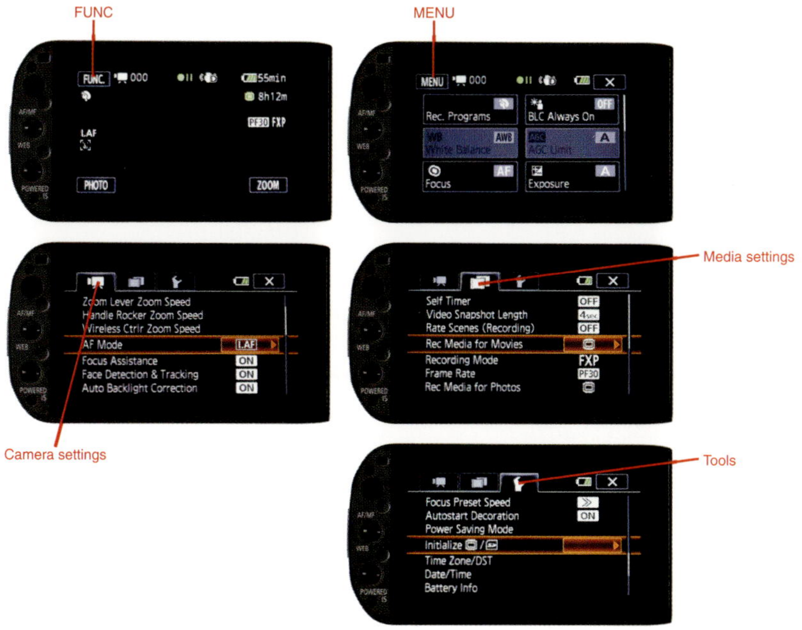

Figure 1.3 Five levels of menu screens: the initial FUNC display, MENU (program modes), and Camera, Film Clip (media), and Tool screens.

when you power up the camcorder. You can set the year, month, date, hour, and minutes by touching their fields and the up/down icons. You have a choice of whether each file is logged as Y/M/D (year/month/day), M/D/Y, or D/M/Y, and whether time is based on 24 hours or 12 hours a.m./p.m. You can later correct or reset the clock time as well as set a time zone for home and travel by pressing FUNC > MENU > Tool icon > Date/Time. A small internal lithium battery runs the clock and holds your menu settings for about three months without recharging. It is recharged as you use your camcorder. If the camcorder is idle for long periods of time, you will need to connect the power adapter to the camcorder once every two to three months overnight so as not to lose your settings.

Initially, the camcorder will automatically record to its internal memory unless you specifically set it to record to one of the removable memory slots. To select a memory slot, turn the AUTO/M/CINEMA mode switch (on the upper-right side of the camcorder; refer to Figure 1.2) to M or CINEMA; then tap FUNC > MENU > Film Clip icon > Rec Media for Movies. This will give you a choice of Internal, Memory Slot A, or Memory Slot B, as well as choices for simultaneous backup recording or relay recording as each chip gets full to maximize your total recording time. The display will provide the approximate available recording duration for the selected memory card and the current quality mode.

The camcorder can operate at lower quality levels with memory cards as slow as Class 4 SDHC, but 32GB Class 10 Secure Digital High Capacity (SDHC) or the newer 64GB Class 10 SDXC "extended" capacity memory cards are recommended to record at the two highest quality levels. This considerably accelerates transfer times and minimizes reading/writing errors, stalling, and lost frames. Note that to read SDXC extended-capacity cards, Mac computers need system 10.6.4 Snow Leopard or later, and PC computers need Windows 7, Windows XP with service pack 3 plus KB955704 update, or Windows Vista with service pack 1 or later. An incompatible computer will signal an SDXC card as defective or unreadable and will prompt you to initialize it. Initializing it would be a mistake, however, as it would erase any files you had recorded. Also, if the computer was incompatible with SDXC to begin with, it would not properly initialize the card anyway. Newer computers will not have this problem, but all memory cards should be initialized in the camcorder. A 64GB Class 10 SDXC with a speed of 45Mbps is a good choice if your computer system is compatible; otherwise, use 32GB Class 10 SDHC cards with a speed of 20Mbps or higher made by major manufacturers like SanDisk, Toshiba, and Panasonic. To insert external memory, turn the power off and wait until all indicator lights are dark. Slide back the memory slot cover and insert the card with its label facing the front of the camcorder and its indentation upward and toward the slot. Push the memory card in until it clicks. Figure 1.4 shows the memory slots (and several other features).

Caution

The memory card absolutely *must* face the right direction (label forward, indentation upward). Electronic components are packed so tightly in the G10/XA10 that forcing a memory card the wrong way can crack a circuit board and cause extensive internal damage.

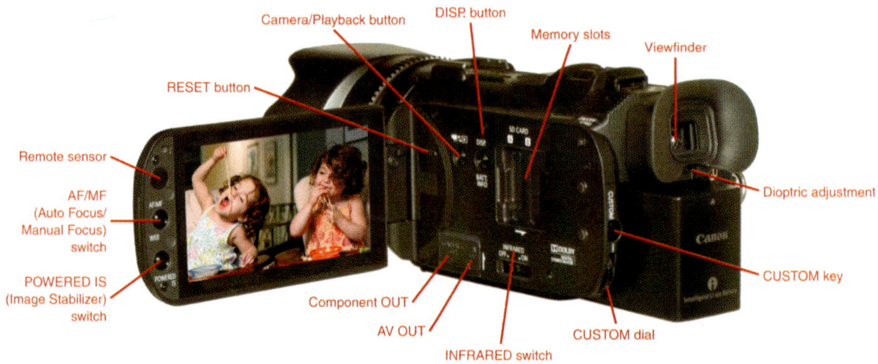

Figure 1.4 Controls on the left side.

To remove a memory card after recording, the power must be turned off, and all indicator lights dark. Press the card in once and it should release for removal. See Chapter 18 for details on transferring, storing, and archiving your video files.

Initializing

Your camera will ask you to "initialize" a newly installed memory card. Alternatively, you may choose to erase a previously recorded card to record new material. The camcorder's built-in memory comes pre-initialized. So, you will not go through this process for internal memory until after you have recorded on it, copied and stored any files you want to keep, and are ready to erase and re-record. To initialize, start by choosing FUNC > MENU > Film Clip icon > Rec Media for Movies > Circuit Board icon (for internal memory) or Card icon (for external memory) > slot A or slot B > Initialize. (Look ahead to Figure 1.5.)

This first Initialize command simply clears the file allocation table from the memory and allows for recording over existing files. Previous video files will appear to be gone because they are no longer catalogued and the camcorder can now record over existing files, erasing them file-by-file in the process (just like recording over a previously recorded videotape). Under certain conditions, earlier video files can later be recovered if they have not been recorded over. After the "initial" initializing step, you have the option to Complete Initialization, which will physically erase all the data from the card and thus minimize potential problems by providing a completely clean space for recording. After the second stage of initialization, all previous files that have not been stored elsewhere will be lost. Touch X when you want to exit the menu.

Selecting the Recording Quality

The Recording Mode setting, which you access by choosing FUNC > MENU > Film Clip icon > Recording Mode (with the AUTO/M/CINEMA mode switch set to M or CINEMA), determines the data rate and compression, and consequently the quality of your image. (Look ahead to Figure 1.5.) Select MXP for highest quality. Alternatively, to operate with 40 percent more recording capacity, select FXP for good quality. Both of these modes record a full 1,920×1,080 image. 64GB of memory will provide nearly six hours of recording time at the highest data rate of 24Mbps. So, the built-in storage in the XA10 plus two 64GB SHXC cards in the removable memory slots can accommodate 18 hours of high-definition footage at 24Mbps, the highest quality level, without reloading. Table 1.1 outlines various AVCHD quality modes.

Table 1.1 AVCHD Quality Modes

Quality Mode	Data Rate	Compression	Record Time
MXP	24Mbps	Highest quality/lowest compression/largest file	64GB=5h:55m
FXP	17Mbps	Good quality	64GB=8h:20m
XP+	12Mbps	Moderate quality	64GB=11h:30m
SP	7Mbps	Low quality	64GB=19h:10m
LP	5Mbps	Lowest quality/highest compression/smallest file	64GB=24h:30m

FXP at 17Mbps and all slower rates can be authored without re-encoding onto standard DVD discs for direct playback as a special "AVCHD disc" that some, but not all, Blu-ray players and media consoles can read. Compatible Blu-ray players will usually have an AVCHD logo. MXP exceeds the data rate standard for AVCHD playable discs, but MXP can be recorded as a data file (as opposed to a playable disc) for storage on 25GB or 50GB Blu-ray discs as well as single-layered 4.7GB or double-layered 9GB standard DVDs. These files can then be played or edited when transferred from the disc to a high-speed hard drive and appropriate computer.

MXP is the AVCHD acquisition format for maintaining the highest quality. Unless you intend to exhibit only on AVCHD-playable discs recorded on standard DVDs, MXP is the mode of choice for all high-quality projects. Some post-production programs edit AVCHD files directly, while others expand each file into an intermediate format and transcode again on export to yet another kind of file or exhibition format. Starting with MXP will ensure the highest quality. The transcoded output of an editing or authoring program can be authored to an actual Blu-ray movie disc playable on any Blu-ray deck (as opposed to an AVCHD disc, which is a standard DVD containing an AVCHD file playable on certain Blu-ray decks).

The middle- and lowest-quality modes save file space by even greater compression and by recording the video's 1,920 pixel width across only 1,440 pixels, which are later expanded in playback. This results in a significant loss of horizontal resolution. The lowest modes might be used for minor video postings on the Internet or in situations where image quality does not matter. It's always best to record in the highest quality mode and then down-convert the image for Web compression in postproduction. Vimeo and YouTube both accept HD video for playback over the Web. YouTube accepts HD video up to 4K in resolution.

Selecting Frame Rate

On the G10 and XA10, the default frame rate in full AUTO mode is 60i and in Cinema mode is PF24. In the M mode, the labeled choices of frame rate are 60i, PF30, PF24, and 24P. To set the frame rate, choose FUNC > MENU > Film Clip icon > Frame Rate (with the AUTO/M/ CINEMA mode switch set to M). All these rates are nominally referred to in whole numbers but are actually 0.1 percent slower than labeled. This is due to the fact that when the U.S. set standards for color television in 1953, it needed to accommodate an additional color reference signal that had to fit within the same bandwidth that formerly carried a full black-and-white signal. This was accomplished by slowing the frame rate from 30 frames per second (fps) to 29.97fps, and because each frame is composed of two interlaced fields, the field rate becomes 59.94fps. Now that we are in the digital age, it is possible to record, broadcast, and view a whole range of frame rates, including a true 24, 30, or 60—or 0.1 percent slower as well as a true 25 (the PAL standard). Camcorders made for use in the United States typically run 0.1 percent slower than labeled in order to be the most compatible with America's pre-existing formats, editing software, and broadcast standards.

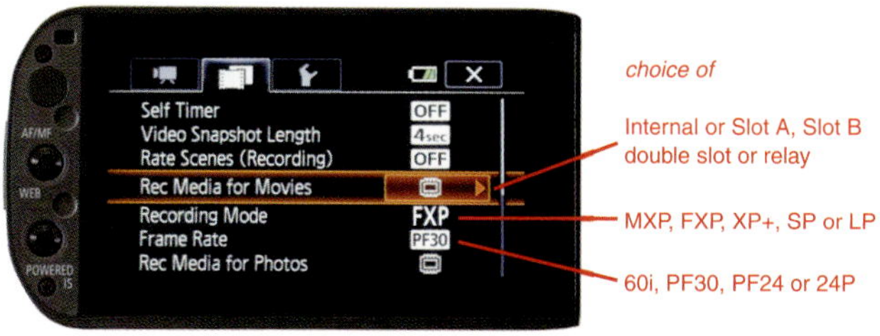

Figure 1.5 Selecting memory, recording mode (quality), and frame rate.

So the Vixia's 60i setting is really 59.94 "fields" per second that are interlaced together to present 29.97 frames per second. This has been the standard for analog television in the United States since 1953. In interlaced video, each frame is composed of two alternating interlaced fields that contain only the odd or the even scanning lines. An interlaced image creates smoother motion that is less likely to strobe, but at the expense of the greater resolution we are able to perceive when an image is scanned progressively as on a computer screen. 60i is a holdover from analog television, yet is one of the main standards for ATSC digital television introduced in 1996, and is still prominent today. It is the rate most compatible with old analog TV sets and with mastering on actual tape. Consequently, many cable and broadcast stations use 60i more than any other frame or field rate. Modern LCD digital TV sets actually take the 60i (59.94i) signal and de-interlace it to 30p (29.97p) for sharper viewing, although some sets do this better than others.

Canon's PF30 setting is actually 29.97 fps scanned progressively for maximum sharpness but then divided into separate fields and recorded at the 59.96i standard for compatibility with tape, editing software, and the widest range of TV sets. If it had actually been recorded as a progressive 30 (29.97fps) file, it would have been called "30P" instead of "PF30." This is a very good-looking setting that produces a live camera feeling to the recorded image. It is useful for most purposes, including broadcast and DVD on digital televisions, and particularly the Internet, where video files are often down-converted to 15 fps to be manageable on most servers and computers. With progressive scanning, there is a danger that movement at certain speeds will have a noticeable strobe effect. Professionals keep this under control by avoiding situations that would produce a pronounced strobe, such as a moderately fast pan across a black iron fence in front of a light background. Many videographers are willing to accept minor strobing in return for greater sharpness and the absence of interlacing artifacts.

The PF24 setting is actually 23.976 fps scanned progressively for maximum sharpness but then recorded at 59.96i through a process called 3:2 pulldown (or 2:3 pulldown). This process creates extra interpolated frames by selectively combining interlace fields derived from the original progressively scanned images. PF24 produces a motion-picture film look or more precisely a film-to-video look recorded in a format ready to use with the widest range of editing software, monitors, TV sets, and tape. Through a lifetime of cultural conditioning, viewers psychologically associate this 24-frame look with Hollywood films, international films, and high production values. Contrast and color settings under Cinema mode may further enhance the film look. If you wanted to record at PF24 but edit and exhibit in a true 24p, some editing software can accomplish reverse 3:2 to de-interlace and convert the files back to 24 progressive frames. This is unnecessary in the M mode, however, because the G10 and XA10 offer a true 24p.

The obvious question is, what is the difference between PF24 and 24p? The 24p setting is actually 23.976 progressively scanned frames per second recorded as such (not transcoded to 60i). Choose this setting if you want the film look and your editing software and exhibition situations can handle true 24p (23.976p) files. The advantage of a true 24p (23.976p) is that the files are ⅘ the size of PF24, PF30, or 60i formats, and they have undergone no extra processing to interpolate and render new frames or interlace fields. It is possible to shoot, edit, master, and release a project on standard DVD or Blu-ray entirely in 24p. A project in 24p will play on modern LCD television sets, computer monitors, and multi-sync video projectors. If a version is needed for broadcast, tape, or compatibility with older TV sets, then Final Cut, Avid, or Adobe Premiere editing software can convert and re-render the edited 24p project as a 60i HD or standard definition master file. However, the Canon camcorder itself cannot convert 24p to standard definition as it can with the 60i,

PF30, and PF24 speeds. 24p is a favorite among film students who have the appropriate editing software and plan to exhibit on DVD, Blu-Ray, or a computer screen.

Shooting 24 images per second instead of 30 or 60 may produce slightly more motion blur if the shutter speed is slowed to 1/48 instead of 1/60. Video and film can shoot at slower shutter speeds than still photography and maintain a relatively sharp appearance because the viewer's eye can perceive detail and sharpness in a sequence of slightly blurred images in motion through a process of perception called "temporal resolution." Under certain conditions, blur helps blend motion from frame to frame, softening some of the strobing of progressive scanning, but in general you will see more strobing at 24 than with 30 or 60, particularly with subjects of high-contrast.

Depending on the input preferences on the editing software, Canon's 60i, PF30, and PF24 speeds can presumably be edited together because their files are actually recorded at 60i (59.94i). However, they each look slightly different even though the editing program sees them all as 60i. So in most cases, you want to set your frame rate to be consistent within an entire project.

The Lens Shade

One of the important tasks you need to do before shooting is install the tulip-shaped lens shade on the camcorder. The shade serves several functions. First, the lens shade allows for cleaner, sharper images because it prevents light coming from just beyond the boundary of your frame from hitting the front elements and bouncing inside the lens barrel as unfocused light, which ultimately affects exposure, degrades your image, washes out contrast and color saturation, and potentially produces glare and lens flare. You get the maximum optical quality of your lens when the shade is in place. Second, most of the lens of the G10/XA10 is buried in the body of the camcorder; only a shallow amount of it protrudes from the front. Without the shade, it is very easy to get your fingers in the shot as you hold the camcorder, particularly as you reach beyond the viewfinder to turn the focus ring.

The tulip contour is a sophisticated design that blocks the maximum amount of extraneous light with the minimum profile, without the shade itself darkening or vignetting the edges of the picture. The tulip lens shade perfectly matches the light-gathering area of the widest angle of the lens and offers reasonable protection for most of the zoom range.

To install the shade, first remove the lens cap. Then align the lip pattern of the shade onto the front of the lens at a 45° rotation and turn clockwise to lock it in place. When the shade is installed, the lens cap can fit on or off the lens, so re-capping the lens is not an issue. The shade not only keeps your fingers from getting in the shot, it prevents you from accidentally touching the front element of the lens when the cap is off.

If your camera case will accommodate the added length, the lens shade should be permanently left on the camcorder.

Shooting in AUTO Mode

With the lens shade in place, with a charged battery, and with memory location and recording mode selected, you are now ready to shoot in auto focus and auto exposure by sliding the mode switch to AUTO. After turning the power on, just press the START/STOP button to begin recording, and press it a second time to stop. Tally numbers will accumulate on the LCD screen while recording, and the access light will blink as the camcorder writes data to memory. In full AUTO mode, the camcorder will determine focus and exposure, and most of the camcorder's settings will not be adjustable on the touchscreen menu. No matter what frame rate you may have selected in M mode, the frame rate reverts to 60i in AUTO mode.

Until recently, most professionals would never shoot video in AUTO mode. Auto exposure could jump to extremes as you pan past a bright window or when a person wearing a white shirt enters or leaves the frame, and auto focus could easily lock on an unwanted detail in the background or indecisively waiver between two points, producing unusable footage. The default AUTO settings for focus and exposure on the HF G10 and XA10 are more intelligently designed and more subtly articulated than previous models. The camcorder's logic circuit which includes SMART AUTO is in full effect when you shoot in AUTO mode. SMART AUTO recognizes 38 different scene types to more selectively adapt to faces, landscapes, foreground/background relationships, and lighting conditions. There may be times when you have no choice but to rely on AUTO mode. As you get accustomed to the camcorder, it would be very useful to test full AUTO mode in a variety of lighting and focus situations to find what you can trust it to do and what its limitations are.

The next chapter more completely explains SMART AUTO and explores more sophisticated semi-automatic controls like Touch Focusing, Touch & Track, Face Recognition, programmed settings, and custom keys while shooting on the fly.

Playback

To review your footage in the camcorder, press the button that toggles between Camera and Playback on the left side of the camcorder (next to the DISP. button). You can also press and hold the Camera/Play button on the wireless remote for about two seconds to enable playback. The LCD screen will display a thumbnail storyboard of the initial image of each shot. The Zoom lever on the top of the camcorder adjusts the storyboard to display the initial frame of either six shots or 15 shots at a time.

Four icons under the storyboard lead to submenus for selecting memory source and date, filmstrip or Rolodex storyboard format, basic editing, and shot information. (See Figure 1.6.)

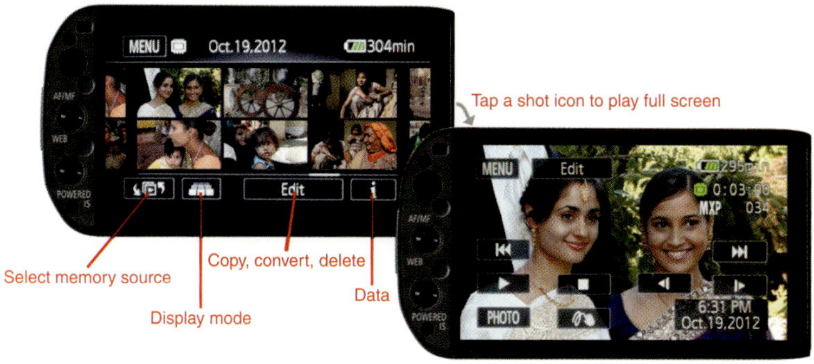

Figure 1.6 Playback menus and controls.

Tap the image of a shot on the camcorder's LCD and it will instantly play full screen. If you tap the screen after a shot has been selected, controls appear for play/pause, stop, fast forward, reverse, previous shot, next shot, volume, and decorative effects. Tapping the screen while in Pause mode will toggle the playback controls from visible to hidden. During other playback functions, the controls disappear on their own after a few seconds.

To locate a shot, scroll the storyboard display with your finger. Shots are grouped according to recording date. The filmstrip storyboard format is easiest for locating an individual shot within a particular date. The Rolodex format, which Canon calls "3D Flip View," is easier for efficiently scrolling among many recording dates because it presents a compact stack of picture icons for each date.

After you initiate playback from either of the storyboard displays, each subsequent file plays automatically. To stop playback, tap the screen so that playback controls appear; then press the Stop symbol.

For playback on a larger screen, connect a cable from the mini HDMI output below the hand strap of the camcorder to the full size HDMI input of a monitor or digital video projector. A six-foot mini-HDMI-to-HDMI cable costs from $3 to $7 at amazon.com and similar sources. HDMI, which stands for "High Definition Media Interface," carries both picture and sound signals to modern HDTV monitors and projectors. If your monitor accepts 1080p (progressively scanned) signals, press the Camera/Playback button to select Playback; then choose MENU > Tool icon > HDMI 1080p Output > ON.

Turning on Control for HDMI (an additional option under the Tool icon just above HDMI 1080p Output) allows monitors equipped with HDMI-CEC (Consumer Electronic Control) to operate the playback functions of the G10/XA10 from the monitor's remote control. If you do not want to use this function, make certain it is off, and playback control will remain with the camcorder. Checking HDMI Status, under the Tool icon, will verify the standard of your HDMI output signal. Connecting to the HDMI output will disable the camcorder's other video outputs.

For connecting to an HDTV through "component" inputs, you will need two cables. For the picture signal, attach the cable that ends with red, green, and blue RCA plugs to the monitor and the plug on the opposite end to the camcorder's Component OUT on the left side of the camcorder. For audio, connect red and white RCA plugs to the monitor and the ⅛-inch mini plug into the camcorder's A/V Output. Go to MENU > Tool icon > AV/Headphones > AV.

For connecting to an analog standard definition monitor (much lower quality), use the ⅛-inch AV OUT from the camcorder and the yellow, red, and white RCA plugs to the monitor's video and audio inputs. Of course, you can transfer your video files to a computer and view them there. This option will be discussed in Chapter 18.

2

Run-and-Gun Shooting

In basketball, "run-and-gun" is a strategy of training for and playing a fast-paced game with little time to think, scoring as quickly as possible before the defense is set. In video games, "run-and-gun" is a genre involving quick reflexes, often with characters on foot dodging and defending against bullets, missiles, or an overwhelming adversary. Sports, gaming, and hunting metaphors apply easily to the process of making motion pictures. In film or video, the term "run-and-gun" refers to shooting on the move in ongoing conditions, with minimal or no assistance, little or no time to prepare, adapting to available light, and having to make quick choices.

The G10/XA10's lightweight body, versatility, and semi-automatic modes make it the ideal camcorder for shooting under these conditions. However, it takes discipline and a thorough knowledge of the camcorder to do this kind of production well. Event videography, surveillance, sports, news, documentary, and advocacy video often demand a run-and-gun approach, as might "stealth video" and "guerilla television." At times, home video, diary, experimental, and even fiction may call upon the skills of instantaneous shooting and adapting to ongoing conditions. Academy Award–winning cinematographer Anthony Dod Mantle filmed moments when the fictional characters in *Slumdog Millionaire* were amid actual street scenes.

The most important thing before any shoot—and all the more important for conditions that may be chaotic—is to be prepared ahead of time. The camcorder should be charged and ready to go with all the appropriate presets, plus spare batteries and adequate time remaining on recording media.

Upgrading the G10/XA10 Battery

The G10/XA10 comes with battery pack BP-808 with a capacity of only 720mAh, which lasts only about an hour or so. This is an undersized battery that only partially fills the chamber, making it a bit hard to remove. The single biggest complaint of G10/XA10 owners is that for the price, Canon should have shipped a full-size battery in the original package. After all, one of the primary reasons for using a camcorder with up to 192GB of memory is to shoot for hours at a time if necessary. To be prepared for several hours of shooting, you will need to purchase a full-sized battery, the BP-819 ($79 to $99) with a capacity of 1780mAh which lasts over two hours, or the extended-run BP-827 ($120 to $130) with a capacity of 2670mAh (three to four hours of recording time).

Checklist

Whether you or someone else last used the camcorder, you need to go over a checklist of important settings before you shoot. (See Figure 2.1.)

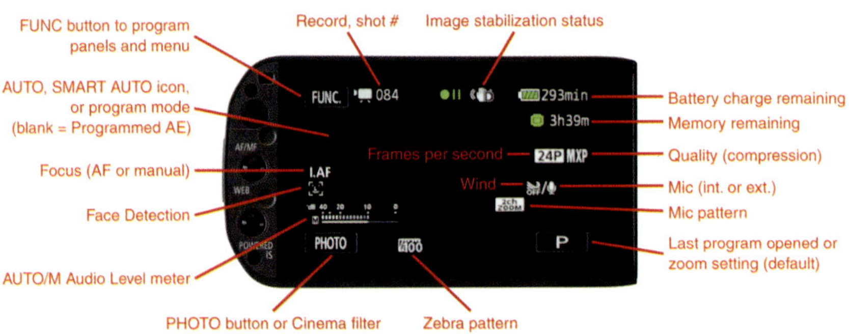

Figure 2.1 Status indicators on the touchscreen display.

- **Check the battery.** This is so essential that Canon created a direct and immediate test as the first thing you do before turning the power on. Simply press the BATT. INFO button (the same as the DISP. button) on the left side of the camcorder while the power is off. For five seconds, the full touchscreen will display the capacity of the battery as a percentage on a color-coded graph and as remaining minutes of recording time. You should adopt the habit of checking the battery every time you prepare to shoot.

- **Check the operating mode.** Look at the AUTO/M/CINEMA mode switch on the upper-right side of the camcorder to see if it is appropriately set for AUTO, M (manual), or CINEMA. You don't want to mistakenly shoot in one mode while intending to be in another.
- **Check the program mode.** When you turn the power on, immediately verify your program mode in the upper left of the touchscreen, just below the FUNC button. If the upper left says "AUTO," then you are in full AUTO mode and control is determined by the camcorder. If you are operating in M or CINEMA mode, this checkpoint is extremely important for identifying a specific program mode, and some of the information will appear only briefly. If you are in program AE (Canon's term for Auto Exposure while in M or CINEMA mode), the letter P will appear for three seconds in the upper left, then disappear. If you are in Portrait, Sports, Night Scene, Snow, Beach, Sunset, Low Light, Spotlight, or Fireworks mode, the name will be spelled out for three seconds in the upper left of the touchscreen then disappear with only its icon remaining. If you are in Av (Aperture value) priority or Tv (Time value) priority, its symbol will remain constantly in the upper left along with its aperture or shutter value. If you are in Manual Exposure mode, the upper left displays the f/stop, shutter speed, and dB gain settings, which stay visible as long as you remain in Manual Exposure mode.
- **Check the memory.** In the upper-right area of the touchscreen, memory location is indicated by an icon of a circuit chip or a memory card (indicating internal, MC1 or MC2). Next to this is an estimate of remaining recording time on the memory chip. If status information like this does not appear after startup, press the DISP. button. It is important to know which memory location you are recording to and how much memory space you have left. For long-duration shooting, you may want to set memory for Relay Recording so that when a memory card gets filled, recording automatically continues on the next available card. To select this setting, choose FUNC > MENU > Film Clip icon > Rec. Memory > Relay.
- **Check the frame rate and record quality mode.** The two are displayed together on the middle-right side of the touchscreen. If only the quality mode appears (MXP or FXP, for example) with no indication of frame rate, then the camcorder is running at its default rate, which is 60i. Any other frame rate will be displayed.
- **Check the microphone.** Verify the microphone source by its icon on the lower-right side. The icon for the internal mic also indicates the directional pattern, equalization, and digital windscreen. Make a sound or gently tap the microphone to see that the Audio Level meter on the lower left responds.

- **Check zebra patterns.** You will need to know whether zebra patterns are on and whether they are calibrated for 70 percent or 100 percent. If zebra patterns are on, a striped icon appears near the bottom left with a 70 or 100.
- **Check the method of focus.** An icon midway on the left side will indicate I.AF (instant auto focus), M.AF (medium auto focus), AF (normal auto focus), Face Detection (a rectangular smiley face), or MF (manual focus).
- **Check the color balance.** There will be no indication of color balance in AUTO mode or in program modes that have a predetermined value or preset automatic white balancing. Otherwise, if the White Balance setting is something other than Automatic, there will be an icon indicating the type of balance midway on the left, next to the icon indicating the method of focus.
- **Check for any unintended functions.** See if there are unexpected icons on the touchscreen (for example, Image Effects, x.v. Color, or Reverse Scan) and run the camera to see if everything works as you expect, including zoom control and focus parameters. Make certain you are not in Decoration, Digital Zoom, Conversion Lens, Backlight On, or Video Snapshot mode unless you intend to be.

If you need to change anything, the touchscreen is fairly easy to navigate once you get accustomed to the five display layers: FUNC, MENU, Camera/Play settings (indicated by the Camera icon), media settings (indicated by the Film Clip icon), and tools (indicated by the Tool icon, which resembles a wrench). Tapping an icon or word activates it. Gently moving your finger up or down the screen will scroll to other items on the menu. Tapping X will exit a menu layer and will enable any adjustment you made while in that layer.

To get out of an unwanted program setting, tap FUNC > Rec. Programs > and select the program setting you want instead. Basic media parameters like memory location, shutter speed, and record quality can be located while in M mode by pressing FUNC > MENU > Film Clip icon. (See Figure 2.2.) Other basic settings from screen brightness to headphone level to initializing memory are under the Tool icon. Not everything under each menu is intuitive. If you have trouble locating what you need, see Appendix C, "Menu Map," available at www.courseptr.com/downloads.

The alternative to the preceding checklist is to take the time to systematically check and set every menu item, particularly if you are going to shoot in M or CINEMA mode. Press FUNC to examine or select the options in the program panel:

- Rec. Programs P (AE, Tv, Av, Manual Exposure, or Scene)
- BLC (backlight correction)
- White Balance

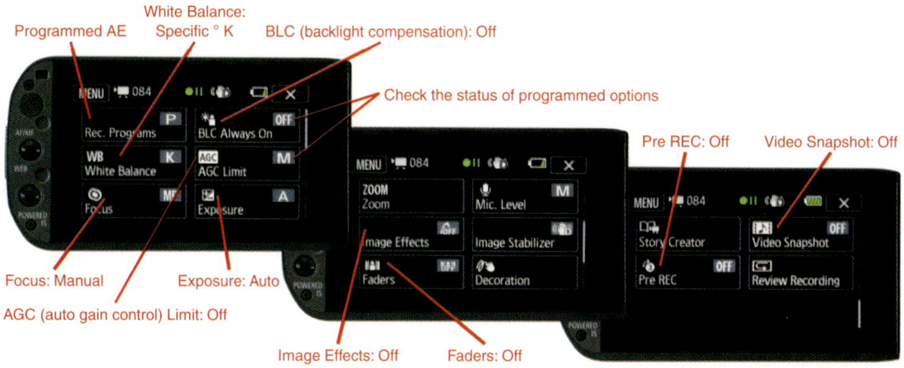

Figure 2.2 Status indicators in the program panel selections. Press FUNC and scroll to access these screens.

- AGC Limit (auto gain control)
- Focus
- Exposure
- Zoom
- Mic. Level
- Image Effects
- Image Stabilizer
- Faders
- Decoration

Do a similar thorough check under the Camera, Film Clip, and Tool icons. The options are spelled out in Appendix C.

Run-and-Gun Focus

Here are the features and techniques that allow for quick and easy focus under ongoing run-and-gun conditions:

- **Face Detection.** Face Detection is the camcorder's ability to recognize and give focus and exposure priority to faces. It works in AUTO, M, and CINEMA modes.
- **Touch & Track.** Touch & Track enables the camcorder to track focus and exposure of a face or an object that you have selected, wherever the image moves within the frame.

- **Touch Focus panel.** Using the Touch Focus panel located at FUNC > Focus in M and CINEMA modes, you can lock the point of focus to a selected part of the composition. The focus remains locked to that distance until another point of focus or until automatic is selected. This is particularly useful for run-and-gun shooting.
- **Toggling between AF and MF.** The AF/MF (auto focus and manual focus) switch on the bezel of the touchscreen allows you to toggle between manual and automatic focus. This is also well suited for run-and-gun shooting. It allows you to instantly choose when you want to be in auto or manual mode. In addition, in run-and-gun conditions, it allows you to lock a good auto focus setting to manual so that it does not wander. The AF/MF switch frees the touchscreen for other functions.

None of these take the time of full manual focus, but they all allow a degree of selection and control as part of the focus process.

Note

Full manual focus, Face Only (coupled with manual focus), the focus ring on the lens, and focusing aids are discussed in Chapter 5, "Selective Focus and Depth of Field," which covers focus in greater detail.

Run-and-Gun Exposure

Here are the options and techniques that allow for quick automatic or semi-automatic control over exposure under ongoing run-and-gun conditions:

- Full AUTO mode with SMART AUTO
- Programmed AE (Auto Exposure)
- Touch Exposure
- Tv (Time value) priority
- Av (Aperture value) priority
- Scene program

These semi- or fully automatic program modes determine exposure along with other parameters like white balance, color saturation, and whether additional controls are activated. Full manual exposure and record program modes with manual overrides are covered in Chapter 4, "Controlling Exposure." However, beyond discussing fully automatic exposure, we will introduce the basic elements of Touch Exposure later in this chapter because Touch Exposure particularly lends itself to run-and-gun use.

AUTO Mode

Let's examine your options if you decide to approach a run-and-gun situation in full AUTO mode. Whatever frame rate you have set in M mode will revert to 60i in full AUTO mode. However, the following functions remain active if they are first set in M mode before switching to AUTO mode:

- Recording mode (quality), the Mbps setting
- Memory location for video files and photos
- Auto focus speed (instant, medium, or normal)
- Zoom speeds and Soft Zoom
- Audio input, internal mic pattern, equalization, windscreen
- Image Stabilization settings, including the POWERED IS button setting
- Video Snapshot setting (turn this off unless you want to be restricted to shooting two-, four-, or eight-second clips of predetermined length)

Even though you are in full AUTO mode, you have a powerful semi-automatic/ semi-manual control for selecting focus on the touchscreen in run-and-gun situations. Face Detection and Touch & Track are always activated in full AUTO mode, even if previously turned off in the menu while in M or CINEMA mode.

You can adjust how quickly the G10/XA10 responds in auto focus to suit your style of shooting. A quick response snaps focus into place nearly instantaneously using both through-the-lens (TTL) and external auto focus sensors. The extra sensor adds accuracy and minimizes searching, which is particularly useful in run-and-gun scenarios. On many camcorders, a quick auto focus often has an annoying mechanical look, but on the G10/XA10 the I.AF (instant auto focus) setting glides smoothly into position and works well in most run-and-gun situations. This setting ensures the maximum duration of a focused image, which can be useful in post production as shots are trimmed and assembled in the editing process. The camcorder's M.AF (medium auto focus) speed may be a good compromise for moderate and slower-moving action. In this mode, focus changes that happen during sustained long takes can seem to glide into place without calling attention to themselves. The relatively slow AF setting (which Canon calls normal auto focus) might be appropriate for situations in which the action itself is in a decidedly slow rhythm—for example, panning among people doing yoga or tai chi. A slow setting is useful for a lingering focus pull from a nearly static image in the foreground to one in the background or vice versa, and its rate might be intentionally chosen for that type of shot. But the G10/XA10's fastest setting will probably work best for shooting on the move while adapting to a variety of ongoing conditions.

Face Detection and Touch & Track

In full AUTO mode, Face Detection and its related feature, Touch & Track, operate by default. Within any auto focus situation, the camera's focus and exposure will seek out faces with a higher priority than other kinds of images. When its logic system detects faces, it places a frame around each one in the LCD screen—as many as nine faces simultaneously. The camera focuses on the most prominent face and displays a white frame around it, with dark gray frames around the secondary faces. (See Figure 2.3.) As characters move, the logic system swaps focus among them to whichever face is momentarily prominent in the composition; the screen will indicate the area of focus with a white frame. At this point, you are in Face Detection but not in Touch & Track.

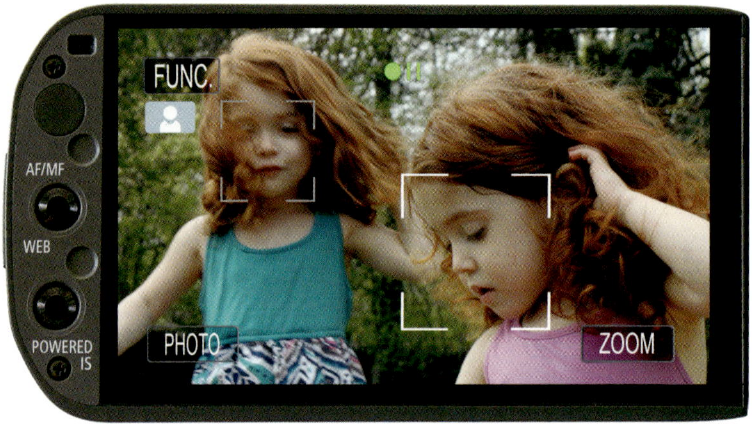

Figure 2.3 Face Detection indicators.

If you tap a face on the touchscreen, even a secondary one, focus will shift to that individual (along with the white indicator frame); you will have moved into Touch & Track mode while still in Face Detection. As long as features are distinctive, the logic system can identify one person from another and will track the selected face, adjusting focus and prioritizing that person's exposure as long as the face is visible on the screen. When the selected face is no longer present in the shot, the logic system returns to regular AUTO mode and will behave as it did before you touched the screen, selecting automatically among faces in the composition or focusing on other prominent details when no face is present.

The ability to track focus and exposure in full AUTO mode is not restricted to faces. The same Touch & Track mechanism can lock onto an object, an animal, a car, or a piece of scenery if you select it on the touchscreen. As an indicator, the display places a white rectangle around the selected object. The object you select must have distinctive features that differentiate it from other images in the frame.

Initially, the logic system will seek out faces in AUTO mode unless there is no face present or until you select a non-facial image. Only then will the camera's logic drop its face-seeking priority. In the M and CINEMA modes you can turn off Face Detection while in auto focus or toggle Face Detection in or out with an assignable button for use in manual focus. We will discuss these options in Chapter 5.

Image Stabilization

The Powered IS (Image Stabilization) feature is particularly useful in run-and-gun situations when you find that you suddenly need to become a human tripod. To know for certain that Powered IS is functional, test it by pressing the POWERED IS button on the left bezel of the touchscreen. The hand icon on the upper part of the screen should turn from white with the letter D (for Dynamic IS) to yellow with the letter P. If Powered IS does not operate, its button has been re-assigned to some other function. To restore it, choose FUNC > MENU > Tool icon > Assign Button 2 and select Powered IS. In addition, you can set Powered IS to operate only while the button is physically held down (the default mode), or to toggle on and off. You might choose the latter setting if you anticipate long static moments; otherwise, the default mode works best for most on-the-move situations. Remember that Powered IS is for keeping the camera very still, not for stabilizing the moving camera. This is why you want to easily get into and out of this function.

One quite effective run-and-gun strategy is shooting in full AUTO mode, manually selecting faces or other points of focus with your thumb on the touchscreen (which reverts to auto focus when nothing is selected), and holding down the POWERED IS button for moments where you need maximum stability. Powered IS seamlessly reverts to Dynamic IS to handle motion when the button is released. These functions work well together and rarely compete with each other. Your subject is usually already locked in focus and being tracked at the point you need to hold the frame in place.

SMART AUTO

As you shoot in full AUTO mode, icons for portrait, landscape, backlight, sunset, extreme close-up, and other characteristics will replace the word AUTO in the upper-left area of the touchscreen as SMART AUTO circuitry recognizes compositional clues in your subject and adjusts accordingly. Canon's computerized scene detection considers parameters like front light versus backlight; stationary versus moving subjects; portraits; landscapes; blue, grey or sunset skies; close-ups; extreme close-ups (tele-macro); spotlight; or night scenes, and the touchscreen displays one of 38 icons indicating how the scene has been analyzed. (See Figure 2.4.)

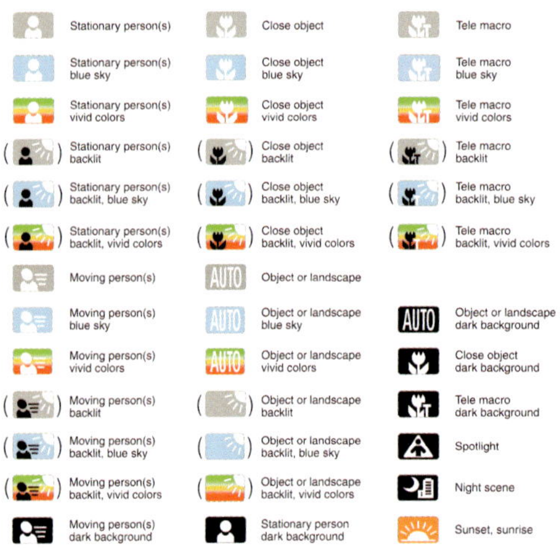

Figure 2.4 SMART AUTO icons.

Pay attention to these icons. They are purely informational; you cannot adjust them because they occur in full AUTO mode. But the icon is still useful, particularly if you notice one that indicates the camcorder is misinterpreting your subject or your intentions. This is your cue to switch to M mode and select a record program consistent with your intentions—for example, Programmed AE, which does not have the SMART AUTO function—or to take complete manual control.

Of course, in an ongoing run-and-gun situation, you might not have the time to switch to a semi-automatic program or to manual control. If you prefer to stay in full AUTO mode, you might simply alter the framing until the icon changes back to AUTO or to an icon that represents a more appropriate interpretation of the scene.

Semi-Automatic

The so-called M (manual) setting on the AUTO/M/CINEMA switch is a misnomer. Most of the choices in M mode are still automatic—or at least semi-automatic—like Programmed AE, Portrait, Sports, Night Scene, Snow, Beach, Sunset, Lowlight, Spotlight, Fireworks, Auto White Balance, and Auto Backlight Correction. Many choices allow you to set one function manually while others remain semi-automatic, like Av (Aperture value) priority, Tv (Time value) priority, +/– Exposure, and Auto Gain Limit. Canon might just as well have called this mode "P mode," or "program mode," instead of "M mode."

Full Manual Exposure is only one choice of 13 exposure programs in the M mode. The remaining 12 settings are automatic but optimized for a particular type of situation or are semi-automatic settings allowing you to set one parameter. Several of these could be perfect for run-and-gun shooting, depending on the nature of your shooting conditions. To access the semi-automatic/semi-manual Rec. Program techniques described in this chapter, set the AUTO/M/CINEMA switch on the upper-right side of the camcorder to M (manual). Then choose FUNC > Rec. Programs and select one of the following:

- Programmed AE
- Tv Shutter Priority AE
- Av Aperture Priority AE

In run-and-gun situations, one of the most useful controls in Programmed AE is the ability to toggle between auto focus and manual focus. Programmed AE mode is a basic automatic exposure, which differs from full AUTO mode in that you will not have the camera's logic system additionally invoking SMART AUTO interpretations and adjustments. Unlike full AUTO, Programmed AE allows you to selectively add manual overrides for some of its functions, including choices between auto or various manual settings for white balance and adjusting aspects of exposure. Within Programmed AE, you also have the possibility of Touch Exposure (+/– Exposure) compensation.

Among the other selections in the Rec. Programs panel, you have the choice of full manual exposure, which is discussed in Chapter 4, or one of the nine content-defined scene programs like Portrait or Night Scene. When you enter Rec. Programs (choose FUNC > Rec. Programs while in M mode), the last previously accessed scene appears with the letters "SCN" among the other program choices in the panel. If you want a content-defined scene, tap the SCN button regardless of which icon it shows, and the icons for all nine content-defined scenes will appear (see Figure 2.5):

- **Portrait.** If your run-and-gun situation is exclusively waist high, chest high, and shoulder high shots of people in a fairly intimate space, then Portrait is a viable option. Face Detection operates in this mode and adjusts both focus and exposure to optimize human faces. Portrait mode lowers the gain setting so that the lens aperture will open to compensate. A nearly wide open aperture provides a shallower depth of field, which will emphasize and better separate a portrait subject in sharp focus from a softer background.
- **Sports.** Sports emphasizes more distant focus and accommodates fast action.
- **Night Scene.** Night Scene exposes for the highlights and limits gain so that areas of the composition remain black.

- **Snow.** Snow brings out detail on the subject, which otherwise might underexpose amid white surroundings. It also minimizes the blue tint that occurs as a snowscape reflects the sky. This is intended for a sunlit scene, not shade, overcast, or falling snow.
- **Beach.** Beach is similar to Snow but with a different color balance. It brings out detail on the subject, which otherwise might underexpose with a background of bright sand under sunlight.
- **Sunset.** Sunset provides saturated colors and exposes so that detail emerges from the glare of a sunset (or sunrise), which may silhouette foreground images.
- **Low Light.** Low Light enables slower shutter speeds and higher gain for greater visibility in dark areas.
- **Spotlight.** Spotlight exposes for the highlights in situations where a pool of light illuminates a small part of the composition while the rest of the area is dark.
- **Fireworks.** Fireworks is not likely to be chosen in run-and-gun situations. It emphasizes distant (infinite) focus and rich color in a predominantly dark environment.

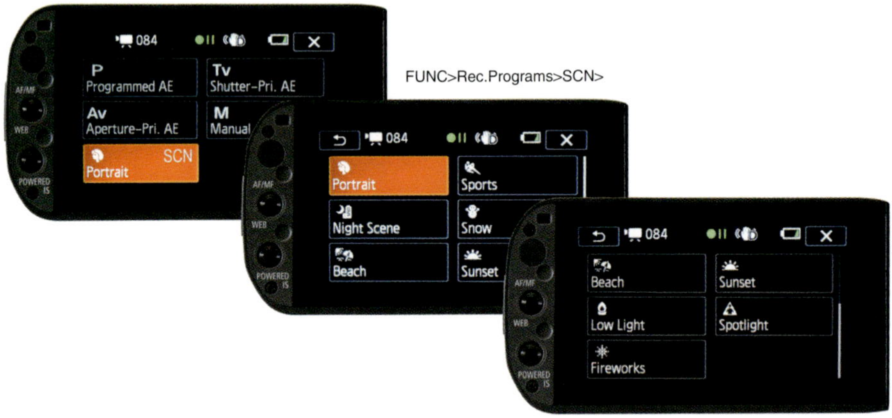

Figure 2.5 SCN on the program panel leads to nine content-defined scene modes.

Note

Sunset, Night Scene, Spotlight, and Low Light are discussed in Chapter 9, "Lighting Techniques," and Chapter 10, "Shooting at Night."

Custom Settings

A menu item that you need often could be re-programmed onto the two mechanical buttons on the left bezel of the LCD screen if you want to forego the ability to either toggle between manual and auto focus or use the POWERED IS button for steady telephoto shots. Most videographers will find that these two buttons are extremely useful at their original assignments and probably will not want to reassign them. But depending on your style of shooting, some of you may consider reassigning one or the other button to be able to toggle into Backlight Correction or Auto Focus/Face Detection (within manual focus), or a swap between a current and a preset white balance value versus automatic. These reassignments are effective only in M and CINEMA mode.

To reassign a button, choose FUNC > MENU > TOOL > Assign Button 1 or Assign Button 2. Then choose one of the following:

- BLC Always On
- Face Only AF (set to work in manual focus)
- WB Priority
- IR Light (XA10 only)
- AF/MF (default setting for Button 1)
- POWERED IS (default setting for Button 2)
- Off

Fixed Focus

An effective strategy for unpredictable run-and-gun situations is to shoot in manual focus almost exclusively in wide angle as if the zoom didn't exist at all, and pre-setting the focus to a fixed distance. Wide angle provides the deepest depth of field and least camera shake, issues that are discussed further in Chapter 5, "Selective Focus and Depth of Field," and Chapter 12, "Controlling the Moving Camera." Having to physically move farther or closer with the camcorder to create long shot, medium shot, and close-up more dynamically positions the spectator in the world of the event compared to zooming, which simply magnifies and de-magnifies images from one point in space. The deep depth of field of a wide angle also allows for composition in depth with near, medium, and far images in sharp focus within the same frame. Staying at a particular focal length also provides a visual consistency to the scene.

In full wide angle, manual focus can be locked at a fixed point just beyond your closest expected image—for example, at a distance of 38 inches. The depth of field in wide angle is so deep for this particular lens that when you focus at 38 inches, about 19 inches to infinity will be in focus. There will be no need to refocus as long as you remain in full wide angle and do not get closer than 19 inches. With this approach, you will have completely eliminated unwanted focus shifts that can easily occur under run-and-gun conditions. You will be able to do spectacular z-axis compositions in depth, with foreground and background in dramatic focus, and wherever you pan will be in focus. The trade-off is that in order to obtain a variety of shots, you have to become a human zoom, physically moving in tightly with the camera for a close-up, back for a medium shot, and farther back for a long shot.

Seeing a Wide Angle in Action

In D.A. Pennebaker's 1967 landmark documentary *Don't Look Back* on folk and rock icon Bob Dylan's tour of England (available on DVD), the close-ups in the early parts of the film were shot in telephoto and are consequently shaky and sometimes soft focus. As Dylan eventually got used to the presence of the camera, Pennebaker shot almost exclusively in wide angle with its inherently deep depth of field, moving to within a couple feet for close-ups and composing with deep focus. The focus, steadiness, and visual consistency of the film are noticeably better as Pennebaker's run-and-gun strategy moved to wide angle.

Shooting exclusively in wide angle can free you to concentrate on visual composition and controlling exposure in run-and-gun situations. One thing to be careful of, however, is that your focus does have to be preset for an appropriate distance that maximizes your depth of field. Check out the depth-of-field charts in Chapter 5. An incorrect setting could result in the entire field of view in soft focus.

The +/– Exposure panel interface enables Touch Exposure, which allows you to select a point within the composition on which to base exposure, along with the ability to lighten or darken the selection using a slider control, or lock the exposure to manual, or toggle back to auto exposure. (See Figure 2.6.) These controls are particularly useful if your subject of interest is lighter or darker than the rest of the composition. The Exposure panel is available in M mode in all record programs and all content-based scene modes except full manual exposure and Fireworks. To access it in M mode, you must be operating in a compatible record program; choose FUNC > Rec. Programs and select a program or scene mode and press X. Then, when you want to use Touch Exposure while shooting in your selected mode, choose FUNC > +/– Exposure.

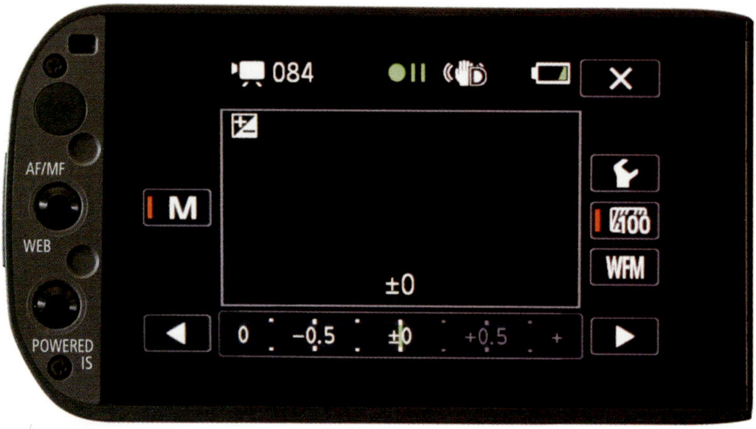

Figure 2.6 The +/– Exposure panel. Touch Exposure can be performed in the central rectangle.

> **Note**
>
> The Exposure panel also provides access to exposure measuring instruments, zebra patterns, and a waveform monitor. We will discuss the Exposure panel in greater detail and the instruments for measuring exposure in Chapter 4.

Coverage Strategies

Even in hectic run-and-gun conditions, there is a need for discipline, structure, and coverage as events are unfolding. It is important to record a meaningful selection of shots that have everything you will need in the editing process for emphasis/de-emphasis, progression, development, point-of-view, and meaning. This can involve a kind of storyboard thinking, in which you continually ask yourself structural questions during the act of shooting—for example, what should the next shot be? Or, phrased in a few other ways:

- What is the complement or visual answer to the current shot?
- Does it need to change angle?
- Where can the camcorder be placed for a meaningful relationship between the spectator and the subject?
- Should I be inside the circle of action, on its edge, or outside?
- Should I favor one character over another?

- Should the composition change because the nature of the moment has changed?
- Should the camcorder remain stationary and let the subject move, or should it follow the subject, lead, react, move in counterpoint, or seek out new angles or other images?
- Do I need detail shots, establishing shots, cutaways, and inserts, or simply an evolving long take?

Among these choices, you want to make sure you have enough coverage. One aspect of coverage is simply having shot ample material in your shooting ratio to be certain you have enough footage and, hopefully, the right footage. Some Direct Cinema observational documentaries by filmmakers like Ricky Leacock or Fred Wiseman have shooting ratios of 50:1 up to 100:1 (100 hours of footage to make a one-hour film). Another aspect of coverage is the concept of the alternative shot or alternative angle. If all the footage is primarily from the same angle, it will be very difficult to cut together without jumps in continuity. Sometimes coverage represents a completely alternative strategy in case the primary footage does not work out in the editing. More often, a coverage angle is chosen because it could be a viable change of vantage point that would cut well with the primary material.

Note

If you are shooting for the purpose of editing, see Chapter 3, "Visual Composition," and Chapter 17, "Production Strategies," for establishing shots, cutaways, B-roll, room tone, *et cetera.*

Pre-Record

A particularly useful aid in situations that are difficult to predict is the ability of the G10/XA10 to automatically pre-record three seconds before you press the Record button. In run-and-gun shooting, you may want to routinely activate this feature. It works particularly well when the camcorder is on a tripod or already has the potential moment well framed. Human reaction time is about [1/10] of a second, but the camcorder can take up to an additional second to start recording. Pre-record will ensure that you lose none of this. Even if you had not been well framed, capturing the camcorder's visual reaction or at least the three seconds of lead-in sound can be useful in the editing process.

Pre-recording is not available in full AUTO mode. To engage the Pre-Record function, choose FUNC, scroll down to Pre REC, and choose ON while in M or CINEMA mode. (The Pre REC option is found at the bottom of the MENU screen.) When the function has been activated, an oval icon with a 3 in its center appears in the lower right of the touchscreen. To de-activate Pre-Record, simply follow the same procedure but tap OFF.

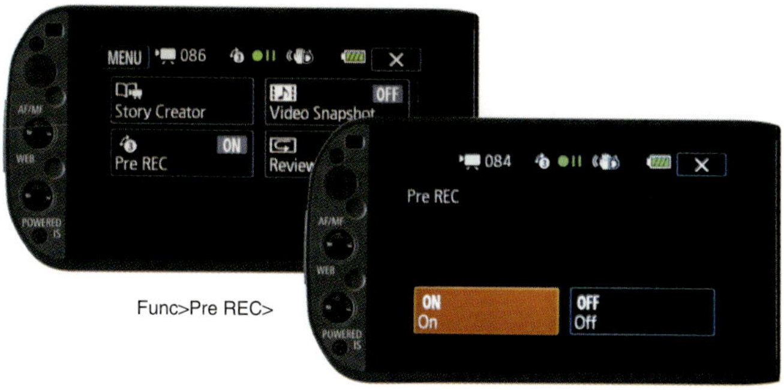

Figure 2.7 The Pre-Record panel and its control screen.

If you are depending on Pre-Record, be certain that its icon appears on the touchscreen. A number of actions will automatically de-activate the Pre-Record function. These include the following:

- Five minutes of inactivity
- Changing the AUTO/M/CINEMA switch
- Activating Video Snapshot
- Entering Playback mode
- Entering Standby by closing the touchscreen
- Tapping any of the program panels, like White Balance, Gain Limit, Image Stabilizer, Faders, Decoration or Review Recording

In addition, the Pre-Record function cannot record a full three seconds if you press Record less than three seconds after initially activating the Pre-Record function or less than three seconds after the end of the previous shot.

Another form of coverage during run-and-gun situations is to record extensive continuous takes of audio while shooting intermittent video. This can be done if you have a separate high quality audio recorder for "double system" sound. Double system recording is discussed in Chapter 7, "Improving Sound."

3

Visual Composition

Composition in video, film, and photography involves mastering the ability to select and compose within a frame. The rectangular frame itself is a convention; natural vision is not limited by a rectangle and reality doesn't come neatly packaged in ready-made 16×9 borders. A frame positions the spectator in relation to the world on the screen and focuses attention on relationships of the subjects within the frame to each other and to their surroundings.

Level Horizon

The human eye sees somewhat differently from a camera. The eye makes quick saccadic movements back and forth across points of interest, scanning detail that it projects across the densely packed area on the retina called the "fovea." Vision consists of interpretations by the brain of these scanned images cross-referenced with other information, including our sense of balance from the semicircular canals in our ears. So if we tilt our head from side to side, the world that we perceive stays upright. A camcorder, on the other hand, shows every moment of imbalance. So, an initial compositional challenge, if we want to create an image of the world the way we perceive it, is to consciously level the camera.

The G10/XA10 has a built-in level guide that consists of a horizontal line that bisects the screen, as shown in Figure 3.1. It would have been really elegant if Canon had instead engineered a floating line that remained truly level regardless of the tilt of the camera, alerting the operator whenever the frame is askew. But the level guide in the G10/XA10 is simply a stationary reference line with a cross-hatch in the center.

The horizontal line is a useful guide for finding a center point and for leveling two-dimensional subject matter like shots of text or graphics, but completely ineffective as a guide for leveling the camcorder in a three-dimensional space unless the camcorder is exactly perpendicular to a table edge, ceiling beam, baseboard, or other horizontal image in the three-dimensional world. A horizontal architectural detail viewed at any other angle actually should appear as a slant due to the laws of perspective. Consequently, the horizontal marker is almost useless as a leveling aid when shooting live action.

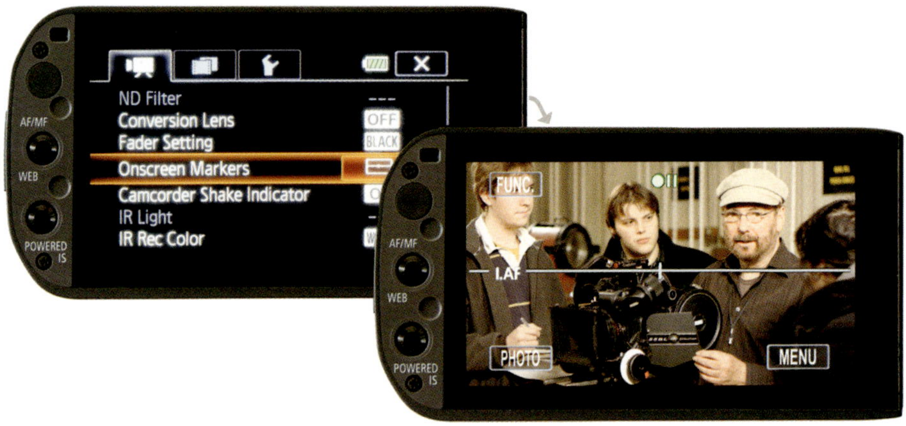

Figure 3.1 The horizontal onscreen marker.

A vertical line near the center of the frame would have actually been more useful for the purpose of leveling. If a vertical image in this part of the composition appears upright, like the vertical edge of a doorway or the corner of a room, then the camera is level and horizontals will appear in perspective at their appropriate slant. Fortunately, the G10/XA10 does provide a grid pattern that will serve this purpose and is an aid for many other compositional concepts. To enable the grid or the level, choose FUNC > MENU > Camera icon > Onscreen Markers; then choose Level, Grid, or Off.

You can choose whether the grid is white, which is probably too distracting, or gray, which I recommend. Two horizontal lines and two verticals—each a third of the distance from the edge of the frame—divide the grid into nine rectangular panels: upper left, upper middle, upper right; middle left, center, middle right; lower left, lower middle, and lower right. This is actually much more useful than a single horizontal line across the center. You can use one of the vertical lines to keep your camera level by lining it up with the image of a column, a doorway, or edge of a building. The grid is particularly useful for composing shots using a compositional concept called the "rule of thirds."

The Rule of Thirds

Let's say you are shooting a series of interviews or actions and you balance every composition to be central. This soon becomes problematic. Always composing for symmetry relegates editing to an act of popping everything into the same spot on the screen. This results in a visually impoverished series of central compositions that disregard the uniqueness of how subjects occupy space and how they relate to each other. In contrast, if the composition for each interview or each action had its own sense of balance (or imbalance) and represented the subject's particular relationship to his or her surroundings, then changing from scene to scene, or person to person with unique positions on the screen, could have significance in making a visual statement about opposition, similarity, continuity, or change.

Often, an off-balance composition or a composition that achieves balance in a more dynamic way than centrality can imply a variety of ordinate and subordinate relationships within the on-screen environment, as well as relationships to off-screen space and spatial relationships from shot to shot. The rule of thirds is an outgrowth of this concept. As shown in Figure 3.2, Canon's grid is horizontally and vertically divided into thirds. Aligning a subject of interest on a one-third division line or intersection can create a kind of dynamic tension and balance.

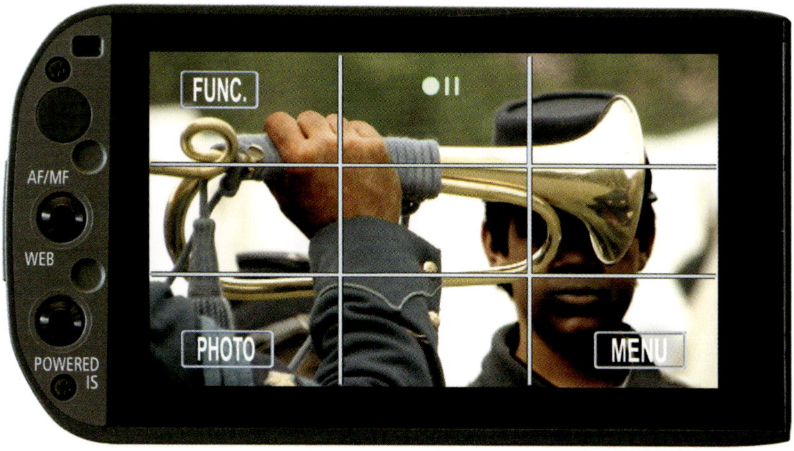

Figure 3.2 The grid marker divides the frame into vertical and horizontal thirds.

The rule of thirds is not actually a rigid rule; it is a convention. The concept is similar but not identical to the "golden ratio" or "golden mean," which goes back 2,400 years to the classic Greeks including Pythagoras. The rule of thirds was first written about in the late 1700s and is the idea that aside from dead center, a compositional subject of interest placed one-third or two-thirds of the way to the left or right (or up or down) also achieves a kind of a balance. In this way the volume on one side at the one-third point in a framed composition is balanced by a void or a view of the background on the remaining two-thirds. This simple mathematical relationship creates a sense of intentionality without being overly contrived as dead center sometimes seems, and is watchable for a period of time.

Not every shot should obey the so-called rule of thirds. Sometimes, a subject should actually be central as a statement of super balance or of finality. Such a statement of extraordinary balance is possible only if most of the other shots are non-central. And sometimes, visual composition demands outright imbalance or a balance achieved by something other than one-third divisions. The main point is to not be overly dependent on centrality and to look for compositions that best represent the relevant relationships of the subject and environment.

Aligning the horizon in a landscape or aligning the subject's eyes in a portrait at exactly the halfway mark creates a self-conscious division that hinges on the horizon or on the eyes. This will look almost as awkward and self-conscious as placing the horizon exactly on the bottom of the frame or placing the upper limit of the frame exactly on top of the subject's head. Aesthetically, the frame is not a container or a box with rigid borders; it is a selection from a world that is larger than the frame.

If you need an aid for composing shots, Canon's grid is an effective tool. It can give you a compositional sense of where you might want to place subjects of interest. Using it can jolt you out of continually placing subjects dead center by default.

Look Space

If a subject is looking at the camera, dead center is only one of several places to put the subject. Alternatively, you might find compositional clues in the environment for whether the subject should be more to the left or right. When a subject is looking to the left or right, a concept called "look space" is a rationale for an off-center composition. The gaze direction of a subject can imply a relationship with off-screen space. If the subject is looking to screen left or screen right, the frame will usually include more space on the side of the gaze direction, often close to the rule of thirds. If the next shot shows the object of the subject's gaze, the object will usually be off-center on the side to which the subject was looking. In this way, the gaze of the subject connects with the general direction of the object of attention, and during a cut, the look space of the outgoing shot is replaced by the object of attention in the incoming shot. The cut is immediately understood by the spectator's unconscious mind as connecting the subject's gaze from the previous shot to whatever occupies that part of the screen in the current shot. If a composition is made with cramped look space, with the subject looking toward the near edge of the frame, it will suggest that the subject is looking away or avoiding looking.

In preparing a series of interviews, some media makers will create a storyboard or a shot list with one subject shot toward the left, another toward the right, and another in the center to compositionally differentiate each when eventually cutting from one to the next. Dramatic scenes are often composed with one character left of center and the other right of center when they are reacting to each other in individual shots. Off-center compositions should not be arbitrary; they should be based on justifications and implied relationships. The spectator feels oriented by these compositional choices.

The 180° Rule and 30° Rule

The 180° rule is a framing and sequencing convention that helps maintain continuity when taking consecutive shots of the same subject. A composition with more than one subject usually sets up a left/right orientation in the mind of the spectator. Even a shot with a single subject implies a left/right orientation if the direction of the subject's gaze is to the left or the right. This line between points of interest or interaction is called the "line of action." Any subsequent shots taken on this side of the line of action will maintain the same left/right relationship. But any camera position that crosses that 180° line will flip the left/right relationship. Editing this image into a sequence that was shot from the other side could disorient the audience, causing whatever was expected on the left to pop up on the right and *vice versa.* If you are setting up two cameras, their images will have a matching left/right orientation if both cameras shoot from the same side of the line of action. If you are taking many shots of the same subject with a single camera with the intention of cutting them together, you will maintain a coherent left/right relationship by staying on one side of the 180° line. (See Figure 3.3.)

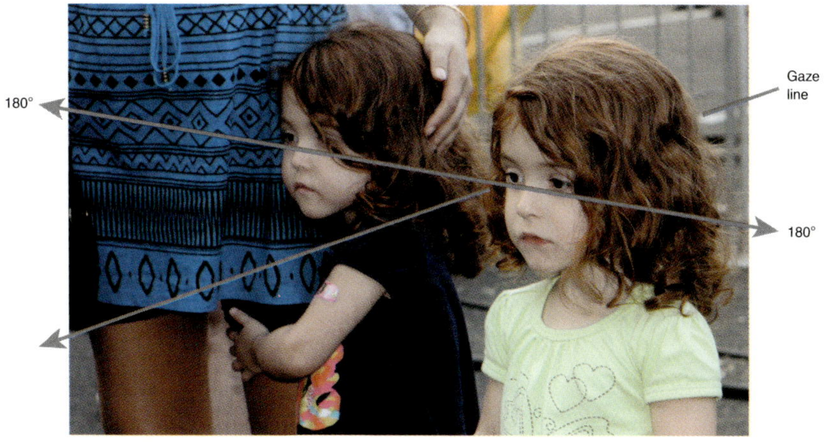

Figure 3.3 The 180° line between two points of interest and the gaze line.

Continuity editing is a lot easier if you follow the 180° rule when filming, but this does not mean you must never cross this imaginary line. If everyone slavishly obeyed this convention, then we would never see the fourth wall of a room (like the missing fourth wall of a stage set). In addition, potential visual development could be inhibited if there is something worth seeing from the other side of the line. The 180° rule is simply a convention for helping continuity, there are lots of ways around it. At certain moments in films like *Taxi Driver* and *The Conformist,* directors Martin Scorsese and Bernardo Bertolucci blatantly make 180° cuts to purposely disorient the spectator. However, they tend to make a pattern of it through several cuts so the violation feels intentional instead of like a mistake.

At times, the viewer may sense no disorientation when left and right are reversed if the incoming shot is meaningful and rewarding the moment it pops on the screen. There are also ways of crossing the line while maintaining continuity—for example, if the actions of your subjects move within the shot to create a new 180° line or if the camera itself physically crosses to the other side while filming. Another technique for crossing the line is to insert a neutral shot between footage from two different sides of the line (like a cutaway or detail that has no relevant left/right orientation). The 180° rule applies only when two shots of the same subject (or the interaction of the subject and object with a left/right relationship) are directly cut together for continuity.

The 30° rule is another continuity convention. It says that when cutting together two or more shots of the same subject, there must be at least a 30° shift in the axis, the angle of view, or both. This is based on the idea that if a shot changes, it should bring enough new information to warrant the cut. Sequential shots of the same subject, in the same scale, from the same view will result in a "jump cut," where any slight variation in facial expression or gesture will be a noticeable discontinuity and the cut itself will seem trivial if all we see is a slightly disrupted version of the previous shot. Cutting a head-and-shoulders view from straight-on to three-quarters (which is a 45° shift) or to profile (which is a 90° shift) will more effectively flow together as long as there are not any major gestural discrepancies.

Aside from shifting the axis, a significant shift in the field of view will help shots of the same subject flow together, like cutting from a head-and-shoulders view to a full-face view or to waist-high view as long as there is no major mismatch. Of course, the cut will have more of a sense of continuity if the change of shot has meaningfully revealed something worth showing or emphasizing. What this means on the practical level is that shooting for continuity with two cameras on the same subject or when changing positions on the same subject with a single camera, the axis or the field of view of one should be at least 30° different from the other (and on the same side of the 180° line). Of course, this convention, too, can be circumvented—by inserting a cutaway shot in between, by trying to elide over a jump cut with a quick dissolve or fade (as is often done with documentary interviews), by intentionally creating a style or pattern out of jump-cutting, or by providing an incoming shot that is so rewarding that any discrepancy of continuity is disregarded by the viewer.

Eyeline

Another compositional consideration is eyeline. The idea of eyeline is that in a waist-high, chest-high, shoulder-high, full-face, or a partial-face composition within a frame, the eyes are usually placed above the center of the frame at about the two-thirds height (varying from between three-fifths to four-fifths). This convention goes back hundreds of years in portraiture. Eyeline is a very pervasive convention. Some of its effectiveness is functional, caused by not wanting wasted space above a subject's head in a typical portrait, and in tighter compositions wanting to provide compositional space for the mouth as a secondary point of interest. Therefore, the eyes fit well at a two-thirds position. Some of its effectiveness is also purely conventional and cultural. When things have been done that way for six centuries of portrait painting and almost two centuries of photography, they set up expectations and a sense of familiarity in the spectator.

In full shots and long shots, the focus is not usually on the eyes and the position of eyes in the frame is not that significant. In shots that emphasize the face, the concept of eyeline provides a way to communicate normalcy by following the convention. Alternatively, you can communicate the opposite by choosing an unusually low or high eyeline. If you wanted a shot to create the sense that a person is short, is seated while others stand, has stepped down into a hole, or is a young child in the presence of adults, you might place his or her eyeline below center. Alternatively, in the case of the last example, you might create an image in which the child's eyeline is normal while the adults' eyelines are abnormally high or at the higher end of normal. What you are doing is orienting the spectator using compositional expectations developed over centuries of portraiture that eyes will appear in a certain space in the frame.

Within a composition that emphasizes the face, you usually want to put eyes in a prominent place, and they will seem more normal if they are above the halfway mark. (See Figure 3.4.) In full-face and wider compositions, a two-thirds eyeline leaves some space above the top of the head (called "head space" or "head room"). Consequentially, the frame does not box the face, nor does the subject's head seem to support the upper part of the frame like a caryatid, an ancient Greek architectural column in the shape of human being. Occasionally, a low eyeline is justified when something of interest in the upper part of the composition balances off the face, like in Christian iconography the dove representing resurrection flying overhead.

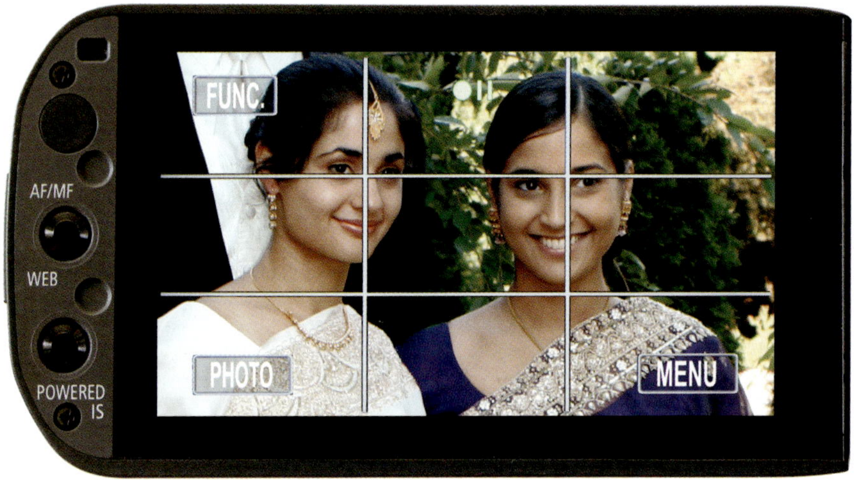

Figure 3.4 The eyeline convention.

There are lots of reasons to disobey the eyeline. You may want to create a quirky composition or portray a character reclining or hanging upside down, and that's fine. But if you want to use the viewer's expectations that eyes look normal at three-fifths through two-thirds to four-fifths the height of the frame, the audience does not question this position and accepts the subject as a normal height.

In shots that emphasize a human face, the spectator makes contact with the subject's eyes. We even judge height not by looking at the top of someone's head, but by looking at how high someone's eyes are. In editing, one of the valuable functions of the eyeline convention is that when you cut from partial face to full face, head and shoulder, chest high, or waist high (and at times to an even wider frame), the eyes will remain in the same part of the frame if the eyeline convention is followed. Consequently, the person's apparent height continues through the cut, the spectator's point of focus to the subject's eyes is unbroken, and greater continuity is achieved. If you completely disregard this convention, then continuity editing will be more difficult and a subject's face, apparent height, and physical relationship to others will arbitrarily jump around from cut to cut.

Figure and Ground

There is a difference between the world we perceive when we are physically present and the world as recorded. In the real world, it is easy enough for us to separate figure from ground. When we occupy the same physical space as we look at someone, the person's face does not blend with the lamp behind his or her head. We know the space (knowledge is part of perception), and all of our senses are working. Our eyes produce three-dimensional binocular vision. Our eyes, ears, and other sensory organs feed information to our brain, which constructs a sense of where something is positioned in space. When we shoot with a camcorder, however, all the information we have is two dimensional within a 16×9 frame. We have to make an effort for the recording to seem as dimensional as we perceived it by using compositional techniques to separate figure from ground.

Major ways of separating figure from ground include movement, selective focus, chiaroscuro, and backlight. If the subject moves and the background stays still (or if the subject is still and the background moves), we do not feel that one is fused to the other. When there is constant movement, like framing a person inside a moving car as the exterior continuously passes by, separation of figure and ground takes care of itself. Otherwise, we need to enhance separation.

In everyday life, our eyes have a very deep depth of field. Chances are, if you look around the room right now, you will see nothing out of focus because your eyes instantly follow-focus, and they scan points of interest through rapid saccadic movements, which the brain constructs into a sharp image. Selective soft focus with a camera lens is not so much a natural phenomenon than a screen convention used to replace the lack of binocular vision, saccadic vision, the orientation of being in the same actual space, and the coordination of eye, ear, and brain in their roles in spatial perception. We encounter shallow focus more often in still photos or motion-picture images than in the real world, but we unquestioningly accept it in film and video as one of the clues of emphasis and de-emphasis and separation of figure from ground.

Small-format camcorders have an inherently deep depth of field. That is their advantage—and when you want shallow focus, it is their curse. The ⅓-inch CMOS chip in the G10/XA10 has more control of selective focus than the ¼-inch chips that usually come in palm-size camcorders but considerably less than larger camcorders, DSLRs, and motion-picture cameras. Selective focus is discussed in Chapter 5, "Selective Focus and Depth of Field."

Chiaroscuro is one of the other major ways of separating figure from ground. In the visual arts and photography, chiaroscuro is the compositional concept of playing off light against dark and dark against light. If you examine paintings by Caravaggio and others from the Baroque period, you will see extremes of light and dark, often with the brightest part of the subject in front of the darkest part of the background and *vice versa.* Even with the soft window light of a Vermeer painting, the darkest part of the figure is often contrasted with a lighter area of the wall. This concept is used in video composition by paying attention to foreground and background relationships and controlling where you place the subject, where you place the camera, and set dressing, or by adding light to or subtracting light from the foreground or background. Sometimes, placing the camcorder two steps in one direction or another will make a difference between a shot in which the subject blends into the background or stands out. *Citizen Kane*, which uses deep focus extensively, employs chiaroscuro as its major means of separating figure from ground. The effect of chiaroscuro is that subjects have more dimensional identity from their surroundings, more like the world we perceive. (See Figure 3.5.)

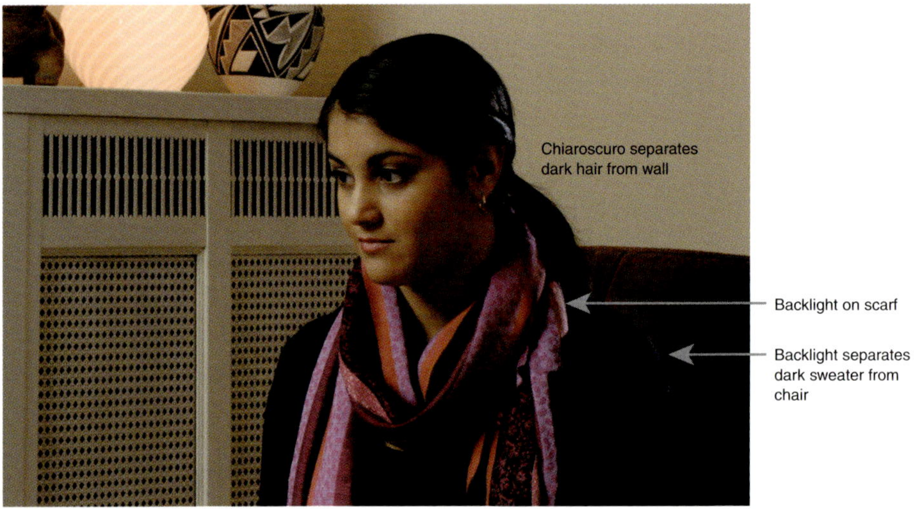

Figure 3.5 Separation of figure and background.

Another way of separating figure from ground is backlight. Coming from three-quarter rear to fully behind the subject, backlight is usually a hard light (that is, not bounced or diffused), so you can control its spill and flag it off the camera if necessary. A large soft light coming from behind would not produce as sharp an edge of backlight on the subject as hard light and would probably create issues of spill and lens flare. Although skylight (or even a simulation of skylight) coming through a window is fairly soft, it might, at times, be used for backlight to provide a little intentional flare of daylight entering an interior space. In most cases, crisper, more controllable hard backlight without flare is preferred. Hard backlight is typically used to create a small outline of light around what would have been the darker side of the subject. This prevents a medium or dark subject from blending into a medium or dark background. The main purpose of backlight is to separate figure from ground and to provide an extra dimension of modeling on the subject.

Video itself provides a certain amount of separation of figure from ground through what is called "contour enhancement," which is the Sharpness control in the Image Effects menu of the G10/XA10. The Sharpness control electronically exaggerates differences so that, for example, an image of a person has a mild electronic line around it.

Although this makes it easier to shoot video compared to film, this electronic contour is rather artificial looking compared to the effect achieved through lighting and chiaroscuro. When sharpness is set too high, it separates skin irregularities and makes video grain more visible. So the Sharpness control should never be abused. Images will look less electronic and have much better dimensional and photographic qualities with Sharpness at 0 or even turned to a negative number, provided the lighting and composition have independently created the appropriate emphasis and separation.

Selecting Shots

Even though you have a small handheld camera that lends itself to run-and-gun operation in situations where you may be constantly improvising, you need to shoot in a disciplined manner to produce useful footage that will help you tell your story. If you are moving along handholding the camera and something of interest happens, it can be important to become a stationary human tripod for a while. Hold certain moments in a well-composed frame and let the subject do the moving as opposed to following every one of the subject's micro-movements with the frame. At times, you can even let the subject move into or out of the frame, because you may compositionally need an entrance or an exit in the edited piece. Footage is very difficult to edit if the subject is in every frame. In many kinds of productions, there are compositional needs for action/reaction shots, cutaways, distant establishing shots, intimate details, and even sometimes the absence of the central character.

Whether shooting reality or fiction, novice media makers often feel as if they have to match each shot with the next for the sake of continuity. However, shooting real or dramatic events for action/reaction between characters is more likely to move the structure along more dynamically than shooting solely for continuity with the main character in every shot. In fact, continuity itself is rather bland, particularly if it is excessive. Some shot changes might be conceived as contrast, oppositional forces, or separate elements of the whole, and others as ellipses, jumping forward in time. If 90-minute feature films had absolute continuity, they would always be about 90 minutes of a person's life. Some shots should propel us forward (or backward) in time in relation to the previous shot, while others should shift us elsewhere in space. Otherwise, films and video would be as statically contained as stage space.

Compositionally, look for how the frame sets up relationships. Every photograph implies a position from where the view was seen. The camera places the spectator into seemingly objective, subjective, interpretative, reflexive, intimate, distanced, privileged, or even voyeuristic relationships to the subject or event on the screen. Is the camera within or outside the circle of action? The act of framing calls attention to relationships among subjects within the frame as well as to relationships to the foreground and background and between on-screen and off-screen space.

An important consideration, particularly for run-and-gun types of shooting, is to make sure you get the variety of shots that you need—not simply for variety's sake but to create emphasis, progression, continuity, cutaways, details, and a shape to your scene with a beginning, middle, and end. Most kinds of productions need B-roll images (potential insert and cutaway shots), including establishing shots and close-up details that could be relevant in the editing. If you have been following a subject intimately within the social space, you might also move back and take a full view of the action or take an external view of the location when you get an opportunity. If all you have is the same subject in every shot in the same place in every frame, your choice in editing is only to jump cut. If you are compositionally shooting for action/reaction and shooting to represent relationships, including from person to person and person to environment, you may need a range of shots. It takes rigor to make sure you get these extra materials.

Does your production have a need for any of the compositional choices in the following list?

- An establishing shot
- A long shot (LS), medium shot (MS), and close-up (CU) (at appropriate moments)
- An entrance into the frame
- An exit from the frame
- An eye-level, high-angle, and low-angle shot (at appropriate moments)
- An extreme close-up of detail
- A z-axis composition (showing relationships on the depth axis)
- An off-center composition
- A shot that uses or implies off-screen space
- A reverse shot (an opposing view without crossing the 180° line)
- An over-the-shoulder (OTS) shot
- A line-of-sight (LOS) shot (sharing line of sight, even in high or low angle)
- A point-of-view (POV) shot (through a character's eyes)
- A well-planned tracking shot (pan, dolly, hand-held, or steadicam)
- A counterpoint camera movement (in relation to the subject's movement)
- A reveal (a moving camera that discovers something of significance)
- A sustained long take that replaces LS, MS, and CU in its development
- A set of action/reaction shots

- Coverage (a second view to provide alternative shots from another angle)
- An effective concluding shot

In terms of visual composition, the cliché idea is that close-ups have impact, medium shots have less impact, and full shots have the least impact. But this has no basis in film theory or actual practice. If your primary form of communicating to the audience is limited to facial expression, then of course, a facial close-up will have more impact than a long shot. But human interactions are articulated by much more than facial expressions, and this is a pretty impoverished way to think about all the possibilities of visual expression.

In the era of daytime TV soap opera, domestic dramas were shot primarily in close-up and medium shot with three or four cameras on studio sets that represented bedrooms, living rooms, and hospitals. Even though these productions abounded in close-ups, they were visually uninteresting. In comparison, Hollywood films and even made-for-television dramas have an expressively greater range of space that includes exteriors as well as interiors and the potential for action, interaction, and overview. Some have casts of thousands or special effects; even a modest film or video may have elegant—even breathtaking—moments that happen in long shot. Long shots have just as much potential to be expressive as close-ups; they simply express different things.

Significant moments can also happen in medium shot, where the emphasis is on human relationships within the frame. An example would be in Jean Renoir's *Grande Illusion* when French and British prisoners of war rehearse for a variety show and a fellow prisoner enters the rehearsal dressed in costume as a woman. Everyone falls absolutely silent and stares. The impact of the collective reaction is expressed in medium long shot and is far more potent than showing an individual face in close-up. For most forms of video, you need to master the expressive potential of medium shots and long shots in addition to close-ups.

Many beginners tend to shoot in medium shot by default. They might do this out of shyness—not wanting to get too close. They not only miss close-ups and long shots, they often fail to fully exploit the real potential of medium shots themselves. In medium shot, look for meaningful character-to-character and character-to-environment relationships and develop how you use the frame for emphasis, de-emphasis, selection, and visual development. Because of its depth of field, the G10/XA10 is a really good camcorder for revealing relationships at medium distance, particularly when composing on the z axis (the depth axis).

Other media makers think of small camcorders as relegated to close-ups. Of course, the G10/XA10 is well equipped for close-ups with its 10× zoom lens and powered image stabilizer. And, in general, it is easy to be intimate with a small camcorder.

With its inherently deep depth of field and natural-looking wide lens, the G10/XA10 is equally capable of expressive long shots if your eye for composition and your creative imagination are up to the task. The point is that visual composition depends on finding the best form to suit the content moment by moment, not a simple formula.

Another tendency for beginning video makers is to take all their shots from the height at which they happen to be standing, regardless of the subject. Whether the camcorder is at the same eye level as your subject, or above or below, is a significant compositional consideration. If you film three-year-olds at a pre-school and shoot from adult height, that choice places the spectator in an adult relationship to the scene. If you shoot from a three-year-old's height by getting down on your knees, using a monopod, or sitting while everyone else stands, then you have compositionally positioned the spectator in the world of the three-year-old. Shooting the scene halfway between adult height and child height creates an even different point of view. It may be that the entire piece has all three (or more) heights at different times, or predominantly stays with one as the best way to interpret the scene. The important thing is that a camcorder as agile as the G10/XA10 frees you to shoot at waist height, positioned on the floor, at the end of a monopod six feet above your head, or nearly any angle you need.

You ought to have a rationale for the relationship of the camera to the event. This is true whether you are shooting a wedding, a dramatic film, or a socially conscious documentary. A major compositional consideration is where you place the spectator—how intimately; how distant; how much higher, lower or on the level as the subject; in the space of the event; at its edge; or outside of it. Sometimes, you select a particular position to align the spectator with a foreground or background relationship, which might demand a straight-on shot, a higher angle looking down, or a lower angle looking up. If the shot is meaningful, it will justify itself.

Not every scene needs the same approach. Some scenes may need very little camera movement and a tripod may be appropriate. Others may need to move intimately within the social space of the event or, conversely, might need to respect a physical distance. Most types of productions need a variety of shots that position us as spectators in meaningful relationships with the subject and the event while providing emphasis and visual development.

4

Controlling Exposure

Exposure is a judgment based on five variables. First and foremost is the amount of light itself. You can turn on more or fewer lights, move your lights closer or farther away, dim them up or down, or choose to shoot in bright daylight or on an overcast day or at night. Each of these choices will affect exposure. The other four exposure variables are shutter speed, aperture (f/stop), neutral density (ND) filters, and gain. Each of these compensates for the amount of light, and each is selectable for adjustment in the G10/XA10. Presetting or changing any of these variables will affect the exposure balance and will have consequences for the other variables. The choices involved in exposure affect highlights, shadow, tonal range, and the aesthetic impression of the shot. In addition, these choices affect motion blur, motion strobing, flicker, depth of field, or the aesthetic quality of the image.

Shutter Speed

Shutter speed is the amount of time that light hits the sensor to expose each frame of video. A too-slow shutter speed produces motion blur and a softer image, whereas an overly fast shutter speed produces a strobing effect, which can be distracting for the viewer if it appears to be too heavy. The typical shutter speed for camcorders in the U.S. is 1/60 of a second for frame rates of PF30 and 60i, and a shutter speed of either 1/48 or 1/60 when the frame rate is PF24 or 24P. The shutter speed is usually a quicker exposure time for each image than the frame rate in order to produce a sharper picture with less motion blur.

In Tv (Time value) Priority mode, you can pre-select and lock a particular shutter speed while the G10/XA10 automatically varies the aperture, ND, and gain for the appropriate exposure. (Choose FUNC > Rec. Programs > Tv [Shutter Priority] and set the shutter speed.) Or in the full Manual Exposure panel, you can individually set the shutter speed along with aperture, ND, and gain. (Choose FUNC > Rec. Programs > Manual Exposure and set all the exposure variables.) See Figure 4.1.

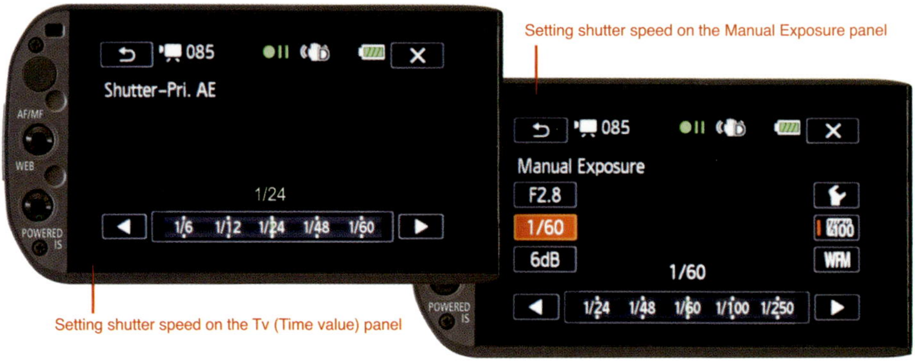

Figure 4.1 Shutter speed on the Tv (Time value) and Manual Exposure panels.

A particular shutter speed is usually set for the entire scene, although in some situations it might vary shot by shot. Presetting shutter speed allows you control when the consequence of a particular speed is important. In situations with potential flicker from fluorescents, sodium vapor, and mercury vapor lights, you should lock the camcorder to a shutter speed of 1/60 in the United States. In Europe and Asia, the frequency of alternating current is 50Hz, so a shutter speed of 1/100 may be appropriate on the Vixia G10/XA10. For international use, it would have been ideal if Vixia models came with a selectable shutter speed of 1/50, which is an even better match to eliminate 50Hz flicker. But that speed is available only on the Canon Legria models sold in Europe and Asia. If 1/100 doesn't minimize 50Hz flicker on the American Vixia model, try a slower shutter speed like 1/24, 1/30 or 1/48, which may be an improvement over 1/60 even though it is not a perfect match.

Slower shutter speeds can be useful for shooting in very low light. 1/30 of a second needs only half the light, and 1/15 needs only one-quarter the light of a standard shutter speed of 1/60. However, very slow shutter speeds from 1/6 to 1/15 will have considerable motion blur. Also, because they are slower than your frames per second, they will display motion with a stylized step-by-step appearance. This could mean sacrificing visual quality to obtain a low-light shot that would otherwise be lost or choosing a slow shutter speed specifically for its stylized look. Music video and experimental productions might exploit how the slow shutter defamiliarizes reality. Even a documentary or fiction production might use a slow shutter to represent an urban nightscape as an expressive smear of headlights and tail lights progressing through city streets or to portray a human gesture as less real and more metaphoric.

A shutter speed of $1/15$ of a second produces motion blur but will not have a step-printed appearance on the Internet, which often uses a display rate of 15 images per second. A shutter speed of $1/24$ matching a frame rate of PF24 or 24p, and a shutter speed of $1/30$ matching a frame rate of PF30 or 60i, are viable options for shooting in less light with only a slight loss in sharpness and a slight increase in motion blur. It will not have the step-printed look of the very slow speeds where the shutter is longer than the frame rate. The extra blur at $1/24$ or $1/30$ can sometimes help blend very contrasty motion that might otherwise strobe at $1/48$ or $1/60$. Images shot at shutter speeds of $1/30$ or slower will generally look softer when handheld. Image stabilization helps improve the image at these speeds, as does mounting the camcorder on a monopod or tripod.

Fast shutter speeds are used to help maintain proper exposure in very bright situations and to produce crisp, motion-frozen images on each frame. The strobe effect increases with fast shutter speeds because there is less motion blur to help the spectator's eye blend progressive positions of a moving image into a continuous motion. Fast shutter speeds might be selected for shots that will be subjected to frame-by-frame motion analysis or freeze-framed or shots where the strobe effect is aesthetically intended. $1/500$ should produce clean images of a jumper mid-air. $1/2000$ should produce sharp images of every droplet in a water spray. See Tables 4.1 and 4.2 for the effect of shutter speed on the appearance of the image and the amount of light needed.

Table 4.1 Possible Shutter-Speed Settings for PF30 and 60i

Shutter Speed	Effect/Light Requirements
$1/8$ sec.	Extreme motion blur; highly stylized effect; minimum light
$1/15$ sec.	Motion blur; stylized; suitable for Internet; very low light
$1/30$ sec.	Motion blur may reduce strobing; useful for low light
$1/60$ sec.	Normal; slightly sharper; minimal flicker with 60Hz lights
$1/100$ sec.	Minimal flicker with 50Hz lights
$1/250$ sec.	Crisper images; strobing motion; needs more light
$1/500$ sec.	Crisper images; strobing motion; needs more light
$1/1,000$ sec.	Crisper images; strobing motion; needs more light
$1/2,000$ sec.	Motion freezing images; strobing; needs maximum light

Table 4.2 Possible Shutter-Speed Settings for PF24 and 24p

Shutter Speed	Effect/Light Requirements
1/8 sec.	Extreme motion blur; highly stylized effect; minimum light
1/15 sec.	Motion blur; stylized; suitable for Internet; very low light
1/30 sec.	Motion blur may reduce strobing; useful for low light
1/60 sec.	Normal; slightly sharper; minimal flicker with 60Hz lights
1/100 sec.	Minimal flicker with 50Hz lights
1/250 sec.	Crisper images; strobing motion; needs more light
1/500 sec.	Crisper images; strobing motion; needs more light
1/1,000 sec.	Crisper images; strobing motion; needs more light
1/2,000 sec.	Motion freezing images; strobing; needs maximum light

The PAL versions of these camcorders, the Legria HF G10 and XA10, shoot at 25 and 50 frames per second, the European and Asian standard. Legria camcorders have the following shutter speeds: 1/6, 1/12, 1/25, 1/50, 1/120, 1/250, 1/500, 1/1000 and 1/2000.

Selecting an Aperture

Aperture settings on the G10/XA10 lens are available in 1/3-stop increments from f/1.8, letting through the most amount of light in wide angle (which becomes f/2.8 in telephoto at its widest aperture), up to f/8, which lets through the least light. An aperture from f/1.8 to f/8 can be selected and set in the Av (Aperture value) Priority mode or in Manual Exposure mode.

Lenses contain a matched set of glass elements to correct for chromatic aberration, curvature of field, diffraction, and various forms of distortion. A single element like a magnifying glass can bring only one portion of the visual spectrum into focus on the photo sensor. The other two-thirds of the spectrum will come into focus a little before or a little beyond the focal plane, creating soft edges and fringing (which is a condition called chromatic aberration). A second corrective element can start to bring two-thirds of the visual spectrum into focus and produce an achromatic lens that might be photographically usable. It usually takes at least three elements and often four, five, or more to create a correction on a correction on a correction to bring the entire visual spectrum into focus on the same plane with flat edge-to-edge focus instead of a curvature of field and corrected for other aberrations including diffraction.

Zoom lenses have even more elements. The zoom on the G10/XA10 has 12 elements in 10 groupings. One set of elements focuses on the image, another set magnifies or demagnifies the image to create the zoom effect, banks of elements move with a mechanical compensation so that focus does not drift as you zoom, and the aperture changes its physical size to maintain a proportional relationship to the focal length from wide angle to telephoto. So, a zoom lens is both optically and mechanically complicated.

The corrective elements needed when a lens is wide open (like f/1.8), where light comes through the full curvature of each lens element, are not the same as when the lens is set for a high f/stop number (like f/8), where light comes through the central axis and is somewhat defocused by diffraction (bending around the edges of the smaller iris). Because no set of corrections is perfect for the whole range of apertures, all lenses are a set of compromises, usually designed to balance their optical corrections for somewhere in the middle of their aperture range. For the G10/XA10, the lens is the most optically perfected around f/4. What this means is that f/4 will produce the sharpest images on the plane of focus, a pleasing bokeh for images that are out of focus, and the best contrast, gray range, and color rendition that the G10/XA10 is capable of delivering. ("Bokeh" is a Japanese term for the visual quality of an out-of-focus image.) However, by necessity, we often shoot at other apertures to adjust exposure or control depth of field.

Depth of field is affected by the distance from the camcorder's sensor to the subject, the focal length (for example, 4.25mm versus 42.5mm), and the size of the aperture (for example, f/1.8 versus f/8). In spite of some loss in optical quality, the widest or nearly widest apertures might be chosen for working in low light or to create the shallowest depth of field. The highest (f/8 on the G10/XA10) or nearly highest aperture setting might be chosen for working in very bright light or to ensure a deeper depth of field in telephoto. If extremes of depth of field are not an issue, selecting an aperture close to f/4 will produce the best optical quality—provided this can be done with an adequate balance of gain and shutter speed for the optimum exposure.

There are reasons for wanting to lock in a fixed aperture and reasons to let the aperture be variable. Reasons to let an aperture be variable include needing to shoot at a fixed shutter speed and wanting to limit your gain. The consequences of having the aperture vary in auto exposure may be that you are not always shooting at the aperture of highest optical quality and your depth of field changes as the aperture varies. Reasons to set a particular aperture in Av Priority mode or in Manual Exposure mode are to choose f/4 for its optical quality or to choose one of the extremes to control depth of field. The lower the f/stop number, the shallower your depth of field. Although in small-format video you inherently have a deep depth of field to begin with, particularly with wide-angle and normal settings. A high aperture might be needed to adequately extend deep focus to telephoto. Conversely, if you want to take advantage of selective focus with a shallow depth of field, you will need to shoot with your aperture wide open or nearly so.

Neutral Density

Canon has incorporated a series of internal neutral density filters that automatically kick in so the lens never has to get to a detrimentally high aperture like f/16 or f/22. (This saves Canon from having to design a more optically compromised lens with a greater range of f/stops.) The camcorder has an incremental set of built-in neutral density (ND) filters to hold onto the optimum aperture of f/4 for as many exposure increases as possible before continuing to a maximum in bright sunlight of f/8 plus an ND filter that absorbs up to three additional f/stops of light. This is the equivalent of shooting at f/22 but with the optical quality of f/8. Canon's ND system is ingeniously designed to get the most out of your lens.

The internal ND filters progressively reduce the light to ½, ¼, or ⅛ its nominal value, and extend the ability of the lens to prevent overexposure by three f/stops. Auto-exposure, programmed exposure, and full manual exposure modes interpolate these neutral-density values before raising the aperture setting above 4.0 to f/5.6 and above. This is a scheme to maintain the best optical quality from the lens by keeping it close to the optimum aperture of f/4 in situations with bright light. In Av and Manual Exposure mode, an aperture value will appear on the screen that indicates both the f/stop and the ND value—for example, "f/4 ND⅛." If for some reason you prefer to shoot at f/5.6 or f/8 without ND kicking in, you can defeat the automatic ND filters (or activate them if they had previously been turned off) by choosing FUNC > MENU > Camera icon > ND and choosing OFF (or Automatic).

In Table 4.3 you can see how progressive ND filters are used to automatically hold onto the optimum aperture of f/4 as light increases. Keeping ND turned to Automatic is highly recommended. In general, it is better to leave the filters on unless you really need to maximize the depth of field in less light.

The built-in ND filters do not preclude using external neutral density. The front of the camcorder's lens accommodates a 58mm screw-in filter. Adding a high-quality multicoated ND.6 or ND.9 glass ND filter could allow you to move the exposure toward an aperture like f/4 for the best optical quality in bright sunlight or toward something like f/1.8 to 2.8 for more selective focus under less intense light. An ND.6 lowers your aperture setting by two f/stops and an ND.9 allows the lens to open three f/stops.

Table 4.3 Aperture/ND Settings on the G10 and XA10

F/Stop	Description
f/1.8	Lowest aperture in wide angle
f/2.0	
f/2.2	
f/2.4	
f/2.6	
f/2.8	Lowest aperture in telephoto
f/3.2	
f/3.4	
f/3.7	
f/4.0	Optimum lens quality
f/4.0 ND ½	Optimum lens quality
f/4.0 ND ¼	Optimum lens quality
f/4.0 ND ⅛	Optimum lens quality
f/4.4 ND ⅛	
f/4.8 ND ⅛	
f/5.2 ND ⅛	
f/5.6 ND ⅛	
f/6.2 ND ⅛	
f/6.7 ND ⅛	
f/7.3 ND ⅛	
f/8.0 ND ⅛	Deepest depth of field, more diffraction

Gain

Changing the gain does not change the quantity of light that hits the photo sensor as the aperture does, and it does not change the duration for which the light hits the sensor as shutter speed does. Gain simply takes what may already be an inadequate amount of light and artificially amplifies the photo sensor's signal, which also inherently amplifies randomness, visual noise, and grain. Consequently, increasing the gain progressively degrades the image. The ideal setup is to shoot with the lowest gain that will permit an acceptable exposure by manipulating the remaining exposure variables: aperture, shutter speed, and the amount of light.

Gain is the equivalent of the ISO or ASA sensitivity setting in film. High gain settings are like pushing film to make it more sensitive. On the G10/XA10, gain is measured in decibels, and standard gain is 0dB. A one f/stop increase is a gain of 6dB. Every increase of 6dB doubles the sensitivity and allows you to shoot in less light. The XA10 is capable of applying up to 24dB of gain (16 times more sensitive than 0dB) plus a significant step beyond called "Max." The consequence of very high gain is that it amplifies both the signal as well as its imperfections. Try to keep the gain at the lowest setting that will provide an acceptable exposure for your particular subject matter and purpose.

When you are in full AUTO mode, gain is one of the variables that will rise up and down, and there is little you can do about it. When you are in a programmed record mode, the Automatic Gain Control (AGC) program panel enables you to select a maximum limit for gain while leaving the range below that point automatic. The gain limit puts a cap on the graininess and degradation that can be caused by excessive gain. In low-light situations when shutter speed and aperture have already reached their appropriate maximums, the gain limit on the CUSTOM dial can be a useful manual tool to darken or lighten shots. It enables you to balance the choice of visual degradation versus underexposure in these low-light situations.

To set the gain limit, go to the AGC program panel. (While in M or CINEMA mode, choose FUNC > AGC Limit > M Manual and then set the AGC limit, as shown in Figure 4.2.) Alternatively, you can engage and assign AGC to the CUSTOM key. (Press and hold the CUSTOM key for two seconds, dial to AGC, and press the CUSTOM key again to set it.)

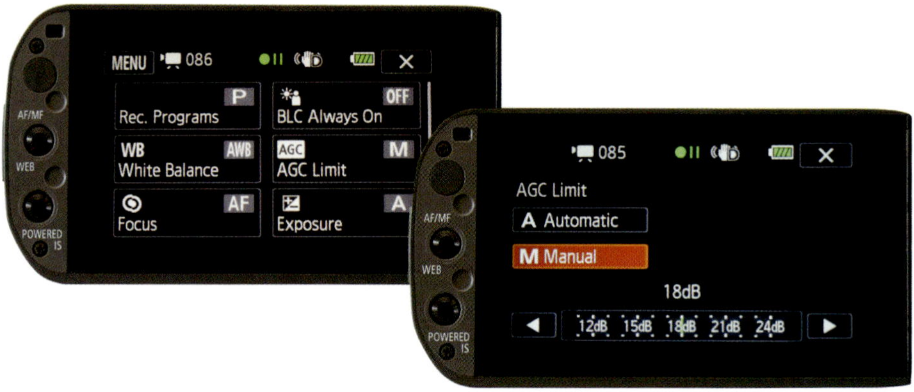

Figure 4.2 Choose FUNC > AGC Limit > M Manual; then set the dB limit.

The gain limit will operate only in Programmed AE, Tv, or Av. Pressing the CUSTOM key now toggles between fully automatic gain versus a gain limit that you can adjust with the dial. It is possible to leave the dial active and manually raise or lower the gain limit as you shoot. In Tv (Time value) Priority or Av (Aperture value) Priority mode, you can lock the shutter or the aperture respectively, then control the gain limit on the CUSTOM dial as your exposure variable while shooting.

Note

If you choose to shoot without adequate gain, you will lose detail in shadows—but for some purposes, denser shadows might look better than getting a grainy, muddy image at full gain.

Shooting in daylight is almost always possible at 0dB (the lowest gain setting). Shooting indoors in available light will typically need 6, 12, or 18dB, and sometimes higher in a room with a ceiling light, a table lamp, or floor lamp. You will have to decide how much gain is acceptable. You can preset the maximum gain so that even in Programmed AE, gain does not rise to a detrimental level. Balancing graininess with the need for visibility will be a matter of choice as you amplify the signal in high gain. In very low light, you eventually face the decision of whether you accept underexposure; raise the gain and accept a degraded image; or raise the base level of the light to improve the image. Bouncing a little extra light into a room might enable you to retain the character of the existing light and save you from having to amplify the sensitivity up to 24dB or beyond. A setting like 12dB will look considerably better.

In auto exposure and in the Programmed AE mode, the G10/XA10 automatically adjusts a combination of the shutter speed, aperture, neutral density, and gain for what it assumes will be an acceptable exposure under average conditions. But auto exposure and Programmed AE are not taking into consideration the unique nature of your subject or your intentions; in addition, the settings will ride up and down as the composition of the frame changes. Individual programmed settings and full Manual Exposure mode give you complete control of exposure and its effect on the image.

In full Manual Exposure mode, you must set each exposure variable individually. Locking to a particular gain setting in Manual Exposure mode tells the camcorder to use that specific setting—no higher, no lower. This has different consequences than simply setting a limit. You will need zebra patterns or the waveform monitor to effectively make the judgments necessary for full manual exposure.

Touch Exposure

An automatic version of Touch Exposure operates when either Face Detection or Touch & Track kicks in. The camcorder's logic system not only focuses on the face or the point of interest you have selected, but the system also bases its exposure on the area that you touched.

To access more complete manual control of exposure with the touchscreen, switch to M mode and go to the +/– Exposure program panel (a.k.a. Touch Exposure). The +/– Exposure panel, shown in Figure 4.3, enables you to select a point of interest within the composition on which to base exposure. Unlike Touch & Track, the +/– Exposure panel operates independently of focus; instead of automatically riding up and down as the shot develops, the selected exposure will not change until you adjust it higher or lower in the interface, select another point of interest, or toggle between manual and auto exposure. This provides a professionally consistent exposure that does not fluctuate as it can in auto exposure.

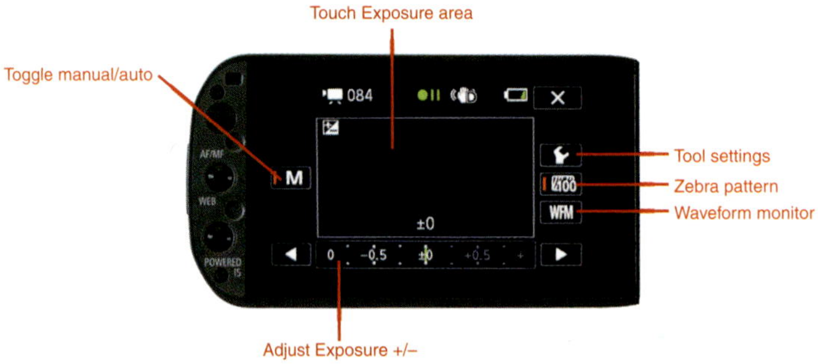

Figure 4.3 Press FUNC and select the +/– Exposure program panel.

Touch Exposure is particularly useful if your subject is lighter or darker than the rest of the composition or when the tonal range of your composition is complex. The +/– Exposure panel provides access to zebra patterns and a small but professional waveform monitor for evaluating and monitoring exposure values. (Zebra patterns and the waveform monitor are discussed later in this chapter.) The Tool icon on the +/– Exposure panel allows a choice of Normal, which averages highlight and shadow when a surface is selected, and Highlights, which bases Touch Exposure on peak values and prevents selections from losing detail by being too bright.

In delicate or complicated exposure situations, you may want to keep this panel open principally for the monitoring it provides and the ability to intercede and adjust exposure at any moment with the tip of your finger. The +/–Exposure panel is available in all record program modes except full Manual Exposure mode and in all content-based scene modes except Fireworks.

CUSTOM Key and Dial

Exposure can be manually controlled with the CUSTOM key and dial at the rear of the camcorder. Some users complain that having exposure adjustments at the rear is inconvenient because the left hand is needed for focus at the front of the camcorder and at the touchscreen for other adjustments. But considering how little space there is near the front of the camera for a key and rotating dial, the placement is reasonable and eliminates any chance of pressing the wrong control by mistake. Besides, these same exposure controls can be selected and operated directly from the touchscreen if you prefer, which disables the key and dial until you exit the controls on the touchscreen.

One might argue that the CUSTOM key ought to be called the EXPOSURE key because the only custom options that can be assigned are various ways to set exposure. You set up the identity of the CUSTOM key and dial in one of two ways. One is to press and hold down the CUSTOM key for two seconds, set the dial to Tv/Av, M, AGC, +/–, or Off, and press the CUSTOM button again. Another is to choose FUNC > MENU > Tool icon > CUSTOM Key/Dial and then choose Tv/Av, M (manual), AGC, +/–, or OFF (see Figure 4.4).

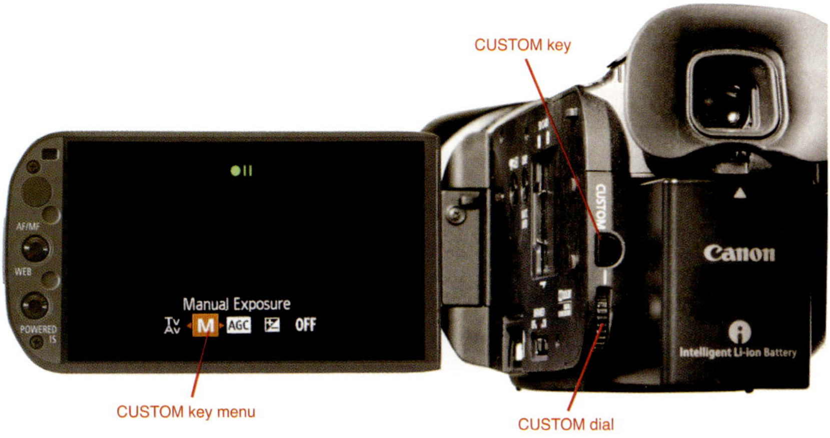

Figure 4.4 The Custom key and dial, and their on-screen menu.

If you intend to use the CUSTOM key to control exposure, you have to select an exposure mode on the program panel and separately select the assignment of the CUSTOM key to control that function or a parallel function. In other words, you have to go through two procedures to enable the CUSTOM key to actually control exposure. You can select the exposure mode itself in the program panel (Programmed AE, Tv, Av, Manual Exposure, AGC Limit, or a programmed type of scene) and then assign the CUSTOM key to a function that is compatible with the selected exposure mode.

If you have assigned the CUSTOM key to read for a different mode than the one you happen to be in, the key and dial will be useless and exposure adjustments can be made only on the touchscreen or not at all. When you activate the CUSTOM key to a compatible function, previous touchscreen control of exposure is deactivated. It would have been much easier and more intuitive if the CUSTOM dial instantly adapted its set of functions to whatever mode you selected in the program panel, and if adjustments were available on both the touchscreen and the CUSTOM dial without one disabling the other. The current arrangement causes frustration among first-time users.

To complicate matters further, the M selection on the CUSTOM key option menu works only when full Manual Exposure mode is also selected in the program panel. Tv and Av work with either shutter or aperture exposure modes on the program panel. AGC (gain limit) works with three program exposure modes, and +/– Exposure is compatible with 11 program exposure modes, but not all. Once you have figured out which sets of controls are compatible with which programmed exposure modes, and have appropriately activated both, you are ready to control exposure with the CUSTOM key and dial. To sort this out, Table 4.4 lays out CUSTOM key options. The first column represents an exposure mode selectable on the program panel after tapping FUNC. The second column represents the CUSTOM key assignment selected from the Tool menu or by holding down the CUSTOM key and selecting with the dial. The numbers in the third column represent one, two, or three toggle positions on the CUSTOM key.

Table 4.4 CUSTOM Key Options

Exposure Mode	**Custom Assignment**	**Key and Dial Can Select and Adjust**
Manual	M	(1) Manual aperture; (2) manual shutter; (3) manual gain
Programmed AE	AGC Limit	(1) Gain limit adjust; (2) auto gain, no limit
Programmed AE	+/–	(1) Auto with plus/minus exposure; (2) auto only
Tv	Tv/Av	Auto exposure with manual shutter
Tv	AGC Limit	(1) Auto with preset shutter; (2) auto with preset shutter and gain limit adjust
Tv	+/–	(1) Auto with preset shutter; (2) auto with preset shutter and plus/minus exposure

Table 4.4 CUSTOM Key Options (continued)

Exposure Mode	Custom Assignment	Key and Dial Can Select and Adjust
Av	Tv/Av	Auto exposure with manual aperture
Av	AGC Limit	(1) Auto with preset aperture; (2) auto with preset aperture and gain limit adjust
Av	+/–	(1) Auto with preset aperture; (2) auto with preset aperture and plus/minus exposure
Portrait	+/–	(1) Auto exposure; (2) auto with plus/minus exposure
Sports	+/–	(1) Auto exposure; (2) auto with plus/minus exposure
Snow	+/–	(1) Auto exposure; (2) auto with plus/minus exposure
Beach	+/–	(1) Auto exposure; (2) auto with plus/minus exposure
Sunset	+/–	(1) Auto exposure; (2) auto with plus/minus exposure
Low Light	+/–	(1) Auto exposure; (2) auto with plus/minus exposure
Spotlight	+/–	(1) Auto exposure; (2) auto with plus/minus exposure
Night Scene	+/–	(1) Auto exposure; (2) auto with plus/minus exposure
Fireworks	—	No control
—	OFF	Exposure controls available only on touchscreen

Note that Fireworks is not adjustable on the CUSTOM key and dial. The alternative for all these settings (except Fireworks) is to control exposure variables on the touchscreen by opening the +/– Exposure panel (Touch Exposure), which deactivates the CUSTOM key.

The LCD Screen

If you set exposure manually, you will need to know what your limits are and when you are getting an acceptably exposed image. You cannot entirely trust the look of the image in the viewfinder. A 3½-inch uncalibrated viewfinder will not really tell you whether you are losing detail by crushing it in the shadows or clipping it in the highlights. To judge exposure in the highlights, you need zebra patterns; and to judge both highlight and shadow detail, you need a waveform monitor. The image on the LCD screen offers an instant indication of whether you have a picture where skin tones look somewhat acceptable and compositional emphasis seems right, but the tiny screen doesn't tell you the subtle details. You wouldn't want to rely on it for determining exposure.

The LCD screen has its own brightness control. It will also look different with different light falling on it. Consequently, it isn't a constant reference. It isn't really going to tell you whether your exposure is giving you the maximum amount of detail, the greatest latitude, or even whether tones have the precise quality you want. When shooting in a very dark space, the LCD monitor's brightness itself may make you think your exposure is greater than you need. When shooting in bright sunlight, it might give the opposite impression. The saturation of color may look different depending on the ambient light hitting the viewfinder. So don't rely on the LCD screen for anything other than a general impression. If you are going to take manual control, you need the zebra pattern and waveform monitor to more precisely set exposure.

Zebra Patterns

Zebra patterns appearing in highlight areas provide a visual indication that exposure in certain parts of a visual image has reached a threshold—for example, 70 percent or 100 percent. Zebra patterns appear only on the camcorder's LCD monitor or viewfinder and are not part of the recorded file. They are an accurate guide for setting exposure based on actual peak brightness values within the composition. To set up zebra patterns, do one of the following:

- Choose FUNC > MENU > Tool icon; then turn Zebra Pattern on and set it for 100 percent or 70 percent.
- Choose FUNC > Rec. Programs > Manual Exposure > Tool icon; then choose 70 percent or 100 percent and turn on Zebra Pattern.
- Choose FUNC > Rec. Programs > +/– Exposure > Tool icon; then choose 70 percent or 100 percent and turn on Zebra Pattern (see Figure 4.5).

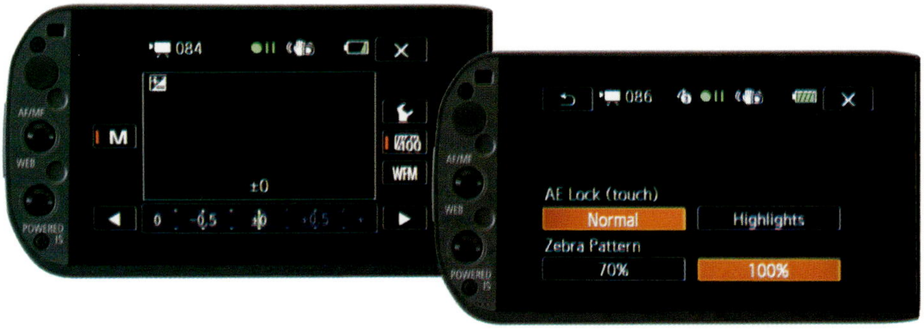

Figure 4.5 The Tool icon on the Exposure panel allows you to set the response characteristics of zebra patterns.

In M mode, you will want to use zebra patterns and the waveform monitor as aids in determining the right exposure. The waveform monitor is available only while in the Manual Exposure setup screen or within the +/– Exposure program panel. Zebra patterns can also be activated and set for 70 percent or 100 percent on those screens as well as in the Tool menu. Once they are enabled, they will stay on after the screen is closed including in the full AUTO mode.

Zebra patterns are slanted stripes that appear on the camcorder's screen as visible indicators that parts of the picture have reached a certain brightness threshold. My preference with other camcorders is to set the zebra threshold to 90 percent (or 90 IRE) and allow them to just barely appear in the brightest parts of the picture as an indication that these points are ½ stop below full exposure. But 90 percent is not an option on the G10/XA10. To use the 100 percent threshold, you increase exposure until zebra patterns just begin to appear in the very brightest white areas in the picture. You might let them remain if you intend for those spots to be overexposed; more typically, however, you back off the exposure to the point where the stripes just disappear. This places white at just below 100 percent but doesn't leave a few stripes in the composition to let the operator know whether the brightest points have fallen lower during the course of shooting. If there is nothing in the composition that ought to be close to 100 percent, hold a white card in the frame as an exposure reference while you manually adjust exposure.

The other threshold on the G10/XA10 displays zebra patterns at 70 percent, which is about 1½ stops below full exposure. At this setting, you expect to see stripes on white and near-white surfaces, and on the highlights of lighter skin tones including the brows and nose ridge. 70 percent is also a useful threshold for setting exposures for compositions that have no white reference or in low light where there might not be enough gain to attain a setting close to 100 percent.

Waveform Monitor (WFM)

In the analog video era, waveform monitors were calibrated in IRE units, named after the Institute of Radio Engineers, who set the technical standards before broadcast television actually existed. An IRE unit equaled 1/140 of a volt. The picture part of the signal stretched from 7.5 IRE (black) to 100 IRE (white), leaving 7.5 down to 0 IRE as a buffer between picture black and control signals (which were minus values below zero). As a measure of brightness, IRE did not actually equal percent because an increase of every 20 IRE represented a doubling of brightness, and monitors were calibrated up to 120 IRE to account for a recorded signal that was up to one stop (one doubling of exposure) above broadcast white (100 IRE). Consequently, the scale of the waveform monitor represents five f/stops (five doublings) from 0 IRE to 100 IRE. A reading of 90 IRE would be half an f/stop short of maximum picture brightness for broadcast.

In the digital era, the signal itself is a stream of digital numbers instead of a varying voltage, and the control signal (below 0 IRE) no longer appears on the visual waveform. Some manufacturers continue to use the term "IRE units" on waveform monitors that read a digital signal. Even though IRE no longer refers to a fraction of a volt, the calibrations 0, 7.5, and 100 IRE have the same relative meanings in the digital era. Other manufacturers, like Canon, have simply replaced the term "IRE" with "percent," meaning percentage of the calibration—not really a linear percentage of brightness because an increase of 20 percent on this scale still indicates a doubling of brightness as it did with IRE. Others have calibrated digital waveform monitors from 0 to 255 (representing the 256 steps in an 8-bit signal, 0 being the lowest step) so that 0 equals absolute black, 16 equals picture black, 235 equals maximum picture white, and 255 equals maximum overexposed white.

I mention these three kinds of calibration because you might see "percent" on your G10/XA10 and IRE or 0–255 on WFMs built into other camcorders, monitors, and editing programs. They all mean pretty much the same thing: absolute black, picture black, maximum picture white, and maximum overexposure. There is some ambiguity about whether there has to be a separation between 0 and 7.5 (16 on a digital scale). The Japanese use no separation and allow picture black to be as dark as absolute black, while many American broadcasters have kept the old standard of starting picture black at 7.5—particularly because so many shows are in rerun that were mastered to that standard. Ultimately it comes down to how viewers have adjusted the pedestal (brightness settings) on their individual monitors, which is obviously not consistent. (Figure 4.6 shows the waveform monitor on the G10/XA10.)

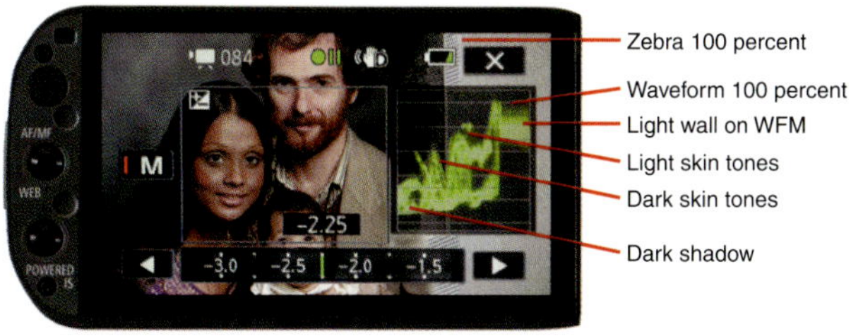

Figure 4.6 When activated in the +/– Exposure panel or in Manual Exposure mode, the waveform monitor appears on the right of the screen.

Sometimes, you will want to find scenes with a majority of tones within a five-stop range or will apply fill light to get the range within five stops. In other cases, you may want a perfectly exposed background with silhouetted foreground figures or normally exposed figures in front of a very darkened or maximum white background. This is where you will have to make a choice on what is best for the scene and where to preserve detail.

Setting Manual Exposures

For full manual control of aperture, shutter, and gain, and for access to the waveform monitor, choose FUNC > Rec. Program > Manual Exposure > WFM; then tap and adjust Aperture, Shutter, and Gain. This gives you complete manual control over exposure on the touchscreen with access to the waveform monitor (as long as you stay in the Manual Exposure program panel) and to zebra patterns even after you leave the window. You set the manual values with an on-screen slider. Any previous setting for gain limit will not be in effect because in Manual Exposure mode, you are setting the gain to a fixed position; there is no need for a limit. You can shoot while in the Manual Exposure program panel if you need continued access to the WFM beyond initially setting up the exposure. When you touch X, you have locked in the exposure settings, and the WFM and other icons leave the screen. The upper left of the touchscreen displays your manual settings for aperture, shutter, and gain. You can assign continued control of the individual manual adjustments to the CUSTOM key by doing one of the following:

- Choose FUNC > MENU > Tool icon > CUSTOM Key > M.
- Hold down the CUSTOM key for two seconds, move the CUSTOM dial to M, and press the CUSTOM key again.

Pressing the CUSTOM key now toggles between the Aperture, Shutter, and Gain settings, which are individually adjustable on the dial instead of the touchscreen.

With the CUSTOM key and dial, you no longer have visual access to the waveform monitor, but the screen is less cluttered with icons and monitors. After setting two parameters, you might leave the dial assigned to the one you prefer to vary while shooting. You can recall the monitor and touchscreen control by pressing FUNC > Rec. Programs > M (Manual Exposure). Alternatively, if an M appears in the lower right of the touchscreen, pressing it returns you there more directly.

For complete control of aperture, shutter, and gain in Manual Exposure mode, choose FUNC > Rec. Programs > Manual Exposure. Then select the following:

- Aperture
- Shutter
- Gain
- WFM
- Zebra
- Tool

Three separate manual exposure parameters are now adjustable on the screen, as is access to a waveform monitor and zebra patterns. If in addition you have preset the CUSTOM key to Manual, you will be able to adjust individual exposure levels with the dial after you exit the Manual Exposure setup screen. Tap the CUSTOM key on the rear of the camcorder to toggle to each of the three choices and rotate the dial to individually adjust each parameter. After your initial settings, you will probably leave the dial set for the exposure variable you expect to adjust the most. In this way you can use the interface like an aperture, shutter, or gain priority, but with greater knowledge and control of all the settings.

In low light, you eventually get to the choice of whether you open the aperture, lower the shutter speed, or raise the gain past the point that degrades the image, or (preferably) raise the base level of the light itself to improve the image. It is sometimes possible to increase the existing ambient light or to bounce in a little extra light without radically changing the character of the original location.

5

Selective Focus and Depth of Field

Auto focus has its limits. It is responsive to images with adequate light and at least moderate contrast with vertical detail. Auto focus may not work well, however, in situations with low contrast, no vertical detail, fast motion, very low light, night scenes, or when shooting through wet or dirty windows.

The G10/XA10 camcorder has three levels of auto focus:

- **Instant (I.AF).** Instant auto focus glides decisively into place.
- **Medium (M.AF).** Medium auto focus moves into focus at moderate speed.
- **Normal (AF).** Normal auto focus moves slowly into focus using "normal" through-the-lens technology.

Instant and Medium auto focus use both through-the-lens auto focus and an external focus sensor just below the lens. The extra sensor helps the camcorder lock into focus more quickly, minimizes the need to hunt for focus, and improves focus in low-light and very bright situations. In comparison, Normal AF operates somewhat slowly. It uses only the through-the-lens sensor and can at times be indecisive, particularly in low light.

The Instant and Medium settings work best for most auto-exposure situations, but they are not available under certain conditions. For example, shooting in infrared is limited to Normal through-the-lens auto focus, as is shooting with an auxiliary converter lens. Attaching a wide angle or tele converter actually covers the external auto focus sensor. If you attach an auxiliary lens, you need to access the Camera menu and let the camcorder know that you are using a wide angle or tele conversion lens;

otherwise, auto focus will try to obtain information from a blocked sensor. To do so, choose FUNC > MENU > Camera icon > Conversion Lens; then choose Wide, Tele, or OFF.

Face Detection

Face Detection and Touch & Track are an integral component of full AUTO mode and cannot be turned off. They are also available in M and CINEMA modes except in Night, Low Light, Fireworks, or Manual Exposure mode. In M and CINEMA modes, Face Detection and Touch & Track can be turned off in the Camera menu or can be toggled to other forms of focus with the AF/MF switch.

As discussed in Chapter 2, "Run-and-Gun Shooting," the camcorder's logic system detects, analyzes, and optimizes faces. In Face Detection, the camera focuses on the most prominent face in the composition and displays a white frame around it along with dark gray frames around secondary faces—up to nine simultaneously. As a shot develops, Face Detection focuses on whichever face is dominant in the composition and the indicator frame changes accordingly. If you tap a particular face on the touchscreen, even a secondary one, the system goes into Touch & Track mode. It locks onto that face and will track-focus wherever the image moves until the selected face becomes obscured or exits the frame. At that point, the logic system returns to Face Detection, which shifts focus to other faces or, if there are no faces, glides into auto focus on a prominent non-facial image.

Touch & Track can also lock onto a vehicle, an animal, or an object with distinctive features if you tap its image on the touchscreen instead of a face. The camcorder then momentarily drops its priority for faces and will track the selected image, keeping it in focus as it previously did with faces.

In M or CINEMA mode, touching the AF/MF switch will toggle to manual focus without Face Detection. This enables you to lock focus into manual at any point or to focus primarily in manual mode and toggle back to AF when you want the camcorder to automatically track faces. As you toggle back and forth, letters on the left side of the touchscreen indicate manual focus (MF) or the form of auto focus you had preselected in the menu: I.AF (Instant), M.AF (Medium), or AF (Normal). I.AF is the default auto focus and for most situations it works best.

If Face Detection and Touch & Track are disabled under the Camera menu, then the AF/MF toggle switch becomes a way to use both auto focus and manual focus without Face Detection, instead of as a means of moving in and out of Face Detection. To enable or disable Face Detection and Touch & Track, choose FUNC > MENU > Camera icon > Face Detection and select ON or OFF.

Face Only

On the AF/MF switch, the manual focus (MF) mode typically operates without Face Detection. However, there is a way to make it responsive to faces. If you reassign the identity of the AF/MF button to Face Only AF, you will be able to toggle between AF (which operates as before) and Face Only, which operates as manual focus until it detects a face. To do so, choose FUNC > MENU > Tool icon > Assign Button 1; then scroll to Face Only AF.

Now the camcorder will track focus on a selected face in either AF or MF mode. The AF side of the toggle switch will always be auto. It will recognize and track faces as long as Face Detection and Touch & Track are enabled under the Camera menu, which is the default position. Under AUTO, the touchscreen says either I.AF, M.AF, or AF (depending on your earlier selection of the type of auto focus) along with a plain smiley face icon indicating Face Detection.

In Face Only, when you press the AF/MF button to enable what would have been the manual focus mode, the I.AF letters turn gray and the smiley face icon has the letter O indicating you are in Face Only mode. When there is no face in the composition, the camcorder is actually in manual focus. When the camera's logic detects a face, auto focus takes over, the letters I.AF light up, and auto focus tracks faces. It will lock on a face if you select one and will track focus until the face is no longer detected, at which point focus reverts to manual if no other face is on the screen.

If Face Only is activated on the Tool menu while Face Detection is disabled under the Camera menu, then ironically, only the manual focus side goes into Face Detection. This gives you one more combination of possibilities: an auto focus that does not recognize faces and a semi-manual focus that does.

The LCD Screen

The LCD screen rotates 270° to allow for normal, high-angle, low-angle, and waist-high filming positions. The screen can rotate up to 90° downward for shooting high angles while holding the camcorder above your head with arms extended or on a monopod. It is also possible to instantly shoot at a very low angle by turning the monopod and camcorder upside down, with the intention of uprighting the shot in post production. For extensive shooting upside down, the camcorder can be set for Scan Reverse in the Film Clip menu, which will render the original files as upright images. To set this, choose FUNC > MENU > Film Clip icon > Scan Reverse Rec; then choose Both (for upside down), as shown in Figure 5.1.

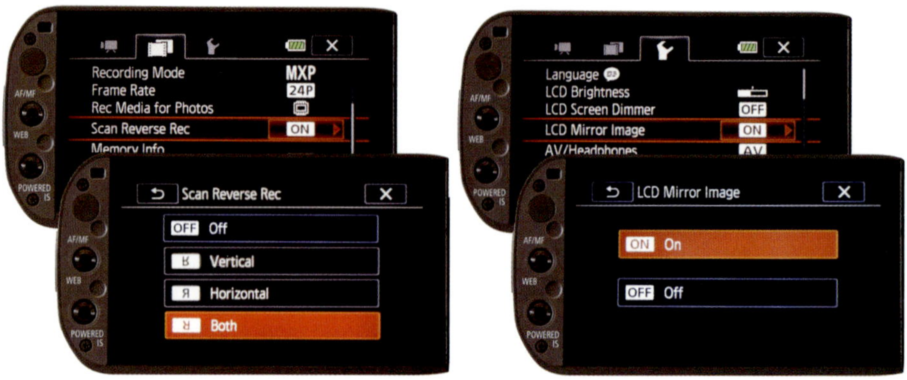

Figure 5.1 Scan Reverse controls are shown on the left, and LCD Mirror Image controls on the right.

Tilting the LCD 45º to 90º upward is convenient for viewing while shooting from waist high and lower angles. When the LCD panel is turned 180º forward so the subject of the shot can see his or her own image (or for filming yourself), the LCD clicks into Mirror mode, which reverses the left-to-right screen image (not the recorded image) like a mirror. This happens automatically with the LCD in the completely forward position, provided the Mirror function has been activated in the Tool menu. (Choose FUNC > MENU > Tool icon > LCD Mirror Image > ON, also shown in Figure 5.1.) The regular (non-mirror) orientation would be disconcerting when viewing yourself live as you and the LCD image of yourself diametrically face each other. With the LCD facing forward for recording and monitoring oneself, the camcorder is usually operated with the wireless remote. The difference between Scan Reverse and Mirror mode is that Scan Reverse actually records a flipped image, whereas Mirror mode simply shows you one when the LCD faces forward but records a standard image.

The LCD panel can also be folded against the side of the camcorder with the screen facing outward. This would allow viewing in tight quarters when there is no space behind the camcorder, or could allow a director to monitor from the side while the operator uses the rear viewfinder.

To change LCD and viewfinder brightness from normal to bright or back to normal, press the DISP. button on the left side of the camcorder for two full seconds. This affects only the monitor brightness, not the recorded image. However, running the LCD or viewfinder on the bright setting reduces the usage time of the battery. There is an additional dim setting on the LCD menu under the Tool icon, for when normal screen brightness might be a distraction.

The Viewfinder

The viewfinder at the rear end of the G10/XA10 could have been better designed. Its magnification is low, it does not tilt, and its rear-focusing dioptric adjustment uses a tiny plastic lever just under the eyepiece. The lever is so close to the eyecup it is very difficult to adjust while looking through the viewfinder—which of course you have to do in order to make the adjustment. The lever should have been larger and in a more accessible place, like the side or top of the viewfinder. Even with these shortcomings, however, there are times when it becomes preferable to use the rear viewfinder instead of the LCD screen—for example, when extreme bright light makes it more difficult to judge the touchscreen image compared to the shielded image in the viewfinder.

Some people prefer stabilizing the camcorder against their face. For some, their visual style changes subtly to become more psychologically motivated as the camera becomes contiguous with the eye and head. Instead of the camcorder being a selection device held at the length of a partially bent arm, where framing a shot is a bit like pointing with your hand, the camcorder held against the face becomes more directly an extension of the eye, head, and brain. For some operators, the frame and its movement take on more human qualities in this position. Shooting through the rear viewfinder can be particularly good for point-of-view shots. People unconsciously respond to the camera as if it is a person when it is held to the face.

A particular occasion for focusing and framing through the viewfinder is shooting while the LCD screen is turned 180° toward an interview subject. The front-facing LCD creates a strong point of eye contact for the subject on an axis fairly close to the lens while also allowing the videographer to monitor the scene through the rear viewfinder. Many camcorders turn off the LCD screen when the viewfinder is activated. Fortunately, Canon allows the possibility for both to operate simultaneously. This makes the G10/XA10 a particularly good on-axis interview camera.

If you view with the LCD panel in its traditional position, the alternatives for an on-axis interview are letting the subject look much further off axis or unconsciously leaning around to address you beside or behind the camera. Simply asking the subject to speak to the camera lens is about as motivating as saying, "Speak to a potato." Documentary filmmaker Errol Morris achieves his riveting on-axis interviews in films like *The Fog of War* by using a live image of his face on a teleprompter directly in front of the camera lens, which shoots through the teleprompter image.

You can begin to approximate this directness and intimacy with the camcorder's LCD facing forward, allowing the subject to make contact with his or her own image while having a conversation with the operator who is on the same axis behind the camera. There is actually something for the subject to see, which is less likely to generate a blank stare. As with recording yourself, the LCD screen needs to be set for

Mirror Image; otherwise, it is a disconcerting experience for the subject to see each gesture appear on the opposite side of the screen as an observer from the opposite side would see. As a menu item, the LCD Mirror Image setting can always be left ON because the mirror effect does not kick in until the LCD screen is turned 180° toward the subject and the inverted image appears only on the LCD screen. The actual recorded image is correct left-to-right.

Dioptric Correction

Before using the viewfinder, you have to adjust the rear-focusing diopter. "Dioptric correction" refers to the use of a magnifying lens (a diopter) to correct for the viewer's eyesight. You need to make this adjustment even if you have perfect eyesight because the aforementioned lever, shown in Figure 5.2, is variable. It can easily be knocked off focus and may not be perfectly centered. Instead of making the rear-focus adjustment while viewing an image, you might point the camcorder at a blank surface or even leave the lens cap on. You are adjusting the optical correction for your eye to the viewfinder's miniature LCD; the focus of the front zoom lens has nothing to do with this adjustment. You need to focus on the pixels themselves. If the pixels and display data look sharp to your eye, you are now set up to judge the focus of images through the zoom lens.

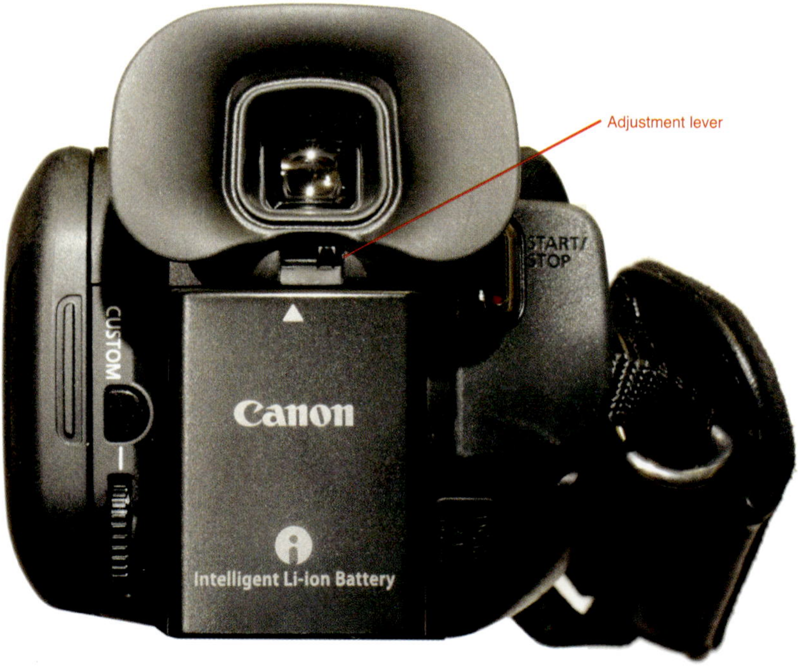

Figure 5.2 The dioptric adjustment lever is just below the viewfinder's eyepiece.

Pull the eyepiece straight back until it clicks. This turns it on. Look through the viewfinder and slide the knob at the bottom of the eyepiece until the pixels and the data information are as sharp as possible. The dioptric adjustment is very small, and unfortunately does not lock in place. It is inconveniently located just below the eyecup. In order to have access to this tiny lever, you will need to hold your eye a few inches away while making the adjustment with your fingernail. At the point you do not need the rear viewfinder, press it forward to turn it off to save battery power.

Tip

If you use the viewfinder instead of the touchscreen, some videographers find it useful to shoot part of the time with both eyes open—one eye composing the frame and the other working almost like peripheral vision scouting the next shot.

The Lens

Focal length is a measure of the optical power of a lens. It is the length from the optical center of a lens to the focal plane when the lens is focused on infinity. A higher-powered lens has a longer focal length and greater magnification. It relation to a particular format size, we can call a lens "wide angle" if it demagnifies, makes objects look further away, and exaggerates depth. We can call a lens "telephoto" if it magnifies in relation to its format size, flattens space, and makes objects appear closer than they actually are. Somewhere in between is a "normal lens" for a particular format size, which makes objects appear in normal perspective—more or less the way we see them with an unaided eye.

The G10/XA10 zoom lens has a focal length of 4.25 to 42.5mm, which is the 35mm equivalent of a somewhat mild wide angle of 30.4mm to a relatively powerful telephoto of 304mm. The setting for "normal" perspective on this lens is approximately 6mm to 7mm, just a bit tighter than full wide angle. The lens features a professional eight-blade iris, which provides a smoother and more natural bokeh in out-of-focus parts of the composition. Most lenses in this price range have a six-bladed iris, which produces artificial hexagons from out-of-focus points of light. The eight-bladed shutter in the G10/XA10 also minimizes diffraction (light bending around edges of the iris). The higher number of iris blades helps maintain image quality in the higher aperture numbers where diffraction can degrade the image.

Instead of a small focusing knob below the lens, as on previous Vixia camcorders, the manual focus ring is actually *on* the lens, where it should be, and glides into focus with smoothness and accuracy. It feels thoroughly professional. Its parameters can be adjusted in the Tool menu in terms of clockwise and counter-clockwise rotation and coarse-to-fine response using the following commands, respectively:

- Choose FUNC > MENU > Tool icon > Focus Ring Direction and select Normal or Reverse.
- Choose FUNC > MENU > Tool icon > Focus Ring Response and select Fast, Medium, or Slow.

The f/number is the focal length divided by the diameter of the lens aperture. This number provides a relative comparison of brightness among lenses of different focal lengths. A telephoto lens lets though a narrower beam of light; in order to be as bright as a wide angle (which lets through light from a much wider area), the telephoto needs a proportionally larger aperture to equal the same f/number. A 10mm lens with an aperture of 5mm would equal f/2 (a focal length of 10 divided by a width of five). A 40mm lens would need an aperture of 20mm to equal f/2. The most relevant f/number is the widest aperture of a lens, which provides a relative indication of low-light capability.

F/stops are a series of lens-aperture calibrations that are multiples of the square root of two: f/1.4, f/2, f/2.8, f/4, f/5.6, f/8, *et cetera*, used for exposure as the iris is opened or closed to regulate light. By being based on the square root of two (which is 1.414), each "stop" represents a halving or a doubling of the amount of light of each previous or next stop. Each stop also affects the depth of field, which is shallowest at the widest aperture and progressively deeper at higher f/numbers (smaller apertures). The higher the f/stop number, the smaller the aperture. At higher f/numbers, there is more diffraction—with light bending as it comes through the smaller aperture opening—which would need a different optical correction than light coming through an aperture of f/2.8, for example.

As discussed in Chapter 4, "Controlling Exposure," lenses contain a matched set of glass elements to correct for chromatic aberration, curvature of field, diffraction, and various forms of distortion. The kind of optical correction needed when the aperture is wide open—say, f/1.8—is different from what is needed at f/8. So, lenses are designed with a series of optical compromises. The highest aperture on this lens is f/8 and its lowest opens to f/1.8 in wide angle. F/4 is the most corrected and least compromised aperture on this lens.

Zoom lenses are designed for the aperture to physically change size during zooming to maintain a constant f/stop setting and constant brightness as the focal length changes. A telephoto lens needs a physically wider aperture because it intersects a narrower field of light compared to wide angle. On some zoom lenses—including the G10/XA10—this proportional adjustment is not possible at the lowest setting when there is no additional space for the aperture to open. So the f/1.8 reading in wide angle becomes 2.8 as you zoom to telephoto, a drift in brightness of nearly 1½ stops. (One stop is the difference between f/2 and f/2.8.) At a setting of f/2.8 and above, the aperture can remain constant throughout the entire zoom range because it has the physical space to adjust proportionately.

Focus Assistance, Peaking, Focus WFM

A quick and easy form of Focus Assistance is magnification. It momentarily enlarges the picture to double size; consequently, you see only the center of the frame for focusing. Manually turning the lens focus ring automatically engages Focus Assistance; any discrepancy in your focus is amplified by a factor of two on the touchscreen or viewfinder while the actual picture being framed or recorded is the full frame. So you can keep recording as you focus, but you cannot use the enlarged image as a guide to framing when focusing. When you have finished adjusting the lens, the enlarged image takes about one full second before it returns to normal scale. For those who find it a distraction when Focus Assistance magnifies the image every time you turn the focus ring, the feature can be disabled in the Camera menu. To enable or disable Focus Assistance, choose FUNC > MENU > Camera icon > Focus Assistance and then choose ON or OFF.

Another major form of assisting focus is a Peaking indicator, as shown in Figure 5.3. It displays sharply focused edges within your composition in a red, blue, or yellow highlight visible only on the touchscreen or viewfinder. You can turn Peaking on in the Focus panel, which is discussed later in this chapter. Its setup comes with a Tool icon that enables you to choose the highlight color and determine whether it is displayed over normal color video or black and white on the monitor screen (not the recorded image). The black-and-white option makes highlighting stand out even more. If Peaking has been activated, it continues to operate even after the Focus panel has been closed in M or CINEMA mode.

The Focus panel also provides a Focus waveform monitor. This WFM is not to be confused with the highly valuable WFM that measures exposure. They handle two completely different waveforms. The Focus WFM graphically indicates the portion and relative position of maximum sharpness within a composition. It is sort of like Peaking but instead of highlighting sharp edges directly on the image, the Focus WFM displays this information in a waveform across the bottom of the touchscreen with peaks that indicate maximum edge sharpness. It is primarily sensitive to vertical edges. The Focus WFM can be used alone or simultaneously with Peaking. If you have never used a Focus WFM before, using both the Focus WFM and Peaking together will help you understand how to read the waveform. For critical focusing, I prefer Peaking, the momentary image magnification of Focus Assistance, and the practice of prefocusing by zooming to telephoto.

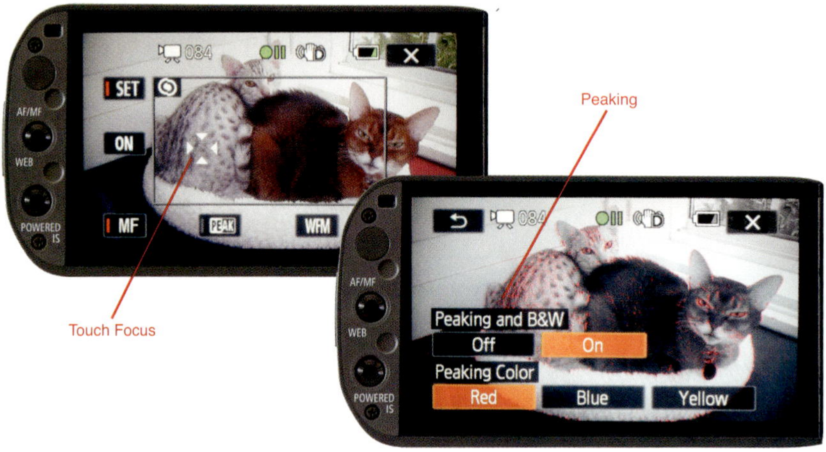

Figure 5.3 The Focus panel and Peaking adjustment sub-panel.

Focus Panel and Touch Focus

In the Program menu, the Focus panel provides a range of tools, techniques, and instruments for critical focus. (See Figure 5.4.) Some of these include auto focus, manual focus, Touch Focus, a rectangular focusing window, a Peaking indicator, a Focus waveform monitor, readouts of focus distance in feet, and the ability to set a prefocused distance to which you can return at any point. In addition, both Focus Assistance (by turning the focus ring on the lens) and the AF/MF switch on the left bezel of the LCD screen continue to be active within the Focus panel.

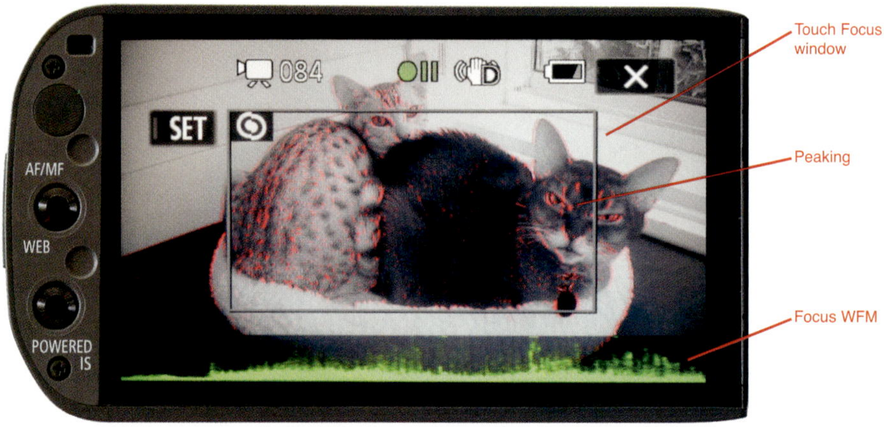

Figure 5.4 The Focus panel with both Peaking and the Focus WFM turned on to indicate points of sharpness.

Touch Focus works intuitively. Simply tap a point anywhere in the inner focusing rectangle. An auto focus indicator momentarily blinks at the spot and disappears when it locks that point in manual focus. The MF letters in the lower left of the panel become highlighted. You can continue to select new points of focus and the Touch Focus will lock to them.

You can switch to auto focus any time by tapping the MF letters in the lower left of the screen or the AF/MF button to the left of the touchscreen. Either method will move your focus back and forth between auto and manual. Tapping a new focus point in the Focus panel will also switch from auto focus (or a previous manual setting) to a new locked-in manual setting.

If Touch Focus does not quite hit its mark or if you simply want to focus the lens directly, you may turn the manual focus ring on the lens. Focus Assistance momentarily magnifies the viewfinder image by a factor of two and focus distance in feet is displayed. When you have finished adjusting the lens, the Focus panel will lock to this focus distance.

When you would like to commit a particular focus distance to memory, tap SET after you have achieved focus by touch or by the manual lens ring. The distance will momentarily display on the screen and the letters SET will be highlighted. As long as SET remains highlighted, the camcorder will remember that preset focus distance. You may now focus by touch, lens ring, or auto focus, but can return to the preset focus any time by tapping ON. This is one tap away when you are in MF mode. However, the word ON disappears from the touchscreen when you are in AF mode. In this case, to activate ON, you need to first tap MF. Touching SET a second time will cancel the current preset focus setting. The preset focus setting will also be canceled when the camcorder is turned off.

All of these manipulations of focus can be done with greater judgment and accuracy when the Peaking indicator or the Focus WFM is enabled. Their access icons are on the bottom of the Focus panel. Peaking will remain active after you exit the Focus panel, even if you turn the camcorder off in between. In contrast, the Focus WFM operates only with the Focus panel screen and is disengaged when you exit the panel.

Zoom Focus

Discrepancies in focus are more apparent in high definition than they are in standard definition; consequently, focus is very critical. Your recorded image is 1,920×1,080 pixels but your LCD screen is 852×480 and only 3½ inches diagonally for an image that will be displayed 15 to 20 times that size on a monitor and even larger on a projection screen. So it is impossible to critically judge focus by simply looking at the image on a 3½-inch LCD screen. An initial technique is to use the zoom lens itself as a magnifying aid.

The lens in the G10/XA10 is what is known as a "parafocal zoom," which means there is no focus shift as you zoom. If you focus in telephoto, the image will hold focus over the entire zoom range. However, if you initially focus in wide angle where the depth of field is nearly infinite, that point of focus will not be precise enough for the shallower depth of field of telephoto where discrepancies are more critical. Prefocusing in telephoto is a safe technique if you are going to be shooting in the mid range of your zoom lens or in wide angle. Focusing in telephoto can be done with the AF/MF switch by simply switching to auto focus (AF) in full telephoto and then toggling to manual focus (MF) to lock in the setting, which will be useful for the whole zoom range.

Zoom all the way to telephoto to enlarge a detail in your subject. The enlarged image magnifies any focusing discrepancy, and depth of field is shallower and more critical in full telephoto. Adjust the image to be as sharp as possible by momentarily pressing the auto focus button to the left of the LCD screen; then press a second time to lock to manual focus. As you zoom back to frame your subject, depth of field becomes noticeably extended in medium and wide angle.

For many camera operators, the instant magnification of Focus Assistance replaces having to zoom in. However, Focus Assistance is only a 2× magnification and full telephoto is a 10× magnification. For even more critical focus, zooming in and Focus Assistance magnification can be used together. In M or CINEMA mode, simply zoom all the way to telephoto and focus manually. As soon as you touch the focus ring on the lens, Focus Assistance will kick in and combined with the zoom's magnification you will instantaneously have 20× magnification.

Depth of Field

Depth of field (DoF) is the near-to-far distance that appears to be in sharp focus within a shot. Three primary factors determine depth of field: aperture (f/stop), focusing distance, and focal length (wide angle to telephoto). DoF becomes shallower in telephoto with longer focal-length lenses, at closer focusing distances, and at lower f/stops like f/1.8 or f/2.8.

Format size also has an effect on depth of field. Small format needs lenses that produce less magnification to provide its wide angle, normal, and telephoto views than would be required of a larger format like 35mm. Because focal length is one of the major factors that affect depth of field, the shorter focal length lenses required by small format inherently have a deeper depth of field. There is also recalculation of what constitutes "sharp" for each format size based on the circle of confusion (CoC), which can be described as a measurement of how large a single point of light can get before its boundary erodes too far into adjoining photo-sensor pixels or film grains and causes soft focus. Cinematographers and videographers never calculate the CoC themselves, but it is factored in for a particular format size whenever they consult a depth-of-field table or computer application that calculates depth of field. The format size for the G10/XA10 is a ⅓-inch sensor; based on its sensor and pixel size, its CoC is 0.011mm (a smaller tolerance than 16mm, APS-C, or 35mm).

Table 5.1 and Table 5.2 show the depth of field for wide angle (rounded up to 4.3mm), medium telephoto (20mm), and full telephoto (42.5mm) for the lens on the G10/XA10, the extremes on the zoom lens. The first column is the focal length and f/stop. The second column is the distance setting on the lens. The third column shows the approximate near-to-far limits that appear to be in sharp focus, which is the most useful part of the information. The fourth column is the depth of field itself, which is how deep the area of sharp focus is (the nearest distance subtracted from the furthest distance). For each combination of focal length and f/stop, the hyperfocal distance is highlighted. Hyperfocal distance is the focus setting that provides the deepest depth of field. Because depth of field changes with focal length and aperture, so too does the hyperfocal distance. If you choose to set your lens at the hyperfocal distance, everything from half its distance setting will be in focus up to infinity.

Table 5.1 Depth of Field in Wide Angle

FL, F/Stop	Focus	Near to Far	DoF
4.3mm f/1.8	1.00 ft	0.67 to 1.47	0.80 ft
	2.00 ft	1.22 to 5.58	4.36 ft
	3.00 ft	1.53 to 85.0	83.5 ft
	3.11 ft*	1.55 to inf	Inf
	5 ft	1.92 to inf	Inf
	10 ft	2.37 to inf	Inf
	15 ft	2.57 to inf	Inf
	20 ft	2.68 to inf	Inf
4.3mm f/2.0	1.0 ft	0.74 to 1.56	0.82 ft
	2.0 ft	1.16 to 7.15	5.99 ft
	2.77 ft*	1.39 to inf	Inf
	3.0 ft	1.44 to inf	Inf
	5 ft	1.78 to inf	Inf
	10 ft	2.16 to inf	Inf
	15 ft	2.57 to inf	Inf
	20 ft	2.42 to inf	Inf

continues...

Table 5.1 Depth of Field in Wide Angle (continued)

FL, F/Stop	Focus	Near to Far	DoF
4.3mm f/2.8	1.00 ft	0.66 to 2.02	1.36 ft
	1.96 ft*	.98 to inf	Inf
	3.0 ft	1.19 to inf	Inf
	5.0 ft	1.41 to inf	Inf
	10 ft	1.21 to inf	Inf
	15 ft	1.26 to inf	Inf
	20 ft	1.29 to inf	Inf
4.3mm f/4	1.00 ft	0.58 to 3.51	2.93 ft
	1.39 ft*	0.7 to inf	Inf
	2.0 ft	0.82 to inf	Inf
	3.0 ft	0.95 to inf	Inf
	5 ft	1.08 to inf	Inf
	10 ft	1.63 to inf	Inf
	15 ft	1.73 to inf	Inf
	20 ft	1.78 to inf	Inf
4.3mm f/5.6	0.99 ft*	0.49 to inf	Inf
	5 ft	0.82 to inf	Inf
	10 ft	0.89 to inf	Inf
	15 ft	0.92 to inf	Inf
	20 ft	0.93 to inf	Inf
4.3mm f/8	0.7ft *	0.35 to inf	Inf
	5 ft	0.61 to inf	Inf
	10 ft	0.65 to inf	Inf
	15 ft	0.66 to inf	Inf
	20 ft	0.67 to inf	Inf

*Hyperfocal distance

Table 5.2 Depth of Field in Telephoto

FL, F/Stop	Focus	Near to Far	DoF
20mm f/2.8	5 ft	4.48 to 5.66	1.19 ft
	10 ft	8.09 to 13.1	4.99 ft
	15 ft	11.1 to 23.2	12.1 ft
	20 ft	13.6 to 37.9	24.3 ft
	42.2 ft*	21.1 to inf	Inf
20mm f/4	5 ft	4.29 to 5.99	1.7 ft
	10 ft	7.5 to 15.0	7.49 ft
	15 ft	10.0 to 30.0	20.0 ft
	20 ft	12.0 to 60.3	40.3 ft
	29.9 ft*	14.9 to inf	Inf
20mm f/5.6	5 ft	4.05 to 6.53	2.48 ft
	10 ft	6.8 to 18.9	12.1 ft
	15 ft	8.78 to 51.4	42.6 ft
	20 ft	10.3 to 365	354.7 ft
	21.2 ft*	10.6 to inf	Inf
20mm f/8	5 ft	3.76 to 7.47	3.72 ft
	10 ft	6.0 to 30.0 ft	24.0 ft
	15.0 ft*	7.49 to inf	Inf
	20 ft	8.56 to inf	Inf
42.5mm f/2.8	5 ft	4.88 to 5.13	0.25 ft
	10 ft	9.52 to 10.5	1.01 ft
	15 ft	13.9 to 16.2	2.30 ft
	20 ft	18.2 to 22.3	4.12 ft
	195 ft*	97.6 to inf	Inf
42.5mm f/4	5 ft	4.83 to 5.19	0.36 ft
	10 ft	9.31 to 10.8	1.49 ft
	15 ft	13.5 to 16.8	3.30 ft
	20 ft	17.5 to 23.5	6.00 ft
	135 ft*	67.5 to inf	Inf

continues...

Table 5.2 Depth of Field in Telephoto (continued)

FL, F/Stop	Focus	Near to Far	DoF
42.5mm f/5.6	5 ft	4.76 to 5.27	0.51 ft
	10 ft	9.07 to 11.2	2.09 ft
	15 ft	12.9 to 17.8	4.90 ft
	20 ft	16.6 to 25.3	8.70 ft
	95.7 ft*	47.9 to inf	Inf
42.5mm f/8	5 ft	4.67 to 5.39	0.72 ft
	10 ft	8.7 to 11.7	3.00 ft
	15 ft	12.3 to 19.3	7.00 ft
	20 ft	15.5 to 28.4	12.9 ft
	67.5 ft*	33.75 to inf	Inf

*Hyperfocal distance

These tables illustrate how depth of field varies with focal length (optical power), aperture (f/stop), and distance. At wide angle, the depth of field on the G10/XA10 lens is infinite at every aperture once you have focused to a little more than three feet. You can also see that the depth of field shrinks exponentially as you move closer to the subject or increase the focal length. In planning a shot, it may be useful to know that your depth of field is only three inches (0.25 feet) when focused five feet away in full telephoto at f/2.8 versus 1.92 feet to infinity in full wide angle at f/2.8. These tables will help you determine the distance, aperture, and focal length you need to keep both the foreground and background in focus or to selectively focus on one while keeping the other in soft focus.

It is nearly impossible to judge DoF on a 3½-inch LCD screen. This is where a DoF table can be useful, particularly for planning a shot that involves simultaneous focus between near and far subjects in the same frame. How far apart in depth can two subjects be with both in focus, or how far apart must they be for you to focus on one at the exclusion of the other? The answers will depend on the aperture, focal length, and focusing distance.

For more detailed calculations of DoF over an entire range of focusing distances, aperture settings, and focal lengths you may want to use an iPhone or iPad application. Consider the following:

- **pCAM.** pCAM is an app for professional filmmakers, video makers, and still photographers that computes depth of field, hyperfocal distance, circle of confusion, field of view, filter factors, exposure variables (frame rate, shutter speed, footcandles, and lux), light coverage, and scene illumination. In addition, it can do conversion calculations between U.S. and metric, and also provides a Siemens focus star for testing sharpness and an insert slate. It handles data for every format including ⅓-inch video, which is the sensor size of the G10/XA10. pCAM won the 2010 Emmy Award for Outstanding Achievement in Engineering Development from the Academy of Television Arts and Sciences.
- **DOFMaster.** DOFMaster is a straightforward, easy-to-read app specifically dedicated to depth of field. Insert your format size—which in the case of the G10/XA10 is ⅓-inch—lens focal length (4.25mm for wide angle up to 42.5mm for telephoto), f/stop, and the focusing distance. Based on this information, DOFMaster calculates the near limit of focus, the far limit, the total depth of field, and the hyperfocal distance, which is the closest distance setting that would achieve the deepest depth of field at that focal length and f/stop.

6

Controlling Color

Daylight is considerably bluer than tungsten incandescent light. Both sources produce light that spans the entire visible spectrum, but with a different balance. Our eyes and brain adapt to these differences when we physically move from one light environment to another. If our perceptual apparatus did not adjust, people would look blue in sunlight and orange in tungsten light, and white surfaces would always take on the predominant hue of the ambient light. Video has to be physically adjusted so as to render color closer to what the human eye/brain perceives; otherwise it would give us orange and blue people. The camera's process of normalizing color in different types of ambient light is called "white balancing." When the camera adjusts so that a white surface is rendered as a true white with no residual hue, then the whole range of color will appear accurate and balanced.

The G10/XA10 provides three methods for controlling white balance:

- **Automatic.** This tracks continuously.
- **White Balance settings.** With the G10/XA10, you have the ability to read and recall two manual White Balance settings and use them as presets.
- **Calibrated custom presets.** You can set calibrated custom presets from 2,000ºK to 15,000ºK in 100ºK increments along with specific settings for daylight, shade, cloudy, tungsten, fluorescent (warm white), and fluorescent H (cool white). (The meaning of the term "ºK" is discussed later in this chapter.)

This is a considerable amount of control over color balance, as shown in Figure 6.1.

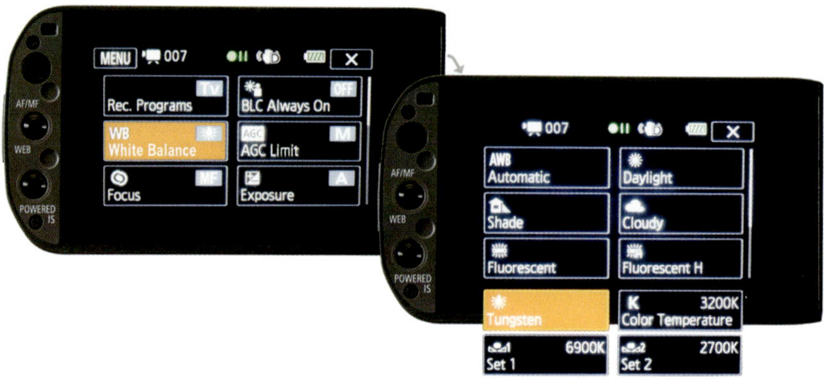

Figure 6.1 Choosing FUNC > WB White Balance reveals 10 choices of automatic, programmed, preset, or manual controls for balancing color.

Automatic White Balance

Automatic White Balance (AWB) is sometimes called auto-tracking white balance. When your camcorder is in full AUTO mode, your white balance runs automatically by default; you have no other choice. In M and CINEMA modes, you have the option to intentionally select Automatic White Balance on the touchscreen. To do so, choose FUNC > WB White Balance > AWB.

If you set the white balance for AUTO, you will get a compromise that continually strives to neutralize variations of the color of ambient light in your scenes. AWB may also introduce arbitrary adjustments—for example, as someone enters or exits the frame. As lighting conditions and compositions change, the camera may alter the entire picture's hue so that red, green, and blue are in balance in the lightest parts of your frame, which the camera assumes ought to be a neutral white or near white. Automatic White Balance may do a better job with some compositions and subject matter than with others, but it may be your best option in uncertain situations where the nature of the light may change quickly.

Manual White Balance

Instead of an auto-tracking white balance, you often want consistency of color within a shot and from shot to shot. You may record at various times during the day with the intent of cutting the shots together with as little color drift as possible. The best way to equalize daylight so that 8 a.m., 10 a.m., 12 noon, 3 p.m., and 5 p.m. render hues that appear identical to each other is to carefully white balance each one manually. Although the directionality of the light and other characteristics may vary, skin tones and other colors shot at different times of day should intercut with less color shift if each scene has been manually balanced.

To read and set a manual color balance, hold a white card or sheet of paper in the predominant light so that the card fills the frame. Next, choose FUNC > WB White Balance and scroll to and press Set 1 or Set 2. Finally, press and hold Set WB for a couple of seconds until the manual white balance icon stops blinking. The white card should now appear neutral. You have now adjusted one manual preset for light hitting the white card.

The camera will allow you to read and store two manual white-balance settings. You might manually balance for two sides of one room, or for indoors plus outdoors, and switch from one preset to another as you move with the camera. The setting of one of the two manual presets for white balance can be assigned to one of the buttons on the left bezel of the touchscreen. Choose FUNC > MENU > Tool icon > Assign Button 1 (or Assign Button 2) > WB Priority. Then choose FUNC > MENU > Tool icon > Set WB Priority and select Set 1 or Set 2. Pressing the button will now toggle between the manual preset and the current white balance value or method you have selected in the FUNC > WB White Balance panel.

Locking to a manual white balance gives you consistency and color control that you do not have with AWB. In a mixed-light situation, the choice of where you take the manual reading will determine where the balance of light will look normal. You might have bluish skylight coming through a window, plus rather orange incandescent light from a table lamp in the interior and the halogen white of a 500- or 600-watt Lowel Omni light bouncing off the ceiling as fill light. In this situation, you would get one color balance near the window, a completely different balance near the table lamp, and another where the fill light is predominant. There may even be a position where the light from all three sources overlaps, which could provide a compromise reading. Choosing where you place the white card and manually balancing for that spot can be a powerful tool in creating a look and interpreting a scene. It's a matter of where you want "normal" to be.

A more elegant way of taking a manual white balance is to use a BRNO baLens white-balance lens cap (see Figure 6.2). The 58mm size fits the G10/XA10 and sells for about $33 from some vendors. Simply replace your Canon lens cap and use the baLens as your regular lens protection. The cap has a white translucent dome in its center. Instead of holding a white card, stand in the light that would be hitting your subject and point the camcorder with its capped lens toward your predominant light source or in a position to receive a balance of light from multiple sources and press FUNC > WB White Balance > Set 1 (or Set 2). (Refer to Figure 6.1.) Then press and hold Set WB until the white balance icon stops blinking. This will become second nature as the last thing you do before removing the lens cap. The hemispherical dome acts as a standard that will give you more consistent readings compared to a white card. In mixed-light situations, a reading from the surface of a flat card will vary with the angular tilt, whereas a hemispherical dome averages the light from a

180º angle. The BRNO baLens is also convenient because it doubles as a lens cap and is always with the camcorder.

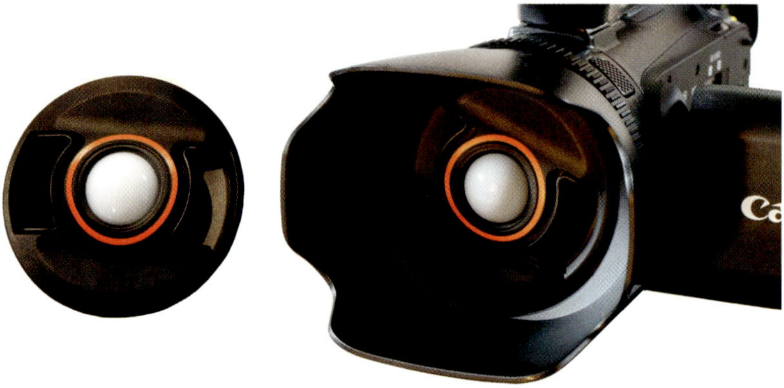

Figure 6.2 The BRNO baLens lens cap with its dome for reading white balance.

It is also possible to digitally filter a scene by tricking the manual white balance. For example, balancing to a yellow card instead of white would cause the camera to produce an excess of its complementary color, blue. The resulting setting can be used to intentionally filter a scene—in this case making it less yellow (i.e., bluer). Experienced videographers often carry a selection of cards with pale hues to produce custom digital filtration. Commercially made sets of color-balance cards are available, but experimenting with and making your own works just as well. Try color assortments of pastel paper from an office-supply or art supply store.

Tip

The BRNO baLens has a replaceable accessory dome that is pale blue in color, which can be used to digitally warm a scene when white balancing.

Digital filters have numerous advantages over glass filters:

- They cost almost nothing.
- They are not as affected by fingerprints and dust.
- There is nothing in the optical path of the lens to degrade the image.
- They produce consistent results.
- The process takes into account and compensates for the actual light falling on the scene while producing its filter effect.

Color Temperature

One of the major ways to produce light is to heat something until it gives off energy. This is the way the filament in an incandescent lamp works, or any object that is heated to the point that it glows. For example, as a metal rod is heated, its molecules move faster and give off infrared radiation. Infrared cannot be seen by the human eye, but you can feel the radiating warmth without touching the rod. If you increase the heat further, the rod will visibly glow red, and even hotter will glow orange. Progressively more heat will cause the rod to produce a yellowish-white light and eventually blue-white at even higher temperatures.

The 19th century British physicist Lord Kelvin discovered that all substances, even a block of carbon, radiate the same colors at identical high temperatures. Among stars, red giants like Antares and Betelgeuse are cooler than our sun, which is yellow-white, and blue-white stars are much hotter, like Rigel, the brightest star in the constellation Orion. A candle flame has predominantly reddish and yellowish areas with a hint of blue in the hottest part. An oxyacetylene torch produces a blue-white flame.

Temperature is actually a measure of the energy (from infrared through the visible range and beyond) produced by molecular movement. When something is as cold as –273° Centigrade (Celsius), its molecules stop moving. At this point, no energy is emitted; there isn't anything colder than –273°C. Lord Kelvin advocated a temperature scale based on Centigrade but instead of 0 representing the point where water freezes, the scale is offset by adding 273 degrees so that 0 on the Kelvin scale is absolute zero.

A tungsten filament of a 60-watt household incandescent lamp actually burns somewhere around 2,700° on the Kelvin scale (which again is 273° added to the Celsius scale). If you were to feed the lamp even more voltage or if it had heavier filaments and created even more heat, its color temperature would be closer to what is called "photographic tungsten light" (3,200°K) produced by a professional 500-, 600-, 750-, or 1,000-watt instrument. 3,200° Kelvin is a whiter white than the orange-white of home incandescent lamps. Hotter still is the surface of the sun, which burns at 5,000°K to 5,500°K. The combination of direct sunlight mixed with diffused light from the sky gives us photographic daylight, which is around 5,600°K. Table 6.1 outlines the color temperature of various light sources.

An overcast day or a shaded area with skylight and no direct sunlight measures from 6,000° to above 10,000° Kelvin. Obviously, skylight in the shade is not physically hotter than direct sunlight. This is because its bluer color is produced by filtration instead of a blue-hot star. The Kelvin scale is a way of measuring color equivalencies within the range of white light, and not all coloration of light is produced by heat and molecular motion. Skylight, which gets its color from atmospheric filtration, and fluorescents, which get their color from phosphors, are examples that can be given a value on the Kelvin scale equivalent to the temperature that a heated body would attain to produce comparable light. The Kelvin scale is extremely useful as a scientific way to describe and compare the apparent whiteness of a light source.

The color temperatures we often encounter in video are 2,700° to about 3,100° for household bulbs; 3,200° if we use professional tungsten lighting instruments; and 5,600° if we are using daylight or instruments to simulate daylight. We might even have higher settings if we are in indirect daylight, skylight, or overcast light. The other temperature we often deal with is around 4,100° Kelvin for cool-white and industrial fluorescents.

Table 6.1 Color Temperature

Degrees Kelvin	**Light Source**
8,000–10,000°K	Sky
7,000–8,000°K	Outdoor shade
6,500°K	RGB monitor; electronic flash
6,000–7,500°K	Overcast day
5,500–6,500°K	"Daylight" fluorescent
5,600°K	Average sun and sky
5,000–5,400°K	Sun at noon (no skylight)
4,100°K	"Cool-white" fluorescent
3,200°K	Professional quartz halogen lights
3,000–3,500°K	"Bright-white" fluorescent
2,900°K	100-watt household lamp
2,700°K	60-watt household lamp; "warm-white" fluorescent
2,200°K	Sodium vapor light
2,000–3,000°K	Sunrise/sunset
1,800°K	Candle flame
1,700°K	Match flame

Warm and Cool

Our everyday experience tells us red is hot and blue is cool, but in the world of high-temperature physics it is the other way around. For tactile sensations, a red glow is already too hot to touch, and most of us have no direct experience with blue-hot objects. We associate blue with shade, with the reflection of the sky in water, and with water itself. Our skin feels cooler when we walk from sunlight into the bluer skylight of the shade. So we physiologically and psychologically associate blue with cool, whereas an actual object heated to "blue hot" would need to be thousands of degrees hotter than the 5,600°K degrees of photographic daylight.

When we talk about the Kelvin scale as a way of defining white light, it would be clearer to use the words "bluer," "oranger," or "redder" or "higher or lower color temperature" or to cite a specific value in degrees Kelvin than to refer to points on the scale as warm or cool, which could lead to confusion. But it is hard to avoid the words warm and cool because they come from a lifetime of visual and tactile experience. So if we talk about making a scene warmer or cooler or warm-white or cool-white fluorescent lights, we generally mean the psychologically reinforced experience of red as warm and blue as cool—not actual temperature.

Color Balance Presets

5,600°K is called "photographic daylight"—a mixture of direct sunlight blended with ambient skylight (which has a bluish hue formed by scattered light filtered by water vapor in the atmosphere). The actual color temperature of sunlight plus skylight will vary subtly from mid-morning to mid-afternoon, and vary considerably at sunrise and sunset. It will also vary in different seasons and in different parts of the world. Certain moments at sunrise or sunset can be even redder than incandescent light, and an overcast winter day might be 10,000°K.

In addition to Automatic White Balance and two manual white balance presets, the G10/XA10 provides presets based on six standard light conditions and 130 settings on the Kelvin scale. To access them, switch to M mode; then choose > FUNC > WB and select Daylight, Shade, Cloudy, Fluorescent, Fluorescent H, or Tungsten. A principal reason for using a preset is to maintain the particular color tonality of the actual light instead of automatically or manually balancing to make the light appear neutral. The best way to show a dance lit by colored gels, the actual color of daylight as it varies through the day, or the vibrant hues of sunset is to select a relevant preset color temperature. In comparison, Automatic White Balance would continually attempt to balance each of these toward neutral until it reached extremes that were beyond its corrective latitude.

For example, 5,600°K is the average hue of daylight. Because the actual balance of daylight evolves during the day, presetting for 5,600°K will capture the balance at that moment and its variations over the passage of time. The appropriate Daylight, Shade, Cloudy, Fluorescent (warm-white), Fluorescent H (cool-white), or Tungsten setting allows you to record the character of how the actual light deviates from a standard, bringing out the unique quality of the light instead of neutralizing it.

In addition to these six presets based on lighting conditions, the G10/XA10 includes the professional feature of being able to preset a light value in 130 increments of color temperature. This means you can scroll across the Kelvin scale to find the setting that balances best for your particular mixture of light and lock in the look that you want for your scene. To achieve this, in M mode, choose FUNC > WB > K Color Temperature and scroll left or right, as shown in Figure 6.3.

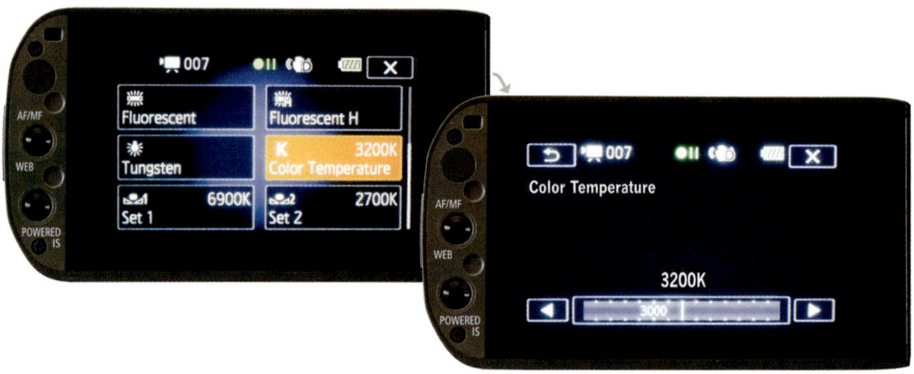

Figure 6.3 The K Color Temperature panel.

You may start off with what ought to typically balance your type of light—2,700°K (household tungsten and "warm" fluorescents), 3,000°K (designer fluorescents), 3,200°K (professional tungsten), 3,100°K–3,500°K (bright-white fluorescents), 4,000–4,500°K (cool-white and industrial fluorescents), or 5,600°K (average daylight)—and then adjust the setting left or right while watching the changes on the screen. You cannot judge accurate color entirely by your camcorder's viewfinder, but you can probably get it in the ballpark. The ability to select from 130 incremental settings to make the scene warmer, cooler, or neutral is a powerful tool.

Fluorescents

The light from fluorescent bulbs is not produced by actually heating a filament to a high temperature. Fluorescents create ultraviolet light through a high voltage gas discharge, which is converted to visible light by a coating of phosphors inside the fluorescent tube. Cool-white and industrial fluorescent bulbs give off a light that might be rated at 4,100° Kelvin. However, there is a difference in spectrum between a fluorescent tube and a source of light produced by heat.

The surface of the sun, the filament in an incandescent lamp, and a candle emphasize a different part of the spectrum at their respective temperature but still emit light across the entire visual range. Once our eyes and brains adjust (which is the biological equivalent of white balancing), we see the entire range of colors in daylight, tungsten, or candle light. The phosphors in cool-white fluorescent bulbs produce enough of the spectrum to create the impression of white light, but segments of the spectrum are uneven or missing entirely. So even if we say that a particular fluorescent burns at 4,100° Kelvin as a reference to its equivalent color, it is not going to behave entirely like a 4,100°K incandescent lamp. The most efficient and least expensive phosphors, and the ones that last the longest, have a high green content and are missing 40 percent to 60 percent of the visible spectrum. Skin tones may not appear as healthy and as complete, and clothing and scenery may shift from the true colors we would see in sunlight or incandescent light.

To shoot in fluorescent light, you can set the G10/XA10 to Fluorescent to compensate for warm-white (which measures from 2,700° to 3,100°K) or to Fluorescent H for cool-white. You could also use the 4,100°K preset on the K Color Temperature panel, but the Fluorescent settings on the G10/XA10 have an advantage in that they try to compensate for the extra amount of green. You could also manually white balance by putting a white card in the light path, pointing the camera, and choosing FUNC > WB White Balance > Set 1 (or Set 2), and then pressing and holding Set WB until the white balance icon stops blinking. The camera will do its best to make the white card a balanced white for the specific spectrum of your fluorescent light.

There are higher-priced fluorescent bulbs that have a more complete spectrum, some of which are called "wide spectrum" or "full spectrum." But in actuality, a mixture of phosphors cannot quite deliver a full spectrum, so bulbs called "wide spectrum" or "full spectrum" have anywhere from about 80 percent up to about 98 percent of the complete range of visible light that the sun or an incandescent bulb would produce.

A fluorescent labeled "wide spectrum" or "full spectrum" will provide a Color Rendering Index (CRI) rating on the bulb or in its catalog description. This is simply a percentage of how much of the full spectrum it provides. The CRI rating for photographically usable fluorescents ranges from CRI 80 to the highest they come, which is around CRI 98. Fluorescents below these ratings are not going to provide true colors, although you still may have to shoot with them under certain conditions because they are so prevalent.

Wide-spectrum fluorescents tend to come in color temperatures of 2,700° to match the "warmness" of household incandescent bulbs or 3,200°K to match professional photographic light, and rated at 5,500°, 5,600°, 6,000°K or 6,500°K to match daylight or indirect daylight. Color temperature is a useful approximation for fluorescents, but the important figure is the CRI rating. Color will look truer with fluorescents that have high CRI ratings once they are white balanced.

Color Bars

If you have a separate monitor for use on location or for later viewing and evaluating your images, it is important to calibrate it so that accurate judgments can be made. Calibration is done with SMPTE color bars, a standard of the Society of Motion Picture and Television Engineers. The G10/XA10 can generate and record color bars. Bars are also available from online sources as downloadable JPEG or TIFF picture files, or as video files that sometimes include an audio test tone. To access bars within the camcorder, choose FUNC > MENU > Film Clip icon > Color Bars. The G10/XA10 offers an option of bars only or bars with audio tone. You can record either of these choices as a video (MTS) file. The camcorder does not allow the option of recording bars as a photo file. (See Figure 6.4.)

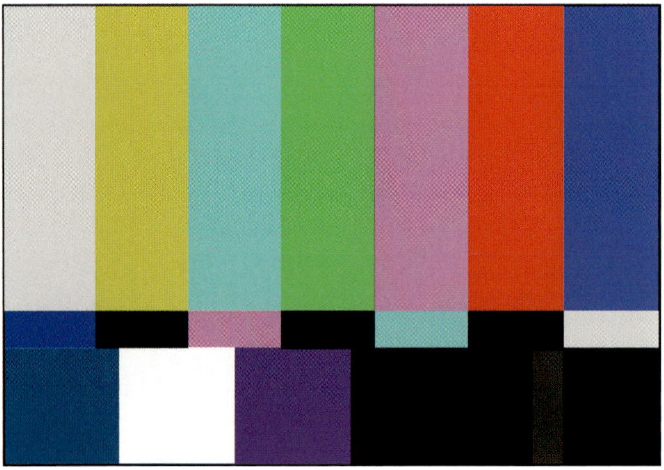

Figure 6.4 Standard SMPTE color bars.

With color bars displayed on your monitor, the first adjustment is usually the brightness (also called the "pedestal" or "black level"). Look for the pattern of three small vertical dark gray bars in the lower right and adjust the brightness until only one small bar remains visible. The darkest bar is blacker than black and the middle bar is just below picture black. The remaining dark gray bar is just above picture black, which is why it should stay visible in a properly adjusted monitor while the other two disappear into blackness.

Now adjust the contrast (sometimes called the "white level"). This sets the upper limit and the overall stretch of brightness. While looking at the bright white square on the lower left, turn the level up and down so that you can see its intensity changing. Then raise the contrast until the square does not seem to be getting any brighter. Back off slightly from this setting.

The next adjustment is hue. Running from left to right, the large vertical stripes in the upper part of the SMPTE pattern are white, yellow, cyan, green, magenta, red, and blue. If your monitor has a blue-only setting or a blue gun, turn it on. These turn off the red and green signal. The bars will now be a pattern where the former white, cyan, magenta, and blue bars are all displayed as blue (because blue light is a component of each of those colors). The former yellow, green, and red bars now appear black because there is no blue content in those colors. Adjust hue (or phase, tint, or color) on your monitor so that all the brighter bars in the upper pattern have an equal amount of blue. Pay particular attention where the former cyan bar had a strip of yellow below it, and the former yellow bar had a strip of cyan below it to see that they now appear to be equally blue. Turn off the blue gun to restore color. Your monitor is now balanced for hue.

If your monitor does not have a blue gun, adjust hue until the secondary colors yellow, cyan, and magenta all seem centered—not orange/chartreuse instead of yellow, emerald/ultramarine instead of cyan, and rose/purple instead of magenta. It could be difficult to judge a precise setting for any one of these colors by itself because there may be latitude in what we might perceive as pure yellow, for example. But a setting where all three seem perfect is a findable narrow point.

The final adjustment is color saturation. This is set subjectively at a point where the colors seem full—neither washed out nor overstated. They should never get to the point where they glow like neon. Using the monitor in a dark space will demand less saturation than in bright ambient light. Many videographers prefer to make the final adjustment of color saturation while viewing the image of a human face. Whether skin tones look pallid, healthy, or artificial can be more precise than judging the color level of abstract bars.

In addition to color bars, viewing the image of a standard Kodak 18% gray card or a ColorChecker chart (formerly called a Macbeth chart) can be used for checking the accuracy of color. The ColorChecker chart has 24 patches of color: six shades of gray, six primary and secondary colors, and the others mimicing the range of natural colors of sky, leaves, flowers, and dark and light skin. Kodak gray cards retail for $16 for a pack of two plus a small card; ColorChecker charts sell for about $70. They are made to very precise specifications. Viewed on a well-calibrated monitor and visually compared to the original, these cards and charts can help you judge the trueness of color. A recorded signal of these charts is useful with field instruments or in postproduction where an RGB parade can test for color neutrality, balance, and hue, and a vectorscope can test for saturation. The RGB parade comparatively graphs the levels of red, green, and blue in a composition, and a vectorscope graphs color saturation and relative hue. Both devices are built into professional editing and color-balancing software.

Image Effects

The G10/XA10's M mode allows you to customize color depth (saturation), brightness, contrast, and/or sharpness. To do so, choose FUNC > Image Effects > ON and adjust the settings as needed, as shown in Figure 6.5. The first three of these settings are very similar to the saturation, brightness, and contrast controls on a monitor, but unlike a monitor, the camcorder's manual controls permanently alter the recorded signal. A monitor simply alters how the signal is displayed. In making these permanent adjustments, it would be ideal to judge their effects on a larger, well-calibrated monitor than on the camcorder's 3½-inch LCD screen.

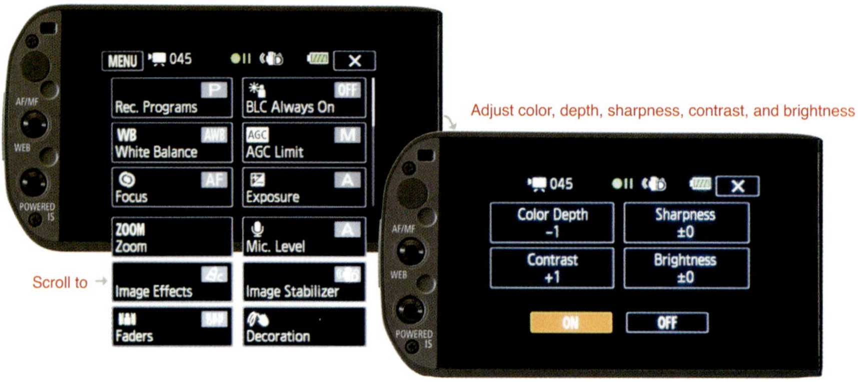

Figure 6.5 The Image Effects panel and its control screen.

Be careful with high settings. Excessive contrast can permanently lose detail in highlights and shadows, and excessive sharpness may create artificial edges or video grain and accentuate irregularities in skin.

CINEMA Mode

CINEMA mode alters color, contrast, and the response curve to look more like film. It provides a choice of nine filters plus individual adjustments under each filter. Switching to CINEMA mode automatically selects a frame rate of PF24. In addition, photos cannot be recorded when the camcorder is in CINEMA mode.

The first CINEMA mode selection is FILTER 1 > Cinema Standard, a film look that allows additional controls similar to the image effects found in the manual mode. The eight other alternatives are as follows:

- **FILTER 2 > Vivid.** The Vivid cinema setting accentuates primary colors and increases saturation. It has a kind of hyper-real look with certain subjects.
- **FILTER 3 > Dream.** Canon describes Dream as a "magical look," but this is a subjective description that some might see as a desaturated reality instead of a dream.
- **FILTER 4 > Cool.** Cool adds a bluish tint.
- **FILTER 5 > Nostalgic.** Nostalgic adds a warm tone, which Canon suggests is like "old TV programs," but here again, this is subjective. With completely different lighting or subject matter the filter may suggest a different interpretation. So, do not be guided solely by Canon's labels.
- **FILTER 6 > Sepia.** Sepia creates a warm, antique, faded look while still retaining a hint of the original color.
- **FILTER 7 > Old Movies.** Old Movies provides an alternative cine look like old Cinemascope with grain and scratches.
- **FILTER 8 > Memory.** Memory softens contrast.
- **FILTER 9 > B&W.** B&W strips the image of color and its three adjustable settings alter levels of contrast.

Note

Cinema filters 2 through 9 provide for more limited adjustments of low, medium, or high.

Setting the AUTO/M/CINEMA switch on the upper right side of the camcorder to CINEMA instantly locks the frame rate to PF24 (not 24P) and activates a cinema filter based on the last setting used. The lower left of the touchscreen displays the filter number, 1 through 9. To change to another cinema filter, tap the lower left of the touchscreen and scroll through the nine selections.

Cinema Standard provides a film look with a response curve (gamma) that should retain more detail in the shadows and highlights. You can further adjust the setting for color depth, sharpness, contrast, and brightness by touching the Tool icon that appears on the right side of the touchscreen. Adjustments for cinema filters 2 through 9 can also be accessed by tapping the Tool icon. (See Figure 6.6.) To exit from CINEMA mode altogether, slide the AUTO/M/CINEMA switch to M or AUTO.

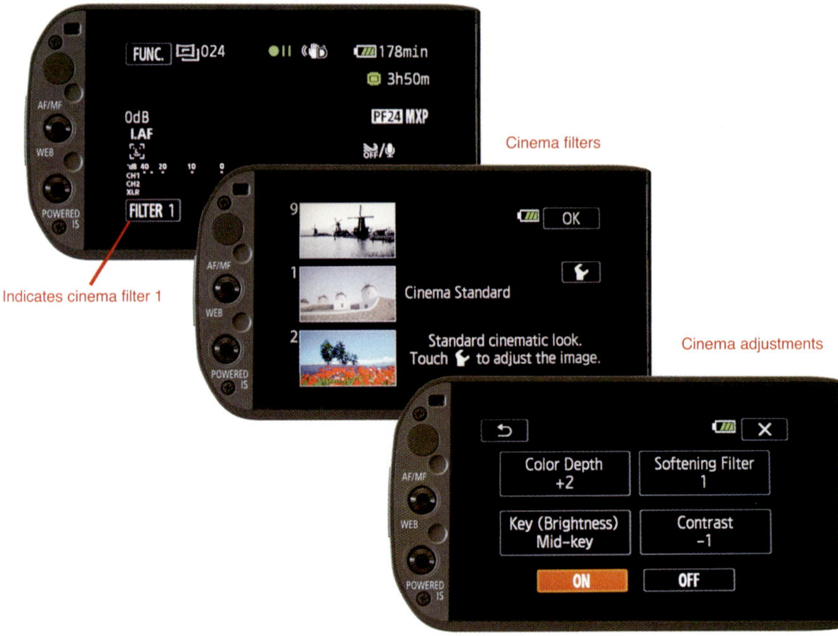

Figure 6.6 Cinema mode filters and adjustments.

xvCOLOR

Almost all video is limited by the NTSC and ATSC range of possible colors. "Illegal" colors beyond the range will glow, clip, fall below picture black, or look unnatural on most TV sets. However, some televisions, monitors, and projectors have allowed for an extended range of color to be displayed with an option called xvYCC, xvCOLOR, or Extended Gamut YCC. The G10/XA10 can record with the xvYCC expanded color palette. To access this setting, in M mode, choose FUNC > MENU > Film Clip icon > xvCOLOR.

xvYCC can be viewed only on monitors and projectors that have the xvYCC option, and the monitor must have its extended gamut feature switched on. DVD and Blu-ray discs do not support xvYCC. The source signal has to come through an HDMI 1.3 cable from a device capable of playing AVCHD, like the G10/XA10 itself or a computer playing an AVCHD file with appropriate software. You should not use this setting for video intended for broadcast, DVD, or Blu-ray, or for viewing on most TV sets and monitors.

7

Improving Sound

Sound is the complement to the picture image, and a significant channel of information, dialogue, aural experience, and meaning in its own right. Sound can enhance or complete a visual image or make us question what we see. Good audio adds presence, sensuality, and dimension to the world within the frame, and evokes the world that extends beyond the frame.

The processes and techniques of recording high-quality audio deserve as much attention as composing, lighting, and focusing the visual image. Let's start with the audio capabilities and limitations within the camcorder itself, then examine external microphones, separate recorders, and professional approaches to field recording.

Using the Internal Mic

The built-in microphone in the G10/XA10 is better than most internal mics. Camcorders that cost somewhere between $500 and $1,800 typically come with the equivalent of a $40 internal X/Y stereo mic, which for many situations is the worst pickup pattern for an on-board microphone. Its emphasis is 45° off center to the left and 45° off center to the right, which in each case is just to the side of where you are pointing the lens.

Naïve consumers assume that stereo is inherently a step up from mono, so manufacturers equip consumer camcorders with cheap X/Y stereo mics simply because that is what consumers will buy. Professionals tend to use a directional monophonic microphone. After all, the primary reason for mounting a mic on a camcorder is to obtain the on-axis sync sound of the image framed in the lens. Building the direct on-axis sound into a stereo track is done in editing.

The G10/XA10 has a rather sophisticated multi-element built-in microphone based on a mid-side pattern, which does pick up direct on-axis sound. For all practical purposes, it works like an audio zoom with a choice of four patterns. Instead of an element pointing 45° toward the left and another element pointing 45° toward the right as in X/Y stereo, it has a main element that points straight forward and an element that picks up sound from the sides. By processing these signals, the camcorder can provide a Normal position, which actually mimics X/Y stereo in that it combines the on-axis sound with the side audio for one track and combines the on-axis sound with a minus version of the side audio to create the other track. With an appropriate balance, you do get what sounds like regular stereo; but because there is in an on-axis element, you do not have a hole in the middle like in X/Y. Then there is a Monaural position, which is useful if you want to emphasize the on-screen sound. Two channel mono records a single monophonic signal on both the left and right tracks. When it is played back in stereo, the sound will be heard as central. During editing, a mono signal can be panned and placed in its proper special relationship within the left and right stereo tracks or within 5.1 surround sound in the final sound mix, along with ambience, music, and sound effects.

The internal mic has a third option, Wide, which emphasizes ambient sound and a broad pickup pattern. This can be useful if you are already recording more focused audio from a radio mic or a boom on a separate dedicated recorder. The fourth option is Zoom, which means that the balance between mid and side elements actually changes in relationship to your visual zoom. This provides sound perspective that can be useful. Sometimes, however, you may want to be zoomed out while still maintaining an audio emphasis on the direct axis of the camera rather than having sound coming from almost every direction. You will have to experiment to decide which pickup pattern works best for your purposes.

To select the mic position, choose FUNC > MENU > Camera icon > Built-in Mic Directionality; then select Monaural (on-axis sound on both channels), Normal (X/Y stereo with medium reach), Wide (wide stereo), or Zoom (pickup pattern linked to the zoom lens position). (See Figure 7.1.)

The internal microphone also has five adjustments for frequency response. To access them, choose FUNC > MENU > Camera icon > Built-in Mic Freq. Response. Then choose one of the following:

- **Normal (unfiltered).** Use Normal when recording voive or music under relatively quiet conditions in a good acoustic environment that is not hampered with excessive reverberation or ambient sounds.
- **Boost LF (Low-Frequency) Range.** Boosting the LF (low-frequency) range increases the bass. Its purpose is to make music or drums sound full, but in hollow locations it could also increase unwanted reverberation, making the sound muddy.

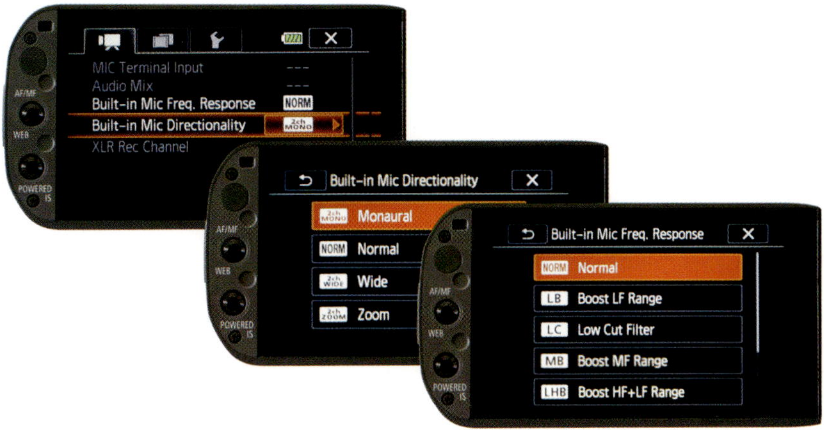

Figure 7.1 Controls for the built-in microphone.

- **Low Cut Filter.** The Low Cut Filter option (also known as a high-pass filter) is useful for shooting on location and is recommended for most location sound. It cuts audio frequencies below approximately 65Hz or 70Hz. This setting diminishes unwanted reverberation, air conditioning, hum, rumble, wind, car engines, and distant ambient sounds (which tend to be low frequency). It is useful for both interior and exterior environments for most situations except for music with deep bass frequencies.
- **Boost MF (Mid-Frequency) Range.** The Boost MF Range setting will help emphasize voice when shooting from a distance. If you need to resort to this filter, your microphone directionality should already be set to Monaural to emphasize on-axis sound as much as possible.
- **Boost HF + LF Range.** The Boost HF (high frequencies) + LF (low frequencies) Range setting is intended to make music sound full and crisp while reducing the mid-range. This is not a good setting for voice. (See the following caution box.)

Caution

Boosting the low-frequency range or boosting a combination of high and low frequency in the camera is not recommended. These two settings—Boost LF Range and Boost HF + LF Range—are completely unsuited for voice. Boosting both high and low frequencies can make music seem more powerful and more brilliant, but this emphasis can easily produce a boomy and possibly muddy sound track when recording on location, and many undesirable sounds that you do not want to boost fall into this frequency range. Do that kind of enhancement in postproduction, not in the camera.

Most professionals do not want to overly filter in the field because audio adjustments can be done with much more precision and better monitoring in postproduction. Low Cut Filter is the only option I would recommend for regular recording in the field.

Setting Levels

You have the option of recording with manual or automatic volume. In manual, you want to provide a record level with adequate headroom by setting the average peak audio at –10dB, –12dB, or even –18dB below the saturation/distortion point as a safety factor. A decibel (dB) is a logarithmic unit of relative volume calibrated so that 0dB equals the saturation/distortion point—the hard limit in digital audio recording. At 0dB, the digital pulses that constitute an audio signal have reached their maximum peak value. AVCHD audio is sampled 48,000 times per second and each sample is represented by a 16-bit digital number with an absolute limit to its maximum value. Any attempt to record at a higher level beyond 0dB changes the relationship between peaks that have maxed out and valleys that are becoming disproportionately higher than they should be. The result is distortion. Levels can eventually get so high that the digital audio circuit cannot distinguish between peaks and valleys at all and produces static, clicks, stutters, intermittent dropouts, or a complete loss of signal. Digital audio distortion that is too severe cannot be repaired in post production.

Control over audio is entirely automatic when shooting in AUTO mode. In M or CINEMA modes, you may select Mic. Level in the program panel and also turn on the Audio Level indicator to monitor the volume levels. To do so, while in M or CINEMA mode, choose FUNC and scroll to Mic. Level. Then select A (automatic) or select M (manual) and set a value using the Audio Level indicator. (See Figure 7.2.)

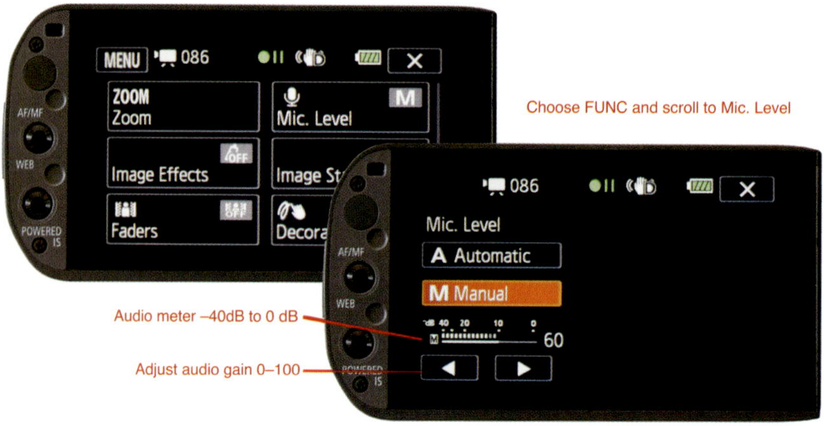

Figure 7.2 Setting audio levels for the internal microphone.

The Audio Level indicator is calibrated at –40, –20, –10, and 0dB. When the Mic. Level panel is set to manual, the touchscreen has a slider that allows you to adjust volume in 10dB increments. You want your average articulated sound to fall between –20dB and –10dB, with occasional peaks above –10dB but short of 0dB. The Audio Level indicator will continue to display after you have closed the panel as long as you remain in the M or CINEMA mode.

Under the Camera menu, the camcorder additionally has a setting for continuous attenuation (ATT) for recording in very loud environments, or auto attenuation (A), which works as an intermittent limiter, which should be the default mode for all other recording situations. To access these settings, choose FUNC > MENU > Camera icon > Mic Attenuator and select A (auto) or ATT (on).

These settings will control the internal microphone or, if selected, an external microphone plugged into the 3.5mm mic input. The professional audio inputs on the XA10 handle have their own attenuator switch and mechanical dials for volume. As good as it is, the internal mic has one huge drawback: Being built into the camera body, it picks up excessive noise from handling the camcorder. If you are solely dependent on this microphone, you need to constantly monitor with a pair of good headphones and practice holding the camcorder, focusing, and making any touchscreen, CUSTOM key and CUSTOM dial adjustments as softly as possible. An external microphone is more physically isolated from these unwanted sounds particularly if it is in a shock mount. And of course, an external mic can be of even higher quality than the one built in.

External Audio for the G10

Sound is very important, and you should invest in a high-quality microphone. The biggest shortcoming of the G10 is the lack of XLR inputs for professional balanced-line microphones. There are some workarounds regarding sound for the G10, including unbalanced semi-pro microphones with 3.5mm mini-plugs, XLR-to-mini-plug adapter cables or converter boxes that accept professional microphones, wireless mics, or using a separate recorder for double system sound.

The Canon DM-100 is an attachable external microphone that receives its power and makes its audio connection through the mini advanced accessory shoe on the Canon G10. It will not operate on the XA10, which uses a universal mount. Canon's proprietary shoe on the G10 provides power and internal connections for specialized accessories such as lights and external microphones. The main advantages of Canon's DM-100 over the internal microphone are considerably less handling noise (because it is more isolated from the camera body) and a moderate improvement in audio quality.

For exterior shooting and general protection, the microphone comes with an attachable wind muff. It has three directionality settings:

- Shotgun for direct on-axis sound (which should be the preferred position for most situations)
- 90º stereo
- 120º stereo with a very broad pickup pattern

Installing the DM-100 on the mini advanced accessory shoe automatically disengages the internal microphone and provides the convenience of perfectly fitting the G10 camcorder with no additional plug-in wires.

Even with its stereo options and mounting convenience, the Canon DM-100 is not quite the audio quality of the semi-professional RØDE mono video microphones. The RØDE VideoMic ($149) and VideoMic Pro ($210–$230) come with an integrated shock mount and are powered by a 9-volt battery. Their mini plug fits the 3.5mm input on the G10 (and the XA10) and puts a mono recording on both left and right tracks. The Pro model has more reach, a three position level control, and a two-step high-pass filter. RØDE also makes a stereo VideoMic but X/Y stereo is not an ideal pattern for an on-board microphone and its audio is not as clean as the mono version. Unlike the XA10, a microphone or shock mount made by anyone other than Canon will not directly fit on the G10. To attach a RØDE VideoMic, you will need a $12–$20 adapter like the Pearstone CSA-II, Satechi MSA-1, or EzFoto mini-to-universal adapter to convert the G10's proprietary accessory shoe to a universal standard shoe. Figure 7.3 shows various mic options.

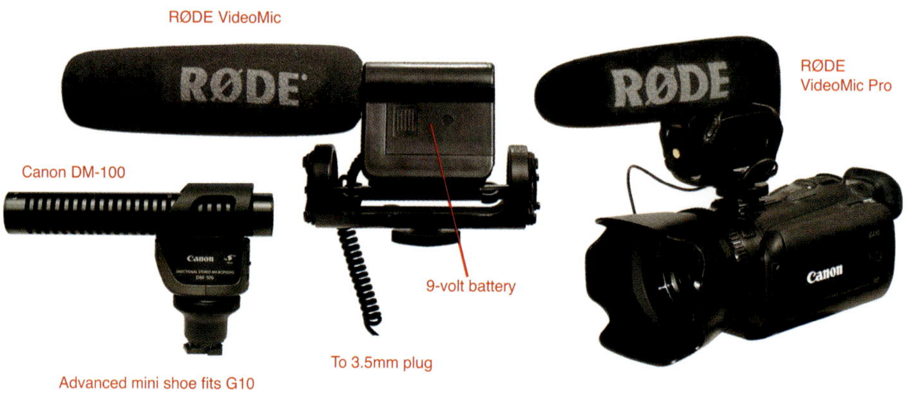

Figure 7.3 Canon and RØDE microphones.

RØDE's newest addition is the VideoMic HD, a short shotgun based on RØDE's top-of-the-line NTG3 professional condenser mic capsule. The microphone itself contains its own built-in digital audio recorder with a small LCD screen, headphone jack, and 3.5mm output. It records to its own memory and simultaneously to cameras like the G10 (and has an XLR adapter for camcorders like the XA10). This opens the possibility of recording long segments of continuous audio inside the microphone while recording video intermittently. The VideoMic HD can also be used as a completely standalone microphone/recorder for double system operation. It records a mono signal on both the left and right track and has a selectable safety mode where it records one mono track 20dB lower than the primary track to virtually eliminate the possibility of digital breakup and distortion from over-modulating. The unit runs on a 9-volt battery and is suspended in a blimp-shaped windscreen and shock mount that attaches to a universal camera shoe. As with other mics, it will need a shoe adapter to mount onto the G10.

The 3.5mm microphone jack on both the G10 and the XA10 is an input that accepts a two-track unbalanced stereo signal from the tip, ring, and sleeve (TRS) of a ⅛-inch plug from a microphone cable. Even though the G10 is limited to the 3.5mm input, professional electret microphones with heavy-duty XLR connectors, like the Sennheiser ME series and the RØDE NTG2, will work on the G10 through a short XLR-to-mini (3.5mm) adapter cable. A range of other XLR balanced-line mics will also work provided they run on batteries instead of phantom power and the cable distance is short because the 3.5mm input does not possess hum-cancelling circuitry like a balanced line input.

Not all adapters are equal. Make sure you use an XLR-to-mini wired for connecting a mono XLR microphone to a stereo male 3.5mm mini-plug. The Hosa XVM-101F ($9.95) is a one-foot adapter cable that will serve this purpose. In addition to being the correct wiring, the XVM-101F uses a right-angled mini-plug that fits snugly against the G10 camcorder. Hosa and many other companies make XLR-to-mini cables wired in various other configurations, and they may all look the same. You want mono-to-stereo, which will put your professional mono signal on both the left and right tracks of the Canon G10. You do not want stereo-to-stereo, which will produce phase cancellation if mono balanced-line audio tracks are treated as stereo in editing or played on a mono television set. Nor do you want mono-to-mono, which will put your signal on only one track, which could cause auto level issues.

Wireless microphones are also an option for the G10. However, the highest quality audio solution for the G10 is to record double system, using a mic on a boom pole with a separate professional recorder and relegating the G10's internal mic to recording reference audio and backup tracks. Wireless microphones and double system are discussed later in this chapter.

External Audio for the XA10

The real value of the XA10 is that it accepts the whole range of balanced-line professional microphones with XLR plugs. The handle for the XA10 includes two XLR professional audio inputs, audio switches, controls, a tally lamp, an infrared light, a microphone shock mount, an additional zoom control, a record switch with lock, and a standard accessory shoe for a second microphone, light, or other accessory. Very likely, the microphone you attach to the camcorder will be a mono short shotgun or a super-cardioid. You might plug a camera-mounted directional mic into one XLR track and a radio mic receiver into the other.

Professional microphones, cables, connectors, and recording circuits use a three-wire balanced-line system with a positive signal, a negatively inverted signal, and a ground that is immune to hum and electromagnetic interference. Balanced-line inputs, outputs, and cables are connected by XLR plugs. An XLR plug is a heavy-duty locking audio connector for professional microphones and audio cables. The three-pronged XLR carries the noise-cancelling balanced-line signal (positive, negative, and ground), and has the potential to simultaneously convey 48 volts of phantom power from the camcorder to a professional microphone. The "X" stands for the Cannon/Switchcraft X series; the "L" for latch, and the "R" for resilient. Three-pronged XLRs are for balanced-line mono microphones, four-pronged XLRs are for battery power cables, and five-pronged XLRs are for balanced-line stereo microphones. The XA10 camcorder has two three-pronged XLR inputs.

Note

Phantom power is a method of sending a 48-volt DC charge supplied by the camcorder or a recorder across the same cable that carries the audio signal to operate a true condenser or the electronics of an electret condenser microphone. This eliminates the need for an external power supply or internal batteries for the microphone.

The mic input switch on the XA10 handle, shown in Figure 7.4, should not have been labeled "INT" and "EXT." It should have been labeled both "INT/EXT" on one side and "XLR" on the other. When set to INT, the XA10's internal microphone is activated unless an external microphone is attached to the 3.5mm input, which overrides the internal mic. Therefore, that position accepts both internal or external microphones. Conversely, the EXT position activates the XLR inputs, but it deactivates any external microphone attached to the 3.5mm input. So the choice is not really between internal and external sources; it is between non-balanced audio and balanced (XLR), which in either case could be external. This is bad labeling. To do this in the limited space of three-letter abbreviations, CAM/XLR might work. Or INT/XLR would at least clarify that one side activates the XLR balanced line (not the 3.5mm external input, which EXT could imply). The XLR audio inputs on the XA10 can be switched from MIC, where the level is measured in millivolts, to MIC+48V, which provides phantom power to a true condenser microphone, to LINE, where the level ranges from 0.2 to 2 volts. Sources providing a line-level signal include mixers, audio preamplifiers, musical instrument equipment, and the line output of a camcorder or recorder.

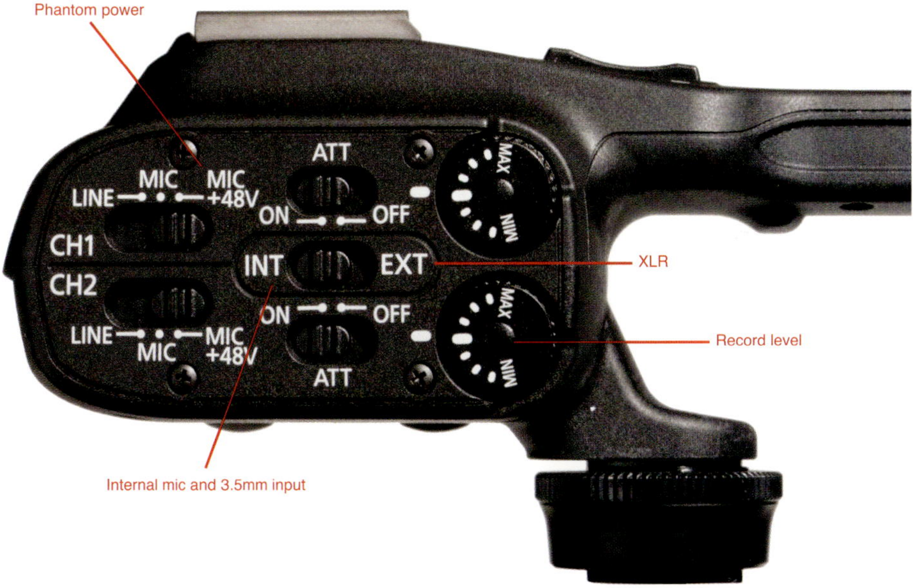

Figure 7.4 Professional audio controls in the XA10 handle.

Microphones come in a number of pickup patterns, and almost all microphones sound good at about one foot away. Omni-directional mics pick up sound equally in all directions and have little proximity effect. But omni mics become very unselective at greater distances. They pick up a lot of unwanted ambient sound unless used close to their source. Conversely, more directional mics, when used closer than six inches, often over-resonate certain frequencies and over-accentuate plosive sounds, breathing noise, lip pop, swallowing, and S sounds.

Unless you can place an omni-directional mic as close as a lavaliere clipped onto the subject, you will need a directional microphone to have selective sound. This will typically be a cardioid (heart-shaped) pattern, a super cardioid, or a short shotgun (lobar) pickup pattern. The more directional the mic, the more reach it will have and the more off-axis sound will be diminished. When the pickup angle of a mic is narrower and more selective, off-axis sound may be somewhat artificialized because high, medium, and low frequencies coming from off axis are rejected at different levels. The extra reach of a shotgun mic can sometimes pick up unwanted sound reflected from the wall behind the subject; very directional mics also have some increased sensitivity directly to the rear. So it is quite possible to have a microphone that is too directional.

Good professional balanced-line microphones for the XA10 include the RØDE NTG-2 and the Sennheiser ME64, ME65, and ME66 in the $250 to $500 range. The ME64 has a cardioid pickup pattern that works if you are fairly close to subjects, like on a boom pole. It has a broad but directional pickup that seems to diminish room noise. It has strong rear-sound rejection and works well as a boom mic. I personally like the Sennheiser ME65. It has a larger diaphragm than the cardioid and shotgun in the Sennheiser ME series. It looks as if it ought to be a handheld mic for singing, but it isn't. The Sennheiser ME65 can be boom mounted or, if you tend to work within two to five feet of your subject, attached to the camcorder with an appropriate shock mount. Its pickup pattern is super-cardioid, which gives it some additional reach for working even a few more feet away when necessary. It has adequate rear-sound rejection. Of this series of Sennheiser microphones, the ME65 is the one that produces sound on location that seems closest to what I subjectively experience live.

The most often used on-camera mic for independent productions, student work, event videography, and electronic news gathering (ENG) is the Sennheiser ME66. As a short shotgun, it has more reach and a narrower pickup pattern than the ME65. It is physically longer and a little boomier sounding. It works well as a boom mic for exteriors. A very comparable choice in audio quality is the RØDE NTG2 ($269), which sells for half the price of the Sennheiser ME66. RØDE is an Australian company whose microphones compete well with industry-standard European and Japanese microphones. The Sennheiser ME series and the RØDE NTG2 are electret condenser microphones that operate with either batteries or phantom power.

If you want even better audio quality, you move into true condenser microphones that must operate with 48 volts of phantom power. These include the RØDE NTG3 ($700), the Sennheiser 416 ($1,000), the Sennheiser MKH-60 ($1,500), the Schoeps CMC6/MK4 super-cardioid ($1,920), and the Schoeps CMIT5U short shotgun ($2,200). If you have chosen the XA10 and are looking for accessories in balance with its price range, you are probably not going to buy a microphone that costs more than the camcorder, so your choice will more likely be the electret condenser mics in the $250–$550 range. However, if the XA10 is a backup for a much more expensive camcorder, you may want to consider these the top-of-the-line microphones. Figure 7.5 shows the Schoeps CMIT5U, Sennheiser ME65, and RØDE NTG2 microphones.

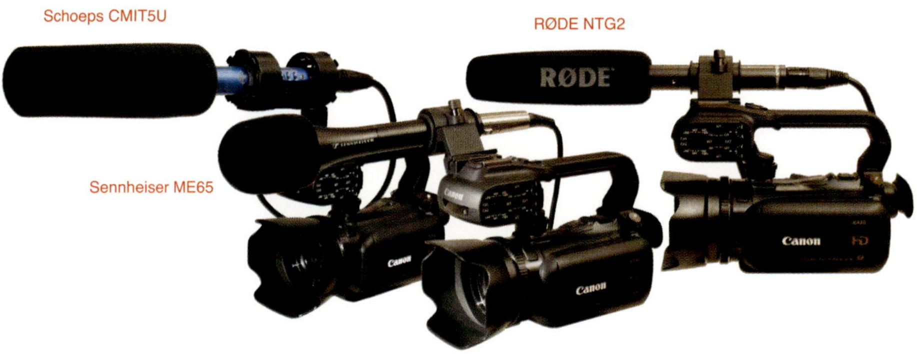

Figure 7.5 Schoeps, Sennheiser, and RØDE microphones.

Almost all professional microphones for film and video are a version a condenser microphone, as opposed to dynamic, crystal, ribbon, or carbon mics. Condenser mics require power from a battery, power supply, or the recorder itself. A true condenser microphone needs 48 volts to place a charge across its condenser plates and run its electronic circuits, which read and amplify subtle changes of capacitance as one of its plates vibrates with sound pressure. Condenser microphones are capable of very high sensitivity and high fidelity with very little inherent noise. The electret is a variant that has condenser plates that are permanently charged by electrostatic means. Electrets still need power to run the circuits that convert changes of capacitance into audio signals. This power is usually supplied from an internal 1.5- or 9-volt battery, but some are designed to run on 48-volt phantom power from the camcorder or recorder like a true condenser microphone. Electrets are usually less expensive than true condensers.

A shotgun (or more typically a short shotgun) microphone is highly directional. It has a lobar pattern that has an acoustic reach akin to the camcorder's telephoto lens and diminished volume from the sides. A short shotgun like the Sennheiser ME66 or RØDE NTG2 is often chosen as an on-camera microphone for picking up on-axis sound. The RØDE NTG2 ($270) has a directional super-cardioid pickup pattern, is 10.94 inches long, and weighs five ounces. On the XA10, the RØDE NTG2 and the Sennheiser ME series mics would use 48 volts of phantom power from an XLR input on the handle. If used on the G10, they will need to be self powered with a 1.5-volt battery and will require a shock mount, a universal shoe adapter, and a 12- to 18-inch XLR-to-3.5mm adapter cable.

Microphone Accessories

The RØDE SM3 is a universal shock mount that accommodates a wide range of microphones. It suspends the mic on elastic bands to isolate it from mechanical vibration and has an adjustable angle with a locking handle on the side, which is useful when mounted on a boom pole. Its base fits a standard photo shoe and also has a ⅜-inch screw hole for mounting on a boom. The RØDE SM4 has the same elastic band assembly for holding the microphone and can also tilt like the SM3. It lacks the photo shoe and is specifically made to fit on ⅝-inch mic stands, ⅜-inch boom poles, ¼-inch tripods, or on a pistol grip (like the $15 Barska Accu handgrip shown in Figure 7.6). The Azden SMH-1 ($28) is a compact, low-profile shock mount made to fit on a camcorder with a standard photo shoe. It also has a ⅜-inch thread for mounting on a boom pole but has no ability to tilt.

Almost all external microphones need a basic foam windscreen because mics react to even a slight puff of wind. A windscreen can also protect the microphone if it gets knocked or dropped. Fur-covered screens that dissipate air pressure and zeppelin-shaped hollow mesh tubes that isolate the microphone in a pocket of air further reduce wind noise beyond the capabilities of a foam screen. Auxiliary wind muffs that wrap around an existing foam windscreen include the RØDE Dead Cat (made of synthetic fur, not road kill), which sells for $39, and the Rycote Windjammer at $46. The RØDE WS6 ($59) is a robust self-contained windscreen that slides over the front of the NTG2 and similar microphones in place of a foam screen, the RØDE WS7 ($59) fits the slightly thinner NTG3 mic, and the Rycote Softie windscreen ($110) comes in sizes to fit most microphones. For an even higher level of wind reduction, the entire microphone is suspended within the blimp-shaped Rycote S-Series Windshield ($269), which comes in an assortment of sizes. Figure 7.6 shows the Rycote Softie, RØDE WS6, RØDE SM4 shock mount, and Barska Accu handgrip.

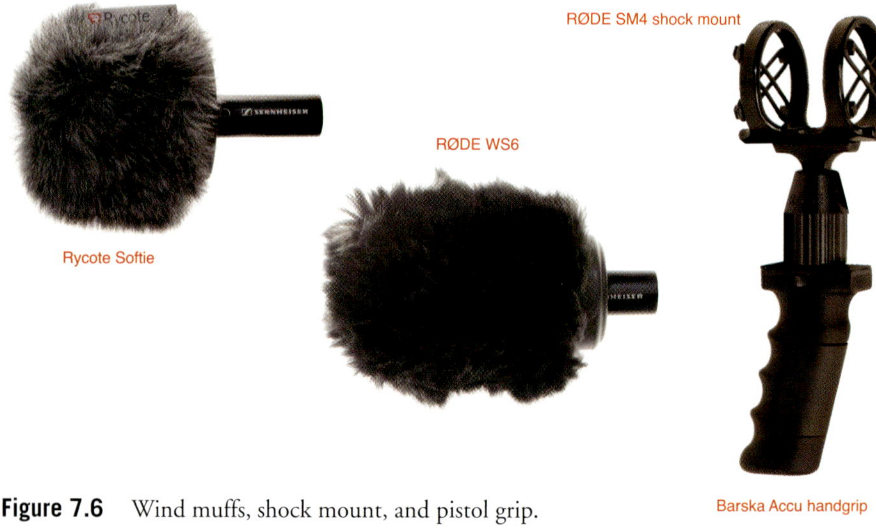

Figure 7.6 Wind muffs, shock mount, and pistol grip.

Often, a cable will appear to be working even though one of its connections is broken or shorted. The result can be hum, low output, susceptibility to electromagnetic interference, intermittent audio, or eventual loss of signal. A Behringer CT100 cable tester ($22) is useful for evaluating XLR and TRS cables and plugs. Its microprocessor circuit can test continuity, correct wiring, proper grounding, intermittent connections, and phantom power, and can provide test tones. It runs on two AA batteries.

Wireless Mics

Canon makes the WM-V1 Bluetooth wireless microphone ($220) for the Vixia HF G10 and XA10 camcorders. Bluetooth has reasonable clarity but a more limited sampling frequency—under 20kHz, compared to 48kHz for digital video and most editing programs. This produces limited fidelity of 500Hz to 7,000Hz compared to more than double that range for a professional radio mic. Even with these limitations, its audio will sound better than the camcorder's built-in mic at distances beyond 20 feet. The WM-V1's microphone is integrated into the transmitter unit, which is about the size of a candy bar. You can clip the transmitter/mic unit onto a lapel, shirt pocket, or belt, but it is a bit awkward. The WM-V1 is much too large and more intrusively visible than a typical clip-on lavaliere mic with a concealable transmitter. The WM-V1 transmitter and receiver each weigh only 1.1 ounces and operate on a AAA battery. Wireless reception is up to 164 feet (50 meters), depending on the environment and line of sight.

It easily picks up handling noise, so it is not an ideal hand-held mic, but it can serve as one if you keep your fingers very still. More typically, the WM-V1 needs to be clipped onto the subject in an area that has no clothing noise. Its sound is clean but a bit thin. The fact that you cannot attach a more convenient external mic is its biggest shortcoming. The whole unit would be considerably improved if the transmitter had an input jack so a much higher quality lavaliere microphone could be plugged in to defeat the built-in mic. Then the transmitter could fit in a pocket while a tiny professional mic is clipped to a lapel.

An interesting feature is that the WM-V1 transmitter and receiver units both have built-in mic capsules and earphone jacks to allow two-way communication, like a walkie-talkie. Only the audio from the transmitter is recorded. This allows the subject to wear an earbud and follow directions from the camera operator up to 150 feet away. The receiver unit clips to the camera strap and its audio output connects to the camcorder's 3.5mm jack. To plug it into one of the XA10's XLR inputs, it would need a male 3.5mm-to-XLR3M adapter like the Sennheiser CL-100.

The WM-V1 is almost identical in design and function to the Sony ECM-AW3 at $149, a savings of $70 (see Figure 7.7). Both brands are omni-directional electret condenser microphones that need to be close to their subject. The Sony ECM-AW3 has a frequency response of 300Hz to 9,000Hz, and each unit weighs one ounce, measures 0.97×3×1.38 inches, and is silver. The Canon WM-V1 measures 1×1.5×2.6 inches and is black. Both the Sony and Canon provide two-way communications while allowing only the audio from the transmitter unit to be recorded.

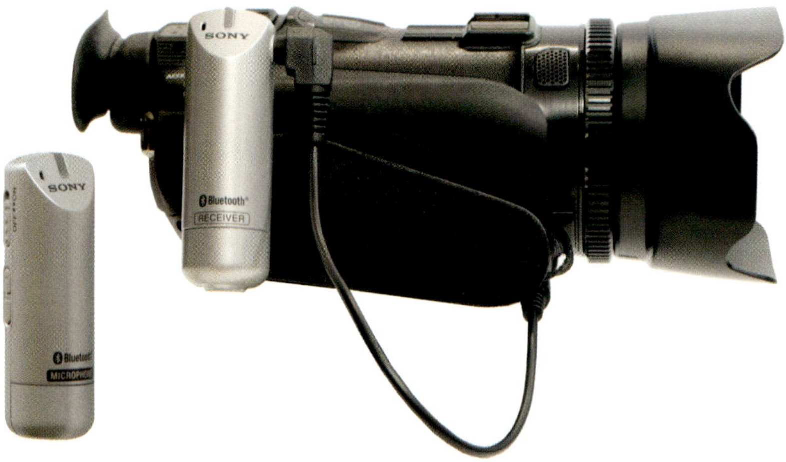

Figure 7.7 The Sony ECM-AW3 Bluetooth wireless microphone transmitter and receiver.

To follow FCC regulations, even professional radio frequency mics have very limited power; otherwise, everyone's mic or wireless telephone would interfere with each other. UHF radio mics work up to about 300 feet depending on conditions. Some frequencies are better than others in terms of transmitting around walls, reflected signals, and metal structures, and avoiding competing radio frequencies in the region. The Sennheiser G3 series is an excellent wireless transmitter and receiver. It accepts a variety of lavaliere mics and each unit has a selectable range of frequencies. "Lavaliere" originally was a term for a pendant or lanyard mic on a string around the neck. As mics became smaller, it was much easier to create versions that simply clipped on. In a professional radio mic system like the Sennheiser EW112PG3A, the lavaliere is about the size of a kernel of corn on the end of a 24-inch wire and it receives its power from the transmitter, which is about the size of a small bar of soap (3.2×2.9×0.9 inches) and weighs 5.6 ounces. The transmitter can be hidden in a pocket, clipped to a belt, taped to the body, or sewn into a costume out of view. The receiver has a 3.5mm or a 3.5mm-to-XLR output plugged into the camcorder.

The best lavaliere mics that fit on a Sennheiser transmitter (or comparable professional unit made by AKG, Audio-Technica, Lectrosonics, Shure, or Sony) are the Sennheiser ME2, the Tram TR50, and the Sanken CO-11D, all shown in Figure 7.8. The Sanken is relatively expensive and may cost around $380 for the microphone alone. Among lavalieres, Sanken is one of the cleanest and crispest—maybe too crisp for some people's taste. It comes in black like most lavaliere mics, but also in tan and other colors. The Tram TR50 is $240 and the Sennheiser ME2 is $140 for the microphone only. Some of these mics come packaged with the transmitter/receiver as a total system for around $600 or more.

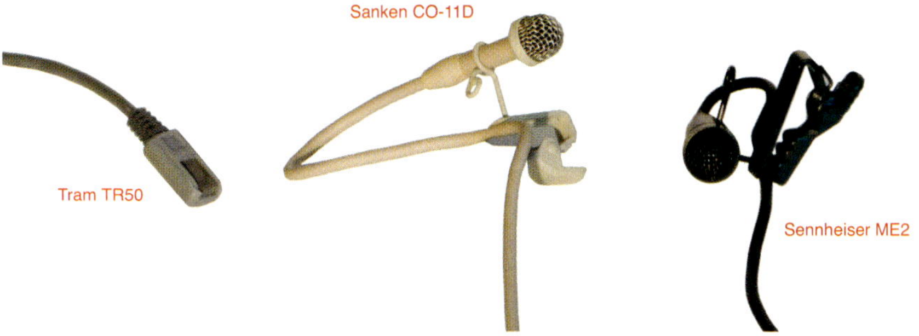

Figure 7.8 Professional lavaliere clip-on microphones.

Instead of having a mic cable from a lavaliere dangling down the front of the subject's shirt, jacket, or necktie, you should put the cable under the shirt or jacket if possible. Bring out the microphone near the collar, on the necktie, or on the lapel. Attach it with about an inch and a half of curved cable clipped underneath the lapel it so that the wire doesn't immediately hang from the mic itself. This helps reduce cable and clothing noise. Depending on personal taste and the individual frequency range, resonance, vocal plosives, and sibilance, certain lavaliere mics may match better than others to a particular voice. Lavaliere mics pick up sound a bit off axis because they are about 6 to 8 inches below mouth level. They are probably about 18 inches away from what the subject's hands are doing. So through proximity to the mouth, they supply a strong emphasis on voice and a de-emphasis of ambient sound. Lavaliere microphones are usually omni-directional. The omni pattern does not change voice quality as the subject turns his or her head. Lavalieres are highly selective simply because they are placed within inches of the sound source.

Sometimes a lavaliere can sound too close, like someone speaking in your ear, and may not sonically match the visual space of a medium shot or long shot. But in many cases, clean sound with too much proximity is better than distant sound marred by less intelligibility and too much ambience. In general, lavalieres lack sound perspective and to some degree lose a sense of the speaker being in a real acoustic space.

A boom mic usually sounds more real than a lavaliere, but lavalieres are useful because they can be tied to a pocket-sized transmitter instead of to the camcorder or can be wired to a small digital recorder hidden on the subject to provide a considerable amount of mobility.

If you want to hide a lavaliere mic under clothing, you have to isolate the mic-chafing movements to eliminate clothing noise. For fiction productions, costumes can be made to conceal a lavaliere and its transmitter using soft, non-abrasive cloth materials like cotton or wool designed with no clothing movement over the mic head. Or you can attach a mic directly to the skin of a person's body under clothing using a Doctor Scholl's Foam Ease Corn Cushion. Designed for protecting a corn or blister, the pad's oval hole serves as a cradle to hold the microphone head. Put spirit gum on one side to hold the pad against skin, and peel the cover off the original adhesive side to secure the pad to the underside of clothing to prevent rubbing noises from cloth movement. Spirit gum is an adhesive that you can buy from a dance store or costume shop. Most people can tolerate spirit gum on their skin, but for some it itches or produces an allergic reaction, so test it beforehand. Isolate the cable a few inches farther down by taping it to skin with adhesive tape so that cable movement is arrested at that secondary point. It is also possible to hide a lavaliere mic in hair or on someone's shoulder or use it as a plant mic hidden within something as long as the person speaking is only a few inches away.

Mixing Internal and External

The G10/XA10 can mix an external microphone in the 3.5mm input with the internal microphone. The ideal would be a mono recording of the internal mic on one track and the external mic on the other. In this way, one would serve as the protection track for the other, or as a wide pickup from the camcorder and an isolated boom mic or wireless emphasizing the subject. They can be mixed in postproduction where appropriate volume levels, compression, and equalization can be applied. Saving mixing until the editing phase allows you to choose whether to blend the two tracks, place them individually in a pan control between left and right, or choose particular moments to emphasize one over the other. But Canon did not provide separate discrete tracks as an option; it simply provides the less useful option of recording external and internal sources irrevocably together.

This is a rather amateur solution for something that can be done with much more judgment and precision in postproduction. If you commit to mixing the two mic sources in the camcorder, there is no way to separate them later. If the professional mic is mounted on the camcorder, one of the problems of mixing it with the built-in mic is that the two are only a few inches from each other. When you mix two mics in close proximity, the result has less fidelity because the same sound hits each mic at a displacement of a few inches. Instead of the sounds being fully added to each other, the spatial delay causes some frequencies to cancel each other and you end up with thinner sound. To minimize phase cancellation and loss of fidelity, the rule of thumb is if you are going to mix two live mics, they should not be aimed at the same subject, and they need to be at least three times farther apart from each other than they are from their source so each mic receives substantially different sound signals.

If your external mic is on a long cable or a radio mic at a considerable distance from the camera's internal mic, the two tracks can be mixed without phase cancellation. But mixing them in the camcorder is still a bad idea compared to having control of each track's level, equalization, compression, pan position, and the ability to cross-fade or choose one track over another moment by moment in postproduction. The alternative is what was called "double system": recording the additional track or tracks on a completely separate professional recorder.

Double System Recording

Double system is the most professional way to record audio for video. This involves having a separate dedicated sound person with the ability to get closer to the primary sound source while you shoot on-screen picture with reference or backup sound in the camcorder. You still might have a professional mic on the camera to get on-axis sound for wherever you point the lens, while someone else with a high-quality digital recorder and a boom pole records from a roving position. One problem with all of this is occasionally getting the sound person in the shot, but with LCD screens and your ability to see what is outside versus inside the frame, you should be able to avoid this.

Double system gives you much better sound, more options, and much more control in the editing process. A mic mounted on the camera has limitations. It does not always sound like the perceived world in the same way that a boom position does. If you shoot straight at someone from a distance of several feet, the mic mounted on the camera will be nearly equidistant from the subject's hands as it is from the subject's mouth. Consequently, the on-camera mic does not make a huge distinction between the noise made by characters' hands, their gestures, clothing, or props versus human voice. With a boom position, the mic is pointed diagonally downward from about a foot and a half or two feet above the subject's head. According to the inverse square law, sound falls off according to the square of its distance; because the boom mic is closest to the subject's voice, everything else is exponentially quieter.

The sound quality of Hollywood film comes in part from using boom microphones. Sound emphasis is placed in a hierarchy when recorded from two feet above with the greatest emphasis on voice, less on hand noise, and least on feet. The overhead boom mic is twice as far from hands as it is from the mouth. Consequently, noise from prop handling, clothing, handshakes, clapping, working, and whatever else that might happen with hands is about a quarter as loud as voice noise because sound falls off according to the square of its distance. Footsteps are maybe about 1⁄16 as loud because they are approximately four times farther from the overhead mic than the voice.

When we occupy the same sonic environment, our brain filters out air-conditioning noise, the resonance of the room, peripheral street sound, clothing noise, and the hiss or hum of lights and appliances, and we focus our attention on voice. We perceive the sound as being relatively clean because our brain is constructing a sonic image from binaural hearing, choosing to select sound from certain directions and cancelling out other sounds by coordinating what we hear and what we see, along with our knowledge and expectations, to create what we think we hear. A microphone from a camera position sounds much noisier and much more distracting than what we perceive when we are present in the actual space. To get the subjective quality of sound that you perceive live at 10 feet, you might have to record with a boom at two or three feet away to replicate the effect of all of that focusing of aural attention that the ear and the brain can do. Proximity is one of the major ways of being selective with a microphone. This is why relatively closer sound from a well-placed boom pole sounds so good.

A boom mic tends to provide a natural sound perspective. When you frame a tight close-up, the boom may be six inches to a foot overhead, it might be two feet overhead in a medium shot, and three or more feet for a long shot. Consequently, the boom produces a different sense of vocal presence and a different balance of ambience from each of those positions that more perfectly matches the pictorial space than the camcorder can. The zoom mic on the G10/XA10 can approximate sound perspective but never as effectively as a boom can accomplish with its proximity and selectivity, which generally need to be closer than the camera.

It is still very useful to have a good-quality mic mounted on the camcorder during double-system filming. The camera provides a reference track, a protection track, and a potentially useful synchronous track of the sound of what you pointed the lens at. The double-system sound is synchronized in the editing process by lining it up with the camera track, after which you can delete the camera's track. There may be occasional moments when the on-camera mic might provide better sound than the double-system boom mic, like when the boom could not get to the right position in time or when the sound perspective from the camera seems more appropriate. With double system, there is the possibility for the boom operator to follow the most significant audio while the camcorder operator follows the most significant visuals. The boom might stay on the speaker while the camcorder is free to pan to a reaction shot.

To aid in synchronization, each take can be slated with a clapboard or a smart slate to provide a precise visual and aural starting point. This would typically be the process when working from a shot-by-shot script for a fiction film. However, as long as the camcorder is recording a scratch track, backup track, or alternative audio track, the high-quality audio from the dedicated recorder can simply be synced in the editing stage alongside the camera's audio track until it perfectly lines up. Then delete the track of lesser quality—usually the one recoded through the camcorder.

Potential drawbacks to a boom mic include needing an extra person, getting boom shadows or the boom itself in the shot, and the fact that some subjects find it disconcerting to have a pole hanging over their head. Whoever operates the boom has to be very aware of boom shadows, the angle of the microphone, coordinating with the camera operator, the dynamics of the situation, and not knocking people in the head. Cardioid mics, super-cardioid mics, and some short shotgun mics work well on booms. A more directional shotgun mic could make the boom angle too critical for following an active speaker or for multiple subjects. Consider some of the same microphones discussed earlier in the chapter, including the RØDE VideoMic HD, which contains its own internal recorder.

One of the best field recorders for professional-quality double-system audio is the Marantz PMD661, which sells for $599. It runs for five hours on four standard AA batteries, has two 48-volt phantom-powered XLR inputs, records onto an SDHC card, and creates 24-bit/96kHz uncompressed WAV audio files. In a lower price range, the Zoom H4n at $279 to $299 is a standout. It is not as sturdy and its preamps are not quite as clean as the Marantz, but it can supply phantom power to run high-end professional microphones. It is very compact (2.75×6.1×1.4 inches), has two XLR inputs, and can record 24-bit/96kHz WAV files onto an SDHC card. The Zoom H4n will last about six hours in standard record mode running on two AA batteries. Figure 7.9 shows the Marantz PMD661, the Zoom H4n, and the aforementioned CT100 cable tester.

The RØDE Micro Boom pole ($49) is a lightweight three-section pole that extends to 6.75 feet and weighs less than 13 ounces. It has a ⅜-inch thread that fits the RØDE SM3 and SM4 shock mounts. More expensive poles are often longer and have built-in cabling and XLR connectors. On a basic boom pole like this one, the simple and direct way to prevent the hanging cable from dragging and creating noise is to grip the cable against the pole with your hand as you hold the boom. A more permanent solution is to use Velcro cable ties, rubberized bands, or cable clips to secure the cable in a couple of places along the pole. RØDE and manufacturers like Gitzo, K-Tek, PSC, and Rycote make longer, more elaborate, and much more expensive booms, but Micro Boom is adequate for lightweight on-the-run productions.

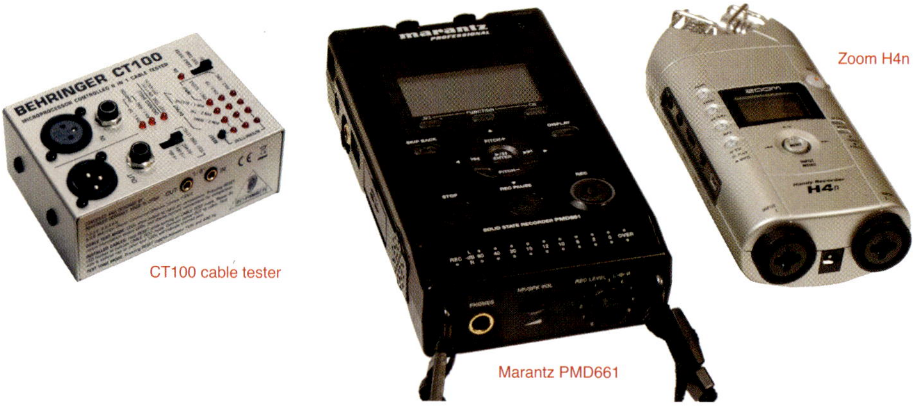

Figure 7.9 Cable tester and audio field recorders.

Air or Room Tone

Room Tone is a 20- to 30-second recording of the "silence" of a location that captures its unique acoustic presence while no overtly articulated sounds are being made. Each space has its own resonance. To label and identify this nearly silent recording, verbally slate the head of the clip by saying, "Begin 30 seconds of room tone." Then, after 30 seconds, say, "End room tone." The volume should be set for the head and tail voice; the room tone itself appears with no noticeable volume level. Room tone, which is sometimes called "air," is used to fill in pauses, clean up noisy moments, and make sound bridges when editing dialogue or action tracks that were recorded at that location.

If you are shooting double system using a separate digital audio recorder, then the verbal slate is your only identification of the air track—in which case you should include the name of the production, the date, the time, and the location in the verbal slate. If you record room tone with the camcorder, you might add a visual slate with the words "air" or "room tone" along with the production, date, time, and location written on a card or displayed on an iPad app like Movie Slate or DSLR Slate. You could otherwise depend on the video picture to identify the location and the AVCHD data files to identify time and date, but when you have multiple air tracks in the editing phase, the visual and audible slates on the clip itself will come in handy.

Here are some tips when recording air or room tone:

- Place the mic at a similar angle and position as for dialogue or action.
- Leave the record level as previously set for dialogue (or at the level of the verbal slate).

- Call for quiet on the location.
- Visually slate production/date/time and the words "air" or "room tone."
- Verbally slate, "Begin room tone (or air)."
- Record 30 seconds of silent location.
- Verbally slate, "End room tone."

Prepping the Environment

Getting the sound you want and minimizing the sound you don't want involves scouting the location and fine-tuning the acoustic environment. Make test recordings and play them back at a high level through high-quality headphones. Listen for cleanness of recording versus unwanted reverberation, hum, rumble, and ambience. Turn off noisy heat, air conditioning, refrigerator, and appliances. Close windows and doors.

If the room sounds too hollow, this is usually because opposing parallel surfaces reflect sound waves back and forth, causing reverberation with a long decay time that muddies each syllable of speech. In an ideal acoustic space for voice, 50 percent of the room is hard and reflective, but each hard reflective surface faces a parallel surface that absorbs sound. If the ceiling is hard, then the floor should have carpet. If a wall is hard plaster or glass, the opposite wall should have drapery, sound blankets, acoustic foam, or soft furniture to absorb or break up parallel waves. Under these conditions, audio will be considerably cleaner.

Environment Checklist

- Scout and record audio tests on location.
- Sound dampen opposite parallel surfaces.
- Break parallel waves with irregular shapes .
- Use sound-absorbing carpet, shag throw rugs, acoustic foam, or blankets.
- Use quieter costumes and shoes.
- Use low-noise props.
- Close windows and doors if possible.
- Turn off heat, air conditioning, refrigerator, and appliances.
- Cover noisy appliances with a "blimp" (a metal or plastic container to block noise) or a "barney" (a soft cover or jacket to absorb and muffle noise).

Field Equipment Checklist

- Use a high-quality mic (Sennheiser, RØDE, Schoeps).
- Match mic/recorder impedance (ohms).
- Match power level (attenuator, mic, line).
- Match mic/recorder wiring (proper cable and adapter).
- Place phantom power in the correct position (on/off).
- Use a windscreen, Rycote, zeppelin, or Dead Cat.
- Shock-mount the microphone.
- Do not move fingers while handholding a mic.
- Mic reasonably close to the sound source (boom position is ideal).
- Position the mic away from unwanted ambience.
- Record double system if possible.
- Record peaks below zero, with average peaks at –12.
- Use balanced-line (XLR) cables.
- Check cable wiring and ground.
- Use the shortest possible cables.
- Loop and secure cable and isolate cable movement.
- Keep audio cables from being near or parallel to AC power lines.
- Always monitor with headphones.

Postproduction Options

- Use high-pass, low-pass, notch, graphic, parametric, and equalization filters.
- Use digital noise reduction (DNR) like Soundtrack Pro, Sound Soap Pro, and ProTools.
- Use ADR (dubbing, looping) to replace bad sound (discussed next).
- Use Foley techniques to create or enhance sound images (discussed below).
- Generate air and room tone as filler and for audio bridges.
- Mask unwanted ambience with music or meaningful ambience.
- Apply compression.

ADR

ADR, short for "automated dialogue replacement" or "additional dialogue recording," is the process of re-recording to improve or change the verbal performance or the acoustic quality of a shot or scene. ADR is usually done while listening to automated (or hand-cued) repeated segments of an original track and recording the subject speaking two or three audio takes of each segment under ideal acoustic conditions.

Dialogue replacement is easy enough to do for an independent or student media maker if the amount of ADR is not extensive. You need a quiet environment, a high-quality recorder, a high-quality microphone at an appropriate distance to match the sound perspective of the scene, and a way to play back clips in the camcorder or on a laptop that can be heard only through headphones. The subject wears headphones and speaks in unison with the original playback audio for a couple of repeats, and then continues in rhythm for a couple more repeats without the playback track (which often produces a more natural take). The replacement dialogue is placed on an editing timeline parallel to the original sync audio track and tweaked until the original and the replacement play in perfect unison. Then the original track is deleted.

Moments within performances can be improved with ADR. In some cases, an actor's voice is completely replaced by another, as in the Italian neo-realist film *The Bicycle Thief* directed by Vittorio Sica, in which the main role is visually played by a non-actor and his voice is dubbed by a professional actor. Most of the time, ADR is used to replace moments that were marred by unwanted ambient sound, a muffed line, or some other unintended problem. Sometimes it is used intentionally where good sync sound was impossible, like when shooting in a noisy environment. So a reference track is recorded with the intention of replacing it with ADR. This opens the possibility that scenes can be verbally coached by the director from off-screen while the camera is rolling because the original scratch track will be deleted.

Foley Sound

Foley is the process of creating, recording, and using sound effects that are added to a scene to provide appropriately expressive acoustic images that match the visuals. Foley sounds are created by watching segments of the production, making a list of sounds that need to be enhanced, and generating them in a sound studio with the proper mic and sound perspective. Sounds like approaching or receding footsteps, clothing noise, a creaking floor, bolting a door, chopping vegetables, preparing dinner, or a punch to the abdomen are created by mimicking actual sound sources and then editing them into the sound design of the production.

Some sounds are created in the pace and rhythm that they appear in the extended scene while watching the scene itself, and others are recorded piece by piece for editing to exact frames. Foley sound images fill in moments where there is no original sound at all, replace the meager sounds of props in an original sound track, or replace real sounds that need to be recorded under better conditions. Having an original track makes it easier to cue and edit the Foley sounds—for example, finding the exact frame to replace an originally recorded door slam with one that has a sense of finality, or replacing the snap of a prop pistol with a full gunshot sound. Not every sound needs to be heard—not even every footstep—only those that should enter or nearly enter the level of the audience's consciousness.

The process is named after director and sound artist, Jack Foley, who pioneered these techniques in the early sound era of motion pictures. Foley sound is often necessary because sync audio recording is optimized for voice and may not produce perfect sound effects. Enhancing a sound specifically to alter our impression of the shot is also called "sweetening." A neutral shot of a dog with its mouth barely open could have a subdued growl, a tired exhale, or a whimper that would change the impression of the shot.

Foley is used all the time in fiction productions. However, it is ethically wrong in news footage and legally wrong in video evidence presented in a courtroom. Foley sound is a complicated issue in documentary. It has ethical ramifications in documentary if it is taken to the point that it misleads and misrepresents material presented as visual fact. However, combat footage from World War I and in most cases from World War II was shot with silent cameras. A documentary presenting the experience of being under fire on the battle field would be an incredible distortion if presented in unnatural silence rather than having visually justified sounds dubbed in with perfect perspective, synchronization, and scale. Even documentary media makers that show us everyday life might record additional actual sounds in the environment to be used later in the editing to flesh out moments when the camcorder's mic failed to capture the aural experience. After all, documentary is not reality itself but a statement about reality made through selection, editing, and juxtaposition of sound and picture. There are ways to do this with integrity and ways that could cross a delicate line into misrepresentation.

Foley sound is not beyond the means of an independent or student media maker. When done well, Foley brings a scene alive without calling attention to itself. Visual images seem more tangible when accompanied with the appropriate sound. Foley can help present the world more like the sensual experience of actually being there instead of the noisy, cluttered, undigested, and often thin sonic experience that is typically captured with a single mic on a camcorder.

8

Shooting in Available Light

The G10/XA10's portability, image stabilization, low-light capabilities, SMART AUTO, programmed modes, and manual controls make it an ideal camcorder for shooting under available light conditions. Available light has the potential to look natural to its location and often provides expressive visuals that are more interesting, more varied, and more justified than conventional setups of artificial light. The challenge for working with available light is to enhance visual meaning and provide emphasis/de-emphasis, composition, and progression primarily through controlling the camera within existing conditions.

When shooting in daylight, the major lighting variables are time of day, weather conditions, and shaping the effect of the light with the camera itself through exposure, color balance, framing, and where you place the camera in relation to the subject, sun, and sky. Positioning the camera in relation to the sun makes the difference between flat frontal lighting, 45° modeling of highlight and shadow, side-lighting that bisects the figure with highlight and shadow, three-quarter backlighting, or a silhouetted figure in backlight. Selective framing shapes the appearance of daylight further through juxtaposing foreground and background relationships: bright subject/bright background, bright subject/shaded background, shaded subject/bright background, shaded subject/shaded background, dark hair/bright sky, light hair/dark foliage, *et cetera.*

One of the most problematic situations for shooting is a partially sunny day with small dense clouds intermittently traversing the sun. You never know from minute to minute whether you have direct light, obscured light, or radical exposure changes in the middle of a shot. At best, the clouds on an intermittently sunny day may provide an interesting skyscape as a background for a low-angle composition. Clear sunlight or completely overcast can be accommodated more easily.

Even shooting on rainy or snowy days has possibilities. Media makers often put off shooting because the weather is bad, without considering that their subject might have effectively been shot in the rain as long as the camcorder is protected from moisture with an umbrella or rain barney, or by shooting from windows, porches, or from within a car. The textural qualities of wetness, water ripples, light reflections from wet surfaces, and the image of rain itself are among a whole range of expressive and visually interesting possibilities with available light.

The process of shooting in available daylight involves checking the weather, then shooting in the bright sun, overcast, rain, fog, sleet, snow, or wind if appropriate; waiting for the appropriate conditions; or rescheduling entirely. Each weather condition has its own challenges. Even bright sunlight offers difficulties because of the extreme contrast between direct sunlight and shade, which extends beyond the range of the camcorder, and the fact that the sun's angle and consequent camera positions change noticeably as the day progresses.

Scouting

To be prepared to use available light expressively, it would be ideal to scout the location the day before shooting. For direct sunlight, log the usable angles of the sun versus time of day, taking digital stills to test for effective camera positions and visual compositions. Shooting location stills like these is an ideal task for the still photo mode of the G10/XA10 because the photos will be taken with the identical lens, image processor, and number of pixels as the eventual video, and are automatically encoded with date and time. This is a perfect reference for documenting the evolving appearance of daylight from particular angles at precise points in time.

Scouting an exterior is done to plan when the light will be optimum and where you can place the camera the following day. It may be that certain kinds of shots can be taken at 10 o'clock in the morning and other shots at three o'clock in the afternoon based on where the sun is and where shadows fall. You may want to exploit a particular time of day—for example, using sunrise or sunset as a background; shooting very early in the morning or late in the afternoon when the sun is low on the horizon, creating very long shadows; or shooting mid-morning and mid-afternoon for a classic balance of light and shadow.

To aid in the scouting process, Sun Seeker is an iPhone and iPad app that uses GPS and magnetometer data to lay out the hour-by-hour path of the sun for a particular location. For planning optimal light conditions, Sun Seeker presents a map view that shows the direction of sunlight for each daylight hour, a flat compass view, and a dimensional augmented-reality camera view. It also calculates precise times for sunrise and sunset.

If you are shooting an exterior event that must happen at a predetermined time, it is useful to visit the location at the equivalent time on the previous day and take test photos to see what problems need to be solved. If you cannot adapt the production schedule to the optimum lighting conditions, then at least know what to expect. Whether you scout or simply adapt as you arrive, your primary controls of sunlight are as follows:

- Dealing with the angle of the sun
- The physical placement of your camcorder
- The composition in your frame, including foreground and background
- Using reflectors to improve or control the light

Using a Reflector

A reflector can shape and redirect sunlight to provide a key light in a shaded area, a fill light in a sunny area to control the density of shadows, a dimensional accent from the side or rear, or a pool of light that heightens part of the background. Shooting under direct sunlight without a reflector can produce unnaturally dense shadows because video cannot detect as much shadow detail as the human eye. On a bright day, opaque shadows will not be noticed in a long shot, but when you move in for a close-up, spectators usually expect to see detail in the facial shadows. With limited crews and equipment, wide shots in contrasty sunlight are photographed without a reflector, whereas close-ups and waist-high shots will typically add fill light to prevent excessive highlight/shadow contrast using a reflector held just beyond the frame. In available light, a reflector is an effective way to regulate shadow detail and keep it from being crushed by the limited range of video. Controlling the angle and distance of this reflector will make the difference between deep dramatic shadows with details on the edge of visibility, to natural appearing contrast, to pale unnoticeable shadows.

Metallic reflectors made from foil, metal sheets, or metallic fabric are pebbled or textured to even out irregularities and hotspots. Smooth mirror-like reflectors can be used only on subjects like foliage, where unevenness will not be detected. Lightly textured metallic reflectors provide a pool of directional light. If you were to make a reflector by covering several square feet of cardboard, foamcore, or plywood with shiny aluminum foil, you should crinkle the foil first and then stretch it out.

Matte white reflectors of cloth or foamcore can be used to produce soft fill light for close-ups. Foamcore (or foam board) is a lightweight polystyrene foam sheet laminated with white poster paper on each side, available in art stores. Compared to metallic reflectors, matte reflectors do not throw as much light and need to be relatively close to the subject. Matte white reflectors are generally flattering and subtle, and simply restore to the shadow side of the subject some of the facial detail that you would expect to see with the naked eye but would otherwise be lost within the narrow exposure range of video.

Covering larger areas, Hollywood films might fill the shadow side of bright sunlight with banks of 10,000-watt arc or HMI (metal halide) lights or use 20-foot-long reflectors, or might even go the other direction by hanging a 20×20 foot overhead cloth mesh called a "butterfly" to diminish direct sunlight while the non-directional light from the sky remains the same on the shadow side. For those of us working with palm-sized camcorders, the instrument of choice is a foldable 42- to 52-inch circular reflector made of cloth (silvered on one side and matte white on the other) stretched over a spring steel hoop. The reflector can be held by hand or clamped to a light stand that has a proper accessory arm.

LiteDisc by Photoflex is a particularly good brand used by professionals. A 42-inch Photoflex circular reflector that collapses and folds to one-third its diameter for storage sells for approximately $45, and a five-in-one model with silver, white, gold, and black surfaces that zip over a 42-inch translucent hoop sells for about $95. For those looking for a bargain, Neewer imports from China a 43-inch five-in-one collapsible reflector (model 110CM) that sells for approximately $13 on Amazon.com. It holds Amazon's number-one sales rank in its category. The stitching on the Neewer model is coarser than on the Photoflex, its surfaces are a bit more wrinkled, and its carrying bag is made of lighter cloth, but the quality and evenness of the reflected light from each brand are nearly identical. The Neewer reflector is so inexpensive, there is no excuse for not owning one. (See Figure 8.1.)

The translucent surface on the Neewer 110CM can be used as a reflector or as diffuser with light passing through it. The black surface is used for negative fill, keeping light off of things. If a shiny object or a bright surface casts unwanted light into the scene, the black disc can be used to block the light. It can also be used to shade the camera from unwanted light, flagging the lens to prevent flare or glare. The silvered surface can redirect sunlight to illuminate something that is otherwise in shade or be used as a key light on the subject when the sun is supplying backlight. The white reflector considerably softens the light and has much less reach compared to the silvered surface. White is used as a subtle fill light, particularly in close-ups.

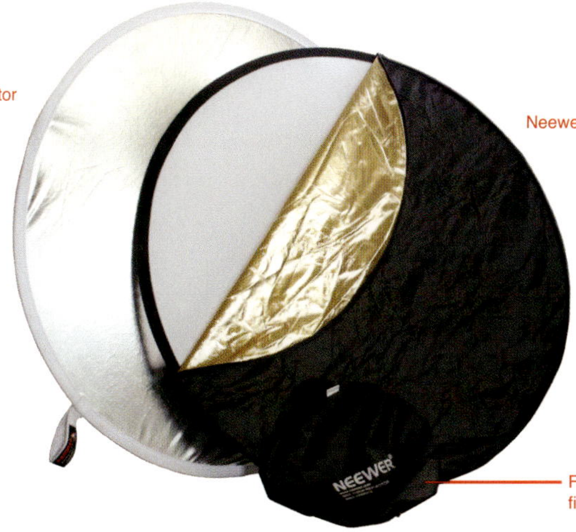

Figure 8.1 LiteDisc and Neewer reflectors.

A gold reflector can be used to warm pale skin or suggest the light from a fire or a candle. Ironically, however, one of the major uses of the gold reflector is actually to cool the background. To do this, you cast reflected golden light on the subject while excluding it from the background. Then manually set the white balance referenced to a white card or diffuser dome held in the golden light. The effect will be a subject with normal skin tones in an environment that is decidedly cooler. If this is done in a crowd, it can create a special kind of emphasis where the subject looks humanized and everyone else looks icy. This technique, whether it is accomplished by the lighting or by a colorist in postproduction, is often applied in feature films.

Exposure in Available Light

Selective exposure is an important control in available-light situations. Bright sunlight (with its inherent deep shadows) and sunny days with intermittent clouds offer particular challenges to finding an ideal exposure and to maintaining consistent exposures that will match in editing. It is absolutely essential to avoid overexposing the highlights, which can easily happen in bright sunlight and light that continually varies. Burned-out highlights that have lost all their detail cannot be redeemed in postproduction.

You might try to deal with available light using SMART AUTO, which lets the camcorder analyze and compute exposure and color balance parameters based on 38 types of scenes. Alternatively, you can shoot in available light with much more personal control in a programmed mode with selected manual overrides chosen to match the conditions, or achieve maximum control by shooting in full manual mode.

As discussed in Chapter 2, "Run-and-Gun Shooting," SMART AUTO is engaged when the camcorder's AUTO/M/CINEMA switch is set to AUTO. It is important to observe the icons in the upper-left corner of the touchscreen to confirm how SMART AUTO is interpreting the scene. The icons will indicate a stationary portrait, people moving, a blue sky background, a gray sky background, vivid red/green colors, a sunset, close objects, extreme close objects (tele-macro), a night scene, a spotlight, and various combinations of backlit situations. SMART AUTO adjusts focus, image stabilization, depth of field, f/stop, shutter speed, gain, color balance, saturation, and contrast to suit each type of scene. If the icons are at odds with your intentions, and if the visual result is not what you want, you should move into Rec. Program mode or full Manual Exposure.

If you simply want plain vanilla automatic exposure that is not second-guessing your intent and your scene's content, switch to M mode and select Programmed AE (choose FUNC > Rec. Program > Programmed AE). In addition to Face Detection and Touch & Track (as you also had in AUTO mode), Programmed AE mode gives you several ways to focus, including the ability to toggle between manual and auto focus, to instantly engage manual focus by turning the ring on the lens, or to engage Touch Focus. Programmed AE also provides selections in the program panel to set a particular white balance, backlight compensation, automatic gain limit, or +/– Exposure control. To access these settings, choose FUNC and select WB, BLC, AGC, Focus, and/or +/– Exposure.

If you want even more specific control over a particular aspect of exposure, then choose FUNC > Rec. Program and select Av (aperture value), Tv (time value), or full Manual Exposure instead of Programmed AE. In Av, Tv, full Manual Exposure, or Programmed AE itself (under +/– Exposure or AGC Limit), an aspect of exposure can be assigned to the CUSTOM key and dial (see Chapter 4, "Controlling Exposure"). The CUSTOM key and dial are particularly useful for ongoing manual adjustments of exposure in the extremes of bright sunlight and shade, and in intermittent clouds and sunlight. Expose so that zebra patterns do not exceed 100 percent in the highlights.

If your available light conditions perfectly fit the Portrait, Sports, Night Scene, Snow, Beach, Sunset, Low Light, Spotlight, or Fireworks settings, then you can select one of these Scene Program modes. When you choose FUNC > Rec. Program, only one scene choice initially appears among the panels. By default, this will be the scene type that had been previously cued (Sunset, Night Scene, and so on). If you tap the scene icon marked by the letters "SCN," all nine choices then appear (see Figure 8.2):

- Portrait
- Sports
- Night Scene
- Snow
- Beach
- Sunset
- Low Light
- Spotlight
- Fireworks

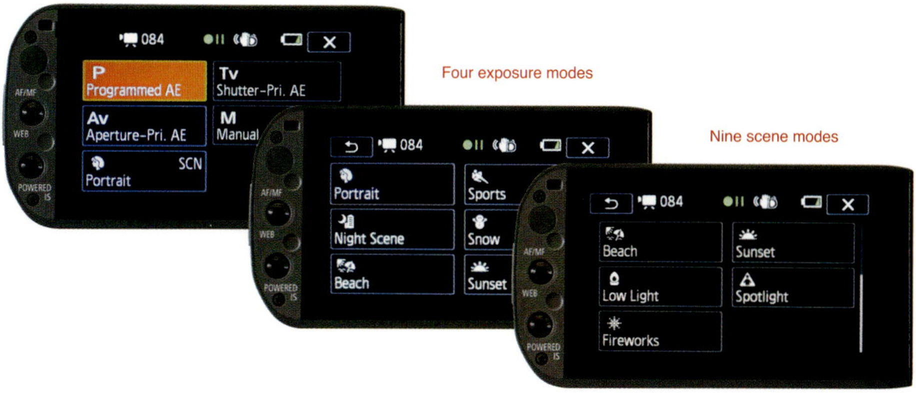

Figure 8.2 P, Tv, Av, and M offer four approaches to exposure; nine scene modes optimize exposure, color, focus, and image stabilization for particular shooting conditions.

Overcast

It is much easier to shoot video on an overcast day. The advantage of such soft nondirectional light is that you can shoot from almost any angle—front, side, back, high, or low—without encountering excessive brightness or loss of detail in shadows. The angle of light does not noticeably change every five minutes the way bright sunlight does. The disadvantage is the subject can easily look flat or bland.

Instead of having to cope with the overly high contrast of direct sunlight, the major problem of an overcast day is the bland lack of contrast. Framing foreground/background relationships with chiaroscuro (playing light against dark or dark against light) can make up for the lack of contrast range in the light itself. Providing one brilliant color (like a red sweater) or including a white reference and black reference in the shot can also keep an otherwise gray scene from being bland.

White reference and black reference are compositional concepts that affect the way the spectator perceives the lighting and tonal range of a shot. If a composition contains a small amount of nearly fully exposed white and a small amount of rich black, then everything in between will look as if it had been intended even if the rest of the composition is overly dark, overly light, or blandly narrow in its range of tones. The eye and brain of the spectator sense that this is normal because white is white and black is black. Psychologically, black does not look fully black except in the presence of white, and our brains understand the relative value of pale, medium, and dark tones when perceived in relation to black and white. In fact, the darkness in a night scene will look more effective if there is a white reference in the shot, and rather gray scenes with a limited tonal range will seem richer and more tangible with a black reference and white reference in the composition. When working with highly diffused light like an overcast day, a black reference and white reference in the composition can compensate for the lack of highlight and shadow and provide the impression of a more complete range of tones.

Full AUTO mode with SMART AUTO will generally produce consistent results on an overcast day. There will be fewer surprises and misreadings because the light itself is more consistent. However, whether shooting in soft overcast light or harsh sunlit situations, shooting in complete Manual Exposure or Programmed AE, Tv, or Av are much better choices because they allow the options of exposure controls on the touchscreen or the CUSTOM dial, plus manual controls over focus when you want them. You can use zebra patterns to establish whether you have a white reference at nearly full exposure in the frame. If you are in either manual mode or +/– Exposure mode, the waveform monitor is the ideal tool for graphically indicating both white and black levels in the composition, as shown in Figure 8.3. (Choose FUNC > Rec. Program > Manual and select WFM or Zebra and set the percent or choose both WFM and Zebra.)

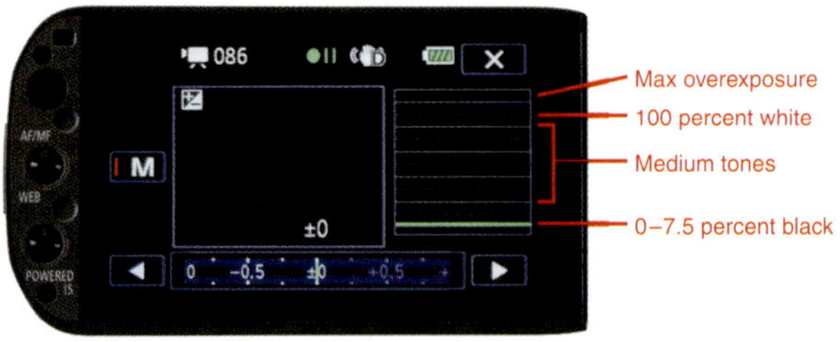

Figure 8.3 Watch out for flattening at the top of the WFM response curve (clipping whites) or at the bottom (crushing blacks).

In the right hands, soft light can be very expressive. Vermeer's paintings often pictured subjects in soft skylight coming through a side window, and Lance Accord's cinematography for *Lost in Translation* makes extensive use of soft light by augmenting the skylight from large room-length hotel windows with KinoFlo fluorescents balanced for daylight.

Seemingly gray overcast moments can be full of color by increasing saturation in Image Effects in program mode, or by using the Vivid cinema filter, or enhancing color in postproduction where you will have more control. A good portion of making an overcast day expressive is in controlling what is contained in the shot. The pervasiveness of bland soft light on an overcast day allows you to be free to explore foreground/background relationships and extensive camera movements. Sometimes, starker costumes might be needed on an overcast day or when shooting during the indirect light of magic hour.

Magic Hour

During magic hour, there exists a form of soft, indirect light that is quite different from an overcast day. Just after the sun disappears over the horizon at sunset or for about 20 minutes just prior to sunrise, when the atmosphere is reasonably clear, you have a brightly glowing sky where the light seems to come from everywhere yet the sun is not visible. This is magic hour. In black-and-white shots, this will be incredibly bland. But in color, you end up with luminous soft light and a blue sky (as opposed to the soft light and a bleak gray sky of an overcast day). Objects are differentiated primarily by their color as in an Impressionist painting instead of by light and shade. Magic hour produces romantic color shifts evolving as the minutes pass, and the color balance changes from typical photographic daylight to or from skylight, to the atmospheric effects of post-sunset or pre-sunrise.

The film *Days of Heaven* was shot by Nestor Almendros extensively in magic hour. Almendros received the Academy Award in Cinematography for this production. The story is about migrant farmworkers who labor from sunrise to sunset and their personal interactions occur in the little periods of time just before sunrise and just after sunset. Magic hour, when indirect light is everywhere, does not provide modeling from light to dark. Almendros exploited this by using low angles to silhouette people against the sky or costumes that had dark black and bright white in them so that they stood apart against the medium tones of the wheat fields. The film's landscapes often featured a luminous ultra blue sky, at times with the remnants of occasional clouds or a few rays of sunset reds and purples that compensated for the flatness and the blandness of the shadowless light hitting most of the landscape. For certain shots, Almendros added a bit of reflected light on a subject's face in the foreground.

In magic hour, under the right conditions, you might see a dramatic skyscape while the light on the landscape and subjects will be as shadowless as on an overcast day. In most cases, magic hour is more controllable just after sunset than just before sunrise, and the results are somewhat different because one progresses toward darkness and the other toward brightness. To be prepared for shooting magic hour before sunrise, you have to anticipate pre-sunrise in the dark and be set up for it while not really knowing how things will look until the effect of the light is already occurring and constantly changing, eventually leading to sunrise or morning mist.

If you set your color on Auto White Balance, you are probably not going to be able to exploit the wonderful pinks, purples, and blues that can occur at magic hour. Auto White Balance will try to make the light neutral. Three strategies for shooting in magic hour are to use the Sunset mode, which intensifies colors; to use the Vivid cinema filter; or to use a manual white balance locked to some fixed point at or between 3,000°K and standard daylight 5,600°K, depending on what looks good in the viewfinder. The Sunset mode, which you select by choosing FUNC > Rec.

Program > SCN > Sunset, does not allow any additional adjustment of color balance. Most professionals would probably not choose the ready-made Sunset mode for this reason. The Vivid cinema filter does allow additional color balance control, but its increased saturation could be done in postproduction instead of committing to it in the camera. Of the various choices, setting a manual color balance allows a greater range of options and control. Similar strategies can be applied to shooting sunrise or sunset.

Sunrises or sunsets can provide beautiful images in their own right (see Figure 8.4). They are also an opportunity to portray a subject in silhouette or modeled with redirected sunlight from a reflector. As with magic hour, automatic settings will attempt to normalize the color during sunrises and sunsets, which may or may not be appropriate. When the camcorder is locked to a manual color temperature, the exceptional colors will stand out. Reds and purples will remain rich and the progression over time to (or from) full daylight will not be negated by a program that continues to adjust. To lock in a fixed white balance while in Programmed AE, Tv, Av, Manual Exposure, or the Vivid cinema filter, choose FUNC > WB > K Color Temperature or lock to Daylight, Tungsten, or some other fixed value.

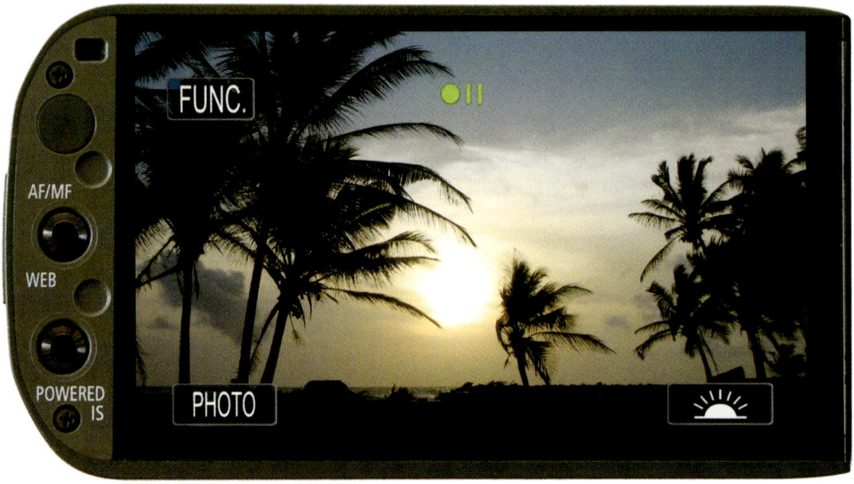

Figure 8.4 Sunset with silhouetted trees in the foreground.

In addition to white balance, you may also want to lock the exposure to manual or to AGC Limit for sunset to maintain the progression toward darkness. Auto exposure would attempt to negate the progression, and eventually create a muddy graininess as it increased gain while trying to compensate as the horizon darkens. Exposure for sunrise is more difficult than sunset. One strategy for a sunrise is to manually preset the exposure based on a recent test—say, at the point the sun just clears the horizon.

Using this setting the next time you shoot, the sunrise will start considerably underexposed, reach a perfect balance at the point the sun clears the horizon, and then proceed to wash out the frame. Of course, a sunset (which is easier to expose) altered in postproduction to play in reverse will look like a sunrise, provided people or birds do not pass through the shot.

Interior Light

Interior available light can be skylight through a window or illumination from a table lamp, floor lamp, or ceiling light. You have some control over this by simply opening or closing blinds and turning existing lights on or off. If you have the time and opportunity, you might increase or decrease the wattage in existing fixtures or exchange bulbs for ones that match color temperature and help create the look you want to design.

If your available light interior has a significant amount of skylight coming through the windows, you may want to balance any additional light in the room to be consistent with daylight by doing the following:

- Using a reflector to redirect window light onto the subject or onto part of the interior
- Using 5,600°K daylight compact fluorescent bulbs in existing lamps and fixtures
- Adding 5,600°K light from a KinoFlo or Interfit fluorescent instrument
- Bouncing a tungsten light with a half-blue gel to bring up the base level with partially corrected light
- Silhouetting the subject against the window by exposing for the exterior and using no additional interior light

Using available interior light often involves shooting under low-light conditions. The G10/XA10 has an unprecedented ability to accommodate low light compared to other camcorders in its price range and even many high-end camcorders. By designing the CMOS chip with exactly 1,920×1,080 photo receptors, Canon was able to make each individual pixel 2.75 microns instead of the 1.7 microns found in most consumer and pro-sumer camcorders. According to Canon, this produces a 25 percent improvement in low-light sensitivity and a 280 percent improvement in dynamic range, which translates into more detail in the highlights and shadows.

Canon recommends a minimum light level of at least 1.5 lux to produce a discernible image, which for most purposes is far from a professionally usable image. So do not expect night vision miracles. The term "lux" refers to the intensity of light falling on an object at a distance of one meter from a single candle, and the term "footcandle" is the intensity of light falling on an object at a distance of one foot from a single candle. In each case, these are standard scientifically calibrated candles, but not that far off from a typical dinner candle. A lux is about 1/10 of a footcandle—1/10.76 to be exact. 1.5 lux is a very small amount of light—the equivalent of a solitary dinner candle about 48 inches from the subject. You cannot really shoot at 1.5 lux without expecting considerable video noise, motion blur, and a degraded image. You will need at least 17 to 20 lux, the light of a typical bedroom or dim living room, to begin to achieve clean results. This is still an impressively low amount of light compared to most camcorders.

In very low light, the gain can rise to the point that you see grain, video noise, unevenness, and eventually an unacceptably degraded image. Every change of 6dB of gain is the equivalent of making the photo receptor twice as sensitive. With the gain at 6dB or even 12dB, the image should still look pretty clean. You will have to decide whether you want to get as high as 18dB or will allow it to max out at 24dB (or even higher if you switch to the Low Light mode). For interior and low-light situations, you need to determine your limit for maximum gain and when shooting provide a base level of enough light so that gain will never have to exceed that point.

Base Level

The term "base level" is used by some to describe the existing level of ambient light at a location—whatever value is already there—to which more light can be added. However, base level is used by others to describe the minimum level of light needed to produce an acceptable picture, a more useful concept. Phrased another way, your minimum base level is the answer to the question, "How much light do I need to shoot at the widest aperture, slowest shutter speed, and the highest gain that I am willing to accept?"

For certain kinds of low-light shooting, it is important to get the image no matter how ugly it looks. In other cases, it is important to have the image only if it looks good. Each would require a different base level of light. You will need to derive a lighting value from previous experience or shoot tests in low light with the gain at 6dB, 12dB, 18dB, and 24dB (or at levels in between) to find the lighting threshold at which the image is acceptable or unacceptable for your purposes. This will be useful information for setting or limiting gain in future low-light situations.

To manually control the Automatic Gain Limit as your major exposure variable, enter Programmed AE by choosing FUNC > Rec. Program > P Programmed AE > X. Then, press the CUSTOM key for two seconds. When exposure options appear across the bottom of the touchscreen, use the CUSTOM dial to select AGC and press the CUSTOM key again. You will now see the dB limit on the left side of the touchscreen and can adjust its value with the dial either for test purposes or as an effective exposure control during low-light shooting. As long as the light is very low, this will also give you the ability to set your gain threshold and to manually underexpose at selected moments by turning the gain even lower. Once you have enough light to shoot at zero gain, the AGC Limit will cease to be a way to manually control exposure, and the +/– Exposure mode would be preferable. (See Figure 8.5.)

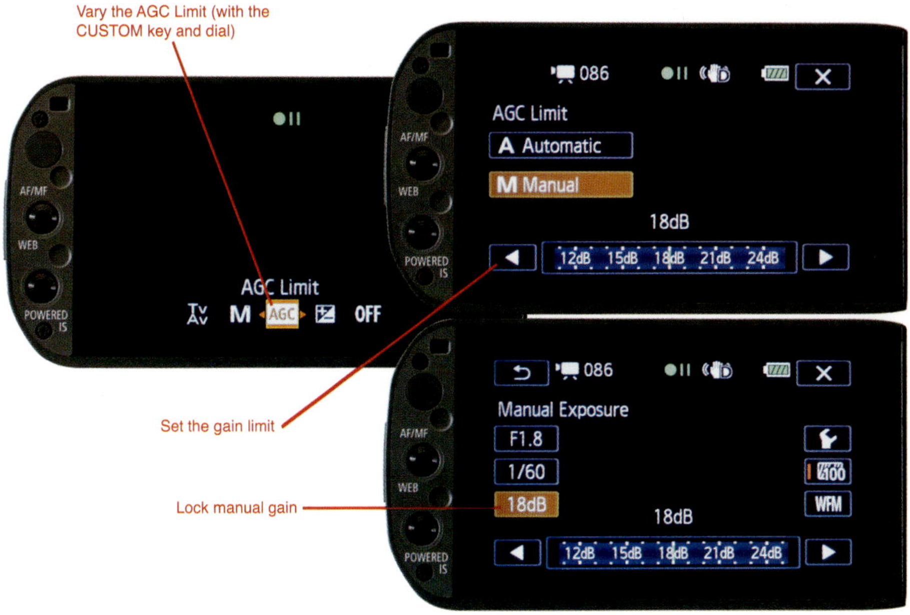

Figure 8.5 The three ways to control gain are shown here.

To obtain enough light, there is an advantage in low light to shooting in wide angle, which opens to f/1.8. Zooming to full telephoto will lose 1⅓ stops at the widest aperture compared to wide angle, which more than doubles the amount of light needed. Also, shooting at a slower shutter speed of 1/30 for frame rates of PF30 and 60i, and 1/24 for PF24 and 24p, will allow the camcorder to attain an acceptable exposure in half the light of the typical shutter speeds of 1/60 or 1/48.

It is also possible to use a light meter on its EV (exposure value) setting to find out if you have an adequate base level of light. (See Figure 8.6.) Set the ISO value on the meter at 100, which many people use as a standard. (You could set it for a calculated sensitivity of the camcorder, but this will change proportionally with your gain settings on the camcorder. For the purpose of reading a base level of light, a sensitivity setting of ISO 100 or any higher value like 400 or 800 will do as long as you consistently use the same number.) The meter reads the light falling on its dome, which should be held in the light and facing toward the camcorder as a substitute for the subject.

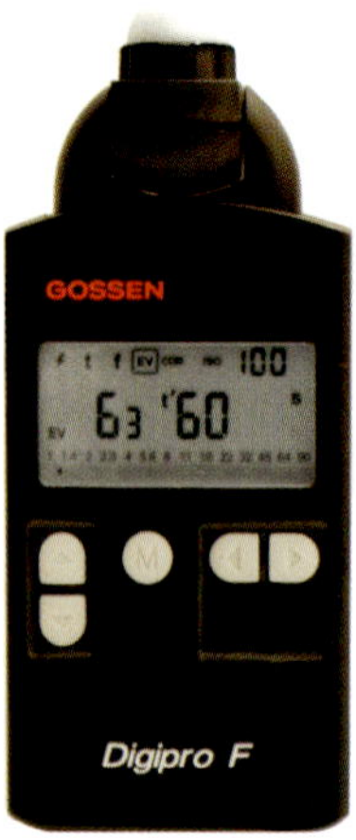

Figure 8.6 A light meter in EV mode is useful for testing the base level of light.

From experience or testing, you will eventually learn what EV you need for your minimum base level of light and can make judgments from that information. If your EV reading does not reach your minimum base level, then your choices are as follows:

- Augment the scene with available light to lower the gain and improve the image.
- Increase the gain and accept a visually degraded image.
- Settle for a dark image.

If you do not have access to a light meter, you can put exposure in full manual mode and use the camcorder as a light meter. Lock the aperture to f/2.0, the shutter speed to your intended setting, and slide the Gain value until you just reach the 100 percent zebra pattern threshold on a white card, or if exposure cannot reach that level, calibrate your zebra threshold for 70 percent—an acceptable underexposure for very low-light situations. You will have to visually judge the quality of the image to determine whether that dB setting is clean enough to be acceptable.

If the gain setting has to go higher than you prefer, your options are to add light to achieve or exceed the minimum base level; stay at the high gain, accepting the degraded image; or purposefully set the gain lower if the composition and nature of the picture look adequate when underexposed (a judgment call). This last option will produce richer blacks and less video noise, but at the expense of losing detail in the dark areas and possibly muddying middle tones. This may be fine for some compositions and types of subjects and not for others. To purposely choose underexposure is an interpretive decision. If you choose to operate with lower gain, this can be done by remaining in full manual exposure mode (choose FUNC > AGC LIMIT > Manual and set the desired dB) or with automatic exposure in Programmed AE or Tv or Av modes (choose FUNC > Rec. Program and select Programmed AE, Av, or Tv), plus setting an AGC Limit.

If you can master manual settings, it really helps to have full control of exposure, even in available light situations. Manual control will permit you to have a purposefully dark shot if necessary or to selectively lock in an exposure based on a selected part of your composition. Otherwise, as you pan around, auto exposure and Programmed AE are going to try to even out what is actually there, which will probably be less expressive than if you let dark areas be dark.

Shooting in very low-light conditions might eventually get to the point that you simply take what you are given, and just as you would outdoors, control the situation more with where you place the camera and how you use the frame. There may be choices in low-light situations that range from expressive silhouette to acceptable underexposure, particularly if there is a white reference in the shot or at least a small portion of the composition normally exposed. Sometimes, the apparent circumstances, the reality of the moment, and rich sound can compensate for less visual information.

Fluorescents

A room lit with fluorescent ceiling fixtures produces an unflattering downlight that leaves eye sockets dark and flattens faces. The phosphors in the brightest, least expensive, longest-life industrial and consumer fluorescent bulbs do not cover the whole visual and photographic spectrum. Consequently, people do not look attractive under them. The light is high in green content, which under-renders skin tones and warm colors. The white balance setting on your camcorder can help correct for some of this, but certain wavelengths of color are entirely missing, and clothing and skin tone can never appear quite natural.

Increasingly, spiral compact fluorescents (CFLs) with a screw base are used where incandescent bulbs had been, as shown in Figure 8.7. Fluorescent bulbs have a Color Rendering Index (CRI) rating that indicates the percentage of the visible spectrum they produce. Anything below 80 percent of the spectrum is not photographically pleasing and may not even have a CRI rating printed on its base or packing. Fluorescents with a CRI in the 80s are called "wide spectrum" and those in the 90s are called "full spectrum."

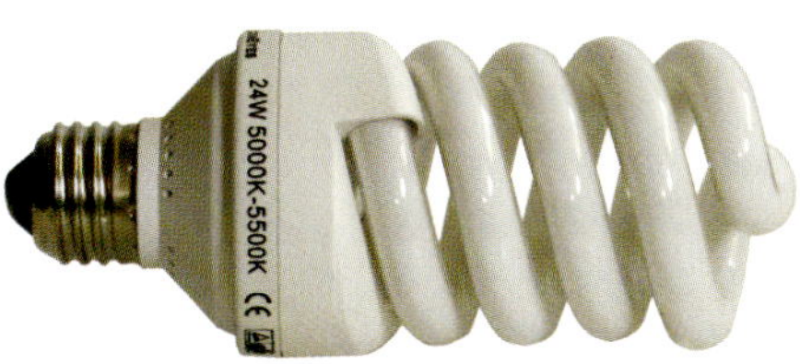

Figure 8.7 A wide spectrum CFL (compact fluorescent lamp) balanced for daylight.

The least expensive tube and screw-in fluorescents for home, school, and industry are bright, efficient, and long lasting but typically have a CRI rating between 40 to 60, which produces unnatural skin tones and skewed colors on video or film. Even after white balancing, a camcorder cannot adapt to the incomplete spectrum as well as the human eye can; consequently, the camcorder appears to exaggerate the effect. Sometimes, the incomplete spectrum is exactly perfect for producing an empty, impersonal mood like the parking garages where reporter Bob Woodward (played by Robert Redford) meets "Deep Throat" in *All the President's Men.* But should a workplace, kitchen, or classroom look like this on video?

There are a number of possible solutions. Photographically desirable fluorescents have a CRI rating from 80 to as high as 98 and will have their rating printed on their base or their packaging. A solution could be to replace industrial- or consumer-quality fluorescents with full-spectrum bulbs. This might be practical for a few fluorescent tubes or for CFL screw-in bulbs, but is not a likely solution for situations involving dozens of lamps in ceiling fixtures, since full-spectrum fluorescents cost three to six times more than regular consumer bulbs. A simpler, quicker solution would be to augment the ceiling fluorescents with full-spectrum soft key or fill light from the side or up to a 45º frontal angle. As it mixes with the ceiling light, the additional light would improve the color rendering, provide visibility in the subject's eye sockets, and create a more modeled, less flattened appearance.

Suitable instruments for supplementing cool white fluorescent light include the following:

- A 500- to 750-watt quartz-halogen light (like a Lowel Omni or Tota) bounced off a white ceiling, wall, or corner through a half-blue CTB filter
- A professional fluorescent fixture like a KinoFlo or an Interfit 9 CFL light with daylight full-spectrum bulbs
- An LED panel light including inexpensive ones made by Neewer

These instruments are discussed in Chapter 10, "Shooting at Night." Quartz-halogen light filtered with half-blue CTB will still look a bit warm compared to 4,100ºK fluorescent ceiling lights, but the two hues will be close enough to create an acceptable color modeling across your subjects. Full spectrum "daylight" fluorescent or LED instruments will be bluer than cool white industrial or consumer fluorescents, but close enough to blend with either fluorescents or skylight through windows.

Practicals

A practical is a source of light that is used as an image within the frame. A practical may or may not supply real illumination to its surroundings, but its image adds to the tonal range of a scene, its mood, and potentially its visual meaning like time, temperature, the nature of the place, or the nature of the event. Images that generate light can be evocative on the screen and available light situations are often full of images that produce light. Examples of exterior practicals include the sun as an on-screen image at sunrise or sunset, the moon, a lighthouse, car headlights, neon signs, storefronts, lanterns, flashlights, fireworks, flares, bonfires, or even a jar full of fireflies. Interior practicals include table, floor, and ceiling lamps; candles; matches; a fireplace; glowing coals; a gas range; heater filaments; televisions; computer screens; indicator panels; molten metal in a foundry; and phosphorescent materials that glow.

The primary problem with practicals is keeping their brightness within the limited exposure latitude of video without underexposing the rest of the picture or overexposing the practical. Solutions include adding fill light so the rest of the picture is closer to the value of the practical and subduing the practical light so that it is more in balance with the ambient level. If a table lamp, for example, appears disproportionally bright, it can be toned down with lower-wattage bulbs or a solid-state dimmer. An inexpensive $13 to $30 dimmer from a hardware store might work, but these often cause the light bulb to produce a 60-cycle hum and possibly a visible flicker at low settings. A professional-quality solid-state dimmer, like the American DJ Uni Pak II shown in Figure 8.8, will provide better results. It sells for $110, weighs three pounds, has a readout of the precise level of power, two Edison outlets, and controls up to 10 amps (1,200 watts).

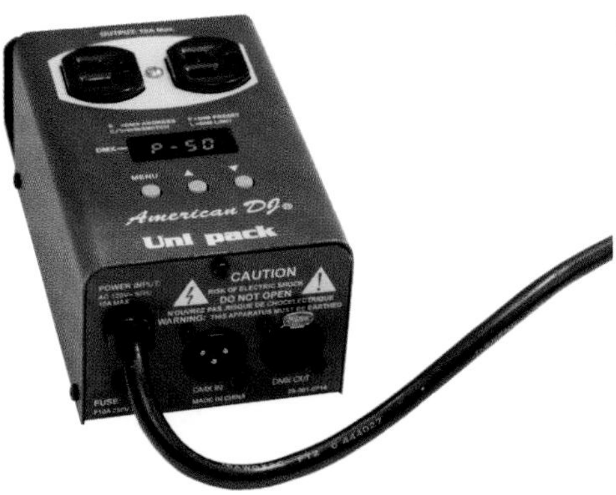

Figure 8.8 A dimmer is useful for reducing the intensity of practicals that would otherwise be too bright in the frame.

In more than one film, cinematographer Vittorio Storaro has strategically placed a scarf over the front of a lampshade to subdue the direct light into the lens while allowing a table lamp to still provide visible illumination to the wall and table. Storaro has also been known to use dimmers. If a scene had a hanging bare light bulb in the shot, cinematographer Andy Laszlo would tone down the side facing the camera by spraying it with soluble brown hair dye—the kind of washable temporary coloring available in drugstores. In this way, the side facing the camera did not bloom and overpower the scene, while the un-dyed portion of the bulb provided some real illumination that was visible on the actors. Laszlo called this "liquid dimmer."

Another way to cinematically deal with an overly bright practical is to expose for the practical itself and allow the foreground subject to be in silhouette or semi-silhouette as you might do with palm trees or lovers in front of a sunset. To produce a silhouette, the camcorder needs to be in +/– Exposure or full Manual Exposure mode with values set to favor the background while the underlit foreground goes dark. The G10/XA10's Backlight mode would have the opposite effect, making a dim foreground subject lighter at the expense of overexposing the background. Allowing the foreground figure to go dark is sometimes a more interesting solution. Silhouette is just one more expressive possibility within the enormous range and variety of available light.

Except for when we look at a light source itself, like a candle, a bonfire, or the setting sun, light is otherwise invisible until it interacts with something. Light is articulated by dust, smoke, or fog or by opaque, translucent, transparent, or textured surfaces. Light does not mean anything until it hits something. A great deal of lighting involves selecting and controlling what light hits and how those surfaces articulate light. The G10/XA10—with its range from SMART AUTO, to programmed modes, to providing complete manual control—is a perfect tool to explore the evocativeness of available light.

In available light situations, you can think less about power cables, light stands, and high-wattage instruments, and begin to explore light by controlling what it strikes: the color and contrast range of the subject (opaque, translucent, transparent subjects); black reference and white reference; surface quality (dry, dull, wet, shiny, metallic, smooth, textured); three dimensionality with highlight and shadow; fog and smoke; dulling spray, wetting, covering objects, shading objects, and placing objects or materials to create shadows.

9

Lighting Techniques

This chapter will be a quick crash course in lighting techniques, terms, and concepts centered on a half dozen lightweight location instruments that are appropriate to palm-sized camcorders like the G10/XA10.

Light serves multiple functions, the most obvious being to provide clarity and visibility. The initial question is whether there is a base level of enough light to photograph a clean image. An acceptable base level will be different for surveillance than for home video or event photography, and considerably different for broadcast-quality documentary or fiction. The issue of base level was discussed in the previous chapter on available light. Beyond simply having enough light to shoot at an acceptable exposure, the principal issues of lighting are concerned with separation of figure and ground, emphasis, expressiveness, and ultimately with meaning.

Basic Concepts

When light comes from a relatively finite source like a light bulb, a welder's arc, or a candle, it spreads naturally and falls off rapidly in proportion to the square of the distance from its point of origin. This is called the inverse square law. Light will be 1/25 as bright at five feet as it is at one foot from its source. Consequently, gradations of light are natural, whereas flat, featureless lighting can be bland and unexpressive and in many situations unnatural. Do not be afraid of uneven light or a range from light to dark. Just make sure through exposure settings or by adding fill light that the extremes are within the recording latitude of the camcorder so you don't clip whites or crush desired shadow detail into blackness.

You learn more about a three-dimensional object if it is brighter on one side than the other, allowing light and shadow to reveal the object's contours, crevasses, and textures. Flat frontal lighting carries much less information. This is why we use the terms "key light" for the brighter light coming from a predominant source on one side versus "fill light," which determines the density and detail of the shadows. Fill light can be rather non-directional, like the luminosity from the sky, which makes shadow detail visible in sunlight. Alternatively, fill light may come from ambient light bouncing from surfaces in a room or from secondary sources that are weaker compared to the key light.

Light is a dynamic component of visual communication. It creates emphasis and de-emphasis, and works as both a modifier and an indicator. As a modifier, light can make a face look younger, older, mysterious, muscular, relatively smooth, or noticeably textured, revealing every wrinkle, pore, and blemish. It can make a bedroom look spacious, claustrophobic, bright, dark, or shadowy. As an indicator, light can make that same space imply midnight, dawn, mid-afternoon, or evening, indicate warmth or cold, or even suggest the light of a particular season. A space can be completely reshaped with light and shadow.

Modeling the subject and modeling the space are often approached as two separate but related lighting problems. To really establish emphasis, de-emphasis, texture, mood, and a sense of place, the background may have certain needs that are not taken care of simply by the spill of the subject's key and fill lights. Think of modeling the subject with an appropriate balance of key, fill, and sometimes backlight, and of additionally shaping and painting the environment with light and shadow. Within the balance between the subject and the environment, light plays a role as an indicator of mood, time, season, temperature, and off-screen space. A background can be darker, brighter, or at the same level as the subject, and different ratios will suggest a range of meanings.

Key and Fill Light

Key light is the dominant modeling light that hits the subject. Usually, it is the apparent source and often the brightest light, although a thin line of backlight might be equal to or brighter than the key light. Positioning the key light is often the first consideration. Determine where the predominant source would logically come from—a window, ceiling, table lamp—and select and place the key light to simulate its hardness or softness and its directionality. Sometimes cheat the angle and axis to create better modeling. Pay attention to where shadows fall and adjust the key light to minimize unwanted shadows or to more precisely place wanted shadows within the visual composition.

Key light is almost never full frontal. It usually comes from an angled position—often ¾ front so as to create light-and-shade modeling on the subject; as sidelight, which bisects the subject in light and shadow; or even ¾ from the rear, which lights the partially visible upstage portion of the subject while leaving a predominant portion in shadow.

After establishing the key light, you might now consider fill light. In natural situations, fill light is supplied by the sky or from ambient light bouncing off walls. Very likely, part of your key light will bounce off surfaces to supply some level of fill light. If you want deep, impenetrable shadows, then you would not add any fill at all. In fact, you might try to limit ambient light by closing blinds, turning off ceiling lights, flagging off spill from your key light, and using black cloth or the black side of a reflector to cover off-screen areas that might reflect light. Removing ambient light in this fashion is called "negative fill."

Conversely, you might add fill light if you want to see detail in shadows. The amount of fill light you add will determine whether shadows on the subject are extremely transparent, normal, relatively pronounced, or highly dramatic. Soft fill light could come from a reflector, from a fluorescent or LED instrument, or from a tungsten-halogen spot or flood light with an umbrella or bounced on the ceiling, a wall, or into the far corner of a room. By its nature, fill light is less intense than key light, ranging from barely visible (say, 1/32 as bright) to about half as bright. Fill light is typically placed somewhere on the opposite side as the key, ranging from slightly behind the subject, to from the side, to any number of positions from the front. Each of these positions will create a different kind of modeling on the subject relative to the key light.

Physical Variables

At least a dozen physical variables affect the appearance and ultimately the mood, emphasis, and meaning of light. One of these variables is exposure, which can be controlled in the camera (as discussed in Chapter 5, "Selective Focus and Depth of Field") as well as further adjusted in postproduction. Exposure itself can lighten, darken, and alter the impression of a scene.

Another physical variable of light is color. Aspects of color can be controlled in the camera's White Balance, Image Effects, and Cinema settings, as well as in postproduction after filming is completed. But a significant amount of the effect of color begins with the choices of the sources and the placement and shaping of natural and artificial light within the actual physical space, where there is an even greater ability to affect the look of the scene. Different lighting instruments come with a color balance of 3,200°K (for tungsten or for "warm" fluorescents), 4,100° fluorescent, or 5,600° daylight. Extremes of tungsten and 5,600° daylight in the same shot will look exaggeratedly orange and blue on video. Added lights are usually chosen to match the color balance of existing ambient light or at least be close enough to allow blending and color modeling.

In addition to color, other physical variables of light include intensity (brightness), angle, axis, coherence (hardness or softness), highlight/shadow ratio, foreground/background ratio, the spread (spot/flood), the throw (distance), the number of sources, and the shape and pattern of light and shadow. Intensity is controlled by the choice of instrument, the choice of lamp and wattage, varying the distance (the throw), adjusting the spot/flood control (the spread), filtering, bouncing (which also diffuses the light), and sometimes with a dimmer.

The angle is the result of the height of the light source in relation to the subject. A typical angle is 45º to 70º high so that light will illuminate eye sockets and will shape the face in meaningful ways. Shadows from 45º to 70º lighting will fall reasonably close to the subject so they are not hitting the upper portions of other subjects and are not distractions on the background. As a natural phenomenon, we are used to light coming from above, but not vertically straight down. The only time the light is at 90º overhead is outside at noon on the equator or when you are standing in the one spot in a room directly below a ceiling light. Most of the time, even in interiors, we are used to light coming from an angle from above. Of course, there are occasional times that justify light coming from much higher or lower angles. The axis is the position of the light falling on the subject in relation to the camera: frontal, ¾ front, sidelight, and ¾ rear.

Hard and Soft Light

Coherence is how hard or soft (diffused) the light is. Hard light produces a coherent, defined shadow and comes from such sources as direct sunlight, a welder's arc, the filament of a bare light bulb, a lensless spot or flood light that produces direct light, or a focused beam from a lensed instrument. Greater distance produces dimmer light but it also produces harder light. So a diffused source like a fluorescent bulb will begin to produce coherent, defined shadows at a great enough distance. Sources of diffused light include an overcast day, skylight, fog, a paper lantern, a translucent lamp shade, fluorescents, lights with frosted or diffusion gels, or bounced light from a ceiling, wall, reflector, or umbrella.

With hard light, the position and angle of the instrument, the camera, and the subject need to be precise. A hard, direct key light calls attention to the angle and position of its source and creates sharply defined shadows that may be harsh or disconcerting if they fall in the wrong places, or may be dramatic and graphically interesting if they are used well. Consequently, hard light needs to be strongly justified by the situation and the nature of the implied practical source. A key light should be hard if it is meant to imitate a source like direct sunlight, a bare unfrosted bulb, a search light, or a light from a distance that produces graphically defined shadows. Otherwise, a soft or partially softened key is subtler and can appear more natural for interiors. The dangers of hard light used inappropriately are noticeable shadows in unwanted places and an artificial, theatrical appearance.

Backlight is positioned to produce a crisp line of light on the edge of the subject for the purpose of separating figure from background. It is almost always hard light because soft light coming from behind the subject toward the camera can create spill and lens flare. The intensity of backlight is usually equal to or brighter than the key light, depending on whether it is hitting a light or dark subject and how much separation is needed.

Note

An instrument's spot/flood control affects the light's spread and intensity. It does not affect hardness/softness. The term "flood" simply means a wide spread of light, which could ultimately be hard light, as with a lensed instrument set to flood position.

In lighting, the term "soft" means diffused. It does not mean low intensity. Soft light comes from a source like a fluorescent lamp, has passed through diffusion media like fog or a frost gel, or was bounced from a ceiling, wall, corner, reflector, or umbrella. Soft light produces amorphous, less-noticeable shadows that lack hard edges. Soft light from a surface as large as an umbrella wraps around the contours of a three-dimensional subject instead of producing defined chiseled edges like direct hard light.

Used as either a key or a fill, soft light is more forgiving in terms of placement. Almost any position that does not spill into the lens could be viable. Diffused light does not produce distracting shadows and it is natural to many situations: an overcast day, skylight, indirect window light, fluorescent interiors, and light from frosted or shaded fixtures. In fact, with the exception of a small reading lamp, we tend to light almost all of our own interior living spaces with soft light. A table lamp, for example, produces soft diffused sidelight through its translucent shade, which also has an opening on the top that allows light to hit the ceiling to produce a spread of bounced soft light from above.

One of the best positions for a soft key light is from the side so that in spite of the tendency of soft light to wrap around and flatten three-dimensional surfaces, it will still produce a modeled brighter and darker side of the subject relative to the camera's view. Fill light is almost universally done with soft light. Diffused fill has the effect of controlling the transparency and density of shadows caused by the key light while not adding any new shadows of its own. Soft light does not call as much attention to itself, which is a particular advantage for fill light. Soft light can be very expressive, but its pitfalls include unwanted spill and flatness or blandness if you do not pay attention to highlight/shadow and foreground/background relationships.

One simple methodology for lighting a scene would be to do the following (see Figure 9.1):

1. Determine the nature of the subject's key light and position it to come from a logically motivated direction.
2. Place the fill light and determine its appropriate level of intensity for effective modeling of the subject, density of shadows, and the nature of the scene. Some situations need no additional fill or may need negative fill.
3. Examine where shadows fall and adjust key and/or fill for better modeling, minimizing distracting shadows or enhancing meaningful shadows.
4. Paint the background with light and shadow so that in relation to the subject, the scene represents the appropriate sense of space, time, temperature, mood, and the nature of the event. This may also include practicals (visible sources of light in the picture, like a candle or a table lamp).
5. If the subject needs more separation from the background, consider a rim of backlight on the subject, or consider lightening or darkening an area of the background so the subject stands out with proper emphasis.
6. Suggest off-screen space with additional light through a window, in a hallway, on the other side of a door, or a hint of light from some other connected but not entirely visible part of the location.

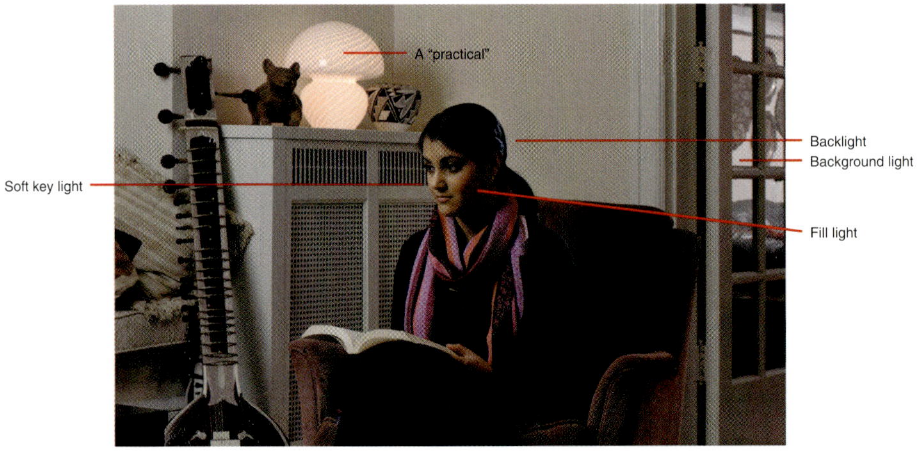

Figure 9.1 Off-screen key, fill, backlight, and background light, plus an on-screen practical.

In each of these steps, you are dealing with issues of emphasis, balance, color, pattern, and their implied meanings. Of course, an outline like this is a simplification. Not every situation will have the same needs, and many things may complicate the process, like the unique demands of working with a combination of natural and artificial light, shooting in a complex or large space with multiple key lights, accommodating complicated and extensive subject movement or camera movement, dealing with reflections, or dealing with inadequate space for placing lights. But this list should give you an organized way of approaching the process.

If you are inexperienced in lighting, you might first explore augmenting available light with soft light. In an interior lit by bland available light, you might add a soft key light from the left or right side to provide brightness to model your subject. Or you might add soft fill light if the existing light already provides an adequate key but you need to lighten shadows.

Tungsten-Halogen Lights

Many professional lighting instruments use tungsten-halogen bulbs, also called quartz-halogen or simply quartz lights. Whether quartz or glass, tungsten lights produce a full spectrum of visible light with true colors once the camcorder is white balanced. A tungsten-halogen bulb has a tightly wound tungsten filament surrounded by iodine or bromine vapor sealed in a quartz glass envelope. Household incandescent bulbs darken with age because their tungsten filaments evaporate over the life of the lamp, darkening the glass, reducing the intensity, and shifting the color temperature. In comparison, tungsten-halogen lights do not darken, shift color, or significantly lose intensity with age. Evaporated tungsten does not adhere to quartz, so as the bulb cools down, tungsten molecules return to the filament itself. Quartz also withstands more heat than glass, which means high-wattage quartz bulbs can be used in smaller, brighter, more efficient instruments.

There are a number of precautions that you must take with tungsten-halogen lamps:

- Never touch the quartz envelope.
- Always use a glove, paper towel, or cloth when changing bulbs. Finger oil etches into quartz, which creates a hot-spot that gets thinner over time and may eventually shatter.
- Work at least five feet away from any open faced quartz light.
- Always warn people when high-wattage lights are being turned on.
- Make certain that light stands are secure. With 500- to 1,500-watt lights, use heavy-duty 14-gauge extension cords and make sure the total wattage does not get too close to the maximum load of the circuit breaker. A 500-watt instrument will draw from 4 to 5 amperes and most modern circuits have a capacity of 20 amps.

In theatrical film production, the most often used lighting instrument is the Fresnel, which features a lens that has had its front curve collapsed into concentric rings. This produces a much thinner lens that has the optical power of a thick lens but can withstand more heat and intersect more light. The characteristics of a Fresnel include hard light that produces sharply defined shadows, an ability to focus its spread from flood to spot, and an even field of light with a natural-looking fall-off in brightness on the outer edges instead of a defined circle of light like a follow-spot. It is this fall-off in edge brightness that makes the Fresnel so useful. Its pool of light imitates the natural fall-off of light over distance and allows subtle blending of the light from one instrument into another to cover wider areas.

Cinematographer Ross Lowell designed the lensless Lowel Omni-light as a lightweight, lower-cost alternative to the Fresnel. It features a 500-watt quartz-halogen bulb situated deeply in a doubly curved parabolic reflector. The reflector's dimpled surface helps smooth the field of light and its double curve helps the edge of the Omni-light's beam fall-off in brightness, which is useful for blending. A knob adjusts the position of the quartz-halogen bulb in relation to the reflector to alter the spread of light from spot to flood. The Omni-light's range from spot to flood is not as long as a typical Fresnel, the field of light is not as even, the edge fall-off is not as subtle, and its direct light produces a slightly double shadow that is not as clean and defined as a Fresnel. But it is a very efficient instrument that produces more usable light per watt than a Fresnel and it comes with accessory arms and slots for holding gels, umbrellas, flags, scrims, and reflectors. It is very versatile and ideally suited for field production with the G10/XA10. (See Figure 9.2.)

The Omni-light can be used as direct hard key light from positions like ¾ front, side, and ¾ rear in situations where you want to produce defined shadows. It can also be used as background light to bring out texture and to cast defined shadows onto or

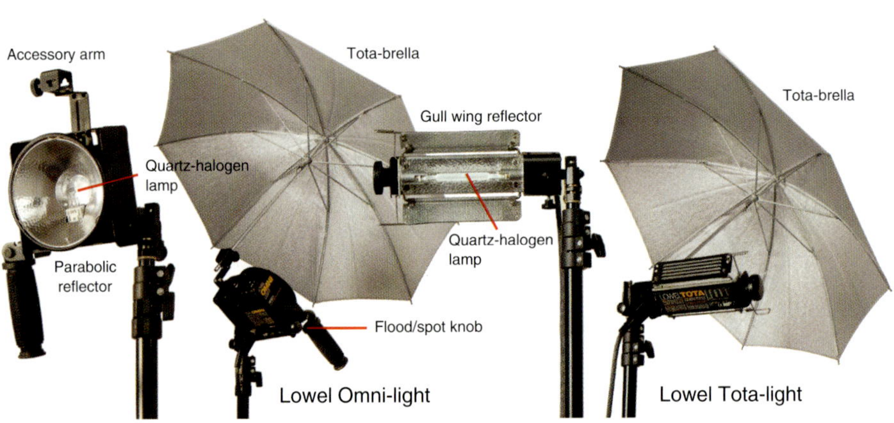

Figure 9.2 Lowel Omni-lights and Tota-lights with and without accessory umbrellas.

within the background, and as a direct backlight to produce a thin rim of light on the subject to separate the subject from the background. Bounced off a white ceiling, wall, or corner or with an umbrella, the Omni-light can be used as a soft key light, often positioned on the side. Bounced from farther away, it can serve as a fill light to control the density and detail of shadows and to bring up the general base level of a location that already has existing illumination. Bounced light will be subtler than hard direct light and less likely to call undue attention to itself. It is also less likely to cause unwanted reflections from windows and shiny surfaces.

The Lowel Tota-light has a 750-watt tube-shaped quartz-halogen bulb mounted on a reflector panel flanked by two gull-wing reflectors. The instrument has no focus controls. Its hinged reflector wings lock into place for the proper and most efficient position for lighting. The wings also fold over the bulb to close the instrument compactly for storage and transport. The Tota-light should never be turned on with its reflector wings closed or partially closed because this would trap enough heat to char and melt the reflectors. It is possible to use the instrument with the gull wings opened beyond the lock point. This would be a way to light all four walls in a room with a single vertical Tota-light facing outward from a corner.

The knob on the Tota-light tilts the instrument 360°, and there are slots for an umbrella, for a gel frame, and for flexible shafts for flags or other accessories. In addition, a second Tota-light can stack and lock onto a first instrument, providing a total of 1,500 watts. Having a tube-shaped bulb, the Tota-light produces shadows with fuzzy elongated edges on one dimension that are not as well defined as an Omni-light or a Fresnel. So, as a hard direct light, the Tota-light is more typically used as backlight on a subject and for lighting backgrounds, taking advantage of its broad spread when mounted horizontally. Where the Tota-light comes into its own is as a soft light, either with an umbrella or bounced from ceiling, walls, or corner. Bouncing spreads the area of the light and loses some light, so the Tota-light's 750 watts and its smaller profile make it an even more effective soft light than the 500-watt Omni-light.

Since the Omni- and Tota-lights have a tungsten filament, they mix with existing tungsten light such as ceiling lamps, floor lamps, and table lamps that may be providing real illumination or are practicals (sources of light used as images in the frame). Incandescent practicals like a candle or table lamp usually burn at 2,600–2,900°K and will look slightly orange compared to the professional 3,200°K light from the Omni- or Tota-light, but the match will be close enough. When used with 4,100°K fluorescents, the Omni- or Tota-light will need a half-blue gel, also called ½ CTB, to come close to balancing. The blue-filtered professional light will help provide the full spectrum that most fluorescents lack and will help counter the excessive green that makes people look so unattractive under most fluorescent light.

Fluorescents

Professional fluorescent lighting instruments can provide a diffused 5,600°K daylight, a cool-white, or a simulated tungsten balance that can be used as either a soft key light or a fill. Fluorescents provide three to four times more light per watt, run relatively cool, and have a useful life of 5,000 to 10,000 hours compared to 60 to 150 hours for tungsten-halogen lamps. The KinoFlo company began manufacturing professional fluorescent instruments in 1987 and received an Academy Award for technical innovation. They engineered high-frequency ballasts to minimize the possibility of flicker, stepped up the voltage to create higher light output, used high-quality full-spectrum fluorescent tubes balanced for daylight or for tungsten, designed fixtures for positioning light units on stands, and provided barn doors and louvers to control spill. A typical unit might contain four 24- or 48-inch fluorescent tubes that could either be dimmed or turned on individually. As fluorescents are dimmed, they retain a constant color temperature—unlike tungsten lamps, which get progressively redder. Instead of dimming to total black, fluorescents eventually extinguish at about 5 percent brightness, but this is no problem because the purpose of dimming (as well as the purpose of individual switches) is to adjust intensity for the desired balance, not to produce an on-screen fade-out. KinoFlo has also designed special units that can light car interiors or fit into tight cramped spaces.

KinoFlos are relatively expensive—often $1,000 or more for a four-light fixture. For those on a budget, there are a number of alternatives, including the Interfit INT110 (see Figure 9.3) and INT216 fluorescent photo floods. Interfit is well known for strobe units, stands, and accessories for studio still photography, but they also make fluorescent fixtures that contain screw-in CFLs (compact fluorescent bulbs) complete with a large parabolic reflector, a light stand, and the fluorescent bulbs themselves at less than 1/5 the cost of a KinoFlo. Using a large reflector and screw-in CFL bulbs, the Interfit lights are not as rugged and compact as KinoFlos. The spiral Interfit bulbs have a Color Rendering Index (CRI) rating of 82 compared to a CRI of 95 for KinoFlo, although you can buy higher-quality CFL bulbs for the Interfit fixture.

Professional fluorescent and LED lights are particularly useful in augmenting existing fluorescent light. Ceiling fluorescent fixtures, as you find in a classroom or an office, provide a bland down-light that does not adequately bring out the three-dimensional features of subjects. In addition, industrial and consumer fluorescents have an uneven spectrum with a high green content that produces unnatural colors. Setting your camcorder to auto white balance, manual white balance, or the Fluorescent H filter can provide only a partial compensation for the irregularity of consumer fluorescent bulbs that are not rated as full spectrum. Under these conditions, camcorders can make white look white, but usually end up with unnatural mid-tones because certain wavelengths are missing entirely.

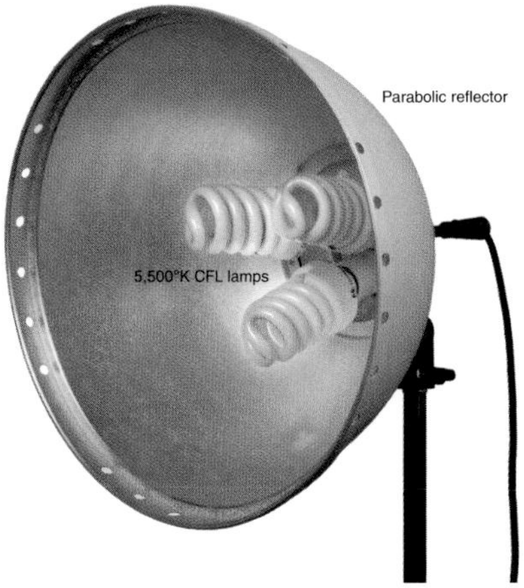

Figure 9.3 Interfit INT110 fluorescent fixture.

Unless there is adequate daylight coming through windows, you will want to augment fluorescent down-light with a 45° or side soft key light to improve the modeling of the subject and improve the color. Appropriate lights include full-spectrum fluorescent instruments like KinoFlo or Interfit, an LED array like Litepanels or inexpensive copies like Neewer and Fancier, or a bounced tungsten-halogen like an Omni- or Tota-light with a half-blue filter.

Lights on the Camera

On-the-camera light can look unnatural. The on-axis position produces flat, unmodeled illumination, and subjects lit with direct frontal light cast an artificial shadow outline onto the background similar to a flash photo. Because the light source is nearly on axis with the lens, it can also produce red eye when light reflects off the subject's retina and makes the pupil appear to glow red. For expressive purposes, the worst position for a light is on the camera. Nevertheless, there are situations that call for on-camera light in news coverage, event videography, and documentary.

Two solutions make lights mounted on the camera more professionally acceptable. One is to purposely use very low powered light that simply brings up more detail and does not call attention to itself in situations that already have some existing light. The other solution is to use softer, somewhat diffused light on-camera, possibly from an array of LED lights.

The Canon VL-5 on-camera video light ($77) is a small, low-wattage light that fits into the powered mini advanced shoe of the G10 but will not fit the XA10, which has a universal standard shoe. The VL-5 is about 2⅜ inches tall and 2½ inches long, weighs less than ⅓ of an ounce, and has a switch for on, off, and auto. At only 5 watts, its purpose is not to light a scene but to simply add to the base level of light for subjects close to the camera, as if the viewer's eye had adjusted to low illumination. This can be useful for highlighting the subject and bringing out details.

Even at only 5 watts, the VL-5 will consume as much power as the rest of the camcorder, cutting the life of a charged battery in half. But there is an enormous convenience in not having to carry an additional power supply for the light. The VL-5 supplies tungsten warm tones at 3,000°K that blend with household and professional incandescent lights or with 2,700°K to 3,200°K "warm" and "bright" fluorescents. In comparison, most LED lights tend to be in the blue range, closer to daylight balance. The VL-5's illumination is low enough that the spotlighting effect of on-camera light is usually subtle enough to appear natural and potential background shadows are obscured or washed out by existing light in the location. The 3,000°K light is very humanizing on skin tones. If the VL-5 is used for nighttime exteriors, the camera will need to be reasonably close to the subject because a 5-watt instrument does not have much reach. In some situations, when the G10 is white balanced for the VL-5's warm tungsten color, the effect will be to cool the rest of the environment, setting the subject apart.

The VL-5 can create marginal visibility in a totally dark room, enabling you to at least get an image at the expense of running the camera in high gain. With no other ambient light to blend with it, the light will have an artificial spotlight appearance. But in some situations, it is important to get the shot even if the image is degraded and the light looks self conscious.

Canon's VL-10Li ($89) is a 10-watt tungsten light that fits in the standard accessory shoe of the XA10 and requires a dedicated camcorder battery cupped to its back. The light and battery make the camcorder a bit top heavy, but it is still well balanced and the dedicated battery means the lighting unit will not drain the camcorder's power. The functions and characteristics are similar to the VL-5 except 10 watts is much brighter. The VL-10Li can also be used on the G10 camcorder with a hot shoe–to–standard shoe adapter.

A more professional alternative to the VL-10Li is the Micro-Lux LK-2104 ($119), which also fits into the standard accessory shoe on the XA10's body or its handle. When mounted on the handle, the additional height minimizes the chance of red eye. The unit will need an external 12-volt rechargeable battery equipped with a four-pin XLR power outlet. Various companies make batteries with XLR connectors or make an adapter for four-pin outlet–to–car cigarette lighter plug that would enable the use of other power sources. The Micro-Lux accommodates a 10-, 20-, or 35-watt MR-11 two-pin miniature reflector bulb. As with the VL-5 and VL-10Li, the reason for using an instrument like this is to provide a warm tungsten accent light.

Its angle can be tilted for bounce lighting and the unit can also be mounted on a tripod or a light stand with an adapter. Figure 9.4 shows the VL-5, the VL-10Li, and the Micro-Lux LK-2104.

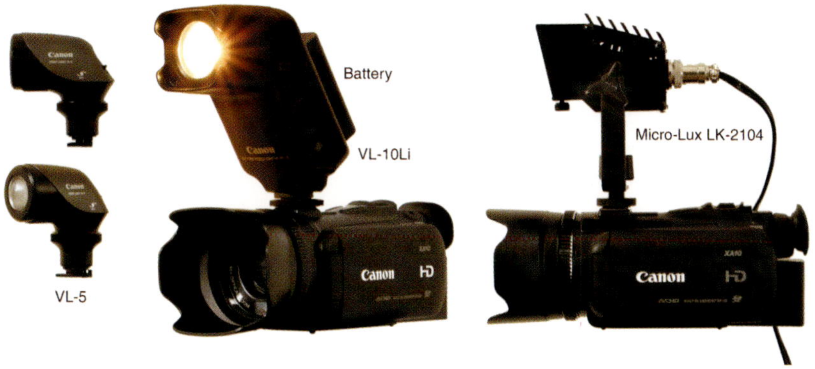

Figure 9.4 On-camera tungsten lighting instruments.

LED Lights

Professional light-emitting diode (LED) on-camera lights by Litepanels start at $275 for the Micro LED, $405 for the MicroPro, and $745 for the MiniPlus Spot or MiniPlus Flood. LEDs have a life of 30,000 hours, compared to 8,000 for compact fluorescents, 1,000 for household incandescents, and about 100 for high-intensity tungsten-halogen lamps. They are mercury-free, which makes them more ecologically friendly than fluorescents. LEDs are so efficient that battery life is approximately three to four times longer than with comparable incandescent light.

On-camera LED arrays usually produce a bluish-white, partially soft light at 5,600°K from an array of 48 to 140 high-efficiency light-emitting diodes. These kinds of lights match well with "cool" and "daylight" fluorescents, skylight, and indirect daylight. Because almost all of the energy in an LED goes into producing light, the instrument does not get hot. To potentially match tungsten light, on-camera LEDs also come with an add-on amber filter, which takes out about half the light. The light produced by Litepanels is dimmable from 100 percent down to zero without flicker or change in color temperature. It is softer, subtler, and brighter, and its reach extends further than Canon's VL-5 and VL-10Li incandescent lights.

Litepanel units are also obviously expensive. What you are paying for is the reputation of the company, brighter LEDs with a precise spread, and accurate full-spectrum color. A remarkably inexpensive plastic alternative is the CN-126 LED Video Light by Neewer (and similar models by Fancier and Opteka), which sells for only $35 to $40. Neewer also makes the CN-160, which sells for $40 to $50. They run on AA batteries or on an adapter for a Sony or Panasonic camcorder battery. They both have a built-in dimmer and come with three interchangeable filters: diffusion, which softens and broadens the light pattern; pale magenta, which reduces green for somewhat truer color; and amber, for approximating incandescent light. Even though the amber filter reduces the intensity by 50 percent, there is still enough light to provide a useful fill or accent in a dim incandescent interior.

A disadvantage of any lighting instrument mounted on the camcorder is the possibility of glaring reflections of the light itself shining directly back into the lens. It is very important to avoid shooting toward glass or other reflective or shiny surfaces. With a shoe adapter, a compact LED array like the CN-126 or CN-160 can be mounted on a clamp or even on a monopod or boom pole held by an assistant. An angle higher than camera height from the right or left should provide better modeling on the subject and reduce the probability that the light source itself will be picked up by the camera.

Litepanels, as well as lower-priced brands like Neewer and Fancier, make LED fixtures with arrays of 500 and 1,000 LEDs that mount on stands. These units can serve as a daylight-balanced, slightly diffused key or fill light. As with the camera-mounted models, the instruments manufactured by Litepanels have truer color and greater brightness, but cost about $1,700. In comparison, the LED500 Light by Fancier sells for $179 and the LED500A model sells for $199. The lower-priced LED500 runs on 120 volts and has individual switches for adjusting intensity by turning on or off rows of LEDs. The 500A additionally includes a dimmer dial and the ability to be powered by either 120 volts or 12 volts. The Fancier LED500A and many other 12-volt lighting instruments use four-pin XLR connectors. If you want to power the LED500A by a car battery, you will need an Arri cigarette lighter adapter to XLR/4 ($39), available from places like B&H Photo. Figure 9.5 shows various LED light rigs.

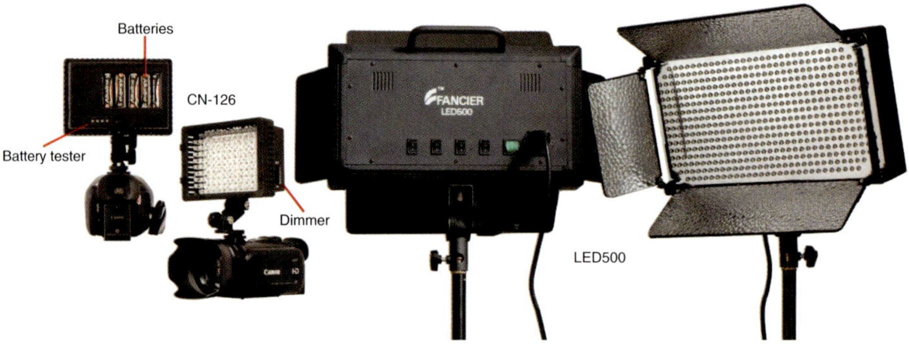

Figure 9.5 Inexpensive LED array lighting fixtures by Neewer (left) and Fancier (right).

Lighting Accessories

Air-cushioned, heavy-duty light stands 9.5 feet tall under the brand name of Impact sell for $39 to $45 at B&H Photo. If one section accidentally becomes loose while a light is attached, the air cushioning feature lets it safely recede into the next section instead of collapsing with a jolt that could damage the light. Impact also makes extension arms with clamps for mounting reflectors and zipper cases for holding lights and stands.

Black aluminum foil under the brand names of Cinefoil and Blackwrap can be very useful for shaping and flagging off light and for creating shadow shapes. Never cover an instrument too completely with Blackwrap; it could trap in so much heat that plastic parts and metal reflectors might char or melt. Always leave space for enough air ventilation.

The Rosco Company manufactures a range of colored gels for film, video, and theater, as well as numerous accessories including diffusion materials, butterfly cloth (for diffusion awnings), reflection materials, fog machines, LED panels, photographic backdrops, and shadow-producing materials. One of the most useful filters for lighting video is a half-blue, such as a Rosco Cinegel ½CTB available from B&H Photo.

Accessories for Lowel Omni- and Tota-lights include silver and white umbrellas, gel frames for holding filters, barn doors, flags for blocking off light, reflector panels, wire mesh scrims for reducing light, and flexible arms for holding some of these accessories. Lowel's Tota-brella fits both the Omni- and Tota-lights, is of particularly good quality, and sells for $17 for white and $20 for silver. The white umbrella is translucent and provides two different qualities of soft light, depending on whether you use the light reflected from its inner surface or the light passing through its white cloth, which has the characteristics of a paper lantern. The silver umbrella provides the highest light output. The Tota-brella's 27-inch size is perfect for Lowel Omni- and Tota-lights. Larger umbrellas will make the light stand off balance.

10

Shooting at Night

The rods in the human eye are sensitive only to light and dark values, and are a thousand times more sensitive than the cones, which sense color. This is why we perceive an otherwise colorful world as dull and desaturated in subdued light and nearly black and white at night. All the colors are still there, but the cones in our retina are not sensitive enough to respond when the light falls below a certain intensity.

Darkening a scene in video does not necessary look like nighttime; it may just look gray or simply underexposed. A successful nighttime scene usually has some portion of the composition fully exposed, even if it is only a car headlight acting as a white reference in an otherwise dark composition. More likely, to replicate how the human eye adapts to low light, we usually expect some areas to be dark and desaturated, other areas to be completely black, while the center of attention, like the highlight portion of your subject's face, has a reasonable amount of visible detail.

For urban exteriors, certain clues tell us that it is nighttime: a black sky, a general lack of fill light (because the sky is no longer luminous), dense shadows, and light from car headlights, store signs, and windows articulating the nightscape. A rural exterior night scene might have different clues: the moon and moonlight, trees silhouetted against a dark gray sky, a lone highway light, porch light, or campfire, along with large expanses of darkness. For an interior, like a bedroom, at 2 a.m., any visible sky through the window is dark. If no lights are on in the bedroom, then visibility is provided by light coming from outside the room, a shaft of hallway light from under the door, or light from a distant streetlamp or the moon casting a Venetian blind or window-molding shadow into the room. In each of these cases, there still has to be some source of light to create a visual scene. Depicting the night environment, whether city or rural, can also depend on off-screen sound because we see less on the screen. The darkness on the screen seems more visual when we hear crickets, the distant hoot of an owl, or footsteps walking through leaves.

In urban areas, there is a lot of light at night. In fact, an urban nightscape is often a composition of extremes: storefronts and small pools of light at full exposure or nearly, plus bright overexposed light sources often visible in the shot, like streetlamps and car headlights, along with a black sky and significant areas of underexposure or complete darkness. (See Figure 10.1.) Some of your options for shooting under these conditions are full AUTO mode, Spotlight, Night Scene, Programmed AE, or with full manual control.

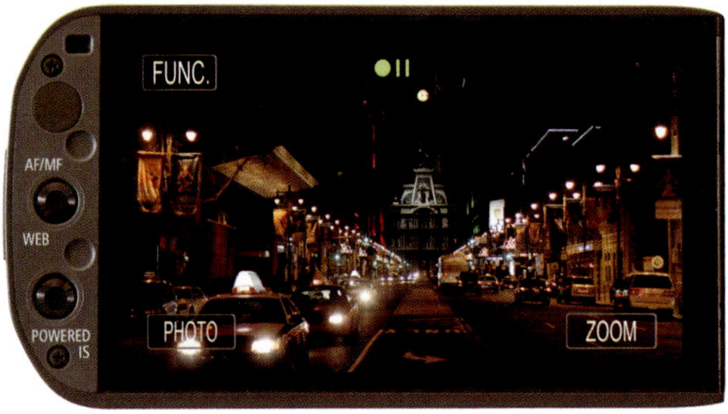

Figure 10.1 Shooting at night in available light.

AUTO Mode at Night

In full AUTO mode, the camcorder's logic will try to decide whether your compositions are simply dark scenes that need to be fully brightened or whether they fall into one of the 38 categories in which SMART AUTO takes over. The danger of this mode is that exposure will ride up and down as the camera's logic system gets different clues. If you are inexperienced with the camcorder or are shooting under such rushed and varied conditions that you have no alternative, then shoot in full AUTO mode. Pay attention to the icons appearing in the upper left of the touchscreen. If it simply says "AUTO," the camcorder has not figured out a more specific interpretation of the scene and will increase the exposure to make the image an average brightness. A head-and-shoulder icon indicates that SMART AUTO has gone into Portrait mode and will expose for skin tones. If the icon shows the sun peeking from its upper corner even though it is nighttime, then SMART AUTO has read the situation as a backlit scene and will raise the exposure to bring out details.

If you intend for your shadows to be dark, as they often should be at night, there is a danger that AUTO mode will bloom and clip highlights while trying to lighten details in dense shadows. In full AUTO mode, you have no direct control over the matter. As you move the camcorder, SMART AUTO may change its interpretation and your scene will have varying exposures. SMART AUTO's 38-scene repertoire does include settings that are well adapted to nighttime, such as Night Scene and Spotlight, but there is no guarantee that SMART AUTO will lock and hold onto these settings when you want them. If SMART AUTO continually misreads the scene or your intentions, then you would fare better using Night Scene or Spotlight in a programmed or manual mode.

The other reason to select programmed or manual control is to have the ability to toggle between auto and manual focus with the button to the left of the touchscreen. Full AUTO mode does allow Face Detection and Touch & Track focus, but at night under low visibility these functions are unpredictable and less reliable. SMART AUTO is a considerable improvement over an auto-exposure system that treats every situation the same, but it is no match for the ability to lock into a single program mode that specifically matches your intentions. Under the M setting, Spotlight, Night Scene, Low Light, Programmed AE, and Manual offer different approaches and different controls for shooting at night.

Spotlight and Night Scene Programs

The Spotlight programmed mode is intended for situations comparable to a follow spot in a theatrical performance: a pool of light illuminating a small part of the composition while the rest of the area is dark. But Spotlight conditions do not have to be on stage or in a theatrical situation. A person sitting under a streetlamp in a dark park or illuminated by a shaft of light from a car headlight or the beam from a handheld flashlight searching a dark space are comparable to spotlight situations. Simple auto exposure will try to bring up details in the black areas and consequently unnaturally gray the dark areas, overexpose the lit area, and increase the video noise. Spotlight, on the other hand, normalizes the lit area and lets dark be dark. To select Spotlight, with the AUTO/M/CINEMA switch set to M, choose FUNC > Rec. Programs > Spotlight.

White balance is automatic in Spotlight, but you are allowed to use +/– Exposure to manually adjust brightness. If exposure is already at maximum aperture, "plus" may not have an effect because this mode sets a limit on gain, but "minus" allows you to darken even further. Spotlight teamed with +/– control can be effective for certain kinds of nighttime compositions that predominantly have a single pool or shaft of light in a dark black environment. Of the programmed modes, Spotlight tends to allow more of the composition to go dark and will do the most to prevent the peak values of highlights from clipping. To operate +/– Exposure control, press the CUSTOM key for two seconds, dial to +/–, and press the CUSTOM key again to activate.

For even greater control of exposure under Spotlight, go to the program panel and press +/– Exposure. A window opens that allows you to select a specific point of exposure on the screen, adjust and lock +/– Exposure values to manual, and monitor on the waveform monitor. (Choose FUNC > +/– Exposure > WFM.)

Under more varied nighttime conditions, the Night Scene program works remarkably well, handling multiple pools of light, neon signs, store fronts, streetlamps, car headlights, points of light in the shot, minimal fill light, and areas of darkness. To select this mode, with the AUTO/M/CINEMA switch set to M, choose FUNC > Rec. Programs > Night Scene. This mode does not allow you to manually set white balance, aperture, shutter speed, or gain. Like Spotlight, it already has preselected parameters, including its own gain limits that work well with most night exteriors. Night Scene does not allow +/– Exposure control with the CUSTOM key. However, it does allow you to use touchscreen +/– Exposure control if you additionally select it from the program panel. (With the AUTO/M/CINEMA switch set to M, choose FUNC > +/– Exposure. Also open the waveform monitor for monitoring.) This gives you a critical element of manual control.

Night Scene will be a little brighter and will bring out more detail than Spotlight. Both modes are viable portrayals of night, but with different levels of black, midtones, and white. To decide between one and the other, you might compare them by directly switching between Spotlight and Night Scene on the Rec. Programs selection panel while looking at your scene. (See Figure 10.2.) This test takes only a few seconds. In addition to exteriors, both Spotlight and Night Scene could be used for predominantly dark interiors that have small areas of light. Both program modes produce a rich nighttime black that minimizes grain and muddiness.

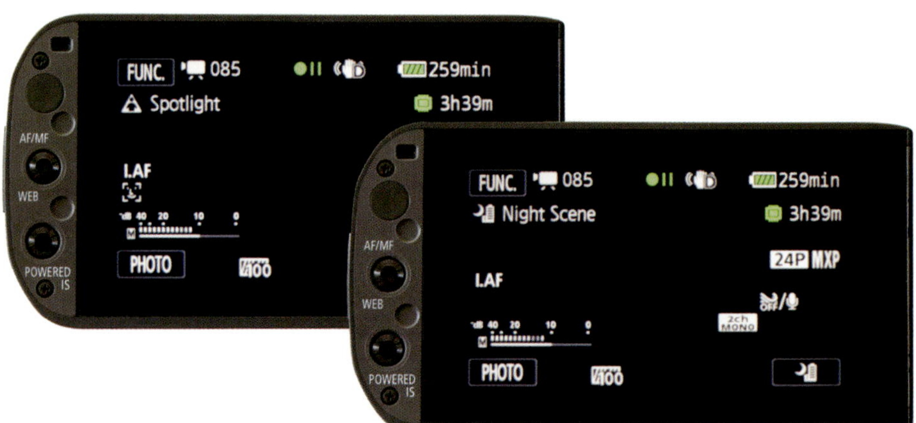

Figure 10.2 Spotlight and Night Scene menu options.

Low Light Mode

The Low Light program does the opposite. It tries to bring visibility to most of the picture by opening to the widest aperture, running at a slower shutter speed if necessary, and raising gain with the ability to go beyond the 24dB maximum until dense shadow is made lighter. This is fine if you must see detail at any expense, but the Low Light mode often grays out the picture and could destroy the feeling of nighttime.

Higher gain produces grain and a degraded image, so you will want to test this program to see if it is appropriate for your purposes. If you want to retain some of the blackness of nighttime in the composition, then Low Light would be a wrong choice. The Low Light program will produce the lightest rendition of nighttime and will push the exposure by going into very high gain. This could produce burned-out highlights on grainy, visually degraded images when the gain reaches maximum. Low Light is the right choice when seeing detail in the image is more important than the look of night.

A candle-flame icon in the upper-left corner of the touchscreen indicates that you are in Low Light program mode. Low Light does not allow you set a gain limit, but it does allow you to toggle between auto and manual focus, to control +/– Exposure on the CUSTOM dial or from the program panel with a waveform monitor as with Spotlight and Night Scene. With any of these programmed modes, it is good to have manual control over focus and some aspect of exposure.

Programmed AE

Programmed AE (choose FUNC > Rec. Programs > Programmed AE) is one more choice that you could try at night. Compared to Low Light, this program allows you to adjust more factors, including white balance, shutter speed, and an automatic gain limit. To control and test exposure (and consequently graininess) in Programmed AE mode, assign the AGC Limit setting to the CUSTOM key. To do so, press the CUSTOM key for two seconds, use the CUSTOM dial to select AGC, and press the CUSTOM key again.

To perfect your nighttime scene, successively test the limit at 6dB, 12dB, 18dB, and 24dB gain settings. Try running one set of tests with Slow Shutter set to OFF and a second set with Slow Shutter set to ON. You may also want to try one additional test using the Low Light program mode for comparison. The Low Light setting does not limit gain at 24dB and also introduces Auto Slow Shutter, so in nighttime conditions, it will probably deliver the brightest but most-degraded picture. You will need to see which produces the best results for your purposes and situation. Or, once you have found your best gain limit, you might visually compare Programmed AE to Spotlight and Night Scene as well as Low Light while in the program panel.

(Choose FUNC > Rec. Programs and then select Programmed AE, Night Scene, Spotlight, or Low Light.)

Manual Exposure at Night

Of course, you obtain maximum control and the fewest unwanted fluctuations under manual exposure. For very low-light conditions, adjust your aperture and shutter speed to low values to transmit the maximum amount of light. (With the AUTO/M/CINEMA switch set to M, choose FUNC > Manual and set the f/stop and shutter speed, as well as the gain. Also turn on zebra patterns, set to 100 percent, and the waveform monitor.) Set the aperture to f/1.8 or slightly above. A setting of f/1.8 lets through the most light, but resolution and image quality improve at a somewhat higher setting, like f/2.0. This is a difference of one-third of a stop, which means you will need 33 percent more light or about 2dB more gain at f/2.0. If you zoom to telephoto, the effective aperture becomes f/2.8, which means you will need double the amount of light or an increase of 6dB in gain compared to remaining in wide angle.

Set the shutter speed to 1/60 if you are shooting at 60i or PF30, or 1/48 if you are shooting at pf24 or 24p. If you are able to hold the camcorder very steady or use a tripod or monopod, you could set the shutter speed to 1/30 or 1/24 to shoot in half the light. Or you could halve that again with a shutter speed of 1/15 or 1/12 if you are willing to accept blur and a step-frame appearance to motion.

You will set gain based on the value that just begins to produce zebra patterns on white or the value that keeps the peak curve in the waveform monitor for a white surface just under 100 percent (for example, at the 90-percent line). If the brightest part of the image is a source of light, then its peak curve can extend just above 100 percent as long as it does not flatten anything that should retain visible detail.

Because you lose light in telephoto, determine the gain setting on readings taken in wide angle. When you expose in wide angle, the image becomes darker when you zoom to telephoto. This is preferable, however, to initially setting the reading in telephoto and overexposing in wide angle. It looks more natural in a nighttime scene to lose some detail in dark areas than to burn out highlights.

Use both zebra patterns and the waveform monitor to judge exposure. In an otherwise dark scene, it is easy to burn out highlights. With the zebra pattern set to 100 percent, you can set an exposure based on placing the brightest part of the image at 100 percent. The waveform monitor provides even more information: exactly how high the peak of the brightness curve extends, how much headroom it has above that point, whether the peak clips (producing a flat top of the curve), and how much shadow detail is crushed in darkness (producing a flat bottom on the curve).

For some scenes, crushed shadows may look natural and justified at night. After all, it is nighttime and we don't expect to see everything. But if shadow detail is important to you, instead of overexposing and clipping whites, you could try going to the Image Effects program panel and reducing contrast. (Choose FUNC > Image Effects and lower the Contrast setting, as shown in Figure 10.3.) Then return to the waveform monitor in manual exposure to see if more shadow detail appears on the waveform.

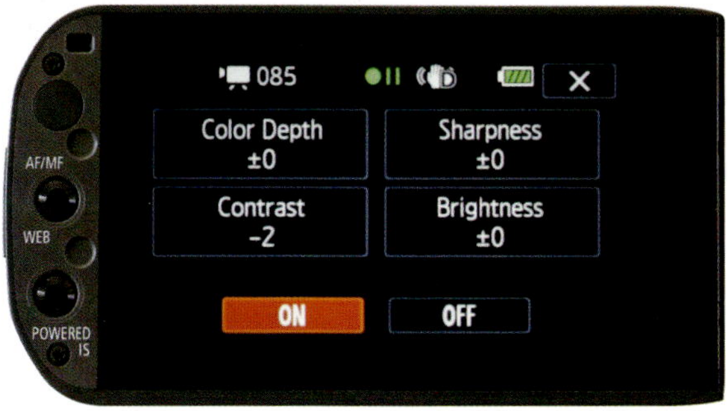

Figure 10.3 The Contrast setting under Image Effects.

Film Noir Lighting

In the 1940s, each of the major Hollywood studios produced about 50 features a year, and would contract with movie theaters to book a package of all 50 films instead of making films available individually. Each studio would make a half dozen high-budget "A" pictures and 40 or more low-budget "B" pictures to fill out the block-booking contracts. Many of the quickly made B pictures were pulp-fiction crime, detective, or domestic dramas that lent themselves to stylishly somber nighttime scenes, which depended on lighting instead of expensive sets. Light could evoke mood, mystery, or imbalance, and could transform the look of a scene through use of shadows, shafts of light, silhouettes, and characters moving from darkness to light and from light to darkness.

At the end of World War II, Hollywood B pictures flooded into Europe. The French called these movies "*film noir*" and considered them high art regardless of their low budgets and quick production schedules. Indeed, some of the most enduring films from 1941 to 1945 are *noir* classics: *The Maltese Falcon* (1941), *Murder My Sweet* (1944), *Double Indemnity* (1944), *Laura* (1944), *Mildred Pierce* (1945), and *Detour* (1945). Post–World War II *film noir* includes *The Big Sleep* (1946), *The Killers* (1946), *Nightmare Alley* (1947), *Out of the Past* (1947), *They Live by Night* (1949), *The Asphalt Jungle* (1950), *Night and the City* (1950), *The Big Heat* (1953), *The Big Combo* (1955), *Kiss Me Deadly* (1955), *The Killing* (1956), *Sweet Smell of Success* (1957), and *Touch of Evil* (1958).

The *film noir* genre often expressed anxiety, alienation, and moral ambiguity that resonated with the period of scarcity in World War II and the tension and paranoia of the cold war in the 1950s. These themes were expressed in a perfect form/content relationship through bleak, hard-edged lighting; ominous shadows; chiaroscuro; and dark angular compositions. *Film noir* died out around 1960 to 1964, as Hollywood moved toward predominantly color productions competing with the emergence of color television. But *noir* set a standard for how to evocatively light nighttime that still has its echoes today.

You can shoot in black and white with the G10/XA10 in the CINEMA mode, but you will have more options if you shoot in M mode and strip the scene of color in postproduction instead of in the camera, which is easy to do. In CINEMA mode, Filter 9 (black-and-white) cannot shoot at night as well as Spotlight, Night Scene, Low Light, or Programmed AE, or offer as much total control as M mode. All the CINEMA modes, including Filter 9 (black-and-white), allow various Rec. Program adjustments to provide partial or plus/minus manual exposure, but they are limited to a maximum gain of 18dB. You have more control over a black-and-white picture if you shoot it in M mode in color, particularly if you are shooting at nighttime and in low light. The Coen brothers' black-and-white film *The Man Who Wasn't There* (2001) was shot with color film and released in black and white.

A production does not have to be in black and white to share the aesthetics of film noir. Examples of "*neo noir*" include Martin Scorsese's *Taxi Driver* (1976), in which cinematographer Michael Chapman evoked the sense of noir in color with a roving taxi on the night shift, steam from street vents, neon signs, blinking lights, storefronts, and street activity of the New York City nightscape. Cinematographer Jordan Cronenweth set a standard for noir in color with evocative shafts of light, backlight, smoke, and rain in the extensive night scenes of *Blade Runner* (1982). His son, cinematographer Jeff Cronenweth, continued the *noir* legacy with *The Girl With the Dragon Tattoo* (2011).

For many decades of television production, there was an argument that video needed a lot of light for an image to show up on home television sets viewed in a lit room. Producers argued that in television, shadows always needed fill light and dark scenes had to be avoided. Yet a series like *The X Files,* which aired from 1993 to 2002, proved the opposite. Commenting on *The X-Files* in an interview in the Archive of American Television, Emmy Award–winning cinematographer John Bartley said, "They thought it was crazy to go that dark, to get things down that far. Sometimes it's a little nail-biting and you've got to make sure that it's actually there—or something's there." Bartley often filmed agents Scully and Mulder from their shadow side, with a soft ¾ rear key light modeling the partially visible opposite side of their faces, in scenes with backgrounds painted with hard-edged light, angular shadows, and expanses of darkness. *Film noir* and *neo noir* provide a lighting vocabulary of how to expressively use light at night, even with a camcorder as small as the G10/XA10.

Nighttime Exteriors

Compared to shooting in direct sunlight, many cinematographers prefer nighttime exteriors. They no longer have the problem of interruptions from passing clouds or a limited window of time for the light to be in the right place as the sun's angle drifts through the day. In addition, nighttime offers inherent expressive opportunities for modeling with hard light, creating and shaping shadows, and allowing parts of the frame to be dark, mysterious, or left to the spectator's imagination.

You can create *noir* lighting with very limited resources. The contrasty, chiseled look is forged by strategically employing very few lights—often a single hard angular key light modeling one side of the subject with no corresponding fill light for the other side. One of the qualities of nighttime is there is less ambient light bouncing around, so there is less fill, and light may conceivably come from a single source such as a streetlamp. There is often an additional sliver of backlight to separate the unlit side of the subject from a dark, sparsely lit background.

Provided you have the instruments and the electricity, lighting a nighttime exterior offers the same element of control as studio lighting, with the ability to put light where you want it. Night lighting is often easier and has the possibility of achieving expressive results with fewer instruments because it usually needs very little fill light (if any), and vast areas can be selectively unlit.

Power for exterior lights can come from a rented portable generator (as it might for a Hollywood production). A 30-amp Honda generator rents for about $25 a day from a hardware store. This will be as noisy as a lawnmower, so it would be appropriate for scenes where the sound track can be replaced. A quiet "blimped" generator rented from a production house will cost much more.

But there are other solutions. Power can be supplied by a 120-volt extension cord for exteriors close enough to an outlet. For more remote locations, a 12-volt instrument like an LED500A or a Lowel Omni-light with a 12-volt quartz bulb can be powered from the cigarette lighter outlet from a car or from a portable car or motorcycle battery. A 12-volt 7AH (ampere-hour) generic sealed lead acid battery sells for as little as $11, and a 12-volt 9AH Bescor MM-9 battery pack with shoulder strap sells for $59. Lightweight LED instruments by Litepanels or the inexpensive Neewer CN-160 powered by lithium ion or AA alkaline batteries are also viable at close range. In makeshift situations, film students and low-budget independents often position a car off-screen so that its headlights throw light on the subject from an expressive angle.

Improving Night Images

You may want the stark look of *neo noir* or prefer a less stylized appearance with additional fill light to bring out more detail. Or, you may limit yourself to only available light at nighttime under streetlamps, at gas stations, or near storefronts. The low-light capabilities, multiple program modes, and manual overrides of the G10/XA10 are up to all of these tasks. For any of these situations, there are several considerations that will improve shooting at night. First of all, focus is more critical in low light. The lens is at its widest aperture, which produces the shallowest depth of field, and auto focus is more indecisive and less accurate in low light. So, if at all possible, this is a time for manual focus.

In auto exposure modes, the appropriate blackness of the dark parts of a nighttime composition can easily become grainy, gray, and degraded through the use of excessive gain. One way to avoid this is to use manual exposure or a programmed mode that allows you to set a limit on gain. Another is to find ways other than gain to bring up the exposure, such as reducing shutter speed, maximizing your aperture, or adding light. If you reduce shutter speeds to $\frac{1}{30}$ or $\frac{1}{24}$ of a second, you may need camera support to prevent softened images from hand-held motion blur. Support will certainly be needed for even slower shutter speeds.

The maximum aperture of the G10/XA10 in wide angle is f/1.8 (an excellent low-light aperture). But this becomes f/2.8 when you zoom to telephoto, a loss of $1\frac{1}{3}$ f/stops of light. Each adjacent f/stop represents a halving or doubling of light transmitted by the previous or next f/stop. The loss of light happens because telephoto intersects a narrower area of light and the physical aperture of the G10/XA10 lens cannot proportionally widen to compensate at the maximum setting. So, if you shoot wide open in very low light, wide angle transmits more than twice the light of telephoto.

Here is a summary of recommendations for getting the highest quality images at night:

- Use a programmed or M mode for maximum control.
- Use manual focus.
- Favor wide angle.
- Consider $\frac{1}{30}$ or $\frac{1}{24}$ shutter speeds.
- Use a tripod or monopod for telephoto or slow shutter speeds.
- Expose for highlights and accept darkness as part of the composition.
- Contain a white reference within the dark composition.
- Set a gain limit to avoid a degraded composition.
- Use chiaroscuro or backlight to separate figure from ground.
- Add light when necessary.

Lighting in a Car

The interior of a car can be illuminated by fluorescent or LED lights. A MiniFlo nine-inch fluorescent instrument is made by KinoFlo, the Academy Award–winning pioneer and innovator in location fluorescent lighting. It has a 12-volt dimmable ballast that can be powered by a car's cigarette lighter outlet. The MiniFlo can be mounted on the car's instrument panel, clipped to a visor, or positioned to shine through a sunroof or car window. It provides about 10½ footcandles at three feet. KinoFlo lighting systems are expensive; a kit with two nine-inch lamps is approximately $1,000.

Luckily, inexpensive LED instruments like the Neewer CN-126 and CN-160 can provide nearly comparable light for about $35 to $50. The CN-126 and CN-160 run on AA cells, have a built-in dimmer, and come with a photo shoe mount and a ¼-inch screw hole. In a car, you do not want to mount the LED on the camcorder because that would be the flattest, most self-conscious angle providing no modeling, not to mention the likelihood of filming an image of the lighting instrument reflected off one of the car windows. You can attach the LED light to the instrument panel, the sunroof, or a window with a suction grip or duct tape. Find a credible angle that provides adequate modeling and no reflection of itself reaching the camcorder. The built-in dimmer is very useful for finding the right level of intensity to balance with the exterior images of landscape, roadway, or city that pass by. If the area beyond the subject is dark, then some backlight should be applied with a second instrument if possible.

Driving at night with a bright light in the car can be a potential safety hazard. Take care that the angle and intensity of the light are not a distraction for the driver. In fiction films, a nighttime car interior is often shot while the car is actually being towed. With black surroundings, a scene shot within a moving car can be simulated using a stationary car rocked occasionally by assistants, along with panning additional lights across the car and a believable audio track of driving sounds. It could even be lit with 120-volt instruments on extension cords.

Infrared

CMOS and CCD photo sensors have an inherent sensitivity to infrared light, which is invisible to the human eye. To prevent unnatural colors, digital camcorders employ a built-in infrared cut-off filter to limit the spectrum to visible light. Engaging the XA10's INFRARED switch retracts the cut-off filter and allows the camcorder to sense infrared in addition to visible light. Infrared capability is one of the differences between the XA10 and G10. Used in conjunction with the infrared LED light source in the XA10's handle, it is possible to shoot video in complete darkness up to 20 feet away.

The XA10 records infrared as a black-and-white image or with a green "night vision" look. Rendering an IR image in full color would look unnatural because infrared is beyond the range of human perception and can never be accurately represented as a visual color. Surfaces that reflect IR radiation often look strange because they have a different tonal value than we are used to, and may reveal details that were less noticeable when illuminated with the visual spectrum. Green foliage often appears off-white under infrared, and warm objects may appear slightly brighter.

In 1997, the Sony Corporation introduced NightShot infrared functionality with full exposure control on some of its Hi8 camcorders. Certain materials, particularly dark ones, can transmit infrared radiation and consequently may look slightly transparent in infrared light. Under precisely the right conditions, it is sometimes possible for a camera to see a pattern or shape through cloth, sunglasses, or dark plastic sheeting that otherwise looks opaque to the human eye. News stories around the world hyped the idea that Sony's cameras had "X-ray vision" that could see through people's clothes and invaded individual privacy, although the actual effect was considerably less graphic or explicit. Under international pressure, Sony weakened the NightShot function on all subsequent camcorders. They also disabled manual exposure controls while in infrared mode, making it impossible to fine-tune the glowing, blooming outlines of the brightest parts of the picture.

Canon's infrared system is designed with the same intentional limitations as Sony's revised version of NightShot. Consequently, night-vision images of high photographic quality are not possible. But the XA10's infrared function does truly enable you to capture video in apparent blackness, which can be invaluable under certain documentary and surveillance conditions. The degraded, voyeuristic, "night vision" look of infrared can also be exploited in fiction, personal media, and experimental work.

To operate in this mode, slide the INFRARED switch on the left side of the XA10 to ON. (This function is not available on the G10.) You must use the menu to enable the IR light in the XA10 handle, which turns on only when the IR switch is activated. To do so, choose FUNC > MENU > Camera icon > IR Light > ON.

The infrared emitter on the front of the handle is nearly invisible to the human eye, yet it provides enough light to capture video in otherwise total darkness at distances up to 20 feet. The fact that this light comes from such a close axis to the camcorder's lens means that subjects are modeled very poorly under flat, direct illumination and the pupils of their eyes glow like demons. These problems can be considerably improved if the infrared light comes from a 45° or side angle instead of directly from the camera.

There are a number of portable infrared lights on the market that can be operated separately from the camera. The Polaroid Studio Series IR Night Light has 36 infrared LEDs and rechargeable batteries, and can be mounted on a camera, light stand, tripod, or monopod pole. For $39, it offers an alternative to the direct IR light from the Canon XA10 that can provide much better modeling. Its major limitation is that the batteries last for about 45 minutes to an hour per charge. Nearly identical is the Sima SL-100IR, shown in Figure 10.4. It also has 36 infrared LEDs and sells for $35 to $45. The SL-100IR contains a built-in lithium ion rechargeable battery with a similar discharge rate to the Polaroid, but it will also run on AC power. (Sima's earlier models did not have the AC option.) For greater intensity and coverage, two or more SL-100IRs can be stacked or horizontally interlocked together. Another possibility is the Phantom Lite Illuminator ($95), which uses 25 high-intensity infrared LEDs and can run for up to 12 hours on a 9-volt battery. It lasts longer in the field and is brighter than the Sima SL-100IR, but its spread is more of a circular spotlight effect than Sima's rectangular flood, which fits the 16×9 screen better. All three of these lights are much brighter than the single LED infrared emitter in the XA10 handle.

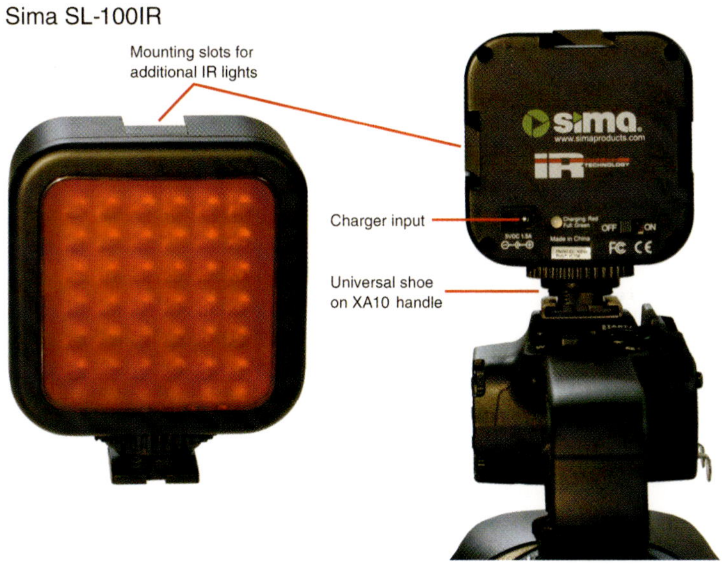

Figure 10.4 The Sima SL-100IR infrared light.

When you are in infrared mode, the letters IR appear in the upper left of the touchscreen. An icon next to the IR will indicate that the built-in IR light is on. IR will not operate in the CINEMA mode because the contrast, saturation, and hue settings that create the cinema look are irrelevant to infrared. A warning will come on the screen telling you to switch to M or AUTO. The M mode allows you to toggle between manual and auto focus, but no exposure controls are available. Images lit with the built-in IR light in complete darkness will be somewhat grainy and low contrast.

With an instrument like the Sima SL-100IR, grain will improve because of the higher IR light level, and contrast will improve with a better modeling angle. In addition to video, still photos can be taken in complete darkness in IR mode.

11

Mounting the Camcorder

Our brain coordinates information from our eyes with our sense of balance and constructs an image of a stable external world that does not bounce when we walk or nod our head. A camcorder, on the other hand, can only partially compensate for shake (with optical image stabilization), and hand-held operation can easily create an unnatural experience of arbitrarily floating, bouncing, and tilting. A well-leveled tripod with a good "fluid head" allows the user to produce video with a balanced horizon, steady framing, potentially sharper pictures, gliding pans, and smooth tilts that are more like the way we perceive the world. A tripod or some other secure mount can be particularly important in situations where stability is critical, such as extreme close-ups, compositions requiring precise framing, and for long takes. Telephoto shooting is a perfect candidate for the solidity of a tripod because telephoto not only magnifies the image, it also proportionally magnifies any instability of the camera.

A poorly used tripod, on the other hand, can seem unnaturally rooted in one place. It can even limit the visual potential of your production if you simply use the tripod for convenience as opposed to clearly determining its position, height, framing, and repositioning based the form/content needs of the production. Physically placing the camera (and a tripod) within a scene positions the spectator. In terms of form and content, should the spectator be inside the circle of action, on its edge, or on the outside? These kinds of considerations are equally important for event videography such as for weddings, as well as for documentary or fiction. The G10/XA10 on a good lightweight tripod is unobtrusive and mobile enough that it can more easily be placed within the social space of the real or fictional event if necessary, and can easily be repositioned.

Obviously, a legal deposition on video is rather straightforward and simply requires a stationary eye-level tripod. But anything more complicated needs careful consideration. Framing a scene creates a relation with the world in front of the camera, and the choices of where to place a tripod and how high to stretch the legs have significant aesthetic consequences. Do you want the spectator to see the scene from an adult's height, a child's height, standing height, seated height, halfway in between, high angle, low angle, or from a meaningful selection and progression of heights? Should the tripod's position, and consequently the position of the spectator, favor one character over another? Should the camera show us a seemingly objective view, a privileged view, or even a disadvantaged view? Should the framing set up a particular foreground/background relationship? Should the camera's position and the limits of the frame imply a relationship to the world that extends beyond the frame?

Whether documentary or fiction, a scene needs to have moments of emphasis and de-emphasis as well as a relevant point of view—not simply one that occurs by default. Most scenes also need visual development. Sometimes these things can be achieved from a single tripod position—for example, in *Citizen Kane* when Kane signs over control of his assets to Thatcher following the stock-market crash. Visual development is achieved in this scene by gradually unveiling the characters. When Bernstein puts the contract down, Thatcher is revealed sitting at the table. Then Kane enters the frame and paces to the far depth of the room before he eventually joins the other two in the foreground and signs away financial control of his fortune. As a form/content relationship, an uninterrupted long take from a single relatively static position effectively captures Kane's sense of defeat and his oedipal resentment of Thatcher. Most dramatic scenes will require a more dynamic position, multiple positions, or movement of the camera to provide progression and development. Documentary, music video, commercials, and event videography share a similar need for effective and meaningful positioning of the camera.

Selecting a Tripod

The four lightweight fluid-head tripods listed in Table 11.1 work well with the size and weight of the G10/XA10. The Manfrotto 190XB.700RC2, shown in Figure 11.1, is 20 percent heavier than the two lightweight Slik models and has a slightly slower quick-release because of its additional tightening screws. The 190XB.700RC2 has no ball leveler, but its central column provides 6½ inches greater height. The Slik DST1 (also shown in Figure 11.1) and DV Travel tripods are, for all practical purposes, identical except the latter model comes with a travel bag. Their advantages are their light weight, the ball leveler, a good quick-release plate, and a smooth fluid head. An extra pound lighter can make a big difference in the field, and the ball leveler in particular speeds up setup time. The principal shortcoming of these two models is that without a rising center column, the tripods do not quite come up to adult eye level. By foregoing a ball leveler, the Slik 504QF-II tripod system has a center column that reaches 60.6 inches. At a price of $130, it's a bargain if you do not mind carrying the extra weight. In addition to its fluid pan and tilt, its head shifts 90° on a third axis to provide vertical orientation for still cameras.

Table 11.1 Tripods with Fluid Heads

Tripod Model	Weight	Height	Material	Leveling Ball	Load	Price
Manfrotto 190XB.700RC2	5.14 lbs	57.5 inches	Aluminum	No	5.51 lbs	$195
Slik DST1	4.32 lbs	51.18 inches	Aluminum	Yes	6.6 lbs	$179
Slik DV Travel Pro	4.32 lbs	51.18 inches	Aluminum	Yes	6.6 lbs	$199
Slik 504QF-II System	5.7 lbs	60.6 inches	Aluminum	No	11 lbs	$130

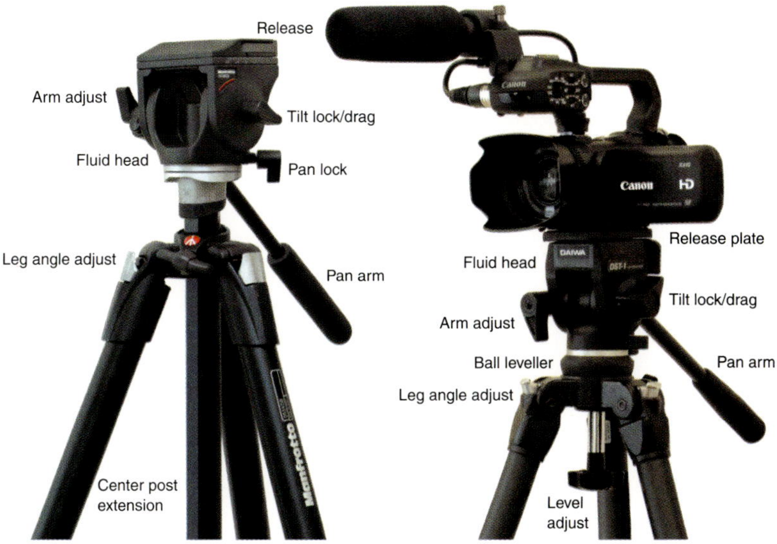

Figure 11.1 The Manfrotto 190XB.700RC2 tripod (on the left) and the Slik/Daiwa DST1 tripod (on the right).

If you want a specific combination of height, weight, and load, or you're particularly concerned with tension, inertia, or fluid movement, you might consider purchasing the legs and head separately. Manfrotto makes many different heads and tripods appropriate for the G10/XA10. Manfrotto products have very similar catalog numbers, which can be confusing; hopefully, Table 11.2 and Table 11.3 will help you differentiate the features of a selected series of models.

Table 11.2 Tripod Legs (Without Head)

Leg Model	Weight	Height	Material	Leg Sections	Load	Price
Slik Pro 340DX legs	2.56 lbs	53.1"	Aluminum	4	8.8 lbs	$80
Slik Pro 500DX legs	5.4 lbs	63.9"	Aluminum	3	10 lbs	$100
Slik Pro 700DX legs	7.05 lbs	70.1"	Aluminum	3	15 lbs	$100
Manfrotto 190XDB	3.97 lbs	57.5"	Aluminum	3	11 lbs	$120
Manfrotto 190XB	4.0 lbs	57.5"	Aluminum	3	11 lbs	$120
Manfrotto 190XBPROB	4.0 lbs	57.5"	Aluminum	3	11 lbs	$149
Manfrotto 055XDB	4.6 lbs	70.3"	Aluminum	3	15.4 lbs	$155
Manfrotto 190CXPRO3	2.8 lbs	57.5"	Carbon	3	11 lbs	$260
Manfrotto 055CXPRO3	3.6 lbs	70.3"	Carbon	3	17.6 lbs	$399

Slik legs are made of a strong aluminum-magnesium-titanium alloy. The four-segmented Slik Pro 340DX is the lowest priced and lightest set of tripod legs on the list. It also is the shortest and least sturdy when fully extended. The other two Slik Pro models are relatively inexpensive, yet sturdy and tall. The Manfrotto 190XDB set of legs is well matched to the G10/XA10 in weight, price, and size. It is a lighter, stripped-down version of the 190XB and 190XBPROB. The other two tripods in the 190 series listed in Table 11.2 have a low-angle adapter that provides a shooting height as low as 3.1 inches. The 190XBPROB also has a center post that tilts 90° to a horizontal position. This is useful for vertical portraits with a still camera or for creating an overhang to point a video or still camera straight down. The Manfrotto 055XDB is heavier than the 190 series, has a longer central post and extends much higher. Carbon fiber tripods are considerably lighter but more expensive. At 2.8 pounds, the carbon fiber 190CXPRO3 is one of the lightest among the models listed in Table 11.2. At roughly triple the price of the aluminum tripods, the Manfrotto 055CXPRO3 has a magnesium top plate and lightweight legs made of strong carbon fiber. Its center post extends to 68.9 inches and it weighs only 3.6 pounds.

Table 11.3 Fluid Heads

Head Model	Weight	Rotation	Tilt	Load	Price
Manfrotto 700RC2	1.14 lbs	360°	–75/+90°	5.51 lbs	$85
Manfrotto 701HDV	1.8 lbs	360°	–60/+90°	8.82 lbs	$130
Manfrotto 128RC QR	2.2 lbs	360°	–60/+90°	8.75 lbs	$80
Slik 504QF-II	N/A	360°	–90/+90°	11 lbs	$70
Davis & Sanford V12	1.95 lbs	360°	–90/+90°	12 lbs	$72

The 700RC2 is Manfrotto's lightest and smallest professional-quality fluid head. It can handle camcorders up to 5½ pounds, which is more than 2½ times the weight of the G10/XA10. Anything larger is overkill, but if you do not mind additional weight, you might also consider the other heads listed in Table 11.3. Each has its own quality of movement and a different design to its release mechanism, pan/tilt controls, and panning arm. The Slik 504QF-11 mounts on legs that provide a ¼-inch screw, whereas the others require a ⅜-inch mount found on most professional tripod legs. The Manfrotto 701HDV weighs 6.6 ounces more than the 700RC2. It is an excellent head if you also intend to use camcorders and still cameras with heavy lenses. The 701HDV and the 701RC2 (shown in Figure 11.2) have an additional centering adjustment and lock so that a camera's center of gravity can be shifted forward or backward on the head.

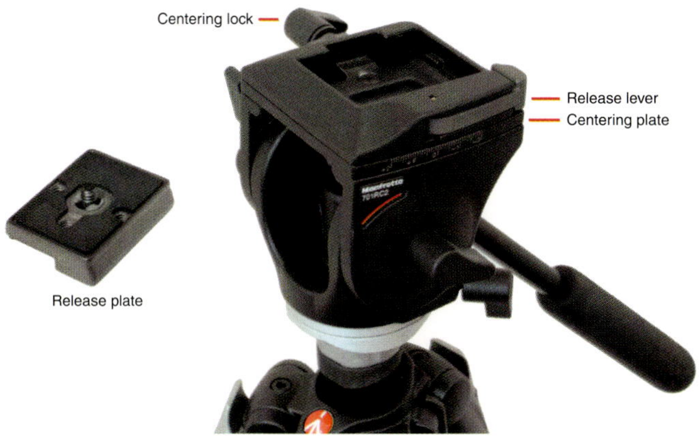

Figure 11.2 Manfrotto 701RC2 fluid head.

The 701HDV and some of the other heads have a more straightforward quick-release mechanism than the 700RC2. To make certain the base plate is secure, the Manfrotto 700RC2 and the Davis and Sanford V12 have a secondary safety catch and an additional video pin that prevents movement of the plate, which add an extra couple of seconds to mounting or removing the camera. Some videographers do not like spending the extra seconds, while others consider it a fair trade-off for a more tightly secured camcorder.

Monopods

Sometimes, tripods are too big, too heavy, too cumbersome, or simply inappropriate for certain shooting situations. In contrast, monopods are lightweight, sturdy, and inexpensive, and require minimal or no setup time compared to a tripod. They provide a flexibility somewhere between the freedom of hand-held and the stability of a tripod, and can enable additional possibilities for shooting, positioning, and stabilizing the camcorder. (See Figure 11.3.)

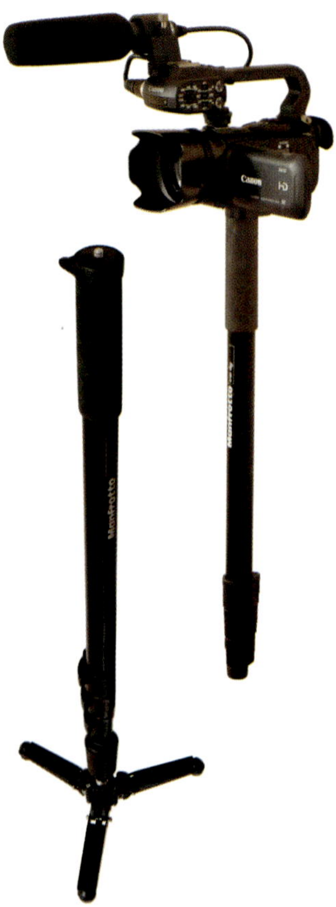

Figure 11.3 Manfrotto 560B and 676B monopods.

In terms of weight, size, leverage, and balance, the best-matched monopod to the G10/XA10 is the Manfrotto 776YB, a.k.a. 676B or 3006B. (As Manfrotto makes slight revisions—for example, in the shape of the latches—the company changes the model number. Manfrotto continually refines its products, so the model number may change again by the time you read this book. Look for a monopod with similar characteristics.) The 776YB has nearly the same general specifications as the 676B Digi monopod ($55 to $65), which is still available from some sources, and the 3006B, which was on the market several years ago.

The 776YB (12 ounces) and the 676B (14 ounces) can handle a load up to 10 pounds. Their leg sections are a rounded, triple-sided shape that bolsters their rigidity and allows them to extend or retract quickly without binding, The triple-faceted shape makes the column easier to hold without slipping or turning in your hand, as can happen with round monopods. Their four-section column extends to a height of 60.6 inches and collapses to a compact 18.9 inches. Manfrotto's ultra compact MMC3-02 weighs 10.2 ounces. It has a gray oval column with five sections that collapse to 15.35 inches. When extended to its full height of 57.28 inches, it is a bit flimsy compared to the other models, and it supports only 3.31 pounds—which is still enough for the G10/XA10. It sells for only $25. For an even lighter mount, Sunpak makes the PRO 424MX carbon fiber monopod for a price of $50 to $75. It weighs 8.8 ounces, can handle a load of 15 pounds, reaches a height of 56 inches, and retracts to 19.5 inches. My personal preference for the G10/XA10 is still the Manfrotto 776YB or 676B.

Some users accessorize the monopod with a base on the top that holds a quick-release camera plate. This could be useful if you anticipate quickly swapping the camcorder between the monopod and a tripod that accepts the same plate. However, if you want the lightest possible rig, simply attach the monopod directly to the camcorder. It takes less than three rotations to attach or unscrew the monopod. Still photographers often add a tilt or ball head to the monopod to shoot vertical compositions, but this is not essential for the G10/XA10 in video mode.

The usefulness of a monopod extends beyond resting it on the ground during long takes or stabilizing telephoto shots. For additional support while mobile, some videographers will park the tip of the monopod leg in a belt pouch or rest it waist-high on a case for small accessories held by a shoulder strap. Even when fully hand-held without the tip resting on anything, an extended or partially extended monopod adds balance while you shoot, like a tightrope walker's pole.

Lifted above the operator's head, a monopod can become an instant hand-held crane, camera boom, or jib. It can shoot over the heads of a crowd or provide a high-angle shot. It can also be used to shoot just inches off the ground by holding the monopod upside down and uprighting the image in postproduction.

The Manfrotto 560B1 ($155) and 560B are current and previous models of a monopod with three retractable feet, which provide a steadier foundation. The big innovation with this monopod is a fluid-damped ball head built into the three-footed base to create smoother panning and more stability when shooting on a tilted angle. The 560B (pictured on the left in Figure 11.3) is particularly useful in tight places over extended periods of time where a tripod may not be allowed, like sports and public events. Its four sections extend to a length of 65.5 inches and collapse to 26 inches. It weighs 1.54 pounds, approximately twice the weight of the 776B.

Vehicle Mounts

One of the advantages of a palm-sized camcorder like the G10/XA10 is the ability to place it almost anywhere—for example, in a car. Cars are an integral part of contemporary life. What would feature films be like without car scenes, or modern documentaries without the ability to film conversations in cars? For many of us, a significant portion of our daily life is spent in a car: traveling, commuting, doing chores, or at leisure. As a container for one or more human beings, a car creates its own hermetic world—a pocket of private space within the larger world that passes by the windows. The enclosed space of a vehicle can even intensify relationships as people share cramped quarters for the duration of a ride.

Iranian director Abbas Kiarostami is a master of writing and directing scenes taking place in cars. Most of his 95-minute feature film, *A Taste of Cherry,* is an extended car ride as a man searches the outskirts of Tehran to hire someone to bury him after he commits suicide. *A Taste of Cherry* won the Cannes Film Festival Palme d'Or in 1997.

Kiarostami's film *Ten* is composed entirely of conversations and interactions during 10 car trips over the period of a day or two as a divorced Iranian woman drives her son, her sister, a praying woman, a prostitute, and others within the city of Tehran. We never leave the inside of a car during the 94-minute production. *Ten* is listed in *Empire Magazine's* "100 Best Films of World Cinema" and named by *Cahiers du Cinema* as one of the "10 Best Pictures of the 2000s." Yet *Ten* was produced with the simplest of technology: two palm-sized camcorders mounted on each corner of the dashboard or windshield—one framing the driver and the other framing the passenger. *Ten* was shot in PAL DV, which has a resolution of 414,720 pixels. In comparison, the G10/XA10 has 2,073,600 pixels—five times the picture quality.

Although I have been describing feature fiction films, the concept of mounting a camcorder in a car equally applies to documentary, music video, commercials, travelogues, event videography, and personal media. You may already have the G10 or XA10; now all you need is a car mount.

The Panavise 809 Camera Window Mount ($26), shown in Figure 11.4, holds up to 3 pounds on a smooth, flat, non-porous surface like a car window. It has just barely enough strength to secure the G10/XA10, which weighs approximately 2 pounds with its battery installed. The Panavise consists of a ball joint that rotates 360º and tilts –90/+90º with a camera screw and locking collar mounted on a strong 3¼-inch suction cup. For a more secure professional mount, the Gripper 115 ($79) made by Film Tools has a 4½-inch suction grip and is rated for up to 50 pounds. Film Tools makes an even heavier Gripper, model 116XL ($110–$140), which has a 6-inch suction grip, metal support rods, and is rated for up to 70 pounds. The 4½-inch vacuum grip should be more than adequate for inside an automobile.

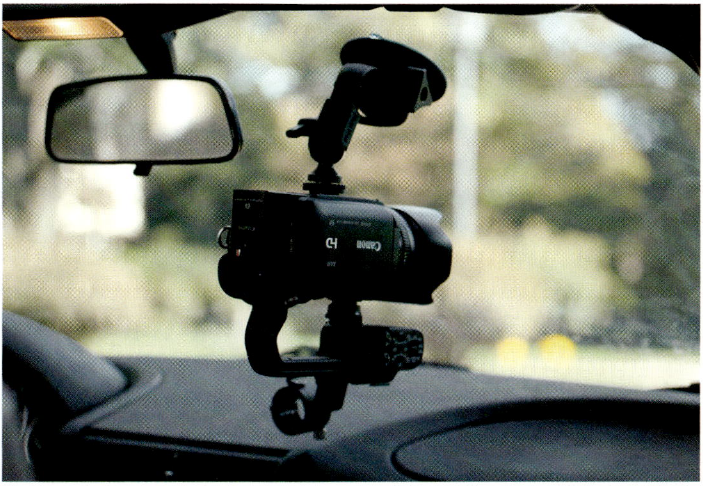

Figure 11.4 The lightweight Panavise 809 window mount for cameras.

The mounting surface must be clean. Also, it is useful to dampen both the surface and the suction cup with water spray. Then, simply press the cup against the surface, press its pump mechanism, and pull up the grip's locking lever to clamp the camera support mechanism tightly against the cup. The camcorder can be pointed at the driver or passenger, or can be turned to shoot through the window on which it has been mounted. If you intend to shoot through the front window, the camcorder will need to be mounted upside down because of the slant of the typical windshield. This is no problem. The image can be digitally turned upright and re-rendered in most video-editing programs. Alternatively, you can correct it to be upright as you record it by using Scan Reverse record mode. Reverse scanning allows you to invert the image horizontally, vertically, or both. Shooting upside down needs both horizontal and vertical correction to create an upright image. (Choose FUNC > Film Clip icon > Scan Reverse Rec > Both.)

A vacuum grip will also mount externally on a flat area of the metal car body, if you are willing to take the risk. You can minimize this risk by also tethering the camera and its vacuum grip to some additional point on the car or to a second heavy-duty vacuum device like the FastCap Handle on Demand ($11), which is a plastic handle mounted on two large suction cups similar to a professional vacuum hand grip. Some cars' suspensions and some road surfaces may produce excessive vibration, particularly with the lightweight Panavise 809. You will need to experiment with the vacuum grip to determine when it will be more effective than simply hand-holding the camcorder inside the vehicle.

A vacuum grip can mount on any non-porous, flat surface that will sustain a vacuum, such as metal, glass, plastic, or Formica. It lends itself to many types of situations, not just vehicles—for example, on a kitchen countertop, a dressing-room mirror, or an upper pane of a house window to get a high-angle shot that would be impossible on a tripod. As with the exterior of a car, you might want to tether the rig to a stationary object or an auxiliary vacuum grip when mounting the G10/XA10 on vertical surfaces like a mirror or house window.

Another kind of car mount simply uses the upper edge of a side window as a vantage point, as shown in Figure 11.5. The Bushnel car-window mount ($27), the Manfrotto 243 car-window pod ($26), and the Giottos professional car-window mount ($54) provide a way to shoot external views with the camcorder from the comfort and convenience of a stationary car instead of setting up a tripod. Unlike the Film Tools and Panavise vacuum grips, these mounts are not intended to be used in a moving vehicle. They fit over the upper lip of a partially lowered car window. You secure them in place by gently tightening a padded clamp against the window glass.

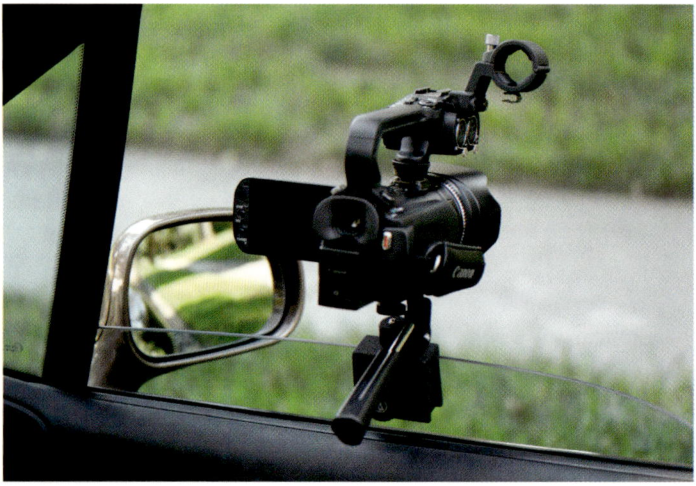

Figure 11.5 The Bushnel car-window mount.

The pan/tilt head on the Bushnel car-window mount is simply for positioning, not for fluid camera movements. The Bushnel mount itself is very lightweight, so users must be careful that it does not slip because adding the G10/XA10 creates a high center of gravity. The Giottos mount has an integrated pan/tilt head like the Bushnel, but is heavier duty. The Manfrotto 243 is quite sturdy, but is simply a clamp base for which you must separately purchase a pan/tilt head. The Manfrotto terminates in a ⅜-inch screw, which allows you to attach a fully functioning fluid video head like the 700RC2 ($76). The 700RC2 can produce smooth pans and tilts, provided the car window is not loose in its tracks.

12

Controlling the Moving Camera

Camera movement is basic to cinematic expression. The fact that the camera (the surrogate for the spectator) can move is one of the major characteristics that makes film and video aesthetically different from theater. Conceptually, the camcorder can move with its subject from a vantage point in front, alongside, or from behind, or can move in counterpoint, setting up a more complex relationship between the camera and the subject. A good example of each of these modes all in one shot is the scene in Scorsese's *Raging Bull*, when Robert de Niro, as boxer Jake LaMotta, comes from the dressing room and through the cramped arena hallways. At first, the camera is traveling in front, then momentarily alongside, and eventually following as de Niro's character enters the cheering, crowd-filled stadium. Halfway down the aisle, the camera and de Niro go separate ways. De Niro continues into the depth of the frame and climbs into the boxing ring while the camera moves to the right and ascends upward on an unseen crane, a counterpoint movement.

In addition, the camera can also move of its own volition. In this mode, the camera serves as the visual narrator of the scene when it searches, seeks, or reveals on its own. An example of this is the end of *Citizen Kane,* where the moving camera explores Kane's warehouse full of belongings accumulated over a lifetime and ends by revealing Rosebud. These two examples of long takes are highly structured. Each shot is engaging, has visual development, creates anticipation, and leads to a moment of significance. In *Citizen Kane,* it leads to a reveal, and in *Raging Bull*, it develops through a changing relationship between camera position and subject, to a grand establishing shot for the boxing match, and a visual summation of the central character's height of popularity. The camera movements are not arbitrary; each internal development could have been a different panel in a storyboard.

Even when shooting an event or an observational documentary, every camera movement should count. Very likely, this will mean holding for long lengths of time while the subject moves within the frame or even enters or exists from the frame, saving camera movements for major actions, reactions, and responses. The spectator is engaged and reassured if camera movements are decisive and meaningful. Shooting with too many camera movements, or following every micro-movement of the subject, over-determines the footage, making it difficult to edit. Arbitrary and indecisive camera movements are not useful at all. There is a need for structure and development within the moving camera shot, and a single moving camera often replaces what could have been many individual shots.

Formal camera movements consist of the pan, tilt, crane, zoom, and dolly and their hand-held and Steadicam equivalents. Devices for aiding the movement of palm-sized camcorders include optical and digital image stabilization, handgrip, fluid pan/tilt head, hand-held monopod, camera stabilizer, wheelchairs, mini dollies, skater dollies, sliders, jibs, and vehicle mounts.

Hand-Held Camera Movement

For hand-held work with the camcorder, cupping your hand under the built-in side strap lends itself to tilted horizons and even a rotational wobble as your wrist flexes. Many users prefer shooting with a pistol grip or a small monopod mounted directly below the camcorder's center of gravity. The Barska Accu Grip ($14) works well.

A wide-angle lens demagnifies camera instability. Conversely, telephoto magnifies any instability, which has ramifications for hand-held work. In addition, telephoto looks like an optically enlarged image, whereas physical proximity in wide angle or normal will feel like actually being close. In fact, some filmmakers adopt a hand-held strategy of shooting primarily in wide angle and accomplish long shots, medium shots, and close-ups by physically moving with the camera instead of zooming. Compared to zooming, this will have a much different feeling that will more physically place the spectator within the circle of interaction.

Image Stabilization

Because our brains cross-reference the information from our eyes with our biological sense of balance, the perceived world does not bounce or rock as we walk, jump, or move through space. If you want to create an image of the world the way we perceive it without unintended dips and jolts, the central problem with camera movement is image stabilization.

Because the G10/XA10 is lightweight, well balanced, has good image stabilization, and is easy to hand hold, it lends itself to mobility. The camcorder has three levels of optical image stabilization. Optical image stabilization uses a set of moving optical elements in the lens that are affected by inertia or powered servomotors. The elements consequently bend the light in the opposite direction of an abrupt movement to correct for camera shake. Standard and Dynamic image stabilization operate solely with inertia-sensitive lens elements. Dynamic image stabilization is the most appropriate for hand-held work, including pans, tilts, and walking with the camcorder. Standard is appropriate for shooting when the camcorder is primarily stationary or when using an auxiliary wide-angle or tele-converter lens. It is also possible to turn image stabilization off for occasions when the camcorder is solidly mounted. To choose image stabilization settings, choose FUNC > Image Stabilizer and then choose Standard, Dynamic, or OFF

When image stabilization is activated, a symbol appears in the upper right of the touchscreen. For Standard stabilization, the symbol is an image of a hand. For Dynamic stabilization, a hand with the letter D appears. (See Figure 12.1.) Dynamic image stabilization is the default mode in the G10/XA10, and it works well in wide angle up to three-quarters of the zoom range. It will cover most of your hand-held needs for stabilization.

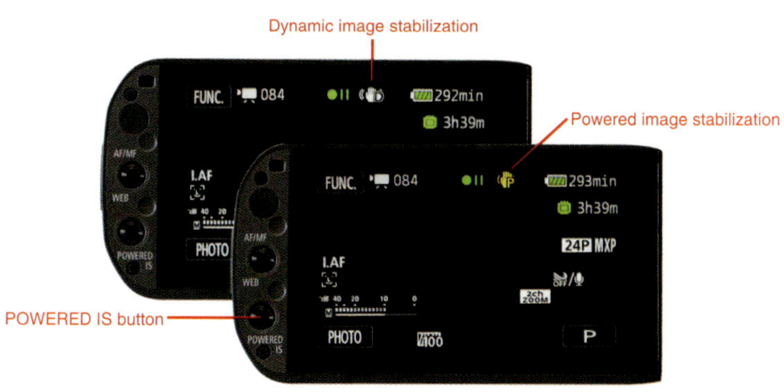

Figure 12.1 Dynamic and Powered image stabilization.

As you approach full telephoto, the lens not only magnifies the size of the image, it significantly magnifies camera shake. Additional stabilization is necessary. The inertia of the camera lens is caused simply by its mass, and is no different when the lens is in telephoto than in wide angle. Yet a 42.5mm telephoto needs 10 times the stabilization of a 4.25mm wide angle. Powered IS is a special stabilization mode that more aggressively holds the frame in one place. It is not intended to handle major camera movements.

For greater resistance to unwanted motion, Powered IS (image stabilization) uses sensors called "accelerometers," which detect subtle movements and send a signal to servo units in the lens that more aggressively position counter movements of the image-stabilizing elements. The G10/XA10's Powered IS attempts to keep points of interest in the same place in each frame. It does this with much less degradation of the image than postproduction techniques because stabilization is accomplished optically.

Powered IS should be used primarily for those times when you need to make a hand-held shot appear as stable as on a tripod or Steadicam while holding a tight frame in telephoto, such as a facial close-up taken from a distance. This mode is intended for keeping the frame in one place, and not for major movements of the camera itself such as quick pans or tilts for which Powered IS will over-compensate, making the image initially blur at the edges and eventually swim and bounce.

Powered IS does not appear as a menu-screen choice in the Image Stabilization panel because it is turned on and off entirely by an external button. Pressing the POWERED IS button on the left bezel of the touchscreen momentarily overrides any existing stabilization setting. The symbol in the upper right of the touchscreen becomes a yellow hand and the letter P, indicating that Powered IS is active.

Powered IS should happen at only selected times—typically, while shooting a tightly framed image. Consequently, it is made to operate only when you manually press the POWERED IS button on the left bezel of the touchscreen and is disengaged when you physically release the button. Upon release, the camcorder automatically returns to the default mode of Dynamic optical image stabilization. The POWERED IS button can be set to operate in either hold on/release off, or press on/press off. If you anticipate a number of static hand-held telephoto shots of extensive length, you can re-program the POWERED IS button to operate as press on/press off instead of its default intermittent mode. To do so, choose FUNC > MENU > Tool icon > Powered IS Button; then select Toggle On/Off (or select Press & Hold to return to the preferred mode of operation).

Note

The Toggle On/Off setting is not recommended. In this mode you must consciously press the button a second time to disengage Powered IS. Leaving Powered IS running for extended periods will drain the battery more quickly. More significantly, it can too easily be left on in situations where it is not appropriate.

Image stabilization can also be accomplished in postproduction. Avid, Final Cut Pro, After Effects, and other programs can magnify the image and re-render each frame so that certain fixed points sequentially appear in the same place relative to the frame.

This is effective for unsteady hand-held shots that ought to be still. It is less effective on tracking shots, but you could try to have a runner's nose, ear, or cap appear in the same place in each frame, as if the camera stayed perfectly locked to this moving image. In either case, digital image stabilization in postproduction usually degrades the image because it has to crop, enlarge, and re-render sequential images to make the frame appear steady for the whole shot. However, if you are able to work in a non-linear software application that provides a 10-bit color space (versus the usual default setting of 8-bit color space), the amount of image degradation will be minimized. DaVinci Resolve and Apple Color enable the editor to adjust to color space accordingly.

Zoom Versus Dolly

A zoom is an optical camera movement that attempts to imitate a dolly. In actuality, the two feel somewhat different. A dolly physically moves the spectator through space, whereas the zoom magnifies and demagnifies a flat image from a fixed position. The zoom feels considerably flat, while the dolly feels more dimensional. A dolly places the spectator more tangibly in the world of the story or event.

Do not zoom excessively. A zoom feels like a self-conscious manipulation of the image. A zoom-in to telephoto can feel like an exclamation point, as if the camera operator is saying "Look at this!" A zoom can easily call attention to itself; excessive zooming communicates impatience and severely limits your options in editing. Most of the time, cinematographers and videographers use the zoom to adjust framing and hold that position for a considerable duration until there is a compelling reason to reframe or change scale.

When you do use a zoom, the G10/XA10 has a number of sophisticated features that help make the zoom less obtrusive and potentially more expressive. These include variable-speed operation and the ability to program 16 constant speeds from as short as two seconds to as long as four minutes, 45 seconds over the entire zoom range. To achieve this, do one of the following (see Figure 12.2):

- Choose FUNC > MENU > Camera icon > Zoom Speed Level and select Fast, Normal, or Slow.
- Choose FUNC > MENU > Camera icon > Zoom Lever Zoom Speed and select Var or Constant (1–16).
- Choose FUNC > MENU > Camera icon > Handle Rocker Zoom Speed and set 1–16.
- Choose FUNC > MENU > Camera icon > Wireless Ctrlr Zoom Speed and set 1–16.

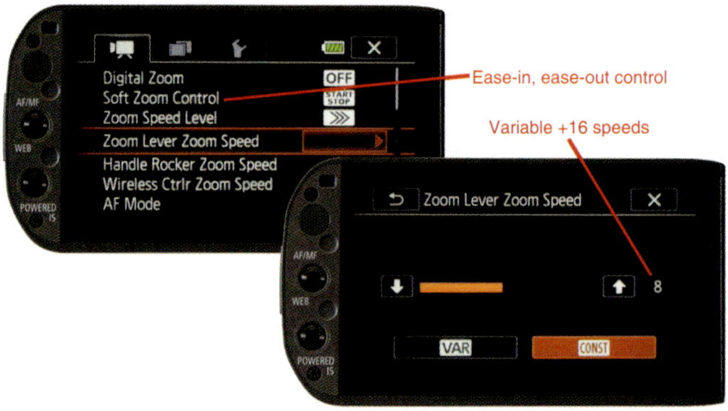

Figure 12.2 Extensive zoom controls.

The XA10 provides access to four different places for controlling the zoom: the touchscreen, the zoom rocker on the camcorder body, the zoom lever on the handle, and the zoom control on the remote. Each of these can be preset to a different zoom rate, which means you can have variable speed on one control. The touchscreen zoom control is accessed in the Programmed Menu (choose FUNC > Zoom).

The menu allows for an overall category of Fast, Normal, or Slow, which affects the rate of all the zoom controls. Fast doubles the speed compared to Slow, and normal is in between. The zoom control on the touchscreen has no additional speed adjustments. The zoom lever on the camera body can be additionally set for variable or for constant with its own choice of 16 speeds. The zoom rocker on the XA10 handle and the one on the wireless remote have independent speed presets from 1 to 16. So you can preset different zoom speeds on different controllers.

Soft Zoom

The G10/XA10's Soft Zoom Control setting enables you to customize zoom movement to seem less mechanical by providing for its speed to ease-in, ease-out, or both at the beginning and end of a zoom. This will help the zoom feel more natural, the way a dolly has to overcome inertia to start moving and has to decelerate to stop. This is a unique professional feature not found in other camcorders in this price range. To change this setting, choose FUNC > MENU > Camera icon > Soft Zoom Control and choose Off, Start, Stop, or Start & Stop.

Tripod

A tripod is just as much an instrument for camera movement as it is for stability, provided it has a good fluid head for smooth pans and tilts. Pan and tilt movements shot in telephoto can particularly benefit from the stability of a tripod. Refer to the previous chapter for a selection of tripods and fluid heads appropriate for the weight, scale, and price range of the G10/XA10.

Just as it is possible to zoom too much, it is possible to pan too much. Excessive pans create the equivalent of a ping-pong match that becomes less interesting with repetition and problematic to edit. A dialogue structured with pan left, pan right, pan left, pan right, pan left, pan right, and so on, will soon cry out for a two-shot of both speakers or holding on one as the other talks off-screen. Pan at significant moments, not every moment.

The fact that a tripod is typically locked in one place means that it can easily feel constrained as a scene develops. This can be countered by finding new physical positions for the tripod so that the scene has visual development. It is also possible to physically liberate the tripod by combining it with other means of motion. Simply combining a pan with a simultaneous zoom can create a compound movement that keeps the tripod from feeling pivoted in one spot and the zoom from feeling like a flat magnification. Other devices that help the tripod break out of its spatial limitations include mounting a jib or a slider on the tripod or mounting the tripod itself on a dolly platform so that it can physically move through space.

Camera Jib

A jib is a hand-operated boom with the camera at one end and counterweights at the other. It is sometimes called a "mini crane." Lightweight models have a six- to 12-foot arm that can be mounted on a tripod at its fulcrum point. Larger and longer ones need a heavy-duty base of their own. The cradle for the camera has controls to remotely adjust its tilt independently of the movement of the arm.

A jib adds the vertical dimension of camera movement. It can take the camcorder through sweeping vertical and horizontal moves that feel more dynamic than simply rotating or tilting the camera on the axis of a tripod's pan head. In addition, a jib can quickly frame high-angle and low-angle shots, whereas a tripod is always stuck at the limited height of its legs. Among the lowest-priced models, the ProAm DVC200 camera jib, shown in Figure 12.3, has an eight-foot arm and sells for $279. Prices for camera jibs can extend into the thousands. Complex models have servomotors and remote monitors.

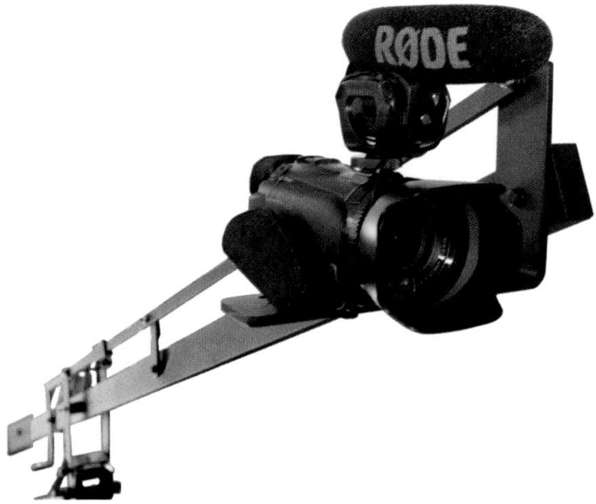

Figure 12.3 ProAm DVC200 camera jib.

Camera Stabilizers

Cinematographer Garrett Brown invented the Steadicam in the early 1970s as a way to physically isolate and suspend the motion-picture camera from the operator to produce spectacularly smooth tracking shots. The Steadicam premiered in feature-length films in 1976 with *Marathon Man*, *Bound for Glory* (winner of the Oscar for Best Cinematography), and *Rocky* (winner for Best Picture). It has been a staple of motion-picture production ever since. Over the last two decades, other companies have started making competing devices, and the term "Steadicam" is sometimes applied generically (like Kleenex for tissues and Coke for a cola drink).

A full stabilizer rig for a 35mm motion-picture camera or large video camcorder consists of a body harness, an articulated arm, a precisely balanced camera mount on top of a vertical armature attached to an ultra-low friction gimbal, and a sled at the opposite end containing counterweights, batteries, and a dedicated monitor. The whole rig with camera included can weigh 40 to 70 pounds and involve weeks or months of training to operate. With the advent of small, professional-quality digital camcorders, models like the Blackbird designed by Camera Motion Research, the HD1000 by Glidecam, and the Merlin by Steadicam are made for lightweight handheld operation without the additional body braces. (See Figure 12.4.)

Instead of supporting a 20- to 40-pound camera, which in turn needs to be counterweighted and monitored, the lightweight stabilizers are designed for camcorders weighing one to seven pounds and depend on the camcorder's LCD screen for monitoring.

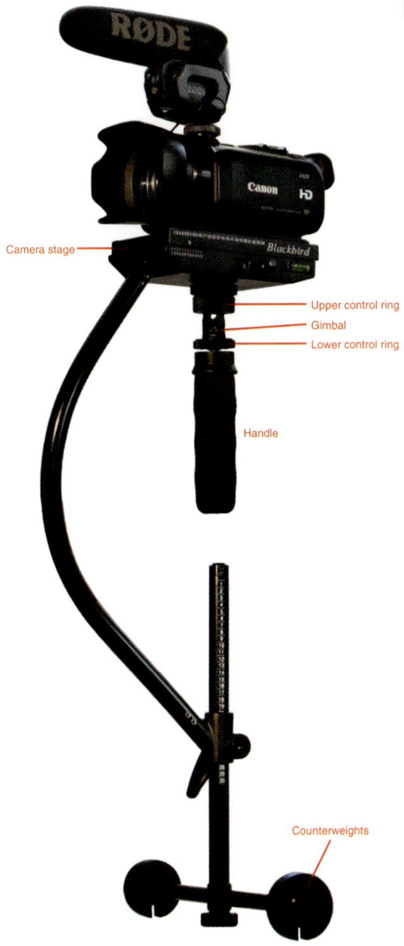

Figure 12.4 Blackbird stabilizer.

The mini stabilizers are simple compared to a full Steadicam rig; are light enough to dispense with the dedicated monitor, articulated arm, and body harness; and are simply held by hand with a handle attached to the gimbal. But even these lightweight models demand a certain amount of practice, finesse, and stamina to achieve professional results. Holding and balancing even four to eight pounds (the camcorder, battery, armature, handle, gimbal, and counterweights) in front of you can become a strain on your arm, wrist, and back over an extended period of time.

People who have never used a Steadicam or similar stabilizer have the misconception that you just strap it on and it does all the work for you. In actuality, it requires practice; coordination of arm, leg, and back muscles; and almost acrobatic dexterity to use a Steadicam well. Even with a hand-held unit, it can take 30 minutes and sometimes longer to make all the adjustments to balance the camcorder on the stabilizer.

The camcorder base must rest perfectly horizontal on the fore and aft, sideways, and rotational planes of the stabilizer's mounting platform. This platform in turn rests on an armature pole connected to a ball socket or ultra-low friction gimbal joint. Then you need to adjust counterweights and leverage at the opposite end of the armature, locate the stabilizer's center-of-gravity balance point, and adjust the gimbal position to be just above the center of gravity. The test for this is when the stabilizing armature is turned horizontal, it almost balances with the camcorder on one side and counterweights on the other, but it slowly uprights itself with the camcorder on top. When all the adjustments are correct, the camcorder is suspended in a nearly neutral position so that the inertia of its own weight and its counterweights, and the leverage of the unit's support armature, resist vibration and abrupt changes.

Now comes physical practice, which can take days or weeks as you develop dexterity. Initially, your arm or back will get sore after about 20 to 30 minutes. First, you will have to practice simply taking a few steps and coming to a stop without the camcorder wanting to rotate, tilt, or move on its own. After you have mastered starting and stopping, you will practice moving backward in a straight line while shooting forward, and walking forward while shooting backward. You eventually move on to making turns and more complex movements with high, low, and angled camera positions. With heavier body-braced rigs, you will wait until you have mastered moving in open spaces before trying to walk through an actual doorway or turn an actual corner without the camcorder bashing into the wall. Later skills include climbing stairs. It is for these kinds of moves that the physical stabilizer, with its counterbalanced weights, leverage, and gimbal, far exceeds what the optical stabilization built into the G10/XA10 can do.

Very likely, you will use the camcorder's built-in image stabilization for most hand-held work and use the Steadicam or comparable device for the occasional long tracking shot over rough terrain or to glide up the steps of the Philadelphia Art Museum as in *Rocky* (1976), which was shot by Garrett Brown himself. Stabilizers appropriate for the G10/XA10 are the Steadicam Merlin ($799), manufactured by Tiffen; the Glidecam HD1000 ($369); and the Blackbird ($469), by Camera Motion Research. My personal preference is the Blackbird for small camcorders like the G10/XA10.

If you cannot afford $369 to $799 for a camera stabilizer the size of a Merlin, GlideCam, or Blackbird, there are several alternatives. One is to shoot hand-held tracking and dolly shots in full wide angle to demagnify camera shake. Another is to hand-hold a monopod. Shots that follow or move along with primary motion within the frame (like running with a runner in the shot) will somewhat justify camera shake, and the moving figure within the frame will call less attention to irregularities of movement of the frame itself.

A Monopod as a Stabilizer

Imagine if you had to carry a teacup filled to the brim by holding it the way we do a camcorder: with your fingers under a leather strap attached to its side. Liquid will spill with the slightest bounce or bend of the wrist. Carrying a dozen filled teacups on a tray might be easier to keep steady, both because of the inertia of additional weight plus the balance achieved by the lateral width of the tray acting somewhat like a tightrope walker's pole. The same principles of inertia and balance apply when you carry a camcorder on a sophisticated device like a Steadicam. They can even apply to a monopod.

A monopod is already much more mobile than a tripod, and it does not always have to rest on the ground. It can be used like a stripped-down Steadicam for mobile shots. Place the monopod horizontally across your index and middle finger to find the balance point between the camcorder and the rest of the pole. This is the center of gravity for the monopod at that particular length. For mobile shots, hold the monopod just above the center of gravity and you will have the maximum stabilization the monopod is capable of providing. If this is combined with Dynamic image stabilization and predominantly wide angle, camera movements can be almost as fluid as a Steadicam.

Sliders and Mini Dollies

Camera sliders are used for two- to three-foot horizontal (and sometimes vertical) movements with DSLR cameras and small camcorders like the G10/XA10. A slider is a three- to six-foot linear metal track or rail with a sliding low-friction mount for a camcorder. The slider can be placed on the floor for low angle, on a table for waist height, or on a tripod for variable height to create professionally smooth linear camera moves. Longer and heavier sliders can span two tripods. Movement with a slider or a dolly looks more dynamic than a pan, which feels rooted on a pivot. Sometimes, a two- or three-foot movement is enough to make the camera feel fluidly alive. To get the most production value out of a slider, you might move across a foreground subject or object that is framed in a z-axis (depth axis) composition. Sliding just enough to change the compositional relationship between foreground and background can create a strong illusion of dramatic movement when in essence you are moving the camera only a few feet.

The camera mount on a slider glides smoothly as you push it along the metal track. More expensive models operate with a geared rubber belt and a crank, and some are motorized. They vary in price from $150 to $1800. The cheapest ones may not be as quiet, nor glide as smoothly, and may not have the ability to be used vertically or on a slant. The versatile belt driven Kessler Pocket Dolly ($649) works horizontally, vertically, and on an angle.

At the lower end of the price range, the Igus DryLin W16-A linear motion system ($159) has many industrial uses, including serving as a camera slider. (See Figure 12.5.) It consists of a ¼-inch aluminum mounting plate on a four-inch carriage that slides on a hefty guide rail slightly over 39 inches (one meter) in length. The carriage has low-friction, lubrication-free bearings for gliding smoothly. The operation makes a mild sliding sound, which means the microphone should be separate from the camcorder, closer to the subject than to the slider.

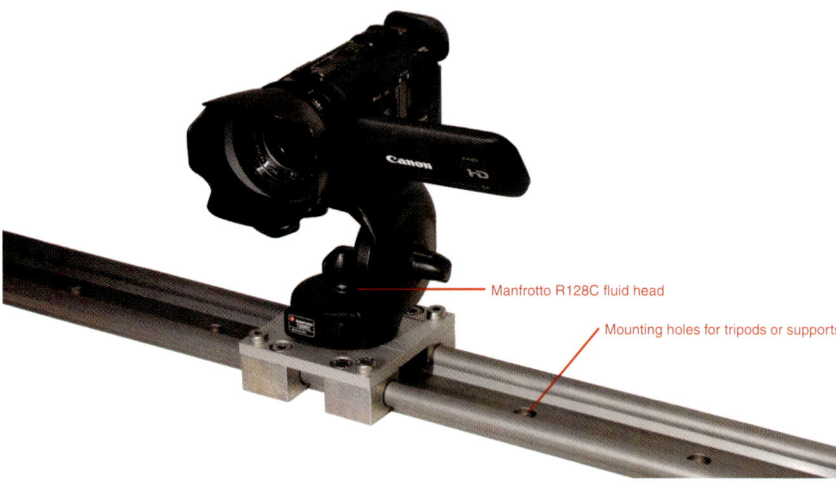

Figure 12.5 Igus DryLin linear slider.

Because this heavy-duty model is modular and customizable for various industrial purposes, it does not arrive ready for mounting the camcorder. You have to drill one 13/32- or 7/16-inch hole through the ¼-inch aluminum carriage plate to accommodate a ⅜-inch bolt for mounting a tripod head. One of the fluid heads discussed in Chapter 11, "Mounting the Camcorder," will do. When you drill the hole, cover sensitive areas with tape and make certain no metal shavings get on the bearings or rail. Igus also sells lighter-weight pre-drilled carriage and rail systems such as the DryLin W1040-B for $114 and the DryLin W1080-B for $150, plus the undrilled DryLin W1040-A for $80. Each of these is also one meter long. For the G10/XA10, the lighter rails are probably just as effective as the heavier model but may be more likely to warp if dropped or abused.

The bottom of the rail plate contains nine evenly spaced mounting holes about 4¾ inches apart. The central hole of the assembly can be attached with a bolt to the head of a heavy-duty tripod. Because the rail is only one meter in length and the camcorder is not heavy, the rail does not need to span two tripods. For the carriage to slide smoothly, it is important to keep the low-friction bearings and the rail clean.

If you are going to operate the assembly directly on the ground or floor, you might use a couple of six-inch pieces of 1×3 pine as protective feet bolted on the bottom of each end of the rail.

The Dot Line Pico dolly ($59) is a table-top "skater" with an adjustable wheel assembly at each end for creating straight or curved camera movements. (See Figure 12.6.) Its body is a 7¾-inch long metal mounting plate with a central hole for a pan/tilt head and additional holes for accessories. The Pico dolly is like an expensive roller skate with slightly softer wheels that has been machined for smooth operation with a small camcorder or DSLR. It can be used on a table for close-up videography, on a smooth floor for low-angle dolly shots, or on a 1×6 plank mounted across two tripods for horizontal moves at higher levels. The ball-bearing wheels produce some sound, so the microphone should be closer to the subject than to the dolly. It is compact and convenient and comes with a zippered nylon carrying case.

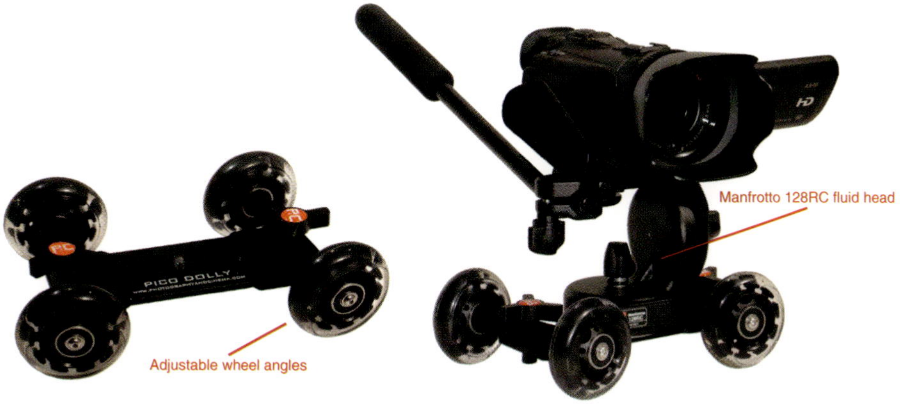

Figure 12.6 Pico skater dolly.

RigWheels are a portable and customizable way to provide mobility for the camcorder. They consist of four small carriage assemblies with four one-inch wheels per carriage with a 5⁄16-inch bolt for mounting each carriage. They can be configured as a floor or track dolly by bolting them to a plywood base wide enough to fit your tripod. As a dolly, it can run on a floor provided the floor is very smooth. But wooden, tile, ceramic, linoleum, cement, and even marble floors are typically uneven, and carpet would be impossible. RigWheels are more effective as a track dolly running on inexpensive 1⅛- to two-inch diameter PVC pipe from the hardware store. Lay out two rails of track, align the width between them to the spacing of the wheel assemblies on your platform dolly, and secure the track to the floor with Mylar packing tape. Dolly movement is now perfectly straight and smooth, and the four small wheels on each carriage unit perfectly straddle the PVC pipe.

As an alternative, RigWheels can be bolted to a smaller base of plywood, plastic, or metal and used as a skater dolly, table dolly, or slider. A price of $115 for four tiny sets of wheels may seem high, but the quality of their construction, the ease with which they can be mounted, and the fact that they glide well on both rounded pipe and smooth flat surfaces make them far less expensive and more versatile than many other kinds of dollies and sliders.

13

Still Photography

Why do you need stills while shooting video? There are lots of reasons, including events that need to be documented by both stills and video, production photos (useful for both documentary, fiction, and many other kinds of productions), and still images that are intended for use in the video production itself. When video is listed in catalogs or submitted to festivals, or when you are designing a cover for a DVD, there is often a need for a frame enlargement from the video itself or an even higher quality photographic image.

Photos produced by the G10/XA10 are in JPEG format, a standard created by the Joint Photographic Experts Group for digitally encoding and compressing still photographic images. JPEG files occupy a small amount of space in memory but lose image quality with successive editing and recompressing. Once you have imported your JPEG files into a photo-editing program, it is useful to convert them into Tagged Image File Format (TIFF) files, which is usually an option under a Save As command. TIFF is a system for encoding still photographic images in uncompressed form or with LZT compression, which reduces file size but has no loss of quality when repeatedly edited and saved. The TIFF standard works particularly well with Adobe software (such as Photoshop) because Adobe owns the copyright to TIFF specifications.

Image sizes of 1,920×1,080 pixels, or preferably larger, are often shot specifically for the purpose of being inserted into video in postproduction: a close-up of the signature on a document, the name on an office door, books on a shelf, a painting hanging on a wall, a street sign. Photographic stills ranging from close-up detail to large-scale shots of buildings, bridges, and landscapes are useful as establishing shots, details, inserts, and cutaways in an edited video sequence. Images much larger than 1,920×1,080 allow for cropping, leveling, blowing up details, and the potential for creating pan-and-scan movements like the archival photos in Ken Burns' *Civil War.* Adding a slight bit of movement to a still image brings it alive, provides a sense that it is being observed in the real world, and gives it emphasis. Otherwise, the extreme rigidity of a still photo can stick out in a sequence of live action shots, and a series of completely stationary photos tends to look like a slide show.

Canon optimized the G10/XA10 for video by using a CMOS photo sensor of exactly 1,920×1,080 pixels to dramatically increase low-light response and eliminate video artifacts from downscaling a much larger number of much smaller pixels. This is an advantage for high-definition video, which is inherently limited to a maximum resolution of 1,920×1,080, but a detriment for serious still photography, which typically uses higher resolutions. Video seems reasonably sharp with a resolution of 1,920×1,080 because each pixel is being replaced 24, 30, or 60 times a second. This provides an apparent sharpness called "temporal resolution." In contrast, a still photograph of 1,920×1,080 allows every pixel to be visible as soon as it is larger than a snapshot. Even though still photography is often an integral part of producing a video, Canon is betting that video makers will not regularly use palm-sized camcorders as their primary means of making still photographs. Market research might support this conclusion.

The best solution for still photography while using the G10/XA10 is simply to carry a separate dedicated 10- to 20-megapixel still camera. A good companion camera might be the Canon Powershot S100, Powershot G12, or Powershot G1-X.

The S100 weighs just 6.1 ounces. It is a very compact, simple-to-operate, ultra-slim pocket-sized camera. The Powershot G12 weighs 12 ounces and has a hinged multi-angle 2.8-inch LCD viewing screen. Both have optical image stabilization and good manual overrides for controlling exposure and focus. They sell for $429 and $379, respectively, and usually outrank other cameras in their price range. The G1-X weighs 17 ounces and has a 3-inch vari-angle LCD screen. It is a full-featured large-sensor camera with an integrated non-removable zoom and is lighter and more compact than a DSLR. The GX-1 sells in the $700 range. These are the point-and-shoot models that professional photographers carry as backups to their $1,500 to $5,000 DSLRs. In the $300 to $370 price range, you might also want to consider the 12.2-megapixel Nikon Coolpix P300 with a 4.2× f/1.8 zoom lens or the 10.1-megapixel Panasonic Lumix LX-5 with a 3.8× f/2.0 zoom.

The G1-X has a 1.5-inch CMOS sensor, which is larger than the micro 4/3 cameras produced by Panasonic and Olympus. It has 14.3 megapixels (seven times the pixel count of the G10/XA10), low-noise image processing, a 4× optical zoom that opens to f/2.8 in wide angle, hybrid image stabilization, and multi area white balancing.

The G1-X was a standout at the 2012 Consumer Electronics Show and made almost every reviewer's top-10 list. The S100 and the G12 are more modest, but either one would be a good photo companion to the G10/XA10. They capture 12.1- and 10-megapixel images, respectively (five to six times the pixel count of the G10/XA10). The S100 uses a 0.588-inch ($\frac{1}{1.7}$-inch) CMOS sensor and the G12 uses a 0.588 inch CCD sensor.

All three cameras are capable of shooting RAW images without JPEG compression as well as standard JPEG photos, and they record on SDHC/SDXC memory cards. All three have a built-in program to produce high dynamic range photos, which retain detail in extreme highlights and deep shadows by combining the best parts of bracketed exposures taken in rapid sequence as the shot is taken. The cameras have SMART AUTO, which intelligently analyzes images and shooting conditions to select an appropriate setting, as well as semi-automatic program modes that match similar functions in the G10/XA10. For users of Canon Vixia camcorders, the icons and menu choices will be familiar.

The S100 features a 5.2mm–26mm optical zoom lens with a 5× range (the 35mm equivalent of 24×120mm), a maximum aperture of f/2.0 in wide angle to f/5.2 in telephoto, and a maximum sensitivity of ISO 6400, although you rarely want to shoot at more than 800 with a small-format camera. The lens will focus as close as 1.2 inches in wide angle and 12 inches in telephoto. The S100 can align and stitch sequential photos together into extended panoramic views. The G12 has a 6mm–30mm optical zoom lens with a 5× range (the 35mm equivalent of 28–140mm), a maximum aperture of f/2.8 (wide) to f/4.5 at telephoto, and a maximum sensitivity of ISO 3200. The G1-X's larger format features a 15.1–60.4mm optical zoom, which is a 4× zoom range (the 35mm equivalent of 28–112mm), and has a maximum sensitivity of ISO 12,800 for extreme low-light capability.

The S100, G12, and G1-X are ideal still cameras for accompanying the G10/XA10. They also shoot video. The G1-X and S100 will shoot 24p video in 1,920×1,080 high definition. The S100 will also shoot slow motion in 640×480 standard definition. These two could be used as a video backup camera for the G10/XA10, although in video mode the tiny S100 would have a short battery life. The video capabilities of the G12 are limited to 1,280×720p, 640×480 standard definition, and 320×240 Internet video size. The G12 is less likely to be used as video backup except in an emergency because it does not match the full 1,920×1,080 standard of the G10/XA10. But specifically for photos, it would be a good choice.

A more upscale option would be a full DSLR like the 18-megapixel Canon T3i (also called the 600D). The camera body weighs 18.2 ounces (516 grams) without a lens and, like the other cameras discussed, uses SDHC or SDXC memory cards. The price for the T3i body without lens is approximately $670. There are package prices that include the body and an EF-S 18–55mm image-stabilized zoom lens at approximately $800. With a maximum aperture of f/3.5 to f/5.6, this entry-level zoom does not have good low-light capabilities. A prime lens would perform one to three f/stops better, needing ½ to ⅛ the amount of light. As a supplement to the G10/XA10 for taking slightly wide high-quality stills that can later be cropped, a 28mm f/1.8 prime lens ($484) or even a 24mm f/2.8 prime ($359) would be much better for available light. The T3i has a flip-out rotatable LCD monitor screen that is useful for shooting at a variety of angles, including high overhead and very low. In addition to stills, the Canon T3i (or the more expensive Canon 60D, 7D, 5D Mark II, or 5D Mark III) would also serve as an excellent companion camcorder for shooting high-quality video at 24p, 25p, or 30p. Canon's DSLRs are impressive video cameras in their own right. (See Chapter 16, "Integrating with Larger Camcorders," for further discussion of DSLRs.)

G10/XA10 Stills

The G10/XA10 produces sharper still photographs than you would expect from a 2-megapixel photo sensor (1,920×1,080 equals a total of 2,073,600 pixels, slightly more than 2 megapixels). Some of the unexpected quality is due to the optics of the Canon lens, and the fact that the exposure system in the G10/XA10 is designed to favor the camera's f/4 aperture where its optical quality is best. The camera is ideally suited for taking preproduction stills of locations, storyboard poses, and in particular lighting tests, because it will show exactly what the image will look like when the same camera is used for video.

As long as large photo files are not needed, the G10/XA10 is an adequate snapshot still camera. Web sites and Facebook pages have become a significant extension of contemporary media production, and they make extensive use of photo images of modest size. Photo files that are 2 megapixels are perfect for the Internet, and are adequate for printing 3×5, 4×6, and 5×7 photos. Prints larger than that would need special software enhancement.

The G10/XA10 allows for shooting stills independent of shooting video, shooting stills while simultaneously recording video, or extracting stills from previous video clips. Live stills can be taken in several modes except while using digital zoom, the digi-teleconverter, or fadeout, or while shooting in CINEMA mode. The rationales for disabling the photo function in these modes are that digital enlargements may create pixels too large for stills, fadeouts are incompatible with still photos, and saturation and contrast are optimized for motion pictures in CINEMA mode at settings that are less effective as stills. However, there is nothing preventing you from extracting still frames from these video files after they have been shot.

Some AVCHD camcorders can take stills with automatic "smile detection" while simultaneously shooting video. This can be useful for home video and event videography. While the video is shot continuously, a camcorder with this feature automatically selects, shoots, and stores the smiling moments as JPEG stills in a separate folder. The Canon G10/XA10 cannot do this as an automatic function. You simply have the options of manually pressing PHOTO while continuously shooting video, shooting photos independently of video, and manually extracting stills from video files after they were shot.

The process of taking still photos with the G10/XA10 is easy. Simply press the PHOTO button at the bottom left of the touchscreen when in record mode. To snap live stills without jarring the camcorder, use the PHOTO button on the wireless remote. (See Figure 13.1.) As mentioned earlier, stills can be taken with or without recording video.

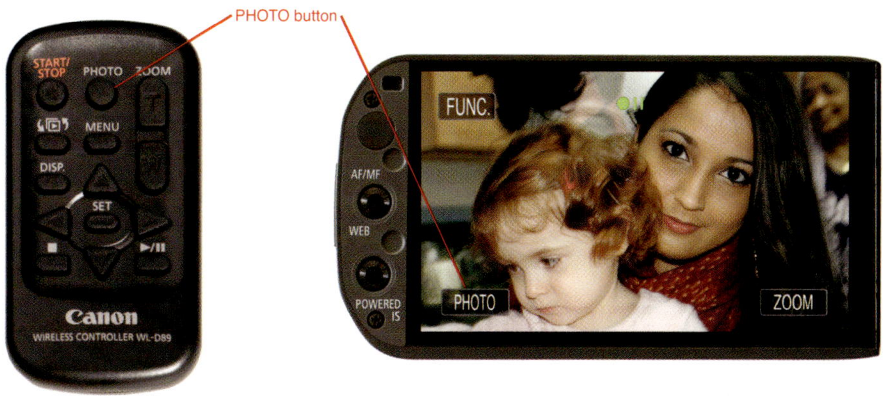

Figure 13.1 Photos can be triggered with the wireless remote or the touchscreen.

If you independently take still photos with the G10/XA10 while not simultaneously shooting video, do not forget that you can turn the camcorder 90° sideways for vertical compositions like individual portraits. A 4×6-inch vertical snapshot cropped from the camcorder's horizontal aspect ratio would provide a maximum of only 720 pixels wide by 1,080 pixels high, whereas tilting the camera to a vertical composition would provide 1,080 wide by 1,620 pixels high—more than twice the resolution in the final cropped image. It is useful to take production stills on location while the subject, background, and light are consistent with the video image, and videos often need vertical shots for DVD covers. Instead of having to blow up a vertically cropped composition from a horizontal video frame, shooting these vertical images with the G10/XA10 tilted 90° provides much better results. Of course, shooting all production photos with a dedicated still camera with a much higher pixel count would provide even better results.

Following are menu items related to recording still photography:

- One of the first things you need to do when setting up the camcorder is assign the memory location for storing photos. To do so, choose FUNC > MENU > Film Clip icon > Rec Media for Photos and select Internal, Card A, or Card B.
- You have the choice of letting your photo file numbers accumulate over months of intermittent shooting or starting from zero with each new project. To set this option, choose FUNC > MENU > Film Clip icon > Photo Numbering and select Reset or Continuous.
- You can select and capture stills from previously recorded video. To enable this, toggle the Camera/Playback button on the left side of the camcorder to Playback; then choose MENU > Film Clip icon > Photo Capture from Video and select Single Photo or Photo Sequence, as shown in Figure 13.2.

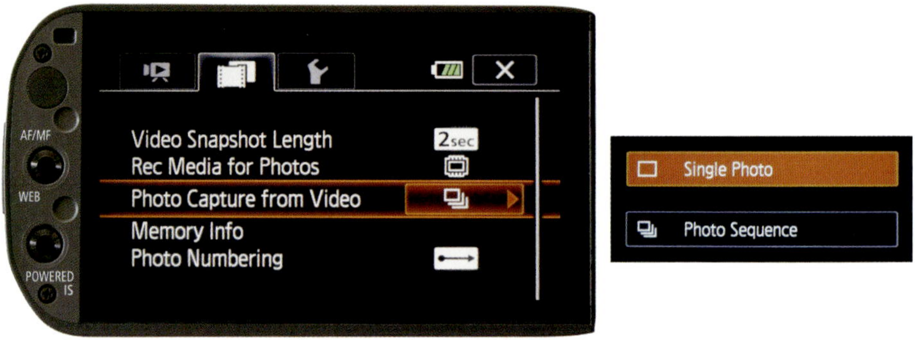

Figure 13.2 Photo capture from video.

To select and capture still photos from a video clip that has already been recorded, follow these steps:

1. Toggle the Camera/Playback button on the left side of the camcorder to Playback.
2. The touchscreen displays a storyboard of video images. Locate and play the video clip, then press Pause at the desired frame.
3. When you pause on a frame, the word PHOTO appears in the lower left of the touchscreen. Press the PHOTO button. The camcorder creates a JPEG photo file and deposits it in the DCIM folder in the memory location you have designated for still images. The photo's file number will be one digit higher than the previous photo, but its date and time information will be derived from the original video clip's data.

Once you have accessed a video clip, you can continue cueing, pausing, and selecting additional stills. If you have selected Photo Sequence instead of Single Photo, the video will automatically advance an additional frame after capturing each still, allowing you to sequentially convert a moment of video frame by frame into stills, up to 100 photos.

To optimize conditions for still photography, you may want to set the camcorder for a progressive mode like 24p, PF24, or PF30, and set a higher shutter speed such as 1/100 or 1/150 to minimize motion blur. As an acquisition method of shooting video solely for the purpose of extracting stills, you might want to set the camcorder for two-second, four-second, or eight-second video snapshots. The G10/XA10 stores JPEG files extracted from recorded video in the same DCIM folder with JPEG files that were shot live, separate from the AVCHD folder that holds video files.

Extracting a photo file from a video clip can be done with greater frame-by-frame control in postproduction, although the process within an editing program will usually take a couple extra steps. The built-in ability to do this in the camcorder provides convenience.

Viewing and Playing Photos

To view photos, toggle the Playback/Camera switch on the left side of the camcorder to Playback. The screen now displays a storyboard of thumbnail images of video clips. In the bottom left of the touchscreen, press the Index icon (it looks like files surrounded by a couple of curved arrows), choose the appropriate memory tab, and select Photos. This opens an Album page that displays either six or 15 photo thumbnail images at a time. (See Figure 13.3.) Moving the camcorder's zoom lever to wide or telephoto determines the number of images displayed. Scroll through the thumbnail images to locate individual photos.

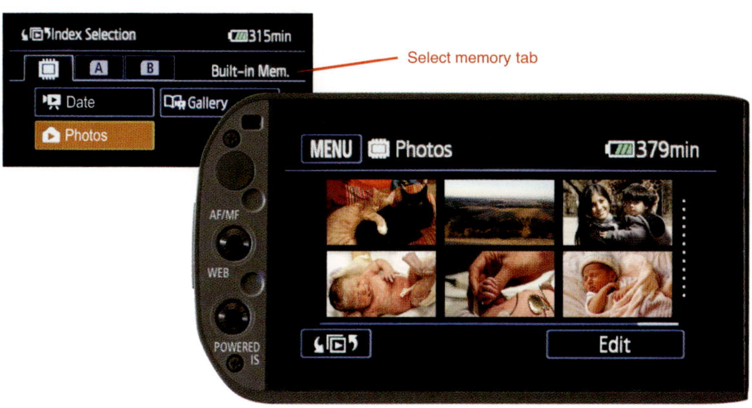

Figure 13.3 An album page of six thumbnail photo images.

Photos are numbered and organized in the sequence of when each file was created as a still image. As you move your finger left or right through the thumbnails, a scrollbar momentarily appears at the bottom of the screen. The scrollbar will allow you to quickly move through a large number of photos, permitting you to navigate through dozens or hundreds instead of albums of six or 15 at a time.

When you tap a particular thumbnail, the photo's image fills the screen. Gently moving your finger left or right lets you scroll one photo at a time. If you tap the full-screen photo, its memory location, sequence number, and file number appear near the upper right of the touchscreen. The top of the touchscreen shows buttons for MENU on the left and Edit on the right. The lower part of the screen has a Play icon on the left, which starts a slideshow; a checkerboard icon in the center for returning to the album of thumbnails; and an icon on the right for accessing the scrollbar.

To view the photos as a slide show, select and tap a starting photo. Press the Play button, which appears when a photo is tapped. To stop the slide show, tap the current photo and press the Pause icon when it appears. To return to the photo thumbnails, press the checkerboard album icon in the center or the scrollbar icon on the right.

To preset controls for viewing still photos, playing slide shows, and displaying photos to external sources, switch to Playback mode and choose MENU > Index icon > Photos. At the head of your menu, a still camera icon appears where the movie camera icon used to be and you have the following controls and options:

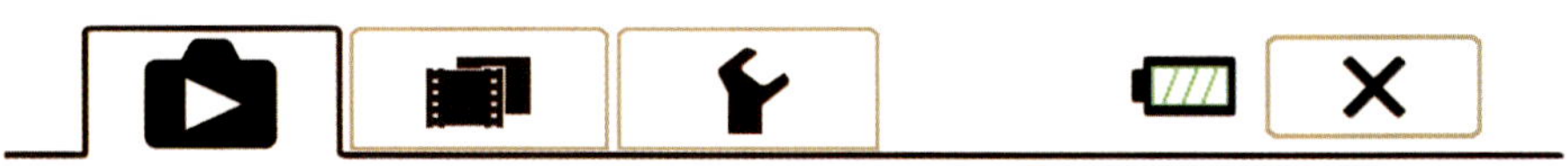

- Select Music (select 1, 2, 3, ON, or OFF)
- External Audio Input (ON/OFF)
- Data Code (to display date/time)
- Slideshow Transition (OFF, Dissolve, Slide)
- TV Type (Normal or Wide)

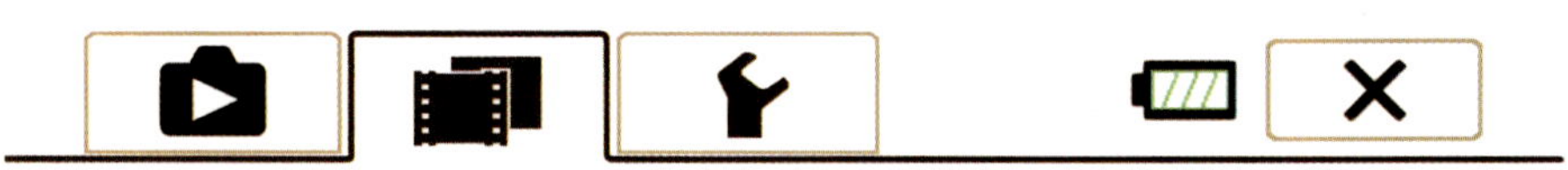

- Memory Info
- Photo Numbering

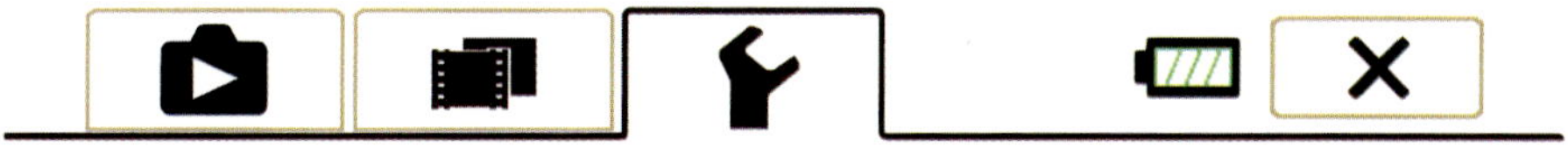

- Output Onscreen Displays (ON/OFF)
- Language
- LCD Brightness
- LCD Screen Dimmer (ON/OFF)
- AV Headphones (AV Outlet or Headphones)
- Volume (1–15)
- Notification Sounds (High Volume, Low Volume, OFF)
- Wireless Remote Control (ON/OFF)
- Power Saving Mode (ON/OFF, 10 Min, 20 Min, 30 Min)
- Initialize (Internal, Memory Card A, Memory Card B)
- Time Zone/DST
- Date/Time
- Battery Info
- Control for HDMI (ON/OFF)
- HDMI 1080p Output (ON/OFF)
- HDMI Status
- Firmware

It is possible to do some limited copying or deleting of photo files within the camcorder under Edit while in Playback mode. To copy files within the camcorder, there must be an initialized card in memory slot B and your source photo(s) must come from the internal memory or memory card A. In Playback mode, locate the photo source and engage the Edit function by choosing Index icon > memory source tab > Photos > Edit and selecting Copy or Delete. Of course, more complex editing functions can be done after the JPEG files are transferred to a computer.

Transferring Images to a Computer

When transferring photo files to a computer from the camcorder, it is advisable to power the camcorder with the compact power adapter. Then preselect the camcorder's memory location that contains the photo files by choosing Index icon > memory source tab > Photos while in Playback mode. Finally, connect the camcorder to the computer with the supplied USB cable.

As shown in Figure 13.4, when the camcorder acknowledges the computer, its touchscreen will say "USB Connection do not disconnect the power source," and the computer screen will display a CANON icon, which it recognizes as an external storage device (although it may show up as NO NAME). Once you have made this connection:

- Do not disconnect power from the camcorder.
- Do not disconnect the USB cable.
- Do not turn off the camcorder or the computer.
- Do not open the memory-slot cover.
- Do not change the camcorder's operating mode.

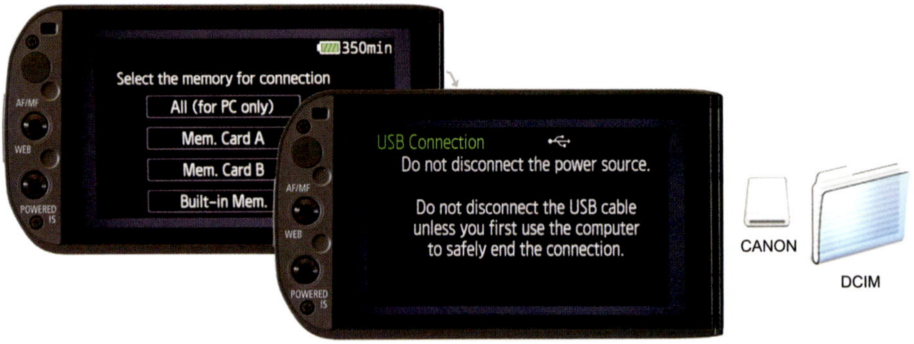

Figure 13.4 The camcorder acknowledges the computer.

Copy the photo files from the camcorder's DCIM folder onto your computer's hard drive as you would for a still camera. You may use whatever image file transfer program your computer has, or you may try a drag-and-drop method. On a Mac, Image Capture and iPhoto will import photo files. On a PC, use Windows Photo Gallery, or try Pixela, the transfer utility included with the G10/XA10 (which does not operate on Macs).

After you have completed the transfer, do not physically disconnect the USB cable, remove a memory card, or disrupt the camcorder's power until you have followed the computer's protocol to disengage the camcorder from the computer. On a PC, use the computer's Safely Remove Hardware function as you would when you eject any other USB memory source. On a Mac, drag the CANON icon to the Eject symbol. After the CANON icon has been removed and the camcorder's touchscreen no longer carries the "do not disconnect" warning, you may then unplug the USB cable. Disconnecting improperly could corrupt or permanently damage files.

If your DCIM file is on a removable memory card, it is also possible to transfer the files to a computer or other USB device through a card reader. Make certain the power on the G10/XA10 is completely off before you open the memory slot door and remove the card. Pressing the card inward should release its latch, popping the card up in its slot. Slide the write-protect tab on the card to the side marked "lock" before inserting it into an SDHC or SDXC card reader or slot on a computer. This is very important for protecting the files on your memory card. The computer will recognize the card as a memory device and may attempt to index or write data to it, which you want to prevent by locking the card. Once the computer acknowledges the memory card, follow the same procedures as just described, including the proper protocol for removing or ejecting the card when the transfer is complete.

Photo Enhancement

If you generate 1,920×1,080 photo files in JPEG, you may want to double or quadruple their resolution and transcode them to TIFF before color correcting, enhancing, or cropping in a photo-editing program. Even a simple color correction of a 1,920×1,080 image may produce noticeable striations of color across what should appear as a continuously smooth gradation. This "color banding" is less likely to be visible when stretched across twice as many pixels. After a still image has been processed in a photo-editing program, it can be imported into a video-editing program such as Avid Media Composer, Final Cut Pro, Premiere, or Vegas, which all have import options for determining how the image will fit the 1,920×1,080 video screen. Within the editing program, the image can be cropped, altered, or re-rendered to a perfect 1,920×1,080. Alternatively, it can be kept as a large file that can be optically panned, scanned, or zoomed with apparent motion. You have the whole range of these options if you have an image significantly larger than 1,920×1,080.

Photo-editing and enhancing software like Photoshop, Lightroom, and Aperture have varying abilities to resample, enlarge, and render a photographic image in a higher resolution. There are also dedicated programs specifically for increasing resolution of photos, such as Perfect Resize 7.0 (formerly called Genuine Fractals) made by onOne Software. Perfect Resize enables you to crop and enlarge JPEG and TIFF images to many times their original size while maintaining sharpness and detail, eliminating edge halos, and minimizing stair-casing of curved edges. Perfect Resize does not simply double or quadruple existing pixels, it uses a patented algorithm to calculate and interpolate new pixels and provides sophisticated controls for texture, sharpening, grain, and the computation of curved edges. It also has controls for enlarging an image to poster size with effects like a tile-mosaic appearance or wrapped edges. But our interest is in the program's ability to maintain image quality while modestly enlarging photo files.

Perfect Resize works as a standalone application or as a plug-in for Photoshop, Lightroom, and Aperture. If you already have Photoshop, Lightroom, or Aperture, you may want to test Perfect Resize before buying it to see if its features offer sufficient improvement for your purposes compared to similar functions in your existing photo-editing and enhancement software. Perfect Resize is available for a 30-day free trial at www.ononesoftware.com/products/suite/perfect-resize.

14

Extreme Close-Up Videography

Most photographic lenses have a close focusing distance equal to about 20× their focal length. However, a macro lens is capable of focusing much nearer to capture extreme close-ups. The G10/XA10 has some built-in ability to work in close range with a self activated mode called Tele Macro.

By one definition, a macro photo is an image taken in the range of a 1:1 ratio between the size of the subject and the size of the negative or photo sensor. A ratio of 1:1 on a ⅓-inch photo sensor would mean an image the size of a kernel of corn would have to fill the screen, which the G10/XA10 does not even come near achieving. Others define magnifications of 1:1 or greater as the beginning of photomicrography and define macro as the ability of a lens to focus closer than 20× its focal length. By this second definition, the G10/XA10's ability to extend focus manages to just enter the macro range. If you consider that 20 multiplied by the 42.5mm telephoto focal length equals 850mm (33.4 inches), focusing closer than 33 inches in telephoto (measured from the CMOS chip deep in the camcorder, not from the front of the lens) can be called macro under some definitions.

According to Canon, the camcorder's normal minimum focus distance in AUTO mode for full telephoto is about 3.3 feet (one meter). The camcorder's logic system, SMART AUTO, analyzes the subject and the shooting conditions, recognizes when you have exceeded the standard minimum distance while shooting in or near full telephoto, and automatically activates Tele Macro mode. You will know that you have entered Tele Macro mode when you see the AUTO button in the upper-left corner of the touchscreen change into a tulip icon with a letter T, as shown in Figure 14.1.

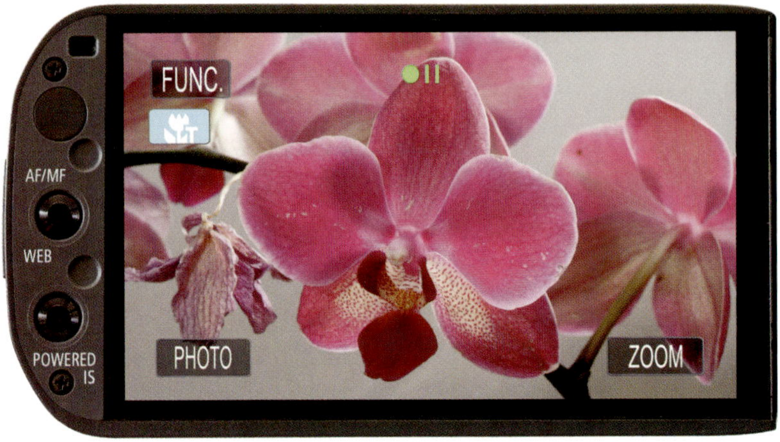

Figure 14.1 The tulip icon with a letter T indicates Tele Macro mode.

Tele Macro increases the camcorder's image stabilization and shifts lens elements toward macro position, which provides focus up to approximately 2 feet from the front of the lens and possibly closer under very bright light. (Canon literature says as close as 1.3 feet.) Aside from this ability to focus a few inches closer while in AUTO mode, the principal thing that SMART AUTO does when it enters Tele Macro mode is select the foreground object for focus as opposed to somewhere else in the composition.

Being able to focus at 2 feet instead of 3 feet does not produce a spectacular result, but it does give you some additional extreme close-up capability and allows the full AUTO mode to hold on the foreground subject. Canon's advertising singles out Tele Macro as a significant feature. However, Tele Macro is basically an assurance that if you shoot in full AUTO mode, SMART AUTO will recognize that an object in telephoto at 2 feet from the lens is an intentional element of the composition and will focus on it. If Canon were serious about providing macro capability on the G10/XA10, it would have designed an even closer focus range and would have made the feature available in M mode with options for manual controls of focus and exposure.

According to Canon, Tele Macro is available only in full AUTO mode. However, there does not appear to be much difference between letting the lens enter Tele Macro while in full AUTO versus using manual focus in the M mode under Programmed AE or Manual Exposure. With the telephoto lens fully extended, both can focus at about 2 feet, which is a few inches less than 20× the focal length (in other words, slightly into the macro range). Each provides a field size of about 3⅞ inches in diameter. So if the M mode allows you to get close enough, you may prefer the ability to use manual focus and manual exposure. Working at extremely close distances often requires the precision of manual controls.

Auxiliary Lenses

Some may be disappointed with the limited macro ability of the G10/XA10. But an auxiliary close-up lens called a diopter or a reverse-mounted prime lens from a DSLR provide ways of working even closer.

A diopter lens functions identically to a magnifying glass or eyeglasses for reading. The diopter threads onto the front of the camcorder's zoom lens. It brings close objects into focus and alters the ability of the lens to focus in its normal range. A diopter will allow you to shoot in full AUTO mode, but its real advantage is the potential of having semi-automatic or full manual control in the M mode.

The term "diopter" refers to both an optical measurement and to a magnifying lens that is measured in diopters. A #1 diopter comes into focus at 1 meter away, and would provide a working distance of 1 meter and closer. A #2 diopter comes into focus at ½ meter (about 19.5 inches), a #3 at ⅓ meter (about 13 inches), and a #10 at ⅒ meter (about 4 inches). The closer the focusing distance, the greater the magnification.

Single-element diopters are the least expensive way to achieve macro photography. Tiffen (an American manufacturer of filters) and Hoya (a division of Tokina Optical) make single-element diopter lenses that can fit on the front of the camcorder's zoom lens like a filter. A Tiffen or Hoya set containing three close-up lenses with a 58mm thread size costs from $11 to $20. The three diopters in the set allow for macro photography at seven different working distances, depending on whether they are used individually or in combination.

These diopters permit focusing at close camera-to-subject distances, but single-element lenses cannot optically provide a flat field of focus or edge-to-edge sharpness, and cannot bring all colors into sharp focus on the same plane for professional image quality. Sometimes these defects escape notice because they are obscured in the very shallow depth of field inherent in extreme close-ups. But only a multi-element lens can provide edge-to-edge sharpness and minimize chromatic aberration and distortion.

The 10× High Definition II macro lens from Opteka, shown in Figure 14.2, sells for $19. This is a four-element #10 diopter that is 40mm wide, adapted to fit a 58mm filter thread (the size of the camcorder's lens). Because this is a smaller-width lens in a 58mm mount, the outer limits of the image become masked in a circle of black in the wider third of the zoom range, but are not affected in mid-range or telephoto. It allows you to focus at a distance of ⅒ meter, approximately 4 inches from the lens. Opteka does not claim that the lens is "achromatic," which means it is probably not sufficiently corrected for chromatic aberration. But it should be an improvement over a single-element diopter if you do not need the full zoom range.

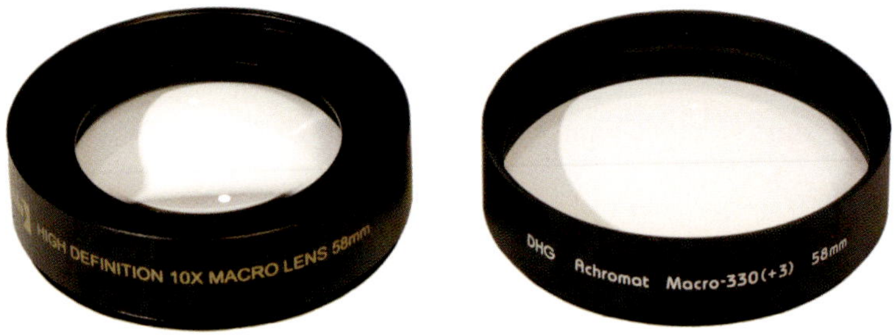

Figure 14.2 Multi-element diopter lenses by Opteka and Marumi for macro photography.

For higher image quality in a 58mm diameter, Canon makes the 250D achromatic close-up lens, which sells for $212 to $299. This is considerably more expensive than the $20 Hoya single-element lens or $19 Opteka. Its 58mm thread attaches to the front of the camcorder's zoom lens and its 250mm focal length changes the camcorder's maximum focusing distance from infinity to ¼ meter, or 9.9 inches.

Far more affordable is the Marumi 58mm DHG Macro 330 Achromat, also shown in Figure 14.2, which sells for $65. This is a professional quality +3 multi-element achromatic close-up lens made in Japan. It has an anti-reflective coating to minimize reflections that could degrade the image, and like the Canon 250D, it operates as an auxiliary lens that screws onto the front of the zoom. As a +3 diopter, it alters the maximum working distance from infinity to ⅓ meter, approximately 13 inches. This provides a little more working distance for lighting the miniature subject

Macro photography can also be accomplished by mounting a high-quality prime lens from a still camera to the front of the camcorder's zoom lens. They are attached to each other with a lens coupler that screws into the filter threads of both lenses, tying them together front-to-front. For example, the Canon 50mm f/1.4 prime lens for a DSLR has a 58mm thread to accommodate a potential filter. (Other DSLR lenses have sizes that range from 49mm to as large as 72mm.) A male-to-male, 58mm-to-58mm lens coupler with threads on each side reverses the DSLR prime lens and mounts it face to face to the 58mm front of the camcorder's zoom, as shown in Figure 14.3. The camcorder's lens shade would have to be removed for the zoom lens to accommodate the Canon 50mm prime lens. The two in combination become a high-quality macro system for shooting extreme close-ups with a field size of about ⅝ inch.

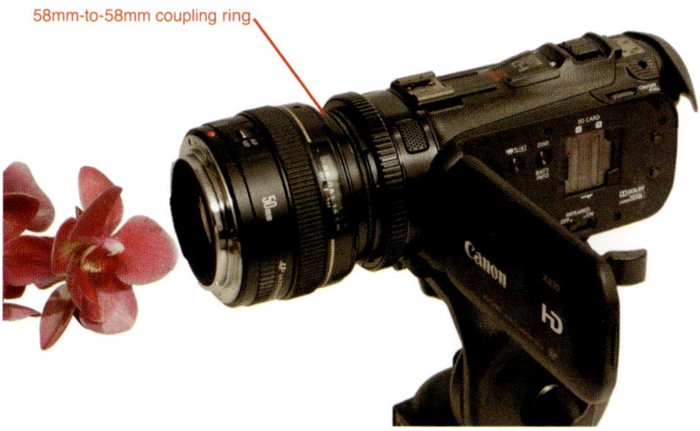

Figure 14.3 Canon 50mm f/1.4 prime lens, mounted in reverse.

Shooting in Macro

Macro video opens a different world full of creative and expressive possibilities for the videographer. Extreme close-up becomes a way to evoke an almost tactile sensation through visual means as the video image approaches the 1:1 scale of touch. An otherwise mundane everyday image or action can be defamiliarized when experienced on a macro scale and consequently compel the spectator to freshly see beyond that which is familiar or taken for granted. Defamiliarization is an aesthetic concept that comes from art theorist Viktor Shklovsky and is a central idea in dada, surrealism, formalism, and postmodernism.

In macro, even tiny movements become enormous. Some macro images may need Tv (Time value) Priority programmed mode to set a high shutter speed to minimize motion blur, vibration, and camera shake. Conversely, if the camera is well stabilized and motion blur is not an issue, Av (Aperture value) Priority programmed mode might be set to f/8 to achieve a deeper depth of field to get more of a miniature, three-dimensional object in focus. At normal video working distances, depth of field is measured in feet and focus may extend to infinity at times. At macro distances, depth of field is measured in millimeters and can become so shallow that you have to choose between the head, the wings, or the torso of an insect because the depth of the entire insect cannot be brought into focus. (See Figure 14.4.) Setting the aperture at f/8 will help. Even then, depth of field may be so shallow that you will have to settle for achieving critical focus on only the most important part of your subject.

A camera slider (or at least a tripod) is highly recommended to minimize shake, vibration, and motion blur, which can become enormously exaggerated when working in extreme close-up. A slider can make fluid camera moves when in extreme

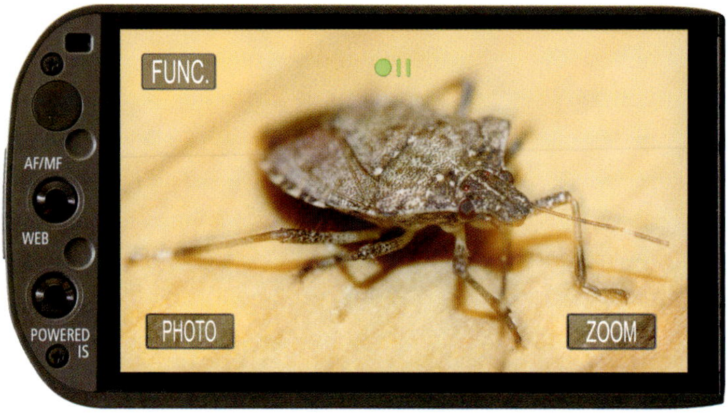

Figure 14.4 Extremely shallow depth of field is inherent in macro photography.

close-up and can even be used to rack focus by slowly gliding the camera physically closer or further instead of using the focus ring. To prevent jarring the camcorder, you may want to use the wireless remote for triggering the camcorder's functions.

When you are working very close, the inherently shallow depth of field will soften the background and will help create emphasis on the subject. But sometimes even in soft focus, the background can be too busy, too distracting, or less than ideal for your subject. Working on such a miniature scale, it is sometimes preferable to replace the background with a white, black, light gray, or sky blue card. Being completely out of focus, the card will look natural. It will give you one more element of control over the composition.

Extremely close images sometimes need to be slowed down to amplify time in a manner comparable to the amplification of visual scale. Because the G10/XA10 does not have slow-motion speeds, this can be done in postproduction by re-rendering the video at ½ or ⅓ speed in an editing program. In some cases, this may look more natural than standard speed. Sound, too, might be amplified or wholly invented to enhance the macro scale visuals. What is the appropriate Foley sound for ants attending to a queen or a spider wrapping up a fly in threads of web silk?

Lighting

The main problem with lighting in macro is the short working distance between the subject and the camcorder. LED lights are good solutions because they can be used at close distances, are ideal for small areas, and do not generate heat. LED arrays like Litepanels or the inexpensive Neewer CN128 or CN160 can work as key or fill light. You have to be careful that the proximity of the camcorder's lens does not cast a shadow on the subject.

If additional fill light needs to come from the front, there are LED ring lights that fit around the lens. The Neewer LED macro ring light sells for $35 and comes with six adapter rings (49mm, 52mm, 55mm, 58mm, 62mm, and 67mm) to fit a variety of lenses. Shown in Figure 14.5, it has a controller to turn on all of its 48 LEDs or just the right or left half. The unit can be powered by two AA batteries or an AC adapter. Ring lights by other manufacturers range in price from $64 for the Bower SFDRLM with 12 LEDs to the Litepanels RM-FT Ringlite Mini System for $2,065, with 72 full tungsten-balanced LEDs on a 10.5-inch ring for large professional lenses. All the LED rings produce a soft, shadowless fill light for macro photography. With only the right or left half illuminated, a ring light can also function as a soft key light.

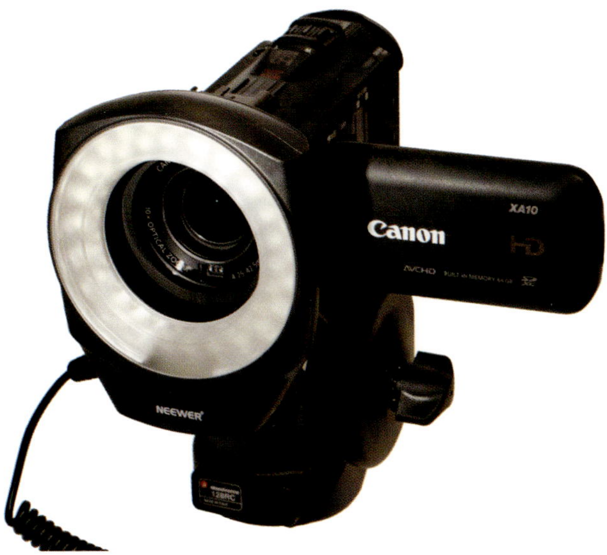

Figure 14.5 Neewer 48-LED macro ring light.

A small instrument with a single LED point source of illumination is ideal for providing a crisp, hard light in a small area for use as a key or backlight. The Ikan iLED ONE comes with a single 60° high-intensity tungsten-balanced LED bulb. It has a swivel mount that fits on a universal shoe or a ¼-inch thread like a tripod. The Ikan iLED ONE costs approximately $90 if it is purchased with its AC power supply, which provides 12 volts. It is about $220 with a heavy-duty field battery and charger. For an even sharper edged light using the iLED ONE, you can purchase interchangeable LED lamp units for $35 with a narrower, more concentrated 40° tungsten or a 40° daylight bulb.

If you already own the Canon VL-10Li II video light, which normally mounts on the camcorder, this could also serve as a crisp key light or backlight for macro photography. With a shoe adapter, it can be mounted on a lightweight tripod or small stand to provide a suitable angle. The VL-10Li II has a tungsten miniature reflector bulb (MR11), which would balance with any ambient tungsten light hitting the miniature subject.

15

Special Features

The G10/XA10 is filled with special features, such as an f/1.8 zoom lens with an eight-blade iris and a manual focus ring; 16 zoom speeds plus variable control; ease-in/ease-out zoom motion; a native 1,920×1,080 CMOS sensor; neutral density filters that automatically keep the lens at its optimum aperture; a built-in waveform monitor; an edge monitor; powered and dynamic image stabilization; Face Detection; Touch & Track; and most of the functions of Canon's XF series of professional camcorders packed into a palm-sized camera body. In addition, the XA10 accommodates professional balanced-line microphones with 48 volts of phantom power, and has the ability to shoot in infrared light. All these features are discussed in depth in other chapters. This chapter is an opportunity to cover a few additional features that have not been described in as much detail.

CINEMA Mode

Like many camcorders, the G10/XA10 has a built-in CINEMA mode—in this case with a choice of nine customizable cinema filters plus some other options. Switching to CINEMA mode automatically sets the frame rate at PF24 (not a true 24p). Canon has made the assumption that you want your CINEMA mode clips shot at 24 (23.976) progressive but converted to 60i (59.94 interlaced fields), which allows them to be matched to many other forms of video in editing. However, if you want to edit a true 24, most editing programs have a reverse 3:2 mode that eliminates the extrapolated fields that the camcorder generated to make 24 progressive frames into 60 interlaced fields. Reverse 3:2 converts your video back to 24 de-interlaced frames per second.

The nine cinema filters are as follows (see Figure 15.1):

- Standard provides a film look, with a contrast response curve that retains more detail in the shadows and highlights.
- Vivid accentuates primary colors and increases saturation.
- Canon describes Dream as a "magical look" but, as discussed in Chapter 6, "Controlling Color," this is a subjective description and some might interpret its de-saturated look as bleak reality instead of dream.
- Cool adds a bluish tint.
- Nostalgic adds a washed-out warm tone, which the menu suggests is like "old TV programs," but illustrates this with a car from the 1920s or 1930s. Broadcast television did not even exist in the 1920s and 1930s. Television was black-and-white in the 1940s and 1950s, and had rather garish color in the 1960s and 1970s, not a faded, nostalgic look.

Note

Do not be guided solely by Canon's descriptions. With completely different lighting or subject matter, the filter may suggest a different interpretation.

- Sepia creates a warm, faded look while still retaining a hint of the original color.
- Old Movies provides an alternative cine look with simulated scratches and an extremely wide letterboxed screen reminiscent of Cinemascope of the 1950s and 1960s.
- Memory softens contrast, and the frame has slightly vignetted (darkened) edges.
- B&W strips the image of color and has three adjustable levels of contrast.

To enter the Cinema menu, press the Filter icon that appears at the lower left of the touchscreen when the camcorder's mode switch is on CINEMA. The nine selections in CINEMA mode provide various degrees of preset color and contrast to look like different kinds of film transferred to video, along with individual adjustments that can be accessed by tapping the Tool icon under each filter. Table 15.1 outlines the various CINEMA mode adjustments that can be made.

However, there is actually a 10th choice for creating a cinema look: switching out of CINEMA mode to M mode and setting the frame rate for 24p (23.976) by choosing FUNC > MENU > Film Clip icon > 24p. This will provide a true progressive-frame look with cinema characteristics. In addition to the wide range of exposure and

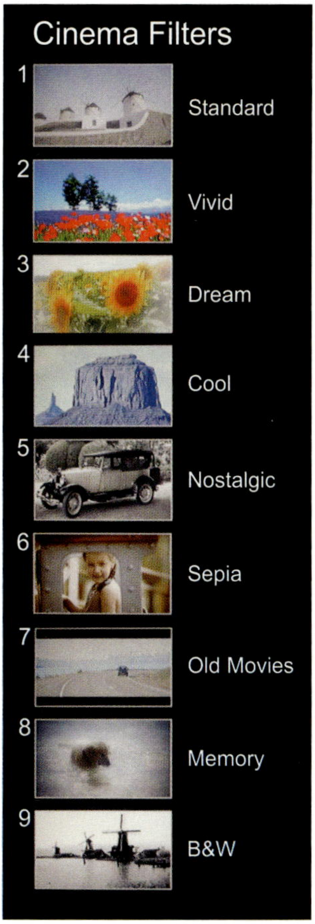

Figure 15.1 CINEMA mode options.

Table 15.1 Cinema Mode Adjustments

Filter Number	Cinema Effect	Adjustments
Filter 1	Standard	Color depth, brightness, contrast, sharpness
Filter 2	Vivid	Low, medium, high effect
Filter 3	Dream	Low, medium, high effect
Filter 4	Cool	Low, medium, high blueness
Filter 5	Nostalgic	Low, medium, high effect
Filter 6	Sepia	Low, medium, high effect
Filter 7	Old Movies	Low, medium, high effect
Filter 8	Memory	Low, medium, high effect
Filter 9	B&W	Low, medium, high contrast

white-balance choices under M mode, you can choose FUNC > Image Effects to customize your settings for color depth, brightness, contrast, and sharpness. These Image Effects adjustments are very similar to the Standard cinema filter, but the video signal is actually recorded as 24p instead of PF24 and you have the ability to select other programmed adjustments and scene-based programs that are unavailable in CINEMA mode.

Saving and Loading Menu Settings

One of the most useful special features on the G10/XA10 is the ability to collectively save and reload all the customized adjustments that you have set on the camcorder. Your entire range of menu settings—such as color depth, brightness, contrast, and sharpness under Image Effects; CINEMA mode filter settings; audio settings; white balance; frame rate; assigned keys; zoom rates; language; and other setup functions—can be saved to an SDHC or SDXC memory card in slot B. To do so, choose FUNC > MENU > Tool icon > Backup Menu Settings (see Figure 15.2); then tap Save and tap Yes. (If a Menu Settings file already exists on memory card B, saving the current settings will overwrite that file.)

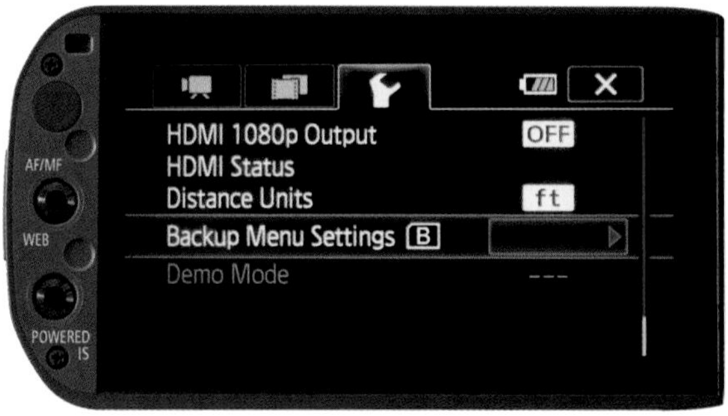

Figure 15.2 Access Backup Menu Settings under the Tool menu.

To load previously recorded memory settings from an SDHC memory card in slot B, choose FUNC > MENU > Tool icon > Backup Menu Settings; then tap Load (instead of Save) and tap and Yes. This will replace all the values on the camcorder's setup menus, and the touchscreen will momentarily go black as it restarts. You could keep several less expensive 8GB SDHC cards with different menu presets for different projects or different production strategies for use in memory slot B.

There is a RESET button on the body of the camcorder, which looks like a tiny hole to the left of the Camera/Playback switch. It can be engaged with the end of a paper clip while the battery and power source have been removed from the camcorder.

This action will restore all functions back to their default values when the camcorder is turned back on. This is much more extreme than saving and loading your favorite configurations of settings on memory card B. If you prefer the default mode for every function, pressing the RESET button might be a way to go. Otherwise, the RESET button is more typically used as a corrective measure if the touchscreen displays abnormal characters or the camcorder operates erratically and turning off power and restarting does not seem correct the problem.

Chroma Key and In-Camera Decorations

Chroma key is a special-effect technique of combining two video images in which a uniformly colored portion of the first image is digitally processed to become transparent, through which we see the second image. Almost any color can be used as long as it is completely absent from the parts of the image that are to remain opaque. Green works particularly well as a chroma key color because it can be kept off of skin tones and costumes. A green-screen chroma key process was used, for example, to create Iron Man flying through the sky out of footage of Robert Downey Jr. suspended on wires in front of a uniformly green background, combined with aerial footage and computer-generated images that digitally replaced everything that was green. *Iron Man 2* used an enormous green screen that covered an area 600×200 feet. Compositing of two layers of images is typically done in postproduction using special-effects programs from companies like Autodesk and Adobe, although most editing programs have the capability to perform chroma key composites at 1,920×1,080 resolution.

In a crude way, chroma key can actually be done in the camera with the G10/XA10 during the recording process with a preshot still image that has a uniform green area into which the camcorder will "key" moving video. Choose FUNC and scroll down to Decoration; then, in the Decoration panel, choose Mix Screen (indicated by an icon showing one screen over another). Next, tap ON to open the chroma key screen and press the plus (+) or minus (–) button as many times as needed to locate and select your pre-stored image. Finally, tap the Return arrow icon in the upper left to matte your selected still image over live video while you record. (See Figure 15.3.)

The camcorder's built-in memory comes pre-initialized and already contains 27 prepared JPEG images for use as chroma key mix frame mattes along with a few music files. If you re-initialize the internal memory, all your video, still, and data files will be erased, but the pre-installed music and image mix frames will be restored after initializing. Most of the supplied image mix frames are keyhole mattes, where you see through an opening in a graphic or a photograph to live action that you will shoot.

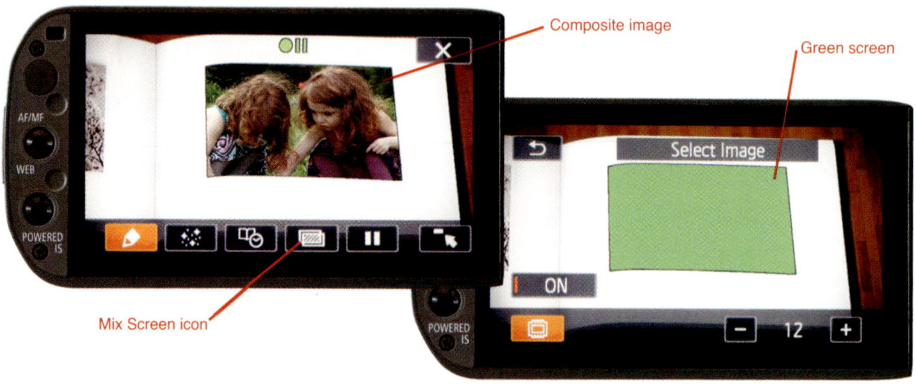

Figure 15.3 A stored still image is chroma keyed in the camera over live video.

You can make your own mix frame mattes by photographing a composition in front of a green screen using the camcorder's Photo mode or with a separate camera. Monochrome green-screen backgrounds can consist of green paper, cardboard, a painted wall, or canvas. The Rosco Company, which manufactures theatrical gels, makes a green-screen paint; in addition, green-screen fabric can be purchased in various sizes over the Internet. When the camcorder is attached to a computer, a JPEG file of a green-screen photo can be taken from the DCIM folder or imported from your computer and dropped in the MY_PICTURES resource folder. It is important that the file is JPEG format and is exactly 1,920×1,080 pixels and uses a numbering convention similar to the file names already in the folder.

Before inserting your green-screen image into MY_PICTURES, you can enhance it in a program such as Photoshop. Using the Magic Wand tool, lasso the green-screen area and drop in a 100-percent green or enhance the area to make it absolutely even. If the photo was taken at a higher resolution, use the Crop tool to resize it to exactly 1,920×1,080 and export the file as a JPEG.

When you choose FUNC > Decoration > Image Mix and select a photo you have placed in the MY_PICTURES file, there will be additional prompts for selecting green or blue and adjusting a slider to tune to the particular color. Pressing ON will enable the effect. Exiting the Decoration panel will turn the effect off, and returning to the Decoration panel will restore it.

Decoration mode also allows you the choice of drawing over an image or by tapping the screen, adding a time/date or caption, and momentarily placing an animated stamp over the image like wiggling musical notes, stars, or sparkles. These can be done while recording. Go to FUNC, scroll down to Decoration, and tap the pencil, stars, clock, or Mix Screen icon, which respectively represent Drawing Pens, Animated Stamps, Captions (for date/time), and chroma key.

In-camera decorations and the chroma key feature are intended primarily for non-professionals. Everything that can be done here can be accomplished with much more control entirely in postproduction in an editing program, a graphics program, or an effects application like Adobe After Effects, and would not be restricted to a still image as an overlay.

Scan Reverse

Changing the scan direction allows you to reverse the image horizontally, vertically, or both. Shooting into a mirror requires horizontal correction to restore left-to-right orientation and readability. Shooting upside down requires both horizontal and vertical correction. This is very useful to correct for the orientation of the camera on a copy stand, on a car-window mount (in which case you may lack enough space to mount the camera upright on a slanted windshield), and very low-angled shots where the camera is simply held upside down on a monopod. Manfrotto makes a tripod with a center pole that can swing 180º to place the camera between the tripod legs near the floor for low-angle shots.

There is seldom a call for a reversed vertical scan by itself, but the G10/XA10 also includes that option. A reversed vertical scan might be used if you want to create the appearance of an upside-down mirror image or to correct an image that appears reversed and upside down because it was shot facing a mirror on the floor. A regular upright mirror image needs only horizontal correction. To scan-reverse an image or to remove the effect, choose FUNC > Film Clip icon > Scan Reverse Rec and choose Off, Vertical, Horizontal, or Both. (See Figure 15.4.)

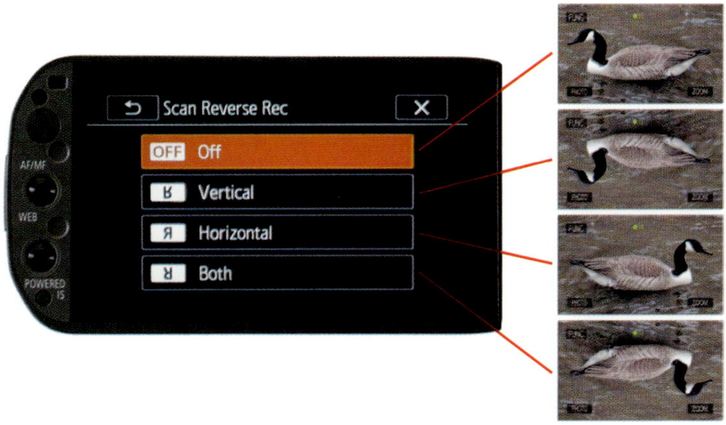

Figure 15.4 Scan reverse settings.

Note

The Scan Reverse setting is not the same as LCD Mirror Mode, found under the Tool icon. The difference is that Scan Reverse actually records a flipped image, whereas Mirror Mode simply shows you one when the LCD faces forward toward the subject while a standard image is being recorded.

Assignable Buttons

You can re-program certain menu items that you need often onto the two mechanical buttons on the left bezel of the LCD screen. You might do this if you wanted to forego the ability to toggle between manual/auto focus or to use the POWERED IS button for steady tight telephoto shots. Most videographers will find that these two buttons are extremely useful at their default assignments and probably will not reassign them. But depending on your style of shooting, some may consider reassigning one or the other button to be able to toggle into Backlight Correction mode, into Face Only detection mode in manual focus, or between a current and a preset white balance value. To re-program these buttons, choose FUNC > MENU > Tool icon and choose Assign Button 1 or Assign Button 2. Then choose one of the following:

- Backlight Always ON
- Face Only AF
- Story Creator
- Video Snapshot
- White Balance Priority
- Infrared Light
- Audio Output Channel
- AF/MF (button 1 only; the default setting)
- Powered Image Stabilization (button 2 only; the default setting)

Pre-Record and the Self Timer

The G10/XA10 can automatically pre-record for three seconds before you press the Record button. This will be the most useful if you already have the subject or an entrance point in frame while you are waiting for a significant moment to begin. To engage this pre-record function, called Pre REC, while in M or CINEMA mode, press FUNC and scroll down to Pre REC and press ON. The next shot you record will begin three seconds before you press the START button. If the function has been pre-activated, an oval icon with a three in its center appears in the lower right of the touchscreen. To de-activate Pre REC, follow the same procedure and click OFF. The Pre REC function cannot record a full three seconds if you press Record less than three seconds after activating the function or after the end of the previous shot.

The Pre REC function automatically deactivates after five minutes of inactivity, when you move the AUTO/M/CINEMA switch, when you activate Video Snapshot, when enter Playback mode, when you enter Standby mode (by closing the touchscreen), or when you tap any of the other program panels. After you have recorded a shot using Pre REC, the function automatically turns off at the end of the shot and the icon with a three in its center will disappear.

The G10/XA10 also has a self timer, which you access by choosing FUNC > MENU > Film Clip icon > Self Timer and selecting ON. The self timer is really a 10-second delay—sort of the opposite of the Pre-Record function. When in Self Timer mode, a clock icon appears in the upper part of the touchscreen near the left. When you press the Record button, the camcorder beeps once a second for the first eight seconds of the 10-second countdown, then six quick beeps at the number two, and a lower-pitched beep just as recording begins. The timer automatically reverts to OFF position after a timed shot. Figure 15.5 shows the Pre REC setting and the Self Timer setting.

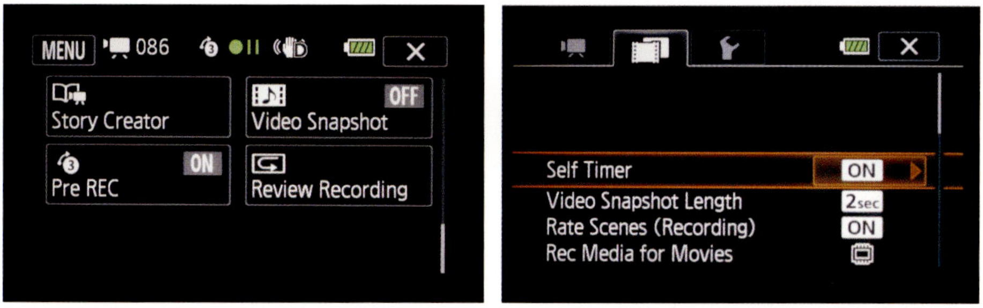

Figure 15.5 The Pre REC setting (left) and the Self Timer setting (right).

Rating Scenes

The camcorder allows you to rate scenes immediately after recording each clip. To enable this function, choose FUNC > MENU > Film Clip icon > Rate Scenes Recording. After each clip, a set of ratings will appear across the bottom of the screen and the option to touch the ellipsis (...) button to leave it unrated. Scenes can be rated in all recording modes, including full AUTO, but the function has to be enabled under the Film Clip menu while in M or CINEMA mode. In Playback mode, you have the option to play scenes within the camera that have been prioritized by rating. This may help in reviewing footage in the field and in playing back selected shots in Story mode while the clips are still in the camcorder.

Eye-Fi

The camcorder will support an Eye-Fi card inserted in memory slot B. Eye-Fi will enable you to wirelessly auto-upload stills and any video files you have converted to standard definition to a video-sharing website.

For Web quality, MTS files can be individually or batch down-converted to standard definition inside the camcorder itself. (See Chapter 18, "Managing and Storing Video Files," for more information.) You must install a supplemental network to configure Eye-Fi; follow the instructions that come with the card. If you are within lock-in range of a configured network, uploading will start automatically and an Eye-Fi icon will appear to show the status. If the icon is grayed out, communication is not established. If the icon is flashing, it indicates that the camera is connecting; if it is animated, upload is in progress. An exclamation mark over the icon indicates an error. The word "OFF" over the icon indicates that Eye-Fi is turned off in the Tool menu. To turn Eye-Fi communication on or off, choose FUNC > MENU > Tool icon > Eye-Fi Communication and select Auto or Off. Photos recorded onto memory card B will upload automatically when the camcorder is switched to Playback mode and Eye-Fi communication is enabled.

Tip

When using the camcorder abroad, check to see if Eye-Fi has been approved for that region.

Fader

The camcorder has two built-in transition effects: fade-in/fade-out and wipe open/wipe closed. The fade and wipe effects can be set to operate for a single shot or for a series of shots until you return to the Fade panel and select OFF. The effect is available in M mode and in all CINEMA mode filters except Old Movies (which is probably the very place you would want to use it, as fades and wipes are old movie conventions). To enable these effects, choose FUNC > Faders and select Fade Once, Fade Always, Wipe Once, or Wipe Always. To disable these effects, choose OFF. You can also select whether to fade to black or wash to white. To do so, choose FUNC > MENU > Camera icon > Fader Setting and select Black or White.

After the effect has been turned on and you have exited the Faders screen, an F1 (fade) or F2 (wipe) icon will appear in the lower right of the touchscreen. The fade or wipe effect will operate automatically each time you press the regular START/STOP button to shoot a clip if you had selected Fade Always or Wipe Always. The audio also fades in and out simultaneously with the picture. In addition to being unavailable in Old Movies mode, fades and wipes will not operate in Decoration mode, Video Snapshot, or full AUTO, or when three-second pre-recording is activated.

Note

Of course, anyone seriously adding effects to video will do it in postproduction, when you can precisely cue the in point and out point and will have dozens of 2D and 3D effects to choose from.

Digital Zoom and Digital Tele Converter

The camcorder's optical zoom has a range of 10×, from 4.25mm in wide angle to 42.5mm in telephoto. Its image quality is quite good. Through digital processing, the zoom range can be extended from 10× to either 40× or 200×. Once you come to the end of the optical zoom's range, Digital Zoom seamlessly continues the zoom by magnifying pixels. Digital Zoom is available only in the M mode. It cannot be used in AUTO mode, CINEMA mode, or for taking still photos. To activate Digital Zoom for 40× or 200×, choose FUNC > MENU > Camera icon > Digital Zoom; then select 40×, 200×, 2.0× Digi Tele-conv., or Off. (See Figure 15.6.)

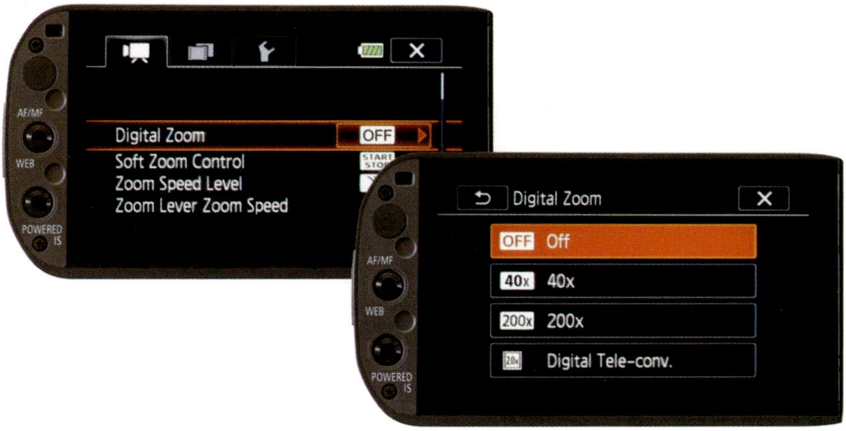

Figure 15.6 Digital Zoom settings.

The 2.0× Digital Tele-conv. choice operates differently. This feature is intended to look like the effect of adding an optical telephoto converter lens, which would magnify the whole zoom range as opposed to eliding from optical zoom into and extended digital zoom. Setting 2.0× Digital Tele-conv. in the Camera menu causes its icon to appear in the Zoom program window but does not activate it. Digi Tele-conv. operates only when you open the Zoom program screen (choose FUNC > Zoom) and tap Digi Tele-conv.

The effect is very similar to 2× Focus Assist. The image instantly magnifies by a factor of two. The difference is that the magnification of Focus Assist appears only on the LCD screen and viewfinder, whereas Digi Tele-conv. magnifies the actual recorded image. By the way, 2× Focus Assist does not operate when you are on the Zoom program screen.

Both Digital Zoom and Digital Tele-conv. degrade the image by magnifying pixels. I do not recommend using either function unless your purpose is to provide an image with noticeable pixels that is explicitly meant to look like blown-up video. The seamless move from optical into digital magnification might be useful under some circumstances, but if a zoom really has to be magnified, recropped, or zoomed into, it could be done in postproduction with programs like After Effects that can re-render the image with less noticeable degradation.

16

Integrating with Larger Camcorders

Using an HF G10 together with an XA10 on a two-camera setup will match perfectly as long as they are both running with the same settings, including program mode, exposure and white balance. There is similar compatibility between the G10/XA10 and Canon's XF professional line of camcorders, the XF100, XF105, XF300, and XF305, which range in price from $3,000–$7,500. In fact, the G10/XA10 has so many features in common with Canon's XF line, it could be used as a directly matched companion. G10/XA10 will also hold its own as part of a production strategy with other professional camcorders and with HDSLR (high definition single lens reflex) still cameras used for video.

XF Camcorders

Although they occupy a more compact body, the Canon Vixia G10 and the XA10 provide almost all the functionality of Canon's XF series of professional camcorders. They share the same f/1.8 zoom lens, the same eight-blade shutter, the same ⅓-inch native 1,920×1,080 CMOS image sensor, and the same image processor (with its features like Face Detection and tracking) as the XF100 and XF105.

The G10 and XA10 are much more compact because the functions of the numerous physical switch controls on the XF100 and XF105 have been reallocated to the touchscreen. The XF100 and XF105, however, can record in slow and fast motion—in other words, at a different frame rate from the playback rate. The most significant difference is that the XF100 and XF105 can record 4:2:2 color space onto Compact Flash cards at 50Mbps, whereas the G10 and XA10 record 4:2:0 onto SDHC cards at 24Mbps. On the practical level, most viewers will not be able to see the difference between 4:2:0 and 4:2:2 except in circumstances like chroma keyed special effects, which could show fringing and edge artifacts in 4:2:0.

4:2:2 color sampling has double the color resolution of 4:2:0, providing finer color transitions and microscopically cleaner edges, which can be important in processes like chroma keying and advanced compositing effects or in printing video onto 35mm film. Otherwise, unless closely compared side by side, 4:2:0 images from the G10/XA10 can be hard to distinguish from 4:2:2 images from the XF series camcorders.

The XF100 and XF105 files are in Material Exchange Format (MXF), a professional industry standard. MXF files are similar to the MTS files of AVCHD but differ in that metadata is embedded in the video files themselves and the bit rate can go as high as 50Mbps (double the information with half the compression of 24Mbps, the highest quality mode on the G10/XA10). Editing programs that handle MTS files can usually handle MXF files and mix them on the same timeline or transcode them to a common editing codec.

Because the XF100 and XF105 use the same lens and sensor as the G10 and XA10, the image will match in optical quality and depth of field. Images from the XF100, XF105, XF300, and XF305 are more customizable in the camera than those from the G10 and XA10. The four XF camcorders can manually set a variety of image adjustments and store them as nine different presets. Up to 20 presets may be saved to an SD card. These include adjustments for gamma (the contrast response curve), black level, master black, low key saturation, knee, sharpness, overall and selective noise reduction, skin detail, color matrix, white balance, color correction, and setup level.

The highest end of the series, the XF300/305, uses three ⅓-inch chips for finer processing of each primary color. Like the single-chip XF100/105, the XF300/305 records a native 1,920×1,080 image in 4:2:2 color using MXF files on Compact Flash cards with bit rates up to 50Mbps. The XF300/305 has an 18× zoom lens, 4.1–73.8mm (29–527mm equivalent) that opens to f/1.6–2.8. The camcorder's tools include both a waveform monitor and a vectorscope. It weighs 5.8 pounds, which is more than three times the weight of the G10/XA10.

Here, too, the G10 and XA10 will have the same depth of field and very similar if not identical lens quality to the XF300/305. In comparing the G10 and XA10 to the XF100 and XF105, viewers would be hard pressed to tell footage shot on one camcorder from another unless they were able to view the images side by side.

Integrating with Other Camcorders

At times, you may need to mix camcorders of different brands and different qualities on a multi-camera shoot or use the G10 or XA10 as a backup for a higher-end professional camcorder of another brand. (See Figure 16.1.) Here, a more aggressive attempt must be made to make the images of dissimilar camcorders visually contiguous.

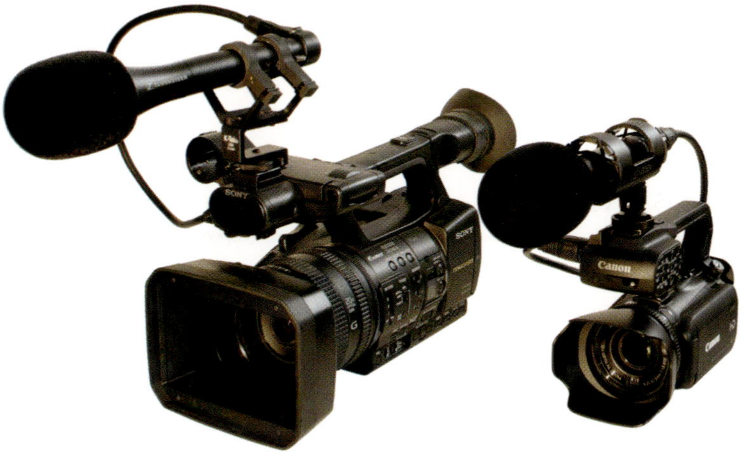

Figure 16.1 Sony's three-chip NX5 and Canon's single-chip XA10.

If possible, shoot comparative tests to see what matches and what stands out. One of the techniques for balancing two or more camcorders to each other is to focus each on the same subject and feed their image into a common field monitor set for split screen. White balance and exposure need to be equalized before anything else is considered.

If each camcorder has an internal or external waveform monitor, they can be set so that black and white levels are more precisely matched. Other instruments like a color RGB parade (a triple waveform monitor that shows red, green, and blue waveforms in a side-by-side comparison) and a vectorscope (which shows color-saturation levels and predominant hues) are useful for measuring and comparing color balance, hue, and saturation. But even without these instruments, a split screen allows a direct comparison in which differences and similarities are immediately apparent and many adjustments can be made by eye.

For making adjustments within the G10 and XA10, start with white balance and exposure. Then, you might want to consider image effects, which enable you to customize color saturation, brightness, contrast, and sharpness. Choose FUNC > Image Effects > ON and then adjust the Color Depth, Brightness, Contrast, and Sharpness settings as needed. As discussed in Chapter 6, "Controlling Color," be careful with high settings under Image Effects. Excessive contrast can permanently erase detail in highlights and shadows, and excessive sharpness may create artificial edges or video grain or accentuate irregularities in skin tones. Do not set image effects unless you can judge the output on a well-calibrated monitor instead of the camcorder's 3.5-inch LCD screen. Otherwise, leave these kinds of adjustments to postproduction if you cannot verify them on location.

Not all matching has to happen in the field. The most important considerations in the field are that each camcorder is white balanced and exposed as correctly as possible. The G10's and XA10's waveform monitor is a big help in fine-tuning exposure. You can precisely identify whether white areas are clipped due to excessive exposure and determine whether important shadow detail is crushed. White balance each camcorder to the actual lighting conditions. Color grading in postproduction can usually take it the rest of the way to equalize skin tones, contrast, background hues, and saturation as long as it does not have to radically correct poor white balance, irredeemable exposure errors, or degraded images.

If two or more camcorders are going to be used together repeatedly, save their setup parameters so they can be instantly matched for future shoots. (Refer to Chapter 15, "Special Features," for more information.) Develop a strategy that exploits what each camcorder is best suited for.

Integrating with HDSLRs

HDSLR (high definition single lens reflex) still cameras are digital 35mm, APS-C, and mini 4/3 cameras that have the ability to record full-motion video. HDSLRs have been hot items for the past several years because they fill a gap in a price range of $800–$12,000 that existing camcorders did not previously cover—namely, providing interchangeable prime lenses, a 35mm or near 35mm image size, and selective focus with shallow depth of field. The television series *House* shot one highly publicized end-of-season episode with a Canon 5D Mark II DSLR as an experiment, but they have not adopted it for regular production. However, numerous fiction and documentary feature productions, including Sundance winners, have adopted HDSLRs. (See Figure 16.2.)

As for price, a Canon 5D Mark III body alone costs more than $3,400 with a couple of batteries and two 32GB recording chips. By the time you add two or three L Series Canon lenses at $900 to $2,500 each or two or three Zeiss prime cine lenses at $3,900 each, a cine viewfinder or portable HD monitor, a separate digital audio recorder with a professional microphone (because the 5D has amateur sound), and Zacuto braces to make the camera stable, you are in the $9,000 to $24,000 range for each package. The Mark III makes sense for still photographers making the transition to video (for example, wedding photographers) who may already have an investment of $5,000–$20,000 in still-camera lenses that they can now use for video.

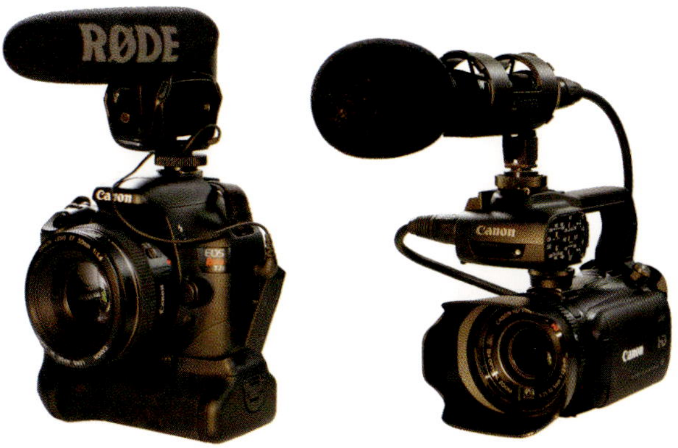

Figure 16.2 Canon T2i HDSLR equipped for video and the Canon XA10.

At the low end of HDSLRs is the Canon T3i body (and its predecessor, the Canon T2i), which has the same video functionality as the middle-level Canon 7D in an APS-C size CMOS sensor. The T3i body sells for $799 with an inexpensive but slow 18–55mm zoom lens. The price plus longer-term batteries, 32GB memory chips, and a separate middle-quality prime lens totals about $1,500. Adding a second prime lens plus sound equipment will bring the price closer to $2,000. This puts the T3i squarely in the price range of the XA10 and would be a strong alternative for a student or an independent media maker.

The shooting style of the HDSLR lends itself to carefully set up shots, a tripod, a slider, a mini dolly or Steadicam operation, a 12-minute limit between cool-down times, shallow depths of field, and avoiding situations that may provoke skew, aliasing, and moiré artifacts. Footage from HDSLRs can get noisy from heat, and the camera may shut down due to overheating. Because of the real danger of overheating, people who shoot with HDSLRs often alternate between two HDSLRs so one can cool as the other shoots. If you mix an HDSLR with the G10/XA10, plan a strategy to get the most out of the features of each kind of camera. Because most HDSLRs have a limit of a 12-minute take, the G10/XA10 becomes the long-take camera and very likely the more mobile camera because of its dynamic image stabilization.

The main problem with using HDSLRs is working around their limitations. With HDSLRs, image stabilization is an issue. Unlike the G10/XA10, image stabilization in an HDSLR is not designed for shooting video. Image stabilization is available only on certain individual SLR telephoto lenses and is designed to take sharp still photographs, not to smooth out the bounce of walking when moving with the camera. HDSLRs will not have zebra patterns and waveform monitors. An HDSLR may have a histogram for measuring exposure, but this function is usually available only for reviewing stills.

HDSLR cameras pose enormous, but surmountable, problems for video production:

- Awkward ergonomics (balance, shape, and controls appropriate for taking stills instead of moving images)
- Inadequate viewfinding without additional attachments
- Limited video controls
- Limited recording time (usually 12 minutes)
- Rolling shutter artifacts
- Moiré patterns
- Workflow issues
- Heat issues (because they were not made for continuous video recording)
- Poor sound

The fact is, HDSLR cameras are simply make-shift tools in digital video production. In spite of all these limitations, however, the images from HDSLRs are often stunning because of the high-quality lenses that can be used, the lower optical and mechanical tolerances needed for a larger format, and the greater potential for selective focus with a shallower depth of field.

Depth of field will be one of the biggest visual differences between the G10/XA10 and a larger-format HDSLR. You do not want to intercut similar shots from different formats together in the same scene unless there is an aesthetic reason to do so because the depth of field will radically shift with each cut. Instead of cutting between shallow and deep space arbitrarily, save the HDSLR for moments that should be shallow or devise a scheme that justifies the change of appearance. It might be possible to shoot with the G10/XA10 in medium to telephoto at f/1.8 to f/2.8 to achieve a shallower depth of field. This may match with a DSLR in normal or mild wide angle and at higher f/stops, where its shallow field is less pronounced. But instead of a strategy of making the spatial representation of each camera match, you more likely will want to exploit the unique look of each camera: the G10/XA10 in wide angle at an infinite depth of field and the large-format camera taking close-ups with a shallow depth of field. The intercutting will be between extremes of scale and depth of field, which can work if there is a consistency and purpose for shallow and deep (like the Sergio Leone spaghetti westerns of the 1960s). Alternatively, allocate the shots that have extensive movement to the G10/XA10 and assign individually set up shots that need to be carefully focused to the HDSLR.

The HDSLR is designed and optimized for taking still pictures and has been retrofitted for video as an afterthought. Excessively fine lines and textures below the resolution threshold of a digital camera create aliasing artifacts as the digital circuit misreads irresolvable detail. To improve performance, an optical low-pass filter is used to better match the threshold of fine detail with the camera's pixel size and the potential number of pixels. However, what is required for a still photographic image on an 18-megapixel T3i or 22.3-megapixel 5D Mark III is completely different from the requirements of the 2-megapixel resolution of 1,920×1,080 video on the same camera. This produces aliasing, false detail, and moiré when a camera designed for still photography is used for video.

When a high-megapixel HDSLR creates a 1,920×1,080 video image, it simply skips lines of in-between pixels that would have been available for a still photograph. This produces stair-casing and intensifies other artifacts. It would be a much richer image if the HDSLR interpolated the in-between information into calculating the 1,920×1,080 video signal. But an HDSLR's processor cannot do this in real time, and is already verging on overheating by taking 24 or more pictures a second when it was designed for simply one picture at a time.

Before the HDSLR revolution, the lowest-priced package that could provide large-sensor capabilities dedicated to video was the RED, starting at $45,000 with professional cine lenses and monitor. Canon's EOS C300 PL is one of the new generation of large-sensor camcorders designed specifically for video. To solve the artifact and heating problems in large-format video, the price tag for the EOS C300 camera body alone is $16,000. The Canon T3i body at $800, the Canon 7D at $1,700, or the Canon 5D Mark III at $3,400 provide a good approximation of the large-format image at a fraction of the price if you can work around the HDSLR shortcomings. The newest camera from RED, the Scarlet, costs $11,700 for a stripped-down body, and about $17,000 for a fully operational camera system that still needs expensive lenses. Competing large-format bodies dedicated to video like the BlackMagic Cinema Camera have come on the market at about $3,000 and will still need another $3,000 to $7,000 in lenses and accessories. Most HDSLRs are still a less expensive alternative for large-format video, but the gap is narrowing.

The Canon T3i has the same video capabilities as the middle-level Canon 7D at about half the price. Both have an APS-C sensor that shoots 24p/25p/30p at 1,920×1,080; and 50p/60p at 1,280×720 which can be used for slow-motion work. Compared to the T3i, the Canon 7D has a heavier-duty waterproofed body and some additional still-photography capabilities. The 7D has HDMI-out during 1080i recording for high-definition monitoring, whereas the T3i reverts to standard-definition monitoring while the camera is recording.

When mixing a G10/XA10 camcorder with an HDSLR on a multi-camera shoot, the ideal is to assign each to what it can do best. You can pre-adjust each to look similar in white balance, exposure, camera profile, and filtration, but the formats will still look different. Figure out a form-and-content strategy that will exploit their different looks. You might assign the camcorder and HDSLR quite different types of shots or completely different subject matter so that matched action and direct shot-by-shot comparisons do not occur. HDSLRs not only look good in shallow focus, to some degree they need shallow focus to look good. Aliasing and moiré disappear in shallow focus. Shallow depth of field is probably the look that you want to exploit with HDSLRs.

An L Series Canon lens on an HDSLR can cost as much as the entire XA10 camcorder. If lens quality is a major comparative difference, then lock the G10/XA10 in Av mode to f/4 for its optimum aperture. Do tests from matching cameras and find the ideal lighting ratio, ISO and gain sensitivity settings, and camera presets. The more expensive camera and lens may be assigned to shoot the primary footage and the G10/XA10 relegated to shooting B-roll. But in certain situations, the opposite strategy might work. If the main subject needs very long takes, run-and-gun mobility, or a deep depth of field, the G10/XA10 excels at that, and a large-format HDSLR might be dedicated to composing and taking exquisite establishing shots and cutaways as B-roll.

When testing and comparing the images of a G10/XA10 and an HDSLR, you might compare the HDSLR's standard camera profile versus neutral, as well as hacked profiles and setups available on the Internet. To further match the HDSLR to video, you might also try a Caprock 2.0 anti-moiré filter to cut the hyper-real look of HDSLR video and its artifacts.

17

Production Strategies

There is a need for discipline, structure, and coverage in almost any kind of production. Decisions need to be made about the goal of the project, form and content, point of view, methodology, and aesthetics. Depending on the kind of production, physical preparation involves research, scripts, outlines, shot lists, storyboards, meetings, location scouting, test footage, permissions, clearances, call sheets, schedules, or rehearsals. Entire books can be written on any one of these aspects of preproduction. This chapter discusses a few selected strategies and relevant production aids for palm-sized production of non-fiction, fiction, student exercises, and experimental media. Let's start with thematic production outlines built into the camcorder itself.

Story Creator

The G10/XA10 comes with a built-in Story Creator tool that provides shot recommendations and outline structures for certain types of productions and themes. It also offers a way to tag shots to points in the Story Creator outline for later grouping for review or playback. Because this feature is primarily for amateurs, Story Creator is one of the few menu items available in full AUTO mode in addition to the M and CINEMA modes.

The first three Story Creator themes relate entirely to home video:

- Travel
- Kids & Pets
- Party

When you select a theme, the touchscreen outlines categories of shots relevant to that theme and presents them in a coherent order. (See Figure 17.1.) Under Travel, for example, the outline starts with introducing the travelers, planning the trip, shopping for the trip, packing, expectations, taking off, and so on. The middle contains entries for eating, landmarks, visits, adventure, funny situations, and making friends. The end has categories for a sunset (or if you take this metaphorically, a concluding shot), memories, thinking about the next trip, and additional scenes. In a similar fashion, the Kids & Pets theme, suggests shots like waking up, breakfast, getting dressed, morning walk and playtime (see Figure 17.1). Story Creator helps completely inexperienced media makers think more fully about the kinds of shots they could be taking for home movies on travel, kids, pets, and parties.

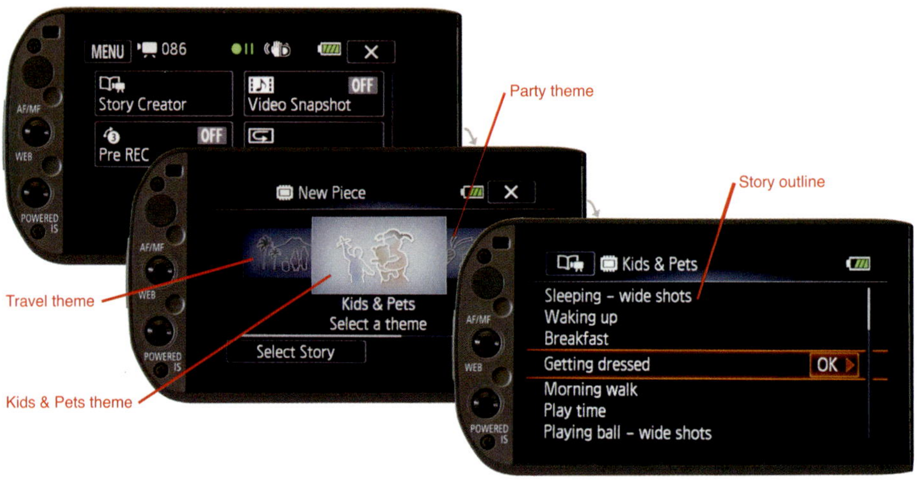

Figure 17.1 Story Creator. To tag a clip that you intend to shoot, press OK next to the outline entry.

The last three themes on the list are also basic:

- **Ceremony.** Ceremony is designed for the amateur, but it could help someone starting out in event videography. It is the most developed outline and is obviously based on a wedding, but could be adapted to other events. The outline suggests interviews with the main character(s) and covering pre-event details like planning, invitations, dress, and rehearsal. It moves on to recording thoughts from the main character(s) or someone else just before the event, backstage activity, and the ceremony itself. The outline includes guest interviews, the dinner, toasts, speeches, and concluding items like last comments, the exit of the main character(s), guests leaving, and a place to tag additional scenes.

- **Blog.** The Blog theme prompts you to identify main characters, identify what is at stake, and do interviews, but is much less detailed than the other themes in providing a model or in recommending a structure (except to suggest obtaining establishing shots and getting both wide views and close-ups).
- **Unrestricted.** The Unrestricted theme simply offers a way to tag shots. No internal structure is provided. It would have been much more useful if the Unrestricted theme had numbered or lettered sub-choices to sort shots more individually. A set of blank A, B, C, D, and E options could have been tags for five separate unrestricted projects, or selective parts within a single unrestricted category. Or this section could have had generic categories like Interviews, Dialogue, Action, Establishing Shots, Extra Scenes, and B-Roll. But unfortunately, the only capability of Unrestricted is to tag shots into a whole undifferentiated category. The easier way to put shots for a single project into one location is to dedicate a separate memory chip to a particular project. The only meaningful use of Story Creator in Unrestricted mode is to differentiate shots from other material on the same memory chip, possibly when shooting a long-term project off and on among other projects, or to identify B-roll from everything else. But then these other clips would have to be one of the other five themes or else go unidentified.

To use Story Creator, choose FUNC and scroll down to Story Creator. Then select a theme and tap the appropriate entry on its outline before taking shots that belong in that category. If you select the Travel theme and a sub-category such as Landmarks, a storybook icon appears on the upper part of the touchscreen and the word Landmarks appears across the bottom of the screen as indicators that the camcorder is in Story Creator mode and is tagging shots for this category.

Remember to close Story Creator when you are no longer shooting that particular item on the outline. To do so, choose FUNC > Story Creator and select Yes to end Story Creator mode. When you close and reopen Story Creator, which could be a few seconds later or even months later, the outline will list how many clips were taken in each category. This feature is useful for instantly knowing you have seven shots of landmarks but no shots of eating, scenery, or new friends. To move onto another item in the outline, you must close Story Creator and re-open it. To make this practical in ongoing situations, you can set one of the re-assignable buttons to toggle Story Creator on and off. This saves having to press FUNC and scrolling down to Story Creator. To do so, choose FUNC > MENU > Tool icon > Assign Button 1 or 2 > Story Creator.

Where Story Creator can have some professional use is in reviewing your footage. To do so, toggle the Camera/Playback button to Playback, touch the Index icon (lower left), select Gallery, and horizontally scroll to and select one of the six story theme icons. To play the entire outline of clips within a story, tap the theme icon.

When a clip plays, the on-screen controls for pause, stop, fast forward, and reverse are similar to controls for regular playback. Instead of directly playing the clips, tapping Story Details (at the bottom center of the Gallery screen) displays information about date, number of clips already shot, total playback time, and provides the ability to play clips by rating. This becomes a way to review culled selections of shots while in the field to see if you have covered everything acceptably.

Tapping Scene List (instead of Story Details) opens a vertical list that displays the icon of each clip, its play time, date, and rating. (See Figure 17.2.) There are also some editing options, including the ability to rate scenes. To access these, scroll to a clip in the Scene List and press the orange arrow to the right of the entry. The Edit Scene window opens; touch the desired rating (zero to four stars) or an editing function (delete, copy, or move the clip within or between stories).

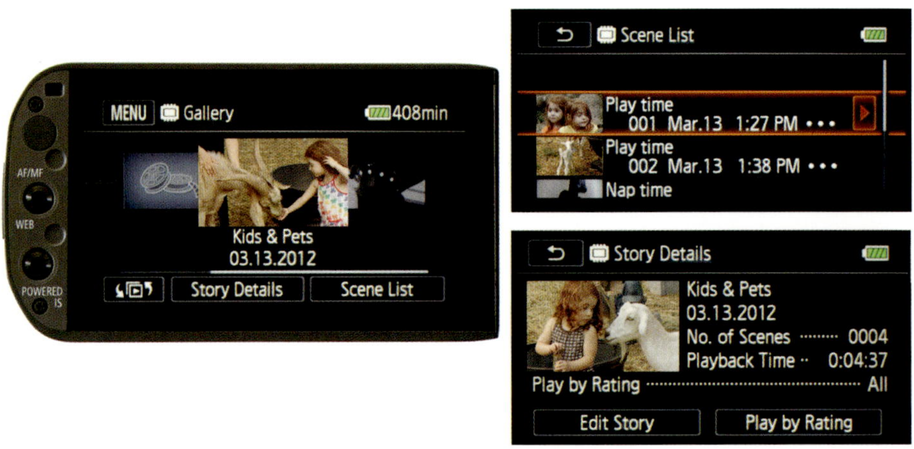

Figure 17.2 Scene List and Story Details allow you to review the clips you have taken for a particular story theme. The orange arrow to the right of the selected entry in the Scene List leads to a screen for rating and editing.

A story's default thumbnail image is the first frame of the first clip in the outline. To change this image, start at the main Gallery screen, choose Story Details > Edit Story > Story Thumbnail, and select the desired thumbnail. A story's default title is its date. To change this to a title of up to 14 characters, start at the main Gallery screen, choose Story Details > Edit Story > Edit Title, and use the virtual keyboard that appears on the screen to type a title. To enter your changes and exit any of these editing functions, tap OK, and then tap the return arrow twice.

Non-Fiction

Non-fiction can include news, event videography, narrated visual essays (typically seen as television documentaries), interviews, historical documentaries with archive footage, ethnographic documentaries, activist media for social change, personal diaries, *cinéma vérité*, and the observational style of direct cinema, to mention a few examples. A production strategy for one kind of non-fiction production would be considerably different from another.

Note

A difference between documentary and TV news is that documentary is usually a more developed form, treating its subject in greater depth than a typical one- to three-minute news clip, and is more interested in the human condition than in the latest development of a current event that specifically categorizes something as news.

News

News gets documented not simply because a camera happens to be present—although this happens more frequently as a vast number of people carry video-capable cell phones and other devices. Professional news gets videoed because the news organization casts a net of assignments to look for news in expected places and reporters cover individual beats like city hall, the courthouse, police, emergency, fire, and anticipated special events. If a station casts a different kind of net, it gets a different story or a different slant on the news. Unfortunately, most commercial news stations present nearly identical news, often with the same lead story. News stories and commercials interweave seamlessly with each other in a pre-planned balance of airtime—until something truly out of the ordinary happens, such as the assassination of President Kennedy, the resignation of Richard Nixon, the Challenger disaster, 9/11, and Hurricane Katrina.

Somewhere in between the catastrophic event and the routine news net (which generates routine news) is space for a more varied approach to the news for a news organization, public television, public access cable, and particularly for those who post on the Internet. Increasingly, it is the viral news story on the Internet that scoops the multi–billion dollar networks. This happens with one-shot postings and with individual blogs that provide ongoing news or commentary.

Camcorders with run-and-gun capabilities like the G10/XA10 have a role in this kind of news gathering, but the G10/XA10 could also pass muster on a commercial news show.

Being at the right place and the right time with a well-positioned camcorder is often more possible with a highly versatile 1.7-pound camcorder than a 25-pound rig.

In 1972, a collective called Top Value Television (TVTV) covered the Republican National Convention with 5-pound cameras tied to 20-pound porta-pak video-recording units strapped on their backs. They provided a completely different slant on the convention by showing rehearsals for so-called spontaneous events and extensively examined the mainstream press, which covered the highly scripted convention yet never looked below the surface.

Direct Cinema

I want to go into one approach to documentary in detail, Direct Cinema, because the G10/XA10 lends itself perfectly to its observational style. Direct Cinema filmmakers include Ricky Leacock, D.A. Pennebaker, Robert Drew, Fred Wiseman, and the Maysles brothers. Landmark films include *Crisis: Behind a Presidential Commitment, Quint City U.S.A., Don't Look Back, Salesman, Grey Gardens, Titicut Follies, High School, Seventeen,* and *The War Room.*

Direct Cinema is an observational slice of life that tells its own story without needing narration or explanation. It is accomplished by shooting a real-life event with an unobtrusive handheld camera in available light within an event's circle of action and paying attention to human interactions, personal values, ideology, and natural drama. For the footage to tell its own story, the filmmaker looks for conflict or at least contrasts and opposing forces within the naturally occurring event. Even within everyday events, the filmmaker tries to find Aristotelian elements of plot structure: exposition, initiating action, complication, foreshadowing, crisis (moment of decision), anagnorisis (moment of truth, discovery, recognition, realization, or revelation), peripeteia (turning point, reversal, gain or loss, or moment that cannot be easily undone), climax (the height of verbal or visual conflict), and denouement (unraveling or settling).

Direct Cinema as a documentary genre is interested in the human experience: social actors in situations that would occur even if the camera were not there. Characters are tested through conflict—in particular when pressed to make decisions in a moment of crisis. Characters are conveyed through their moments of discovery and revelation, the decisions they are pressed to make, and their moments of change—particularly those that result in a gain or loss. The Direct Cinema filmmaker looks for such moments.

Let's contrast this with an event videographer. Shooting a wedding, an event videographer will want to get each element of the ceremony as well as ample footage of the bride, groom, and their closest friends and relatives having a good time. The video will be celebratory and will contain idealized memories of the high points of the occasion, similar to the outline provided in Story Creator. Conversely, a Direct Cinema documentary maker would look for natural drama, conflict, tension, stress, things that went wrong, last-minute decisions, character-revealing moments, the human story behind the ceremony—a completely different documentation of the same event.

Direct Cinema observational video is characterized by the following:

- A central interest in human character (words and actions that reveal inner values)
- A story or event that tells itself

When shooting in the Direct Cinema style, you'll want to keep these points in mind:

- Gain access to private space and privileged intimacy. (For this, you have to gain trust.)
- Do not stage the subjects or ask them to repeat anything.
- Do not interview.
- Look for naturally occurring Aristotelian elements (conflict, crisis, revelation, discovery, character, and plot).
- Look for relationships—people-to-people, people-to-environment, people-to-objects.
- Look for value-laden behavior and psychologically revealing detail (actions, objects, mannerisms, and gestures). Seek "truth in detail."
- Look for existential complexity of characters, including their contradictions.
- Position the camera (and consequently the spectator) intimately within the circle of action.
- Use the unobtrusive hand-held camera as an active, mobile witness.
- Shoot in structured long takes. Do not shut the camera off too soon.
- At appropriate moments, physically move to meaningful new positions instead of always zooming or panning (which creates a static position for the spectator).
- Do not overreact with the camera. Resist the tendency to pan to everything. Determine when major adjustments are occurring and pan or move accordingly.
- Some moments of dialogue and action may occur off frame. This is acceptable if represented by sound or on-screen reaction.
- Be selective with the frame. Use close-ups and medium shots to focus attention; over-the-shoulder and line-of-sight shots to share a view; and occasional full shots, group shots, or establishing shots to show overall relationships.
- Use a high shooting ratio.

Making a Direct Cinema documentary is something like novelist Norman Mailer's definition of American existentialism: "the entrance into a situation where you don't know how it is going to turn out." Be open to what you actually find instead of shooting only what fills your preconceived notions. Shoot a lot of footage (like 20:1, 40:1, or even 100:1) and organize it into a coherent story in the editing.

In Direct Cinema, the camera is unacknowledged. Some erroneously call this a "fly-on-the-wall" approach, but this metaphor implies a kind of aloof and stand-offish approach (like a bank surveillance camera) and does not capture the element of trust that allows the mobile Direct Cinema camera to intimately and actively move within the center of things as they happen. Rather that an inert housefly, the Direct Cinema camera is more like an unnoticed butterfly or firefly that moves in and around the subjects, who are preoccupied with the event at hand. Various other kinds of documentaries may involve more passive observation outside the circle of action or even more intimate first-person observation, or might involve media makers and participants who acknowledge the filmmaking process in what might be called a reflexive mode. The non-intervention of the Direct Cinema observational media maker is quite different from a Michael Moore provocateur or catalyst, which would lead to a completely different set of assumptions and strategies.

I have described one approach in detail, but all of these approaches to non-fiction are viable, and each deserves a well-considered strategy. You need to think out potential relationships between form, content, the documentary process, and the ultimate goal, which in documentary is to say something meaningful and relevant about the factual world.

Interviews

Research your subject. People are used to giving routine, self-serving answers, and what you end up recording in an interview is often their public mask. If you ask a well-known sculptor, "Why did you become a sculptor?" you will get the response he or she gives everyone. Stock questions get stock answers. If you ask, "Why did you become a sculptor instead of a plastic surgeon?" you might get a moment of introspection and a different kind of answer.

Certain formal decisions need to be made before an interview. Should every interview for the production be set up identically or should each have a noticeably different composition and environment? Should the environment reflect the values and personal space of the subject? Should the interview be a static sit-down session, or while walking, driving in a car, or engaged in an activity? Will the interviewer interact with the subject on any level other than asking questions? Will there be an on-camera, off-camera, or behind-the-camera interviewer? Will the subject address the questioner, the camera operator, or the camera itself? Will questions be asked that require a story to answer or simply a yes or no? Will the camcorder be handheld or on monopod or tripod for the interview? Will the interview be recorded with a lavaliere, boom mic, hand-held mic, or camera-mounted mic (in which case the camcorder needs to be relatively close)?

Fiction

One of the most important approaches to shooting scripted material is marking up the script with notes and arrows for camera setups. For example, a dramatic scene might have 20 shots taken from three different setup positions plus an additional coverage angle as backup. These three setup positions could be called A, B, and C and the coverage angle could be D. The footage expected from these positions might be drawn as vertical lines down the script to indicate the in point and out point of each shot within a setup and where overlaps should occur. The coverage angle may cover major portions or all of the scene. In addition to being identified as A, B, C and D, the lines might be drawn in different colors. You are now better prepared to set up the camera and efficiently take those 20 shots from four positions without missing important angles.

Whether it is marked in the dialogue script or exists separately, a shot list is usually preconceived before shooting. This might simply be a list of shots with references back to dialogue cues or could be written down with complete dialogue and descriptions of action to form a detailed shooting script. This too would be particularly helpful if it is further broken down into setups and organized for ease of shooting.

The shot list can also be visualized in the form of a series of storyboard panels, where the opening frame or a significant moment from each shot is hand drawn, photographed, extrapolated from rehearsal video, or computer generated. Not every production storyboards, but most scenes can benefit from the kind of thinking and previsualization that go into storyboards. There are a number of things you can tell by looking at a storyboard, including whether there is a significant compositional change from shot to shot. (There usually should be—otherwise, why change the shot?) A storyboard represents the overall visual flow or shape of a sequence—for example, an establishing shot, a two shot, several waist-high reverse angles, a shift to head and shoulder close-ups at a significant beat within the scene, a two shot in depth as one character leaves, and a concluding reaction shot of the remaining character.

A call sheet is a daily schedule for cast and crew that lists times and locations and is keyed to script pages and eighths of pages. (Call sheets are traditionally based on eighths of a script page.) Based on a thorough breakdown of the script, the shot list, and an analysis of the shooting schedule, the call sheet lists the elements on call for each scheduled scene: actor, stunt, extras, props and set objects, costumes, vehicles, animals, make-up and hair, special equipment, et cetera. There are standard versions of call sheets and computer programs for making call sheets with color coding and with certain kinds of items circled, boxed, underlined, and asterisked. They can also be posted online.

This is simply a hint at the kind of organization you might want to consider for scripted productions. There are numerous books on production planning.

Experimental

Many experimental works attempt to see the world with fresh eyes by inventing a new form/content relationship or by altering or recontextualizing the subject matter. Defamiliarization is a concept from Russian formalism that pervades 20th and 21st century aesthetics. Theorist Viktor Shklovsky claims defamiliarization is the essence of all art. A palm-sized camcorder offers endless possibilities for experimenting with how we represent the world, and human experience can be presented in media in numerous ways.

As a professor at the Danish National Film School, Jørgen Leth used the formalist concept that creativity is spurred and challenged by setting limitations. Jørgen's film exercises for his students would set obstructions on each exercise that would pose a difficulty that would need to be creatively solved. In 2003, Danish filmmaker Lars von Trier, who had become an internationally known filmmaker, turned the tables on his mentor at the Danish National Film School and made a feature film about the process called *The Five Obstructions*. Von Trier had his former professor remake *The Perfect Human* (a short film that Leth had made 35 years earlier) five different ways, with von Trier imposing a nearly impossible condition on each new version. The challenge was in each case to make the film as effective or more effective than the original while being prohibited from doing anything the same way. Each time, the imposed obstacle would cause Leth to have to rethink the whole process. The first obstruction was that every shot in the film had to be 12 frames long (a half second). The second obstruction involved setting up difficult social conditions in "the worst place in the world" under which the new version is shot. Another version involved reconceiving the film as an animation, a form that neither Leth nor von Trier like. Sometimes, artificially imposing obstacles forces the filmmaker to break out of old habits and discover new creative solutions.

B-Roll

B-roll is secondary or supplemental footage. The concept is useful for news, documentary, event videography, and even works of fiction. Part of the production process involves the discipline of getting the additional shots for cutaways, inserts, establishing shots, and background details that may ultimately be needed in the editing stage. A preparatory B-roll shot list or outline can be useful. Do not limit yourself to only preconceived ideas; you should also be open to finding unique and unexpected details on location at the spur of the moment.

The Video Snapshot function is convenient for taking a series of very short B-roll clips that are 2, 4, or 8 seconds in length. You can turn on this function fairly quickly by pressing FUNC > Video Snapshot, and can exit it just as quickly. I will discuss Video Snapshot in greater detail near the end of this chapter.

Comparable to the importance of B-roll for visuals, audio can be just as significant. Plan to record distinctive ambient sounds, wild sound, wild lines, and potential Foley sounds while on location. Here, too, a list can be useful. As part of your audio B-roll footage, record room tone for each location. Room tone is a 30-second recording of the "silence" of an interior location that captures its unique acoustic presence and its sense of space while no other sounds are being made. "Air" is the term for an equivalent 30 seconds of "silence" at an exterior location. The audience can hear the difference between absolute silence, which is perceived as an empty hole in the sound track, versus room tone, which has the character of an actual acoustical environment when it is quiet. Air and room tone are used in the editing process to fill in pauses, clean up noisy moments, and make sound bridges for audio recorded at each particular location. The steps for recording room tone and air are described in Chapter 7, "Improving Sound."

Teaching and Learning

With its unprecedented range of professional features in its price class, the XA10 is a perfect teaching tool for media production. It is capable of operating in full AUTO and program modes like a consumer model, but offers students the opportunity to learn professional techniques with its XLR balanced-line sound inputs, phantom power, waveform monitor, 70-percent and 100-percent zebra patterns, multiple frame rates including 24p, and complete manual control of focus, exposure, and color balance. There is a lot of video technology that can be taught and learned with this camcorder.

Its ergonomic design, portability, and relative ease of use allow the teaching/learning situation to go beyond technology to concentrate on concepts. As a means of teaching yourself, or as assignments for a media class, it is possible to derive assignments from the production strategies discussed in this chapter. Here are some suggestions:

- Shoot an observational, slice-of-life Direct Cinema exercise. Tape approximately one hour of intimate hand-held observational video of a human-centered activity or event that would occur on its own. Edit it into a coherent five-minute

Direct Cinema mini-documentary so that we feel we know the person(s) involved. It should be shot in such a way that the event itself engages us and tells its own story directly with no narration or interview as intermediaries.

- Shoot an interview portrait or an interview oral history documentary with B-roll on an assigned or self-selected topic. Use a similar ratio: an hour of video for a five-minute finished piece.
- Video Snapshot lends itself to short exercises and media assignments on the nature of montage. Classic montage is the process of making a statement through the dynamic juxtaposition and sequencing of images, constructing meaning by stringing a series of shorter shots together. What happens if you preset the camcorder for 2-second video snapshots but assign (or choose to shoot) completely different strategies for creating a metric montage of an event? If this is done as a class exercise, each person might be assigned the same topic or event. The differences will reveal how each has used metric montage. One person might construct a montage based on Eisenstein's sense of collision, where each shot is considerably unlike the previous shot in composition, rhythm, or action. When a sequence is composed of opposing or contrasting elements, we feel the rhythmic change of every cut. Another person might shoot entirely in jump cuts by always keeping the same subject in frame for a sequence of 2-second discontinuous clips that jump from moment to moment. Another might try to build an action/reaction/insert/cutaway sequence while still being limited to 2-second shots.

Video Snapshot Mode

The G10/XA10's built-in Video Snapshot mode can pre-set an automatic limit of 2-, 4-, or 8-second shot lengths. As long as you are in Video Snapshot mode, which you enter by choosing FUNC > Video Snapshot > ON, your shots will be a predetermined length. As an indicator, a blue border appears on the touchscreen. (See Figure 17.3.) At the end of each snapshot, the screen momentarily blinks (an imitation of a shutter closing) to inform you that the shot has ended. You can turn off Video Snapshot by choosing FUNC > Video Snapshot > OFF. Changing the camcorder's AUTO/M/CINEMA switch also turns off Video Snapshot. To set the length of the snapshot, choose FUNC > MENU > Film Clip icon > Video Snapshot Length and select 2, 4, or 8 Seconds. It is also possible to assign a programmable button to turn on Video Snapshot. To do so, choose FUNC > MENU > Tool icon > Assign Button 1 or 2 and select Video Snapshot.

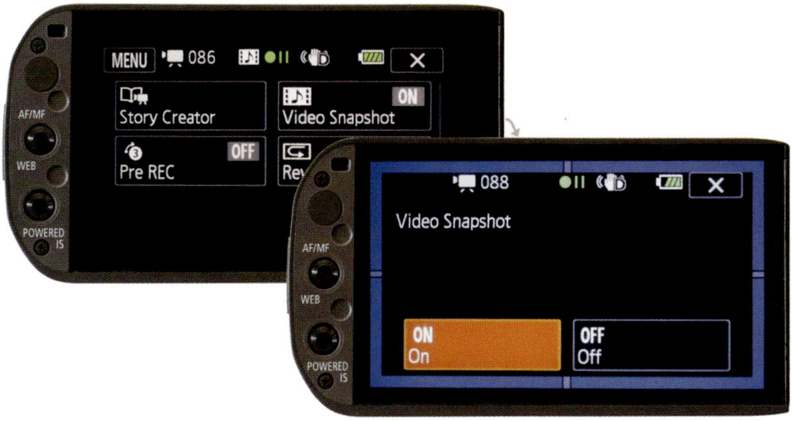

Figure 17.3 After activating Video Snapshot, the blue border remains on screen as a reminder you are in snapshot mode.

- A set of variations of this would be to produce a complete 30-second dramatic, documentary, event video, or experimental scene composed of exactly 15 clips of 2 seconds each. This could be shot in sequence, which for all practical purposes is "editing in the camera," and the challenge would be to completely preconceive the project before shooting. Approached or assigned differently, the project could be edited, which will allow for a combination of production planning along with final shot selection and sequencing of images in postproduction. The project could be an entirely visual exercise with only silence or continuous music or ambience on the sound track. Alternatively, it could be accompanied by the original 2-second sound of each clip as recorded with the video, or a completely developed sound score with sync moments and Foley.
- Create a video storyboard for a short fiction script shot with 2-, 4-, or 8-second video snapshots instead of stills. The shots can be viewed silently to show the visual flow of the storyboard, or can have a one-phrase or one-sentence voiceover description summarizing the dialogue or action in each shot.
- What happens if the 2-second video snapshot is assigned or self-imposed as an obstruction for shooting or redoing a short dramatic script that was not intended for short fragments? Every shot will be of identical length, as predictable as a metronome. The challenge is to make this work effectively. See *The Five Obstructions*, where filmmaker Jørgen Leth had to do it with half-second shots.
- Use the camcorder to defamiliarize. Through cinematic means, transform a banal, commonplace experience by seeing it in a new way. Part of the challenge here is to create an engaging, coherent, and rewarding experience with a beginning, middle, and end. Macro videography is one way to enter a sensually visual

and tactile world that goes beyond everyday experience. Infrared is another, provided you avoid imitations of the *Blair Witch Project* and cable TV stories of haunted houses and try to explore genuinely fresh possibilities with infrared. The defamiliarization exercise can be just as challenging in normal operating modes. Even without special devices, a palm-sized camcorder that you can take almost anywhere offers ways to explore the world with fresh eyes.

Production Apps for iPhone, iPod, and iPad

The iPhone, iPod, iPad and Android have become essential as aids for planning, organization, and various aspects of field production. Their size and mobility are perfectly suited to palm-sized production. Following are some selected apps that are particularly useful:

- **DSLR Slate.** Even though it is called "DSLR Slate," this app works equally well with the G10/XA10. The slate provides a way to display for the camera essential information such as director, producer, project, scene, take, memory card, and date, as well as technical information such as exposure, aperture, shutter speed, and white balance. Recorded clips of this information are useful for continuity notes, retakes, future reference, and organizing. When there is more than a full frame of information to display, the slate will cycle info so that items can be viewed on successive video frames over a 2-second time span. When shooting double system sound or with multiple cameras, DSLR Slate provides a precise audio/video sync mark. It also includes a color chart and selectable timecode.
- **Easy Release.** A release is a legal agreement between the media maker and the performer, documentary subject, crew member, or property owner giving permission for their recognizable image or other contribution to be used in the production. A release usually dissuades frivolous legal actions and can be used as evidence that consent had been given. It is a good practice to obtain releases for any production that will have exposure to venues other than a limited private audience. If you were to license, sell, distribute, or broadcast a production, you may be asked to demonstrate that it was produced with consent. Easy Release allows you to complete the entire release process on your iPhone, iPad, or Android. You can customize the wording of various kinds of standard releases and add your own data including contact information, personal signature, and even a logo. The app is then used on location to take contact information, a photo, and a signature of the subject(s) directly on the iPhone, iPad, or Android. Easy Release assembles these items into a well-formatted PDF document and automatically emails it to both the media maker and the subject.

- **Movie Slate.** This app doubles as a clapper board and a digital slate for displaying production information, shot logs, and notes for shooting by the camera at the head or tail of a shot. It is useful for creating an audio/visual sync mark for slating double system sound with a separate video and audio recorder or providing a synchronization point when shooting with multiple cameras. You can customize its appearance, colors, and fonts. During production, it can also be used as an off-camera note pad for text, voice, photos, logging, and rating shots. This information can be later exported as a production log.
- **ProPrompter.** In ProPrompter, scripts can be imported or typed within the application and then paused or scrolled at controllable speeds as a teleprompter. An iPhone or iPad can be held next to the camcorder for simple teleprompter operation, mounted on a bracket, or incorporated into a professional two-way mirror and anti-reflection hood (which the company also sells) for reading a script while looking directly into the lens.
- **Storyboard Composer.** Cinemek Storyboard Composer is compatible with iPhone, iPod Touch, and iPad. To pre-visualize your production, you can import photos or drawings or take photos within the application itself. The app also supplies a library of pre-existing graphic figures if you need them. Storyboard Composer allows you to crop, scale, rotate, and arrange the visuals with various panel options to which you can add zooms, pans, shot numbers, arrows, labels, notes, and audio. It provides a mobile reference that can be used on location while setting up shots. The storyboards can be exported to PDF, sent by email, or viewed on the mobile device as individual panels, multiple panels, or an animatic (a real-time storyboard slide show with a sound track).
- **Teleprompt+ for iPad.** Teleprompt+ turns the iPad into a professional teleprompter that can import, type or edit scripts, and format them for being read aloud. It provides a countdown, cues, arrows, highlighted text, and controllable scrolling speeds. Like ProPrompter, text can be read directly from an iPad held or mounted near the camcorder. Alternatively, Teleprompt+ can display in mirror mode for speaking directly on–axis toward the lens if used with a two-way mirror rig (a beam splitter) available from other sources.

Green Media Making

Within production planning, you should also examine alternative materials and environmentally friendly practices. These include looking into recycling, reducing waste, purchasing locally made products, donating unused or unwanted items, and offsetting the carbon dioxide and pollutants we generate in making a production.

Working with a palm-sized camcorder and the minimal support equipment it needs is a step in this direction. Using augmented available light instead of 2,000–20,000 watts for each scene is a considerable energy savings. LED lights are highly efficient per watt. They last 20,000 to 50,000 hours and do not contain mercury as fluorescents do. Exhibiting productions online or uploading copies via the Internet (even if this is simply limited to preview copies) uses far fewer resources than individual copies burned onto DVDs that are shipped in plastic cases surrounded by padding and cardboard mailers. Media distributors themselves have turned to online as a major delivery system for the digital age.

18

Managing and Storing Video Files

AVCHD needs a fast dual- or multi-core computer with at least 4GB of RAM (preferably more), a high-quality graphics card, and a high-speed hard drive or solid-state drive (SSD). In addition, newer editing programs need a 64-bit operating system. If SDHC or SDXC memory cards or MTS files themselves are not compatible with your computer, you may need to update your computer's operating system, RAM, graphics board, hard drive, drivers, or the computer itself.

For editing, you need to place video files on your computer's internal or external hard drive. It is usually good practice to house these source files on a 7,200 rpm high-speed drive separate from the editing application and system drive. Reading and writing between the two drives will be a faster process than if both operations happen on a single drive. It is also a good practice to duplicate your source files one more time to an additional backup hard drive stored in some other location and/or archive the files to Blu-ray data discs.

Whether you edit with a desktop or laptop, an external high-speed drive should connect to your computer's fastest input/output port, which will be FireWire 800, eSATA, USB 3.0, or Thunderbolt. If you have a desktop computer with internal locations for a second, third, or fourth drive, the internal connection (usually Serial ATA 3.0 at 3–6Gbps) may provide your fastest read/write rate.

If you will be offloading your video files directly from the G10/XA10, the connecting cable from the camcorder to the computer is a USB 2.0, which is good enough for transferring or archiving files but not for actually editing them. This is why the video source files need to be relocated from the camcorder onto a high-speed drive that can meet the demands of the editing process.

To transfer directly from the G10/XA10, connect the compact power adapter to the camcorder. Do not do this operation on battery power alone. Turn the camcorder on, toggle the Camera/Playback button to Playback, tap the Index icon in the lower left, choose the memory tab for the location of your video files (Internal, A, or B), and tap the Camera icon. Finally, connect the camcorder to the computer with the supplied mini-to-standard USB 2.0 cable.

When the camcorder acknowledges the computer, the camcorder's touchscreen may ask you to "Select the memory for connection." (See Figure 18.1.) Your choices will be All (for PC only), Mem. Card A, Mem. Card B, and Built-in Mem. After you make your choice, it will then say, "USB Connection, Do not disconnect the power source." The computer screen will display an icon that says "CANON" (or "NO NAME"), which it recognizes as an external storage device.

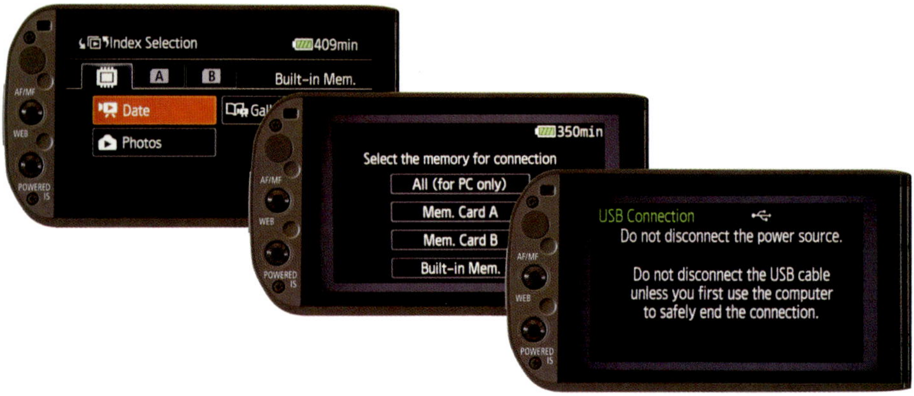

Figure 18.1 Select the camcorder's memory location from which to transfer files.

As with transferring still photos, once you have made this connection, keep the following points in mind:

- Do not disconnect power from the camcorder.
- Do not disconnect the USB cable.
- Do not turn off the camcorder or the computer.
- Do not open the memory slot cover.
- Do not change the camcorder's operating mode.

When you open the CANON icon on a computer, you'll find this folder and file structure (see Figure 18.2):

CANON (overall name)
    DCIM (folder for still photos)
        JPEG files (photo files)
    AVCHD (folder for video files and metadata)
        BDMV (Blu-ray digital media video folder)
            BACKUP (folder)
            CLIPINF (info folder)
            INDEX.BDM (clip file index)
            MOVIEOBJ.BDM (clip description file)
            PLAYLIST (folder)
            STREAM (video clip folder)
                MTS files (your video clips)
        CANON (folder for thumbnail clip images)
    CV INFO
    MY_MUSIC (a resource folder)
    MY_PICTURES (a resource folder)

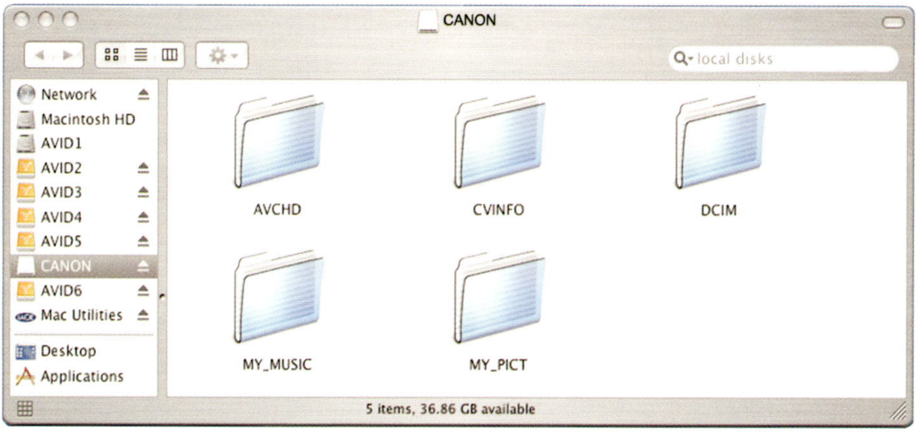

Figure 18.2 The memory card will display these folders on your computer screen.

BDMV, which stands for "Blu-ray disc movie," is the structure on which AVCHD's organizational structure is based. Within the BDMV folder, your actual video clips are the MTS files (short for "MPEG-2 Transport Stream files") in the STREAM subfolder. After they have been transferred to a computer's hard drive, you will be able to play these files as fully rendered video with an appropriate player.

The other subfolders under BDMV contain associated index files, clip data, playlists, and backup data, all of which are considered metadata (data about data). When the MTS and its metadata files are together, as they are in the BDMV folder, an editing program can locate and identify files with access to all the related data if it needs it. Some programs will find it difficult or impossible to track the time, date, file name, and file number; link continuous files; or even locate an individual file if the metadata is unavailable.

Copy the video and metadata files from the camcorder's folders onto your computer's hard drive (internal or external) by dragging and dropping. The quickest and safest way to offload the files from your memory chip is to simply reproduce all of them, but the entire CANON drive may contain music resources and premade photo mattes for green screen that you do not need to transfer. What you really need is the entire AVCHD folder (and the DCIM folder, if you want still photographs). If your software does not need Canon's video thumbnails, I recommend that you at least transfer the entire BDMV folder to your computer's internal or external high-speed hard drive.

Keep your source files and archive copies in their original MTS format along with metadata files. You can edit, transcode, or create master versions in other formats, but whenever you want the highest quality, you should do this from the originals. A transcoded intermediate is simply an interpretation of the information in the original MTS file; it is not the original file itself. You may eventually transcode to ProRes422, DNxHD, MOV, or Cineform format if your editing program works best with one of these. But the algorithms for transcoding these files from MTS keep improving and future editing programs may develop even better codecs. So, archiving your media in its original form makes sense.

You should not rename the files unless you use an editing or file utility that provides a means to do this. If you simply rewrite the name of an MTS file on your own, the file will still play as an individual clip of video, but it may lose connections with its metadata, which could have ramifications for some editing programs.

Disconnecting

After you have completed the transfer, do not physically disconnect the USB cable, remove a memory card, or disrupt the camcorder's power until you have followed the computer's protocol to disengage the camcorder from the computer. On a PC, right-click the Canon icon in the System menu then choose Safely Remove Hardware as you would when you eject any other USB memory source, or use any of several alternative methods. Wait for the prompt that says "It's now safe to remove your hardware." On a Mac, drag the CANON icon to the Eject symbol. After the

CANON icon has disappeared from the computer screen, you may then unplug the USB cable. The "Do not disconnect power" message should disappear from the camcorder's touchscreen and the camcorder can be turned off. Disconnecting improperly could corrupt or permanently damage files.

Verify and test the transferred files before you erase and reformat the memory card or the camcorder's internal memory. Always reformat your memory cards in the camcorder, never on a computer, to be certain their formatting is completely compatible with the G10/XA10.

Using a Card Reader

If you recorded to removable memory card A or B, it is possible to eject the card from the camcorder and transfer the files to your computer through a card reader. A USB 3.0 card reader or a card slot built into the computer itself may read SDHC and SDXC cards faster than the connection from the camcorder (which is USB 2.0). Make certain the power on the camcorder is completely off before you open the memory slot door to remove the card. Initially press the card inward to release its latch so that the card pops up in its slot.

SDHC cards and readers have been around for a number of years. To recognize SDXC cards, which are somewhat newer, Mac computers need system 10.6.4 or later, and PCs need Windows 7, Windows XP with Service Pack 3 plus KB955704 update, or Windows Vista with Service Pack 1 or later. Your card reader itself must also be compatible with SDXC; otherwise, the computer may want to reject or reformat the card.

It is very important to slide the write protect tab on the memory card to the side marked "lock" immediately after removing the card from the camcorder and before inserting it in an SDHC or SDXC card reader. The computer will recognize the card as a memory device and may attempt to index or write data to it, which you want to prevent by locking the card. Once the computer acknowledges the memory card, follow the same procedures as before, including the proper protocol for removing or ejecting the card when the transfer is complete.

Class 6 or class 10 SDHC and SDXC cards are delicate and expensive, so you want to store them in a protective case when they are outside of the camcorder. Leave them write protected without erasing and reformatting until you have completed and verified the whole transfer process and know that your files are safe and playable on a computer's internal or external hard drive.

File Management and Viewing

You should be able to transfer the BDMV folder or full AVCHD folder from the camcorder or memory card to the computer via drag and drop. In some cases, your editing program itself will be able to import directly from the memory card and organize source files into its own locations. There are also dedicated software programs that can streamline the offloading and file-management process. On a PC, you might try Pixela Video Browser, the transfer utility included with the G10/XA10. Pixela opens automatically when it senses the G10/XA10 has been connected; click Video File Import to start the process.

ShotPut Pro ($89–$99), made by Imagine Products, is a highly regarded dedicated application for offloading MTS and metadata files. It is available in separate versions for Mac and PC. One of its most important features is that it can verify transferred data by MD5 or CRC checksums for each file, or byte-by-byte comparisons to ensure error-free clones of your source files. ShotPut Pro automates the transfer process. It can copy files to more than one drive at a time, simultaneously creating a backup drive. It enables you to add prefix names and accumulate numbers to filenames. It visually indicates the progress of all operations and ultimately creates a log of transferred files and a verification report. A demo version is available online at www.imagineproducts.com.

With VLC, a free downloadable application that plays almost every kind of media file and works well on most computers, you can preview and play your MTS files just by tapping the file without having to go into an editing program. It is designed by VideoLan, a non-profit volunteer organization based in France with developers in 20 countries dedicated to producing and promoting free open-source multimedia solutions for the general public. Go to www.videolan.org/vlc.

HD-VU ($99) by Imagine Products is another application that enables you to instantly play or preview MTS clips in their original form without transcoding or entering an editing program. Clips can be played full screen or in a scalable window and can be operated by on-screen or keyboard commands forward, in reverse, and at variable speed. They can be viewed with or without an overlaid timecode that displays minutes, seconds, and frames, and you can view metadata for any clip.

Hard Drives

As discussed, an external drive (see Figure 18.3) holding your editing source files should connect to your laptop or desktop computer's fastest I/O port, which will be USB 3.0, FireWire 800, eSATA, or Thunderbolt. As a source drive for a desktop computer, the alternative is a second or third Serial ATA 3.0 internal hard drive.

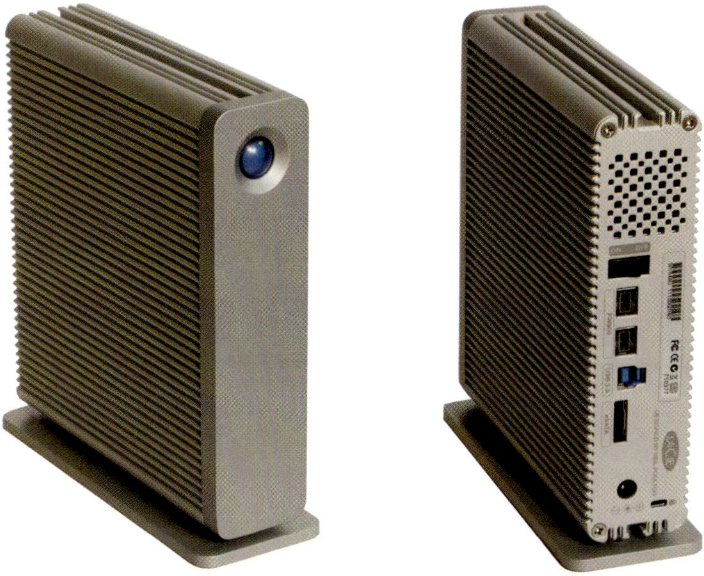

Figure 18.3 LaCie 7,200 rpm Quadra external hard drive with 3TB of memory and FireWire 800, USB 3.0 and eSATA connections.

For editing MTS video files, you will need a high-speed 7,200 rpm (or 10,000 rpm) hard drive with a capacity of 1, 2, or 3TB. The LaCie d2 Quadra v3 hard disk has three types of high-speed I/O interfaces for nearly universal connectivity, or you could choose a comparable model with the single high-speed interface that matches your computer. On the LaCie Quadra drive, FireWire 800 has a burst transfer rate of 85Mbps, eSATA has a transfer rate of 115Mbps, and USB 3.0 has a transfer rate of 130Mbps. In each case, this is many times the rate of USB 2.0. The Quadra series is quiet because its outer shape is a ribbed aluminum heat sink instead of a fan for cooling. The ribbed design is adequate if you are editing in a temperature-regulated area that does not get above the 70s. Otherwise, choose a fan-cooled external drive.

On Macintosh computers manufactured in 2012 or later, Thunderbolt is a very high-speed bidirectional terminal that can transmit and receive data simultaneously. It produces data rates of 8–10Gbps, which is significantly faster than FireWire 800, USB 3.0, and eSATA. The Thunderbolt connector fits all recent Macs. However, Thunderbolt drives and multi-disk RAIDs are currently expensive. The LaCie 1TB Thunderbolt Little Big Disk hard drive sells for $429. To accommodate Thunderbolt's much higher data rates, the Little Big Disk consists of two 7,200 rpm drives within a single enclosure in a RAID 0 configuration acting as a single drive. (This is discussed further in the next section.) It has a 180Mbps data transfer speed.

If you are limited to a Thunderbolt I/O port, third-party vendors sell adapters that let you connect slower FireWire 800 and possibly USB 3.0 drives to the Thunderbolt port. The speed will be limited by the FireWire 800 or USB 3.0 drive.

Editing needs high-speed drives, but additional drives for backup, storage, and archiving can operate with slower than 7,200 rpm speeds. Specifically useful for editing, RAID drives offer the highest read/write rates.

RAID Drives

A RAID drive is a combination of two or more hard drives programmed to operate as a single drive with faster data rates, greater reliability, or both. Preconfigured RAIDs can be purchased, or you may purchase a RAID enclosure that holds multiple drives, which can be striped in various different ways to behave as one drive.

There are various types of RAID:

- RAID 0 needs at least two drives. A single MTS file is written or read as fragments across the two drives working together in parallel. This process creates a higher bandwidth with faster read-and-write rates than a single drive. The 1TB LaCie Little Big Disk ($426) uses a RAID 0 configuration so its two drives in a single enclosure collectively handle 180Mbps with input/output through Apple's ultra high-speed Thunderbolt interface, available on Mac computers manufactured in 2012 or later. Performance speed is great, but RAID 0 does not have error checking. Also, with double the number of drives, there is double the risk of data loss if an error occurs in one of the drives.
- RAID 5 needs at least three drives and is typically set up with four. This configuration builds enough redundancy into the distribution of the data that the system will operate as long as all but one of the coordinated drives are operating correctly (two out of three, or three out of four). The high level of performance is reduced if one drive has errors, turns off, or crashes entirely, but data files are not lost or corrupted. Sans Digital is a well-respected company that makes towers that hold multiple drives configured to operate as RAID 5.

Portable Drives

For immediate and intermediate storage, portable hard drives are very viable ways of carrying your footage from one computer to another. For media files that are worthwhile, you should keep more than one copy when you have time for archiving. It may be that one version is on a very large, fast hard drive or RAID, providing source files for editing, a second duplicate version on another hard drive as backup, and an archived version backed up as data files on Blu-ray discs.

For editing small projects or carrying projects from one computer to another, the 64GB and 128GB Kingston HyperX 3.0 Data Traveler flash drives connect to a USB 3.0 port. The 64GB drive sells for $124, and the 128GB for $259. Solid-state drives are expensive per gigabyte, but the HyperX is fast enough for editing on computers with USB 3.0 terminals and useful for transfers on computers with USB 2.0.

If you need a portable drive of greater capacity, you might consider a 500MB or 1TB hard drive specifically designed for portability. LaCie's Rugged series is compact, air cooled, and shock resistant; has a protective rubber rim on its perimeter; comes with various interface configurations; and receives its power from the computer when connected. (See Figure 18.4.) The 7,200 rpm 500GB model suitable for editing has connections for USB 3.0 and FireWire 800 and sells for $169. The 5,400 rpm 500GB model suitable for archiving sells for $117. Other major brands of hard drives to consider are Seagate, Western Digital, Iomega, IoSafe, and G-Technology. Portable drives are useful for general mobility with a laptop, as well as for more extensive travel, storing separate projects, or interfacing with many computers such as at home, school, work, or a postproduction facility.

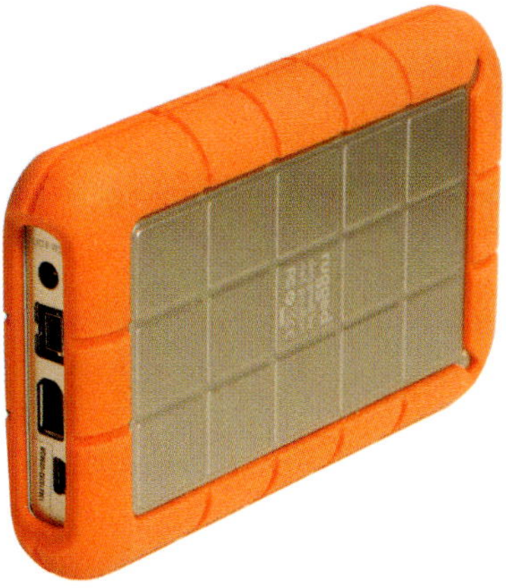

Figure 18.4 LaCie 7,200 rpm 500GB portable "rugged" hard drive.

Archiving

Archive your source files in their original MTS format along with their metadata files. Once you have set up a folder of MTS source files, you may edit and create intermediate or editing versions in whatever other formats necessary from the originals.

Class 6 and class 10 memory cards themselves are much too expensive per gigabyte to be used to archive files. Their function is to be used for video acquisition and transfer, and then reused for acquisition again. Holding data on original SDHC or

SDXC cards offers some short-term protection if you wait until transferred files are verified and playable and don't erase them until you are ready to re-use them. For long-term archiving, a 500GB portable drive, or a 1TB, 2TB, or 3TB external hard drive, is much more efficient and economical by a factor of 10:1 or 20:1. Table 18.1 compares the cost per gigabyte of various storage media.

Table 18.1 Comparative Cost per Gigabyte

Storage Medium	Disc or Drive Price	Cost per GB
32GB class 10 SDHC card	$35–$60	$1.09–$1.88 per GB
1TB ext. USB 3.0 hard drive	$100	$0.10 per GB
2TB ext. USB 3.0 hard drive	$120–$160	$0.06–$0.08 per GB
2TB ext. FireWire 800 hard drive	$160	$0.08 per GB
2TB ext. eSATA hard drive	$140	$0.07 per GB
2TB ext. USB 2.0 hard drive	$100	$0.05 per GB
8.5GB DVD-9	$0.71 per disc	$0.08 per GB
25GB Blu-ray BD-R	$1.00 per disc	$0.04 per GB
50GB Blu-ray BD-R DL	$4.50 per disc	$0.09 per GB

Hard-drive prices vary considerably by manufacturer, the read/write speed of its protocol, and whether the drive runs at 5,400 rpm, 7,200 or 10,000 rpm. So, the figures in Table 18.1 are a very rough guide. The least expensive hard drives will run at 5,400 rpm and may handle only USB 2.0. They will take longer to load and will be suitable for archiving, but probably not fast enough for editing.

Nobody quite knows with hard drives or solid-state memory drives what their life expectancy is. So, source files worth keeping are usually archived on one additional medium like digital data tape or data discs. Up to 8.5GB from an SDHC memory card can be stored as data on a dual DVD-9 disc. If you are using 32GB SDHC cards or 64GB SDXC cards, you can still take combinations of files in roughly 8.5GB bundles and store them as data files on fairly inexpensive DVD-9 discs.

You would need four DVD-9s to hold the information from a 32BG memory card. Save your metadata files for your entire AVCHD folder on the 32GB memory card, keeping the metadata at least on the first disc, or since the files are small, repeat the entire set of metadata folders on each additional disk.

Blu-ray discs used for data storage can hold 25GB per single layer disc or 50GB per dual layer disc, provided you have a Blu-ray deck that will handle dual layer. Blu-ray is an optically recorded disc, so there is no danger of magnetic erasure. Using Blu-ray for data storage (as opposed to a playable Blu-ray disc) is a very viable long-term storage solution, both in terms of its capacity per disc and cost per gigabyte. (See Figure 18.5.)

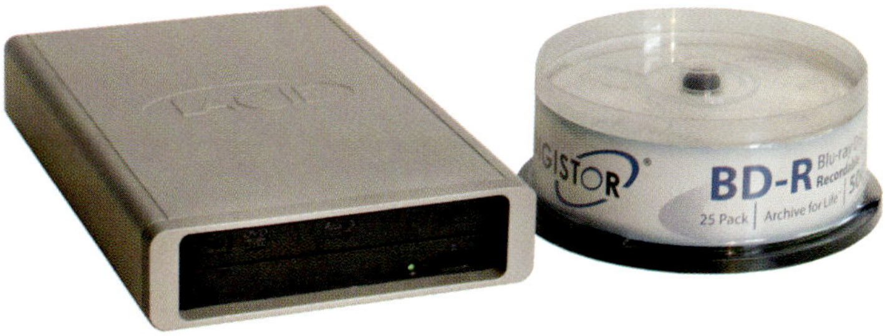

Figure 18.5 The LaCie d2 Blu-ray drive records, rewrites, and plays 25GB and 50GB discs.

In comparison to the complexities of storing AVCHD on hard drives and discs, it may seem that archiving analog or digital videotape was an easy process. Whatever you shot on videotape existed in a physical format that could be stored on a shelf. But in actuality, having to depend on whether that tape would be playable one year, three years, five years, or 10 years later was very problematic. Over time, tape layers stick to each other, and as the binder ages, the magnetic emulsion begins a process of disintegration and dropouts occur. The magnetic signal itself erodes over time. The Mylar or acetate base of the tape expands and contracts with temperature and humidity, causing tracking and timebase errors. Playing or rewinding a videotape always entailed the risk of jamming, scratching, stretching, demagnetizing, or destroying the video signal. Physically locating and cueing a shot was a linear, time-consuming process. Capturing footage from videotape involved setup time, a cue-in time, a cue-out time, and real time for the transfer. As for storing, you would need a shelf of 16 to 40 20-minute Betacam tapes or a lot of mini-HDV tapes to store the equivalent of the video on one SDHC memory chip the size of a postage stamp.

With AVCHD, you have some protections built in and some useful parts of the process that you never had in the tape era, including directories that tell you the time and place that something was photographed and the ability to play the 98th clip in a folder without having to queue through 97 previous shots. Depending on the speed of your SDHC or SDXC cards, the speed of your hard drive, and the speed of your computer, it is possible to transfer seven hours of recorded video to a computer in a fraction of the actual running time.

Noise Reduction

Neat Video Pro ($99–$199) is a digital noise-reduction plug-in for Premiere Pro, After Effects, Final Cut Pro, Motion, Vegas Pro, and Pinnacle Studio. It removes visible noise and compression artifacts from the video image caused by excessive gain or high compression. Neat Video Pro analyzes 1,920×1,080 high-definition video, constructs an individualized noise profile, and allows standard and advanced adjustments to be made by the user. It saves individual noise profiles and noise-reduction settings for reuse with similar footage. Once the settings have been adjusted, Neat Video takes a considerable amount of rendering time for each clip, but it is an effective way to rescue marginal footage.

Standard Definition

The G10/XA10 cannot directly record standard-definition video. But the camcorder does have the ability to play its high-definition clips as standard definition and output them through the A/V analog video output and cable for viewing, for recording on an SD deck, or for quick-and-dirty editing on standard-definition software.

If you want to routinely transfer to a computer running standard DV editing software, you may need an analog-to-DV converter such as the Canopus/Grass Valley ADVC55 ($179), ADVC 110 ($218), or ADVC 300 ($429). The more expensive models offer timebase correction to stabilize the image and individual control of brightness, contrast, hue, and saturation. The ADVC 300 has digital-to-analog as well as analog-to-digital operation. The converter takes the camcorder's AV signal and converts it to DV out through a FireWire 400 cable. Many older computers and editing software programs accept this interface.

For Web quality, MTS files can be batch transcoded to standard definition inside the camcorder itself. Clips can be selected for transcoding individually or in batches based on record date. Make certain there is a memory card in slot B. Then, attach the compact power adapter and turn on the camcorder. Toggle the Camera/Playback button to Playback; then tap the Index icon (lower left), select the Internal, A, or B memory tab, select the date, and press the WEB button (on the left bezel of the touchscreen) to convert all scenes on that date to SD on memory slot B.

The standard-definition clips can be transferred to a computer or can be uploaded wirelessly to a video-sharing website if slot B contains an Eye-Fi card. Your high-definition MTS files still exist in memory slot A or the internal memory. If you want individual clip selections and control of output quality, there is a more complicated route for converting HD to SD. To use it, toggle the Camera/Playback button to Playback; choose Edit > Convert HD to SD; select Internal-to-B or A-to-B; and select the clips individually or by date. Then choose Next (to review selections); tap the Tool icon; set the bit rate (quality); touch Return twice; and press START to convert the scenes. A confirmation screen will appear at the end of the HD-to-SD rendering process.

If your computer is capable of handling MTS files, the best way to produce a standard-definition version is to stay in high definition all the way through editing on a computer, and then use your editing software's options to output to standard definition, including various DVD and Web formats. You could master the entire project in high definition and transcode the master with software like Apple's Compressor or with third-party conversion software.

Deleting Files

The edit function in the G10/XA10 provides you with an opportunity to selectively erase individual files before transferring everything to a hard drive. To use it, first move the Camera/Playback button to Playback. Then choose Edit > Delete and choose to delete by date, by scene, or all scenes.

If you do much deleting and editing in the camera, the memory card will eventually have fragmented memory, which will reduce its recording performance. If recording stops or you suspect reduced performance, save your data to a hard drive, verify the transferred data, and re-initialize your memory card in the camcorder.

If you have many unwanted clips, your other option before editing is to offload all your video files to a computer's hard drive. Then, individually select and delete unwanted MTS files from the editing source drive so they will not be taking up space. You do not have to bother with deleting the associated metafiles because they take up minimal space. In this way, you are certain to have the associated metafiles your programs may need (at the expense of retaining tiny metafiles for shots you have discarded).

19

Editing

In learning any editing program the first things you need to know are how to do the following:

- Open the program.
- Name a project.
- Set preferences.
- Ingest/capture footage.
- Arrange and begin to trim shots.

This will enable you to accomplish some basic functions before you really start learning the complexities of an editing program. This chapter introduces some of the major editing programs and discusses some of these initial steps. Your workflow choice in capturing, importing, or ingesting AVCHD video from the G10/XA10 into an editing program is whether to ingest MTS video files directly from your storage drive (or camcorder), which some (but not all) editing programs allow, or to have the editing program or a separate intermediate program transcode the MTS files into a much less condensed, high quality format best suited for editing.

Major Editing Programs

The major professional editing programs are Avid Media Composer, Final Cut Pro, Premiere Pro, and Sony Vegas Pro. Over the past decade, 70 to 90% of Hollywood feature films and prime-time television programs have been edited on Avid Media

Composer. Avid received an Oscar for Technical Achievement from the Academy of Motion Picture Arts and Sciences, and the ACE Technical Excellence Award from the American Cinema Editors guild. By 2011, Apple's Final Cut Pro 7 was being used by 54% of the broader professional editing community including independents and schools. Features like *The Social Network* and *The Girl with the Dragon Tattoo* were edited on Final Cut. As high-definition video emerged in recent years, Adobe Premiere Pro and Sony Vegas Pro have increasingly been adopted by professional editors, particularly for commercials, documentaries, and music videos. All four of these programs are excellent at cutting, pasting, and arranging picture and sound across a timeline, and they each include advanced tools for titling, visual effects, audio mixing, image correction and mastering.

Final Cut Pro

In 2011, Apple completely rethought the nonlinear editing process and made a clean break from its highly successful Final Cut Pro 7 (shown in Figure 19.1), which had been adopted by a large portion of the professional community. The new version, Final Cut Pro X, does many things more quickly and automatically completes many formerly tedious tasks in the background, but it also left out certain functions. For all practical purposes, it was a completely new editing program designed for the world of file-based, tapeless media production, with little tying it to previous versions. This orphaned the loyal users of the previous version of the software, Final Cut Pro 7, and created an uproar. Independent media-makers, film schools, and professional editors (who continually face heavy production deadlines) strongly objected to having to relearn a completely new interface that used different working methods, employed different workflows, and provided no support or interface for legacy projects in Final Cut Pro 7. For certain functions, Final Cut Pro X was unworkable for production houses that depended on Final Cut Pro's ability to share files and projects among editors, incorporate older projects into newer releases, perform multi-camera editing, work with edit decision lists, and export to tape. Some of these problems, such as multi-camera editing, have since been addressed by incremental upgrades to Final Cut X, and there is now a $10 third-party conversion application called 7toX by Intelligent Assistance that allows older project files from Final Cut 7 to be imported as Final Cut X "events."

Note

Although Apple's Final Cut Pro 7 is no longer available for purchase, many people continue to use it. For this reason, we have included information in this chapter and in Appendix F, "Basic Keyboard Commands: Final Cut Pro," available at www.courseptr.com/downloads, on both Final Cut Pro 7 and its successor, Final Cut Pro X.

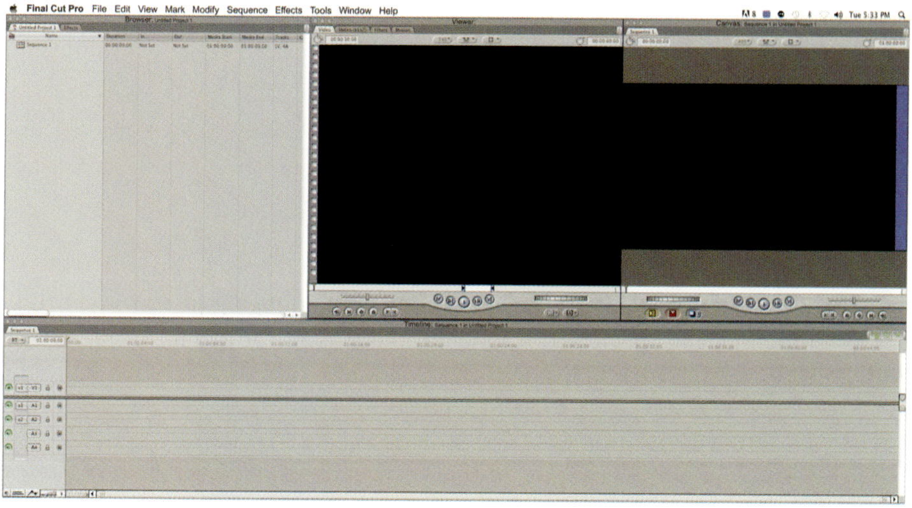

Figure 19.1 Final Cut Pro 7.

Because so much of Final Cut Pro X operates automatically, professionals derogatorily called it "iMovie Pro." In a sense, Final Cut Pro X is intended to work as simply and quickly as a consumer program, but produce professional results. If it provides the results you need, Final Cut Pro X is worth consideration. It costs $299 but does not come bundled with programs like Compressor, Color, Motion, Soundtrack, and DVD Studio Pro, which have to be purchased separately. However, Final Cut Pro X can directly and efficiently work with MTS files from camcorders like the G10/XA10 (as can the latest versions of Avid Media Composer, Adobe Premiere Pro, Sony's Vegas, and Grass Valley's Edius). Apple's previous editing program, Final Cut Pro 7, worked with MTS files only by transcoding to Apple's editing format ProRes 422, which is time-consuming and creates enormous video files in the process. However, many professionals prefer to transcode to a format optimized for editing and have accepted this time-consuming step as part of the workflow.

Avid Media Composer

Another major editing program is Avid Media Composer, which has long been a professional editing standard in the feature-film industry. Avid Media Composer is used on more Hollywood films than any other editing platform. It comes in a software-only version and well as in hardware-accelerated versions. With Avid's free AMA plug-in, Media Composer 6—the latest version of the software—will capture MTS files directly from the G10/XA10 or from a storage drive, making the files available for editing on the timeline without transcoding. Alternatively, Media Composer can transcode MTS files into DNxHD, Avid's high-quality editing codec.

Media Composer works on both Windows and Mac multi-core computers that have high-quality graphics processors.

Media Composer includes a strong assortment of effects, titling, color-correction, and audio controls. It interfaces easily with Pro Tools, which is also made by Avid and is the industry standard for audio processing, mixing, and editing. There are many hardware and software add-ons for Avid Media Composer. With ScriptSync, an add-on sold separately, Avid can automatically locate shots and multiple takes by phonetically analyzing dialogue tracks. It can search, find, and sync these shots to a written script along with groups of alternative shots that share the same dialogue. This is useful for comparing multiple takes and assembling shots for script-based projects such as feature films. With the PhraseFind add-on, Avid can phonetically index and locate sound/picture clips based on a key word or phrase instead of a script. This is highly useful for organizing and editing documentary dialogue and interviews, or for locating a shot or a cut point in many kinds of productions. PhraseFind sells for $495. This may sound expensive for a search tool, but it can eliminate many hours of searching and logging, or in some cases, many weeks of work on projects with high shooting ratios.

Avid Media Composer 6 sells for $2,399 bundled with a whole suite of extra programs for special effects, encoding tasks, and authoring DVDs. There are other package prices that include acceleration and professional input/output hardware as part of the bundle. Avid Media Composer 6 also has an educational price of $295 for those who qualify for an academic discount. The education edition does not include some of the bundled software, but the Media Composer editing program itself has complete functionality at an amazing price.

Adobe Premiere Pro

Adobe Premiere Pro CS6 sells for $599–$799, depending on discounts, with an educational price of $299 for those with academic credentials. Premiere Pro enables you to import and work directly on the timeline with MTS files with most other tapeless formats simultaneously without transcoding or rewrapping. It can run on a multi-core Windows or Macintosh computer with a 64-bit operating system and a high-quality graphics processing unit. It will not run on 32-bit computers.

One of the major strengths of Premiere Pro is its ability to interface with other Adobe software for photography, effects, graphics, and Web development. Adobe's Creative Suite Production Premium 5.5 ($1,145–$1,194) is a bundled collection that integrates Premiere Pro CS5.5 with After Effects CS5.5 (for creating effects, including the Warp Stabilizer tool to correct skew from CMOS camcorders during moments of fast motion), Photoshop CS5 Extended, Audition for multi-track audio editing, Flash Catalyst, Flash Professional, Illustrator, Media Encoder, Device Central,

OnLocation (for monitoring and recording to disc in the field), Encore authoring tools, and Bridge (for organization and browsing among applications). Creative Suite Production Premium 5.5 has an academic price of $449.

Sony Vegas

Sony's Vegas Pro 11 works directly with MTS files and can mix MTS with other kinds of video without having to transcode. The program includes real–time effects preview, image stabilization (including correcting for the skew effect of the CMOS photo sensor), stationary and moving titles, 2D and 3D transitions, and multi-camera editing. Vegas also features an authoring program for DVDs and Blu-ray discs. The editing process involves dragging and dropping media files from the Device Explorer into the Media Pool, the Timeline, or the Trimmer window as well as working with tool icons and keyboard commands.

Sony's MXF file format uses a lower bit rate than Avid DNxHD145 and Apple ProRes 422. Its files will take up less hard-drive space and it will work with less robust computers as long as the computer has a high-quality NVIDIA or ATI graphics board with at least 512MB of GPU memory, 4GB of RAM, and 64-bit processing.

As a nonlinear video editor, Sony Vegas developed from the desktop audio processing, mixing, and editing program called Sound Forge, which Sony acquired in 2003.

Other Programs

In addition to the four previous editing programs (actually, five, considering the two versions of Final Cut Pro), you may want to consider Grass Valley's Edius 6 and EditShare's Lightworks. Edius 6 is a versatile multi-format editing program for Windows that enables you to work natively in MTS files and mix formats and even frame rates in real time without transcoding. Its slogan is, "Edit anything." Edius sells for $729 but you can download a 30-day free trial. There is a special price of $399 if you cross-grade from Avid, Premiere, Final Cut Pro, or Vegas, and an educational price of $159 for those who qualify for an academic discount.

Lightworks by EditShare is an Oscar-winning professional program used over the years in such films as *Goodfellas* (1990), *Pulp Fiction* (1994), *Braveheart* (1995), *Jerry Maguire* (1996), *Moulin Rouge* (2001), *28 Days Later* (2002), *Chicago* (2002), *The Departed* (2006), *Shutter Island* (2010), and *The King's Speech* (2010). Lightworks has a downloadable public beta copy of its current version for Windows available for free. (Mac and Linux versions are in development at the time of this writing.) To find out more, visit www.editshare.com; then click Products and Lightworks. While it does provide the basic editing system without charge, Lightworks makes money on licenses and proprietary plug-ins for some of its professional features.

This meant that as Vegas developed, it always had sophisticated audio editing and excellent audio features. It currently includes Dolby Digital Professional Encoder for 5.1 surround sound. Vegas Pro 11 operates on PC platforms only and sells for $549 or at an academic discount price of $350.

Workflows

Your editing workflow should try to find the best balance between quality and efficiency in relation to the following questions:

- What format and quality level should I shoot in?
- Where and when do I store and back up raw (the original) media files?
- Do I ingest all of my footage for editing or only selected files?
- Do I import from the camcorder, a card reader, or a storage drive?
- Do I import raw MTS files directly or immediately transcode MTS to a high quality editing codec? Or do I initially edit off-line in a lower-quality "proxy" codec and later conform a high-quality master with only the footage needed?
- Do I need to intercut or interface with other formats?
- How do I organize my project in the editing program?
- Which editing procedures should I do first?
- Should I upgrade to a 10-bit high-quality editing codec before color correcting and effects?
- Does the project need to interface with plug-ins and other programs?
- Do I need to share work on the project with other editors (or effects, graphics, or sound people) on other workstations?
- Does the project need the services of a professional production house?
- Do I store all the parameters and iterations of the project?
- What format(s) do I need to export, to where, and for what purpose?
- Do I create and store a completed master, and in what form?
- What are the final exhibition formats for the project?

There is no single set of right answers because there are trade-offs involving time, cost, drive space, image quality, types of equipment and software, ease of operation, learning curves, personal preferences, client preferences, broadcast standards (if applicable), and ultimately what will be acceptable for your purpose with your resources for a particular type of project. The answers were simpler and clearer in the analog age because there were fewer options. Now there are many more variables and many more ways to accomplish each stage of the digital media-making process. The important thing is to find good answers for each of these questions rather than ending up with a workflow by default that may not provide the best results given your time and resources.

Getting Started in Final Cut Pro 7

When you open Final Cut Pro 7, open the Final Cut Pro menu (in the upper-left corner) and select System Settings. Under the Scratch Disk tab, click the top Set button and select where you want your project files to be saved. This creates a Capture Scratch folder where transcoded clips will be placed, a Render Files folder, and an Audio Render Files folder. To name and save your project, click the File menu (upper-left corner) and choose Save Project As.

Final Cut Pro 7 has a Browser window (top left) to organize media in your project, a Viewer window (top middle) to preview and prepare source clips, and a Canvas (top right) to view edited sequences. The Timeline (bottom) provides a graphic layout for assembling and editing picture and tracks. The Tool palette is nearby on the bottom right and the Audio meter is next to the Tool palette. To make a window active, click anywhere in that window. To make sure that the window is active, look for the highlighted window bar.

If your working preferences are not already set in FCP7, open the Final Cut Pro menu and choose User Preferences. Within the General tab, change the Levels of Undo setting (top left) from 10 to anywhere between 30–50. This will enable you to use the Undo function (Command+Z) 30 to 50 times if you make a mistake. In the same tab (General), make sure the Autosave Vault checkbox is checked to further protect your project. Finally, you select and set audio and video settings in the Sequence menu. Highlight a specific sequence, open the Sequence menu (top middle), and select settings for frame size, pixel aspect ratio, and compression to match your video's dimensions (1,920×1,080 and16×9).

As explained in the previous chapter, most editors transfer the media files from the camcorder (or its chip) to a high-speed internal or external hard drive prior to editing. To ingest your media from the hard drive, follow these steps:

1. Open the File menu and choose Log and Transfer or press Shift+Command+8.
2. In the window that opens, click the Add Volume icon (a folder with plus sign).
3. Locate and open the AVCHD folder you want to import. The folder's list of clips will collect on the left.

4. Label the logging fields for each clip or allow Final Cut Pro 7 to automatically name clips by choosing a preset in the Name Preset menu.
5. Select the media that you want to transfer and click Add Selection to Queue.

Media will automatically start transcoding and transferring. Final Cut Pro 7 will warn you that if you stop or pause the process, partially transferred media will not be saved. The transcoded files are stored in your Capture Scratch folder (where you set your scratch disk earlier) and will appear in the Browser window, ready for editing. Final Cut Pro 7 cannot edit with native AVCHD/MTS files. Your MTS files need to be transcoded to Apple ProRes422 during log and transfer and will occupy 3–10× more drive space.

There are several tools that will help you keep your media organized. The Browser window contains projects, which contain all clips, sequences, and effects of your movie. Each project appears as a tab in the window. Bins are folders that keep media organized. To create a new bin, Control-click in the Browser window and choose New Bin from the menu that appears. Sequences are containers for editing dozens or hundreds of clips together into a scene or an entire production. Multiple sequences are often used to create trial edits and alternative versions. To create a new sequence, follow the steps for creating a new bin, but select New Sequence instead of New Bin in the menu. You can drag individual clips and sequences into different bins at any time.

To start the edit, double-click a clip in the Browser window. The video will appear in the Viewer window. Locate in and out points by moving the playhead (the yellow upside-down triangle at the bottom of the frame) and mark them using the I and O keys. Click the center of the video in the Viewer window and drag it straight into the Timeline.

There are two essential tools for editing in the Timeline:

- The arrow-shaped Selection tool (keyboard shortcut: A) is the topmost icon in the Tool palette. The Selection tool enables you to select, move, drag, and rearrange clips within the Timeline.
- The Razor Blade tool (keyboard shortcut: B) in the middle of the Tool palette enables you to perform a straight cut, splitting one clip into two.

To zoom in or out of an area of the Timeline, press Command+plus (+) or Command+minus (–).

Note

Basic keyboard commands for Final Cut Pro 7 are listed in Appendix F. In addition, Moviola's Final Cut Pro Field Guide is a useful app for iPhone or iPad that provides instructions, workflows, troubleshooting tips, and a searchable list of Final Cut Pro keyboard shortcuts.

Getting Started in Final Cut Pro X

To begin a project in Final Cut Pro X, open the File menu, choose New Project, type the name of your project, and click OK. As you work on your project, Final Cut Pro X auto-saves after every change. The layout contains an Event Browser (upper-left window), which displays all the source media. Connected to the Event Browser is the Event Library, where you can see each individual event and the media it contains. Events are folders that hold all the video clips, audio clips, images, render files, and database files. The Viewer (upper-right window) plays back projects and clips, and the Magnetic Timeline (bottom) is where your edits take place.

With Final Cut Pro X, the project settings will automatically match the settings of the first clip dropped into the Magnetic Timeline by default. To find the Preferences, open the Final Cut Pro menu and choose Preferences. In the Preferences dialog box, there are three options: Editing, Playback, and Import. The audio and video settings for the project will change automatically with the media files you use in the edit.

To import media, you will choose between importing selected files or importing all files from an AVCHD folder on a storage drive or directly from a file-based camera such as the G10/XA10. Final Cut Pro X can edit natively with raw AVCHD/MTS and many other kinds of files or edit in Apple ProRes 422. To import files, follow these steps:

1. To import from your storage drive, click the Import Files option found in the Event Browser window; alternatively, open the File menu, choose Import, and select Files.
2. Locate the file(s) you want to import. Designate the event in which the files will be placed. You can add files to an existing event or create a new event.
3. Click Import (bottom right), and the clips will appear in the Event Browser.
4. Alternatively, to import directly from the camcorder, make sure the camcorder is plugged into the computer. Then click the Import from Camera button in the Event Browser window or open the File menu and choose Import From Camera (keyboard shortcut: Command+I).

5. Select your camcorder or device from the list; available clips will appear on the lower right.
6. To import all clips, click the Import All button. Alternatively, Command-click each thumbnail you want to import and then click the Import Selected button.
7. Select the destination for your clips by either adding them to an event or creating a new event.
8. Click Import. The clips will appear in the Event Browser.

Final Cut Pro X gives you options to transcode media:

- **Create Optimized Media.** This transcodes files into the Apple ProRes 422 codec.
- **Create Proxy Media.** This transcodes the files into the Apple ProRes 422 "proxy" codec (for off-line edits at about 30 percent of the 145Mbps data rate of ProRes 422).

Using the Action menu in the Event Browser, selected clips can be sorted and grouped by date created, date imported, reel, scene, duration, and file type.

In the Event Browser, position the playhead to mark in and out points using the I and O keys, respectively, on a selected clip. Then drag the clip from the Event Browser to the Timeline. You can rearrange the clip in the Timeline by dragging it with the Select tool (a cursor arrow), which you can also use to trim a clip by dragging the end of a clip left or right. To remove clips from the Timeline, select the clip(s) and press the Delete key.

Editing tools are located in a pop-up menu in the Timeline (middle left). The Zoom tool (keyboard shortcut: Z) magnifies or demagnifies part of the Timeline. When the Zoom tool is activated, click the Timeline to zoom in. To zoom out, hold down the Option key as you click. Basic keyboard shortcuts for Final Cut Pro X are listed in Appendix F, along with shortcuts for the older program, Final Cut Pro 7, which many people still use.

Getting Started in Avid Media Composer 6

When you open Avid Media Composer 6, a Select Project window presents a list of existing projects or the option to start a new project. For a new project, you need to choose an existing user profile or create a new profile. To create a new profile, click the User Profile drop-down menu and select Create User Profile. The window will prompt you for a name and location where your project will be saved. Select Private if you are working alone on the project. Private will save files to your Users folder on the computer. Select Shared if working with multiple editors who have different logon identities. Select External to save the project anywhere else, like the Desktop or to a specific hard drive.

To set up the project itself, select New Project, give the new project a name, and set the project settings. The Media Composer editing interface opens. The editing windows are very customizable, offering options to configure the screens and tools to suit individual styles of editing. To set the interface to a default window layout, open the Windows menu, choose Workspaces, and choose Source/Record Editing.

Media Composer 6 uses tabs to help keep the workspace organized. (See Figure 19.2.) Like all sophisticated editing programs, there are three, four, or more ways to accomplish the same task using the cursor, moveable tools, icons, menus, or keyboard commands. The Project window (top left) provides access tabs to bins, settings, format, usage, and info. The Format tab enables you to review project settings, and the Settings tab provides a list of settings in Avid Media Composer with options for adjusting.

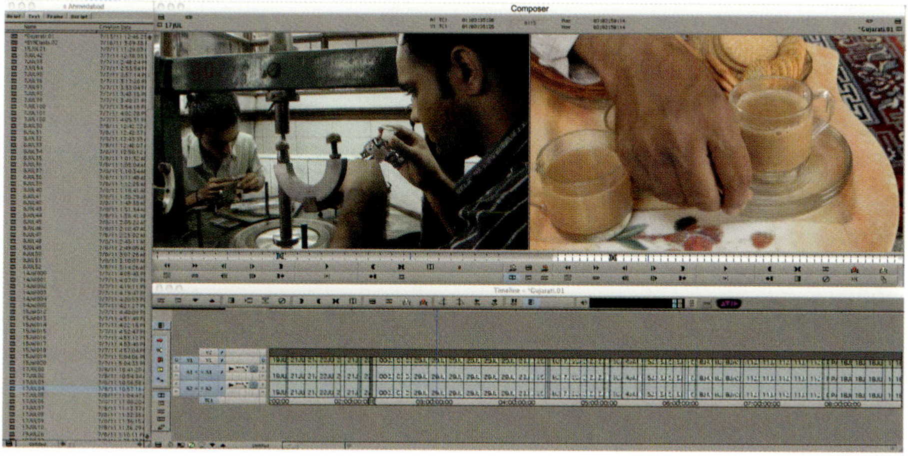

Figure 19.2 Avid Media Composer.

Next to the Project window are the Source and Record monitors for viewing and cueing source media clips (left) and edited Timeline media (right). Below these windows is the Timeline, where you edit your clips. There are many different tools, which you can access from menus, keyboard commands, or panels of icons near the areas they will affect. In the Settings tab in the Project window, you can select All Settings or just Active Settings. Import Settings enables you to adjust for import. Timeline Views displays settings for the Timeline.

Avid Media Composer supports multiple workflows for importing media. Like Apple, Avid Media Composer has its own high-quality video codec, DNxHD, which is optimized for the purpose of editing. DNxHD has three professional-quality bit rates: 10-bit 220x, 8-bit 220, and 8-bit 145. But Avid Media Composer can also work natively in most tapeless formats, including MTS files from AVCHD, RED/RED EPIC, QuickTime, ProRes, HDCAM SR, XDCAM, P2, GFCAM, and Canon XF. To use this function, you need Avid Media Access (AMA), a plug-in that enables the editor to work with native camera files without having to transcode, rewrap, import, and/or copy media. AMA creates a link to the specific volume(s) or file(s) but does not store the media in Avid Media Composer. It only references the media from your storage or backup drive, your media card, or the camcorder itself if you want to keep it attached during editing. To download the free AMA plug-in for your specific format, visit www.avid.com/US/products/Avid-Media-Access/Plug-ins.

Using AMA saves hours of transcoding and enables you to start editing immediately. However, when applying individual effects, titles, and color correction, and eventually creating a master, there will be pauses for rendering. The alternative is to import and transcode into a DHxHD format at the beginning. This involves investing time up front but speeds up effects and color-correction processes because you are working in a high-quality format made specifically for editing.

To import files *without* using AMA, do the following:

1. Open the Tools menu and choose Media Creation.
2. In the dialog box that opens, click the Media Type tab, choose File Format, and select MXF (the most commonly used format for an HD project).
3. Click the Import tab and select the target drives and the resolution, which will be DNxHD145 (unless you are intercutting with even higher resolution footage).
4. Open the bin into which you want to import the files.
5. Open the File menu, choose Import, and mark the video files you want to import.
6. Click Open. Your MTS files will transcode into DNxHD145 and populate the specified bin.

The bin can display the names and data of your clips in four different ways: a brief list (with standard info), a text view (with complete data), a frame view (with storyboard icons), and a script view (which displays thumbnails of each clip similar to the frame view, but with a dialog box that you can use to type notes or script details). Selecting a clip in the bin makes it appear in the Source monitor for examining or for marking in and out points.

There are many alternative ways of assembling your media clips. They can be dragged directly from the bin or Source monitor onto the Timeline and then further trimmed and rearranged, or they can be cued in the Source monitor with IN and OUT points and a keyboard command used to insert or overwrite the shot to a designated point in the Timeline. Basic keyboard shortcuts for Avid Media Composer 6.0 and other recent versions are listed in Appendix G, "Basic Keyboard Commands: Avid Media Composer," available at www.courseptr.com/downloads.

Getting Started in Premiere Pro

As you open Adobe Premiere Pro CS6, you see an Open Project option and a New Project option. To create a new project, click New Project, name your project in the dialog box that appears, and set its location. When you click OK, the Premiere interface is launched. The opening steps involve defining the settings and creating a save location for your project. You can rearrange Premiere's interface to fit individual editing needs by selecting various options from the Workspace menu. The default opening workspace is the Editing mode, in which all the basic editing windows are visible.

The Project panel (top-left window) is where the project files, clips, sequences, and graphics are located. The Source monitor (top-middle window) is used to view and trim raw media. The Program monitor (top-right window) is for viewing the project in progress, and the Media Browser (bottom-left window) is where you can view the contents of your entire computer to find, view, and import files. The Timeline (bottom middle) shows your sequence along with audio and video clips associated with the sequence. The Tools panel (to the right of the Timeline) performs editing functions. The Audio meter (to the right of the Tools panel) monitors audio levels.

Project settings apply to the entire project. To view, set or change project settings, open the Project menu, choose Project Settings, and choose General or Scratch Disk. Be aware that most project settings cannot be changed after they have been set at project creation.

Not many sequence settings can be changed. If major changes to the sequence settings are needed, you need to create a new sequence. To match source media settings and sequence settings automatically, select a desired clip in the Project panel and drag it onto the New Item icon located at the bottom of the Project panel. This will automatically create a new sequence and match the settings. If the setting in question *can* be changed, you can access the setting by opening the Sequence menu in the Project panel and choosing Sequence Settings.

There are two ways to import media with Premiere. The most common way is open the File menu and choose Import. Premiere also enables you to import footage using the Media Browser, which allows you to navigate anywhere on your computer. Once you find your media, you can view it before importing. After you select media to import, double-click on the file(s) or folder, and Premiere will import and place the files in the Project panel. Premiere can natively edit and manage AVCHD/MTS files.

The Project panel uses folders called bins to organize project files. To create a new bin, open the File menu, choose New, and select Bin. To rename a bin, click its current name to select and type the new name.

To edit a clip, follow these steps:

1. Select the clip in the Project panel. It will appear in the Source monitor.
2. Move the playhead (the blue marker) to the desired cue points.
3. Press I to mark an in point and O to mark an out point.
4. Then, click the center of the video and drag it down into the Timeline.
5. Use items in the Tools panel to perform simple cuts, rearrange clips, trim edges, and lengthen, shorten, or divide a clip.

You can use the Zoom tool to magnify and demagnify the Timeline, enabling you to make finer adjustments or larger changes. To remove clips from the Timeline, select a clip and press the Delete key. This will remove the clip and leave a gap where the clip used to be. To delete the clip and close the gap, select the clip, open the Edit menu, and choose Ripple Delete. Alternatively, right-click the clip (or Control-click on a Mac) and choose Ripple Delete from the menu that appears. Basic keyboard shortcuts for Adobe Premiere Pro CS6 (which are also relevant to CS5 and CS5.5) are listed in Appendix H, "Basic Keyboard Commands: Premiere Pro," available at www.courseptr.com/downloads.

Getting Started in Sony Vegas Pro 11

To get started using Sony Vegas Pro, follow these steps:

1. Open the Project menu and choose New.
2. Set Region, Audio, Video, and Project settings.
3. Name the project and set the project's destination folder.
4. Check the Manage Project Files checkbox to save all project files—audio, video, images, *et cetera*—in the project folder.
5. Click OK.

The workspace is divided into three primary areas:

- The Track list (bottom left) displays the track order in the project and contains controls used to determine track compositing and mixing.

- The Timeline (bottom right) is used for arranging and editing.
- The window-docking area (top) is where you can organize frequently used windows into a stack for alternately displaying the Preview window, Trimmer window, Explorer window, Transitions window, FX window, Device Explorer window, and Media Generators window. For quick access, each window has a tab at the bottom with its name on it.

To access preferences in Vegas Pro, open the Options menu and choose Preferences. There are tabs for each category of changeable settings. The General tab includes standard program settings, and the Video tab enables you to control display, video events, and video tracks. The settings in the Preview Device tab enable you to configure an external monitor. The settings in the Audio Device tab enable you to adjust sound-recording and playback options. The Editing tab has preference controls for specific editing options and configurations.

Changing the project properties is different from changing the project preferences. The preferences affect how the Vegas program functions overall. Project properties affect the specific project. Open the File menu and choose Properties to adjust, set, or review settings that are specific to the project. The Properties window contains five tabs: Video, Audio, Ruler (for changing the Timeline scale and ruler), Summary, and Audio CD (for burning "disc-at-once" CDs—an extension of the program's sophisticated audio mixing and mastering capabilities).

To import media, open the Project menu and choose Import. Then locate the media files you want to add to the project media list and click Open. To import media from a device, open the View menu and choose Device Explorer. If the device is connected, it should display on the left side of the Device Explorer. When you select the device, its media files will be displayed. Select the clips, click the Import button, and the clips will appear in the Project Media window, where they can be assigned to bins to organize your project.

When you locate a media file in the Explorer or Project Media window and drag it to the Timeline, an event is created. Events in the Timeline can contain video, audio, still images, or generated media such as titles and effects. In addition to specialized functions that can be performed in the Trimmer, Transitions, and Effects windows in the window-docking area, you can cut, paste, trim, split, or delete events in the Timeline using drag-and-drop operations with the cursor, keyboard commands, and tools like the Cut button. (The difference between a cut and a delete is that a cut places the extracted media on the Clipboard for further use.) Basic keyboard shortcuts for Sony Vegas Pro 11 are listed in Appendix I, "Basic Keyboard Commands: Sony Vegas Pro," available at www.courseptr.com/downloads.

Index

Numerics

A

B

C

Q–R

S